Criminal Justice
Recent Scholarship

Edited by
Marilyn McShane and Frank P. Williams III

A Series from LFB Scholarly

Black Rage in the American Prison System

Rosevelt L. Noble

LFB Scholarly Publishing LLC
New York 2006

Library of Congress Cataloging-in-Publication Data

Noble, Rosevelt.
  Black rage in the American prison system / Rosevelt L. Noble.
    p. cm. -- (Criminal justice recent scholarship)
  Includes bibliographical references and index.
  ISBN 1-59332-100-7 (alk. paper)
  1. Prisons and race relations--United States. 2. African American
prisoners. 3. Racism--United States. I. Title. II. Series: Criminal
justice (LFB Scholarly Publishing LLC)
  HV6197.U5N63 2006
  365'.608996073--dc22

2005031138

ISBN 1-59332-100-7

Printed on acid-free 250-year-life paper.

Manufactured in the United States of America.

Dedicated to Rosevelt Noble Sr., Debra Jean Noble,
my future offspring and the thousands of Black males entangled in the
web of the American criminal justice system.

Table of Contents

List of Tables

ix

List of Figures

Acknowledgements

I would like to thank those individuals whose guidance and comments helped to make this work possible. First I would like to thank Professor Gary F. Jensen, a sociologists at Vanderbilt University, who has been a very important resource for many years throughout the research process for this book. I am particularly grateful for his constructive criticism in early stages of the books development.

Professor Darren Sherkat, a sociologists at Southern Illinois University, was instrumental in the development of my quantitative research skills. Perhaps, I am most indebted to Darren for the candid manner in which he pushed me to perform research with a purpose.

I would like to thank Professor Mary Karpos, a sociologists at Vanderbilt University for introducing me to the realities of American prison life. Her honest and unflinching examination of corrections in America is what sparked my interest in the topic that has now become the center of my research agenda.

I would also like to thank my team of editors, many of which volunteered to graciously spend numerous hours proofreading the text: Robin Kasten, Sheena Walker, Tamara Dood, Crystal Buie, Rae Scott, Kim Perkins, Miko Hudson, and Emile Davidson.

CHAPTER I

Approaching Taboo Topics

Criminologists are loath to speak openly on race and crime for fear of being misunderstood or labeled racist.[1]

The call for a Black criminology is a call for developing and expanding theoretical research on crime committed by Blacks.[2]

African-Americans can no longer passively wait for approval or acceptance of White criminologists to become proactive in theory building and asserting our place at the 'For Scholars Only' table.[3]

Taboo Studies and the "Racist" Label

The study of racial dissimilarities in the American academy often reflects examinations of Black/White differences on a variety of social and personal characteristics (Covington 1995). As a result of these findings, many "physical characteristics, classified as racial, continue to be the basis for inferring major (i.e. racial) differences in culture, cultural achievements, histories, and behaviors of persons who possess them" (Covington 1995: 548). Furthermore, given the moral progression and political correctness of American society, certain topics within the realm of studies examining racial differences between Blacks and Whites are considered controversial or taboo. The "taboo" label has applied to discussions of Black/White differences on topics such as athletic ability (Crepeau 2001), intelligence (Levin 1991), and genetic criminal disposition (Lombroso 1972).

Implied, but rarely stated in academia, is the fact that some topics are taboo, not because of the controversial content of official research findings, but because of the race of the examining researcher. This phenomenon is particularly true when White researchers examine aspects of Black life, whether it is variations in crime rates or cultural issues such as the demise of the Black family. Consider for example, the proliferation of controversy surrounding the notorious Moynihan Report (1965). In March 1965, Daniel P. Moynihan, a White male, working for the Office of Planning and Research of the Department of Labor, completed his infamous report *The Negro Family: the Case for National Action*. The

Moynihan Report (1965: 5) examined the totality of conditions facing African-Americans and concluded that "at the heart of the deterioration of the fabric of Negro society [was] the deterioration of the Negro family." Moynihan (1965: 5) further stated that the Negro family was "the fundamental source of the weakness of the Negro community at the present time." The report also mentioned several additional negative issues affecting the Black community, ranging from the high-level of unemployment among Black males to racial differences in fertility rates and intelligence. Moynihan attributed the problems plaguing the Black community to slavery, the effects of reconstruction on the family, urbanization, unemployment, poverty, and the inability of the wage system to provide a decent family income (Rainwater and Yancey 1967). Yet, despite Moynihan's focus on structural issues and his avoidance of "blaming the victim" in describing the causes for the problems facing the Black community, the report met a fury of controversy and criticism (see Rainwater and Yancey 1967). Many White Liberals and members of the Black community viewed the report as *insensitive* for failing to emphasize the strengths of Black culture. Dissenters further accused the report of neglecting to make mention of those Black families not trapped in the vicious "pathology" described by Moynihan.

The tragic irony of the controversy surrounding the Moynihan Report (1965) was that "nothing in it was really new" (Rainwater and Yancey 1967). Variations of the major findings presented by Moynihan, previously appeared in the research endeavors of prominent Black scholars. For instance, E. Franklin Frazier, an eminent Black sociologist, in his prolific writings such as *Black Bourgeoisie* (1957) and *The Negro Family in the United States* (1939) (to name a few) had previously spoken of the detrimental conditions facing the Black community mentioned by Moynihan. However, Frazier's pioneering works did not draw the controversy evoked by the Moynihan Report (1965). Furthermore, his work continued to receive recognition as late as 1995 when Howard University established the E. Franklin Frazier Center for Social Work Research.[4] Even more ironic was the fact that Kenneth B. Clark, perhaps the most distinguished Black social scientist, published his book *Dark Ghetto: Dilemmas of Social Power* shortly before the release of the Moynihan Report. *Dark Ghetto* provided the basis for much of what Moynihan referred to as the "Tangle of Pathology" affecting the Black community. However, unlike the criticism that Moynihan drew for describing the conditions facing the Black community as "pathology," in 1965 Clark received the *Sidney Hillman Prize Book Award* for *Dark Ghetto* by the Sidney Hillman Foundation.[5] In addition, a year later in 1966, the Society for Psychological Study of Social Issues (SPSSI) awarded Clark the *Kurt Lewin Memorial Award.*[6]

The differential reactions confronted by three researchers making essentially the same statements and reaching similar conclusions about the Black community raises the question, "If nothing was new in Moynihan's Report, what were the reasons for the controversy?" The answer reflects the fact that Moynihan was a White male making perceived negative or detrimental statements about Black culture. On this matter, Russell (1992: 669) commented, "The hackles raised by this report were as much a response to its findings *as they were to the group making the findings*" [emphasis added].

The adverse reaction to the Moynihan Report (1965) resulted in the development of a longstanding taboo against discussing racially controversial topics. One such *off-limit* subject was the connection between race and crime (Sampson and Wilson 1995; Wilson 1987). Serious research on minority problems in the inner city curtailed for a decade "as liberal scholars shied away from researching behavior construed as unflattering and stigmatizing to particular racial minorities" (Wilson 1987: 4). Despite the change in social and political climate since the Moynihan Report, many criminologists continue to avoid the relationship between race and crime. This hands-off approach is primarily "out of concern for emphasizing negative aspects of African-American life and thereby, 'blaming the victim'" (LaFree and Drass 1992: 2). Russell (1994: 305) effectively described this process as the "academic hesitancy to tread race and crime waters."

Compounding the potential controversy surrounding the presentation of research findings that depict African-Americans in a negative light is the added fear of the "racist" label.[7] Researchers engaged in cross-cultural studies walk a fine line between presentation of scientific findings and promoting scientific racism. Although the findings may be highly accurate and/or previously stated, the tone of the research report and the word choices used often decide which side of the line a researcher falls. For example, some Black scholars took issue with Moynihan over the usage of the word "pathology."[8] Fear of the racist label applies in other forms of controversial discourse beyond academic circles as well. A case in point, Lynch (1992) discussed a general fear of the racist label by White males and their objections to affirmative action. He stated, "Even White males directly injured by affirmative action are sufficiently cowed by the threat of being called a racist and they remained silent" (31).

In cases where researchers are able to conquer the fear of having their research misunderstood and labeled racist, they still face a variety of other consequences such as severe harassment and even physical assault (Eysenck 1991; Jensen 1972). For instance, following his suggestion that Black/White differences in IQ might be partly due to genetic causes,[9]

Arthur Jensen received the permanent label as a "racist." Unfortunately, the label was the least of his harassment. In the preface to his book *Genetics and Education* (1972), Jensen mentioned receiving bomb threats on his house, suffering personal attacks, and having his lectures broken up by angry protesters. In the words of Hans J. Eysenck (1991: 217), who experienced similar treatment following his own controversial research,[10] the life of Arthur Jensen "was made a total misery for many, many years." While the treatment endured by Arthur Jensen was an extreme case, his story and that of others such as Moynihan and Eysenck, either forced researchers to avoid studies exploring racial differences or to engage in some form of self-censorship. Through self-censorship, the researcher carefully scrutinizes the tone and word choices used in the final report or intentionally omits certain facts and features from the research findings (Adler and Adler 1989). Fear of the racist label and other possible negative reactions adversely affect the field of criminology by forcing researchers to avoid deep explorations of the link between race and crime. Hence, studies on race and crime in *mainstream* criminology typically focus on superficial examinations of the relationship between the two variables.

Mainstream Criminology and Superficial Examinations of Race

Criminological studies on racial differences in crime and violence focus overwhelmingly on superficial factors that fail to offer suggestions for expanding theoretical paradigms. In fact, "much of the literature on Blacks and crime could be classified as criminal justice research, not as criminology" (Russell 1992: 668). Fear of the racist label coupled with the fact that most criminologists are White, results in *safe* examinations of the connection between race and crime or violence. A case in point, Walker and Brown (1995) conducted a content analysis of contemporary introductory criminology textbooks to explore the tendency of mainstream criminologists to avoid controversial coverage of the race and crime connection. The researchers conducted both quantitative and qualitative analyses of 13 textbooks published between 1990 and 1994. Their results found that none of the textbooks covered core racial issues such as the disparity in arrest statistics, police use of force, bias in charging, plea bargaining and sentencing, or the racial politics of the death penalty (Walker and Brown 1995). Free (1999) conducted a similar content analysis using 18 criminology textbooks published between 1994 and 1997, and reached essentially the same conclusion.
    In general, the racial topics considered in "mainstream" criminology fit under one of three main categories: 1) race and criminality, 2) race, racism and criminal justice, and 3) racism and criminalization (Hudson

1993). In describing the lack of innovation in criminological studies regarding the race affect, Russell (1992) noted:

> Study after study has established the significance of the race variable. However, these studies have consistently failed to develop a broad-based analytical and theoretical framework for explaining the phenomenon of disproportionality. Just how to handle the race variable is the Achilles' heel of the discipline.

As opposed to progressing to deeper levels of examination with the race variable, research involving Blacks and crime focuses overwhelmingly on structural and cultural interpretations.[11] Thus, with few exceptions (e.g. Hawkins 1986; Hindelang 1978; and Katz 1988) criminologists have "abdicated serious scholarly debate on race and crime" (Sampson and Wilson 1995). In large part, the preponderance of superficial examinations of race is due to the over-representation of Whites among *mainstream* criminologists. Given the taboo nature of racial topics and the potential "*Blacklash*" from Black scholars and the Black community, a *Black criminology* offers the best hope for advances in racial theories of crime.[12]

The State of Black Criminology

Russell (1992: 667) loosely defined a Black criminology as "a well-developed, vibrant, and cohesive subfield that seeks to explain crime committed by Blacks." Black criminology attempts to move beyond the well-established fact of disproportionality in offending and attempts to examine the effects of new unexplored variables on the race and crime relationship. Much of the criminology literature on race and crime focuses on established theories; subsequently, the discipline has failed to cultivate or recognize a new subfield that addresses reasons why the race variable is such a significant predictor of crime (Russell 1992). The lack of innovation is largely due to the underdevelopment of Black criminology. While the desire of White criminologists to avoid taboo topics and the fear of the racist label hinders the development of a Black criminology, there are two additional reasons for the slow development of this much-needed subfield.

First, the number of Black criminologists is relatively small (Ross and McMurray 1996), especially when considering the number of Blacks entangled in some aspect of the American criminal justice system. Figure 1.1 presents data from the National Science Foundation (1993, 1997) on the racial distribution of doctoral degrees awarded in criminology from 1980 through 1995. While the number of Black criminologists showed a steady increase from 1990 to 1995, their representation paled in comparison to the number of Black offenders sentenced in the criminal justice system.

Figure 1.1
Racial Distribution of Doctoral Degrees in Criminology

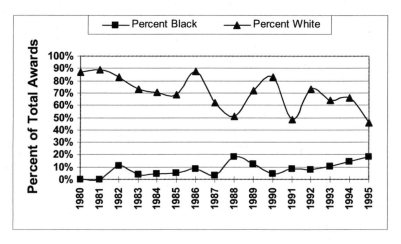

Figure 1.2 presents data from the Bureau of Justice Statistics on the racial distribution of inmates sentenced to state and federal prisons from 1990 to 1995.

Figure 1.2
Racial Distribution of Sentenced Prison Inmates

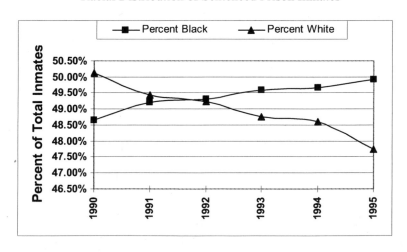

Using the racial breakdown of prison inmates as an indicator of criminality, the drastic racial dissimilarity between the subjects and researchers in criminological studies becomes apparent. For instance in 1995, Blacks represented 18.18 percent of doctoral degrees in criminology, but comprised 49.93 percent of the inmates sentenced to state and federal prisons. If crime is overwhelmingly a *Black problem*, as indicated by the prison statistics and numerous other measures of criminality, then who better to propose new theories and suggest methods of control than the Black criminologists. Naffine (1987: 2) suggested that the goal of a feminist criminology was "to have women fairly represented in the criminological literature and to have their experiences rendered faithfully through rigorous scholarship." The same goal holds true in the need for Black criminologists in the continued development of a Black criminology. Therefore, the first step towards the continued development of this subfield is an increase in the sheer number of Black criminologists.

The second obstacle in the development of a Black criminology stems from the excluded status of past and present Black scholars within the discipline. Young and Sulton (1991) insightfully noted that, "When reading supposedly comprehensive reviews of major theoretical paradigms, the unsuspecting observer would conclude that African-American criminologists have no ideas about crime and delinquency." In fact, Black criminologists have written hundreds of articles, books, and monographs on the subject of race and crime, and other general criminological issues; "Yet their contributions have been virtually ignored" (Young and Sulton 1991: 101).

For example, Greene (1979) compiled and published an annotated bibliography of over 300 literary works written by Black criminologists from 1895 to 1978, nonetheless few of these works receive mention in major theoretical reviews (Young and Sulton 1991). Researchers further contend that Black criminologists face exclusion in a number of other realms as well, such as assistance with the development of public policy, research grants, and media exposure (Ross and McMurray 1996; Young and Sulton 1991).

Black Criminological Theory

The primary effect of the exclusion of the Black perspective is that criminology and criminal justice practitioners have made very little progress towards understanding the connection between race and crime. The theoretical paradigms suggested by Black and White criminologists often differ. In fact, Ross and McMurray (1996) contend that Black criminologists face exclusion in serious academic discourse largely because they tend to challenge many of the basic assumptions proposed by White scholars. Many Black criminologists adopt a more holistic approach to understanding the significance of race and crime (Young and Sulton 1991). In the theoretical models of Black criminologists, crime is typically a symptom of other social problems that occurs within a multidimensional setting (Sulton 1989). Key aspects of this multidimensional setting are the longstanding effects of slavery and oppression. As a group, Black criminologists consistently argue, "racism, discrimination, and segregation are inextricably interwoven with crime and delinquency" (Young and Sulton 1991: 102). Consider for example the argument of Vontress (1962: 108) that crime is attributable to "a mélange of causes stemming from the patterns of segregation and discrimination uniquely imposed on the minority group by the dominant group." More recently, Coramae Richey Mann, professor emeritus at both Florida State University and Indiana University, proposed a quasi-Marxist conspiracy theory alleging that the American criminal justice system was intentionally racist as part of a larger plan to maintain the subordinate position of Blacks'.[13]

The history, drama, and emotion of the Black struggle produce compelling drives towards the study of race for many Black scholars (Watkins 2002). Subsequently, Black criminologists tend to incorporate the effects of this struggle into many of their theoretical paradigms. Unfortunately, the tendency to link contemporary problems plaguing the Black community to the historical significance of slavery and oppression contributes to the exclusion of Black criminologists among the academic elite. Researchers often view Black criminology laced with connections to *the struggle* as propaganda or polemics (Braddock 1978). Because White criminologists cannot understand the preoccupation of Black scholars with race, they claim to engage in scientific research, while viewing their Black counterparts as failing to get past their passions (Watkins 2002). As noted by William Watkins, a Black professor at the University of Illinois at Chicago, "they [Whites] can't understand why we are so preoccupied with the study of our people." Thus, "When Whites study Blacks it is viewed as scholarship, but when Blacks study Blacks it is emotion" (Watkins 2002: 102-103). This subfield of *emotional* scholarship offers great potential to the stagnated state of criminological theory and its inability to explain the race and crime relationship.

The time has come for mainstream criminology to move beyond the traditional theoretical paradigms and consider some of the factors suggested by Black criminologists. The continued absence of the Black perspective from serious criminological discourse, places the discipline of criminology in a "theoretical time warp" (Russell 1992: 675). Criminology can no longer afford to persist with superficial examinations of race. If the discipline is to maintain its academic integrity and influence on public policy, it must cultivate a subfield geared towards explaining *why* the race variable is such a significant predictor of crime. On this matter, Black criminologists offer a unique perspective, given their inclusion and familiarity with Black culture and the "Black experience." As criminologists, we must recognize that "how particular racial/ethnic groups are treated in American society and how they internalize this treatment [has] some bearing on those groups' involvement in crime" (Russell 1992: 672). The inability of White criminologists to comprehend the internalized aspects of the Black experience causes some Black scholars to question whether Whites are "the most qualified to explain all dynamics of crime and justice as they relate to African-Americans" (Ross and McMurray 1996: xxii). Nothing is more upsetting to the Black criminologists than to have persons who do not fully understand the Black experience attempt to explain Black behaviors (Ross and McMurray 1996). Perhaps most disturbing about these explanations are the failures to see the totality of conditions or factors operating in the production of crime. Crime is not an isolated social problem, completely separate and distinct from other social ills plaguing the Black community (Young and Sulton 1991). Based on their likely socialization and network ties, Black criminologists are better able to detail the precise connections between the personal, structural, and cultural factors that produce crime and violence in the Black community.[14] The proposed theory of black rage continues in the holistic tradition of Black criminological theories by drawing on the significance of slavery and oppression to explain violence in prison. Examination of the potential significance of black rage adds to the further development of a Black criminology by assessing the likely influence of previously unconsidered factors in theories of prison violence and general theories of violence.

The Theory of Black Rage

Conceptually, Black rage is an exacerbated state of anger produced by "the irresistible temptation to attribute African-American problems to a history of White racist oppression" (D'Souza 1995). The theory of Black rage suggests that certain interracial crimes or acts of violence, where Blacks are the offenders and Whites are the victims, perhaps stem from anger and frustration at the longstanding subordinate position of African-Americans. For instance, Nathan McCall, author of *Makes Me Wanna Holler* and reporter for the *Washington Post,* vividly recalled an adolescent bout with Black rage. When describing an incident in which

McCall and a group of young Black boys attacked a young White boy, who rode through their neighborhood on a bicycle, McCall wrote:

> We all took off after him. We caught him and knocked him off the bike. He fell to the ground and it was all over. We were on him. We stomped and kicked him. My partners kicked him in the head and face and watched the blood gush from his mouth. I kicked him in the stomach and nuts.

Equating the experience with obtaining some form of racial revenge, McCall goes on to explain his thoughts during the assault:

> This is for all the times you followed me around in stores. And this is for the times you treated me like a nigger. And this is for general principle-just 'cause you White'.

The detailed recount of Nathan McCall provides a classic example of the conceptual model of crime and violence based on Black rage. McCall and his friends saw their oppressor in the face of the little boy, who rode down their street that day. For no reason other than anger at their *Black experience* in a White dominated society, the group took the occasion as a chance to fight back against *the system* by assaulting a defenseless child, who they saw as representing that system. Unfortunately, this line of thought is not limited to adolescent boys, nor is it strictly an underclass problem.[15]   Consider the case of Brent Staples, who in his autobiography, *Parallel Time*, described a game he created while in graduate school called "Scatter the Pigeons." In playing the game, Staples spent his time stalking White citizens in public places in efforts to invoke fear in his victims. In describing the game and the joy it brought him, Staples noted:

> I became an expert in the language of fear. Couples locked arms or reached for each other's hand when they saw me. Some crossed to the other side of the street...I felt a surge of power: these people were mine: I could do with them as I wished. If I'd been younger with less to lose, I'd have robbed them, and it would have been easy.

The stories of two Black authors, one taking place during adolescence and the other during graduate school, depict the manner in which the effects of Black rage can transpire into violence and other forms of aggression against Whites. The last line in the quote by Staples points to a disturbing fact. Staples mentioned if he was younger and had less to lose; he would have perhaps robbed some of his victims. Sadly, thousands of young Black males in America have a lot less to lose, in which case their inhibitions against violent outbreaks are a lot weaker.

A case in point: on December 7, 1993, Colin Ferguson, a Jamaican immigrant residing in Brooklyn, NY, converted his rage against White society into an occasion for mass murder. Ferguson boarded a commuter train and proceeded to shoot passengers at point blank range. In the end, Ferguson killed six and wounded nineteen innocent citizens. Once arrested, notes found in Ferguson's possession stated that he had a personal vendetta against Whites and "Uncle Tom Negroes," both of whom he suspected of conspiring against him. As a testament of African-Americans' belief in the Black rage theory, a *National Law Journal* survey found that 68 percent of Blacks were persuaded by the argument of Ferguson's lawyer that "White racism drove him to his crazed rampage" (D'Souza 1995: 5). Furthermore, Martin Simmons, a Black professor at New York University, referred to Ferguson as a *hero* and mentioned having colleagues who were placing Ferguson's picture on their walls next to Malcolm X (D'Souza 1995).

In addition to crossing age and social class lines, Black rage also crosses gender lines. Bell Hooks in her provocative book, *Killing Rage*, details the manner in which the slightest of racial transgressions can trigger an episode of Black rage. Chapter one of *Killing Rage* begins with the line, "I am writing this essay sitting beside an anonymous White male that I long to murder" (Hooks 1995: 8). The event that brought Hooks to such intense feelings was the fact that the White male boarded an airplane out of turn and occupied the first class airline seat that rightfully belonged to the flying companion of Hooks. Instead of requesting that the White male relocate, the White female flight attendant degraded Hooks' companion. Ultimately, to avoid further conflict, the companion sat in coach while Hooks remained in first class. Although this appeared to be a rather trivial event, the tone and level of emotion expressed by Hooks in describing how she felt about the incident reveals the magnitude of rage "just beneath the surface" in many African-Americans:

> I felt a "killing rage." I wanted to stab him softly, to shoot him with the gun I wished I had in my purse. And as I watched his pain, I would say to him tenderly "racism hurts." With no outlet, my rage turned to overwhelming grief and I began to weep, covering my face with my hands. All around me everyone acted as though they could not see me, as though I were invisible, with one exception. The White man seated next to me watched suspiciously whenever I reached for my purse. As though I were the Black nightmare that haunted his dreams, he seemed to

be waiting for me to strike, to be the fulfillment of his racist imagination. I leaned towards him with my legal pad and made sure he saw the title written in bold print: "**Killing Rage**."

While Hooks used the rage brought on by what transpired on an airplane to write an award-winning book, some African-Americans lack the discipline and focus to channel such anger in a productive fashion. Consequently, without these internal controls, this rage is likely to erupt and surface in some other form, such as the expressions by McCall, Staples, or the violent outburst of Colin Ferguson.

The few pages here covered only four short stories of Black rage, however, the literature in psychiatry, legal studies, autobiographies, etc., are full of stories similar to those mentioned. Yet, despite persistent evidence of the significance of *black rage* on the criminal tendencies of some African-Americans, males in particular, criminologists have ignored this factor in their theoretical paradigms. It is my position that mainstream criminologists have failed to incorporate this factor into theoretical paradigms because of the taboo nature of the topic and the potential controversy surrounding such research endeavors. However, as a Black criminologist, there is a moral obligation to "tread the race and crime waters" that your White counterparts may skillfully avoid. For the Black criminologists, to continue with *business as usual* in regards to what we know about race and crime is to deny the discipline of criminology the opportunity to incorporate internal aspects of the Black experience into theoretical paradigms. One important internal aspect of the Black experience that offers great potential for expanding criminological theory on race and crime is the concept of Black rage. Although I propose and examine the theory in the context of prison violence, the processes and variables described offer tremendous value in explaining other interracial patterns observed in crime and violence statistics.

Black Rage and Prison Violence

Quantitative research regarding the racial demographics of the victims and aggressors in prison assaults illustrates a strong interracial pattern, with Black inmates over-represented among the aggressors and White inmates over-represented among the victims. Furthermore, qualitative inmate narratives provided by Carroll (1974, 1982), Robinson (1971), and Fox (1982) suggests that Black inmates enter the American prison system with an accumulation of rage and anger directed at the larger system of White oppression. Based on the qualitative and quantitative research findings, this study proposes that Black inmates transport *Black rage* into the American prison system, which significantly affects prison violence rates, particularly assaults against facility staff.

The theory of Black rage addresses a major limitation of previous prison violence literature by considering the influence of the race of correctional officers on the rate of staff and inmate assaults. Studies focusing entirely on inmate characteristics assume that guard behavior or demographics do not induce or curtail prison violence. Given America's racial history and the inherent deprivations of prison life, this study contends that the tremendous cultural disparity between the inmate and staff populations in the American prison system contributes significantly to institutional violence levels.

Sociologically, the focus on the effects of differential power on interethnic conflict is central in theory and research on ethnic movements and collective violence. From a practical standpoint, the central research question assesses whether or not the proportion of Black correctional officers in the staff population curtails Black rage and subsequently reduces the level of prison violence. Using institution-level data from the *Census of State and Federal Adult Correctional Facilities*, the current study seeks to develop a theory of Black rage to explain the observed interracial pattern in prison assaults. Theoretically, this study advocates including race and other cultural importation factors pertaining to both inmates and correctional officers into any model designed to explain prison violence. Empirically, this study may provide prison officials with guidance on the management of correctional institutions. It offers the prospect of reducing violence rates by increasing the proportion of minority correctional officers, which should subsequently decrease the racial and cultural discrepancies between the largely Black inmate population and the largely White prison staff.

---

[1] Sampson and Wilson (1995: 2), *Toward a Theory of Race, Crime, and Urban Inequality*

[2] Katheryn K. Russell (1992: 668), Development of a Black Criminology and the Role of the Black Criminologists

[3] Ross and McMurray (1996: 4), Dual Realities and Structural Challenges of African-American Criminologists

[4] http://www.socialwork.howard.edu/SW/FrazierCenter.htm

[5] Since 1950, the Sidney Hillman Foundation has recognized journalists, writers, and public figures for their pursuit of social justice and public policy for the common good. The award reflects the "vision and commitment of Sidney Hillman, president of the Amalgamated Clothing Workers of America (a predecessor union of UNITE), whose tireless efforts to bring dignity and respect to working people left a lasting legacy for the American public" (http://www.hillmanfoundation.org/about.html).

[6] Named for the late Kurt Lewin, a founder of SPSSI and a pioneer in the science of group dynamics, SPSSI presents this award annually for "outstanding contributions to the development and integration of psychological research and social action" (http://www.spssi.org/lewin_award_spoken_addresses_name.html).

[7] White Liberals and Black leaders branded Moynihan as a racist (Russell 1994; Rainwater and Yancey 1967).

[8] For example, Russell (1992: footnote 6) noted, "Some of the word choices used in the report (e.g., "pathology") still would raise eyebrows today."

[9] See Jensen (1969), How Much Can We Boost IQ and Scholastic Achievement

[10] See Eysenck (1971), *Race, Intelligence and Education*

[11] For example, Russell et al. (2000: 47-76) examined 78 sources concerning Blacks and crime that focus disproportionately on the simplistic struggle of culture versus social structure in explaining the race and crime connection.

[12] Russell's (1992) statement about the significance of Moynihan's race in creating the controversy surrounding his report, as well as the differential reactions to the claims of Moynihan versus Clark and Frazier indicate that only Black scholars can safely "air the dirty laundry" of the Black community.

[13] See Mann (1993), *Unequal Justice: A Question of Color*

[14] On this matter Young and Sulton (1991: 110) noted:
"African-American criminologists were raised in predominantly African-American neighborhoods and continue to reside in or regularly visit relatives or friends living in these neighborhoods. As a result, these scholars not only have better access than their White counterparts to those African-American populations that are frequently 'objects of scholarly inquiry' but possess a broad and deep understanding of African-Americans. For these reasons, African-American criminologists are better equipped than their White counterparts to conduct research on the inner-city crime problems."

[15] See Cose (1993) *The Rage of a Privileged Class*

CHAPTER II

Race and Prison Violence

To many Blacks the prison represents White dominance and oppression.[1]

In prison today, races, particularly Black and White, are divided and hate each other.[2]

All the time, all I could think about was killing them niggers because of their attitude towards the White dude.[3]

Previous Literature

The proposed research focuses on three distinct arguments about race and prison violence. The first theme derived from the literature suggests a strong correlation between inmate race and prison violence, with Black inmates contributing overwhelmingly to violence rates. The second theme suggests that Black inmates desire to target their aggression at both White guards and White inmates. The implication is that the interaction between Black inmates and prison "whiteness" is a significant factor in predicting prison assaults. The final theme assumes that incorporating more Black correctional officers among prison staff should control the violent tendencies of Black inmates. The implication is that, because Black inmates engage in racially motivated violence, manipulating the race of prison officers should decrease the inmate's violent tendency towards prison staff. Previous researchers failed to consider these three distinct lines of argument simultaneously. The subsequent literature review discusses each theme individually. The theoretical model presented in Chapter IV combines the literary themes discussed here into the proposed theory of Black rage.

Black Inmate Violent Tendency

Research on race and prison violence largely addresses the violent tendencies displayed by Black inmates. Generally, two theoretical perspectives explain the relationship between violence and race. First, the structural model contends that violence is the product of racial

15

discrimination and socioeconomic conditions (Harer and Steffensmeier 1996). For example, Blau and Blau (1982) state that being Black in urban America is a structural position characterized by high rates of violence because a significant proportion of urban Blacks experience relative deprivation.[4] Second, the cultural model contends that violence is the product of a subcultural value system that condones and legitimates violence (Harer and Steffensmeier 1996). For example, Luckenbill and Doyle (1989) found that Blacks are more likely to follow a code of honor, which demands that a man be able to back his claim of dominance and independence.[5] Following such tenets, Blacks are more likely to engage in violence because of a cultural obligation to respond aggressively to challenges. Regardless of the proposed cause, structure or culture, the general conclusion is that Blacks hold attitudes more favorable towards the use of violence than their White counterparts; a position that is consistent with prior research (Anderson 1999; Brown 1965; Hannerz 1969; Hippler 1974; Rainwater 1970; Suttles 1968).[6]

Dichotomous Group Comparisons

To assess the possibility of Black inmates transporting "pro-violence" attitudes into the prison subculture, criminologists often incorporate race as an importation factor in models of prison violence. Such studies follow one of two research designs: dichotomous group comparisons, and/or cumulative assessments of the influence of race on institutional violence rates. In dichotomous group comparisons, the individual is the unit of analysis. The dichotomy is generally Black versus White only or Black versus all other races combined. The findings based on dichotomous group comparisons are contradictory. Two studies reported that Black inmates were no more violent than Whites (Ellis et al. 1974; Wright 1989). On the other hand, three studies supported the argument that Black inmates had significantly higher rates of prison violence in comparison to White inmates (Carroll 1974; Harer and Steffensmeier 1996; Silberman 1995). A sixth study further contributes to the inconsistency. Petersilia (1983) analyzed data from three states and reached three different conclusions. Specifically, she found that Black inmates in Texas were more violent than Whites, in California, White inmates were more violent than Blacks, and in Michigan, there was no significant difference between the two groups.

Methodological limitations partially explain the discrepancy in research findings from the six studies listed above. The study by Ellis et al. (1974) has three limitations. First, they base their findings on data gathered from a single state. The data collection took place in 55 correctional facilities in North Carolina. One could argue that their results are perhaps state-specific and not generalizable to other areas.

Second, they fail to define the groups, which comprise their Black and White populations. Therefore, one does not know exactly which inmates encompassed the *White* and *Black* samples in their analysis. Finally, the use of ex-convicts as research assistants confounds their study. Ellis et al. (1974) relied on self-reported prison assaults as the dependent variable in their individual level analysis. However, the studies findings were perhaps inaccurate given that Ellis and "a number of ex-inmates, who were hired as research assistants," conducted the interviews (19). Having ex-inmates as interviewers may contribute to an over-exaggeration of reported assaults, potentially masking any true racial differences in prison violence. The protection of one's *manhood* is a defining feature of the inmate subculture (Hawkins and Alpert 1989; Silberman 1995). Consequently, in diverting potential challenges to this manhood, inmates put on a "tough guy image," as one who is quick to resort to violence as a response to all challenges. Therefore, in an interview conducted by an ex-inmate, who may one day be readmitted to the prison or who may still have friends in the facility, the study participant has added incentive to inflate his actual number of prison assaults.[7]

Wright's research (1989) has two major limitations. First, similar to Ellis et al. (1974), Wright based his findings on data obtained from one state. Wright (1989) analyzed data from "several New York State facilities."[8] More so than Ellis et al. (1974), the results of Wright (1989) may not be generalizable to all prisons given the unique racial make-up of New York State. Furthermore, Wright (1989) also distorts the Black-White comparison by including other races among the White sample. For example, his dichotomous race variable records the following values: 1 = Black and 0 = White, Native American, and Hispanic. Combining Hispanic and White inmates does not provide an accurate assessment of the difference in Black and White violence rates since research shows that Hispanic and Black inmates share similar values regarding aggressive behavior. The *machismo* subculture found among Hispanics supports an environment in which aggression is both expected and praised (Davidson 1974). This finding is similar to the series of cultural explanations offered to explain Black violent tendencies. In addition to non-conventional value systems, research also shows that Hispanic inmates have relatively high rates of prison violence due to the importation of gang rivalries into the inmate subculture (Fong and Vogel 1995; Harer and Steffensmeier 1996; Hunt et al. 1993). Therefore, combining Hispanic inmates with the White sample gives the illusion of no significant difference between Whites and Blacks. Wright's data may actually reflect the lack of a significant difference between Blacks and Hispanics.

Carroll (1974) and Silberman (1995) share the same two limitations. First, both conduct their analysis on data obtained from one correctional facility. The major problem facing studies based on one correctional facility is the limited sample of prison assaults. For example, in Carroll (1974) of the 43 Black inmates with reported infractions, roughly 21 percent were for fights and assaults. Of the 69 White inmates with reported infractions, only 9 percent were for fights and assaults. When combined, Carroll (1974) observed roughly 15 *violent* assaults. With such a limited number of actual prison assaults, it is difficult to discern any true patterns regarding racial differences in prison violence. Second, both studies fail to introduce control variables when assessing the racial difference in prison violence. In the absence of control variables, the researchers cannot be certain that race is the only factor accounting for the difference in violence levels between White and Black inmates. For example, age differences between the two groups may explain the observed variance in violence rates. With the absence of statistical controls, we cannot rule out this possibility.

The one limitation found in Petersilia (1983) is primarily a factor of the misinterpretation of her research design and findings by subsequent researchers. Several researchers have cited Petersilia (1983) as a study examining racial differences in prison violence (Harer and Steffensmeier 1996; Bottoms 1999). However, scrutinizing the *weighted* dependent variable used in the regression analysis revealed that Petersilia (1983) studied racial differences in infraction rates, not violence rates. Thus, Adams (1992) used the correct terminology when he described Petersilia's study as an assessment of racial variations in "infraction rates." In creating her dependent variable, Petersilia (1983) combined seven types of infractions: administrative, contraband, threat, violence without injury, minor injury, major injury, and escape. Petersilia created a weighted infraction rate in four steps: 1) assign a numeric value to each type of infraction,[9] 2) sum each inmate's total infraction score, 3) divide each inmate's score by their total number of months imprisoned, and 4) multiply by 12 to get an annual infraction rate. Adding all infractions together prohibited subsequent researchers from making statements about racial variations in prison violence since some of the infraction types summed were not necessarily violent (e.g. administrative, contraband, and escape). In which case, instead of belonging among the literature on prison violence, Petersilia's work (1983) rightfully belongs with studies seeking to explain racial variations in general prison misconduct or infraction rates (Bolte 1978; Flanagan 1983; Goetting and Howsen 1986).

Harer and Steffensmeier (1996) provide the best study to date on the racial differences in prison violence. Their data included information from all 58 male federal correctional facilities within the U.S. They obtained indicators of prison violence from the transcripts of disciplinary report hearings rather than self-report surveys. By narrowing their sample to federal prisons and not relying on self-report surveys, Harer and Steffensmeier (1996) measure real differences in behavior and not the discretionary sanctioning practices of prison staff. Federal employees are less likely to show racial bias in their charges for misconduct, given the due process requirements and necessary evidence for citations (Hewitt et al. 1984). Other improvements implemented in Harer and Steffensmeier (1996) included the consideration of only Black and White inmates. Hispanics and other racial groups were not haphazardly included in the analysis as part of the White sample. They also controlled for both individual and institutional level factors that may have explained the difference in prison violence between White and Black inmates. With the methodological improvements of Harer and Steffensmeier (1996), perhaps their finding that Black inmates are significantly more violent than Whites is more reflective of the true racial pattern in prison violence.

Cumulative Effect of Race

Assuming the findings of Harer and Steffensmeier (1996) reflect the true racial difference in prison violence, cumulative studies should reveal a similar pattern. Cumulative studies consider the influence of the proportion of Black inmates on institutional violence rates. In contrast to dichotomous group comparisons, in cumulative studies, the unit of analysis is the institution and race is a continuous variable (e.g. the percentage of Black inmates). Findings regarding the cumulative impact of race on prison violence are contradictory. Three studies attempted to assess the collective impact of race on institutional violence rates. Ellis et al. (1974) reported that race had only an indirect effect on institutional violence rates through three variables: percentage of inmates under 21, percentage of inmates sentenced for violent crimes, and percentage of inmates incarcerated for more than one year. However, Ellis et al. (1974) operationalized race as the percentage of inmates who were *nonwhite*; hence, their measurement prohibits conclusive statements pertaining to the specific influence of Black inmates on facility violence rates, since their sample of *Black* inmates includes all other nonwhite inmates as well. Gaes and McGuire (1985) also operationalize race as the percentage of nonwhite inmates. However, their results differed from Ellis et al. (1974). Gaes and McGuire (1985) found that a high percentage of nonwhite inmates resulted in fewer assaults against inmates and more assaults against prison staff.

Harer and Steffensmeier (1996) provided a third study assessing the cumulative impact of race on prison violence. Unlike the previous two studies, their work considered the cumulative effect of Black inmates instead of the more general effect of nonwhite inmates on measures of prison violence. Harer and Steffensmeier (1996) included the percentage of Black inmates among the institutional level controls in their dichotomous group comparison. Their analysis revealed that the percentage of Black inmates was not significant in predicting racial differences in individual rates of violence. However, Harer and Steffensmeier (1996) did not include an institutional level violence indicator among their dependent variables. Therefore, their findings prevent statements regarding the influence of the percentage of Black inmates on institutional violence rates. Furthermore, Harer and Steffensmeier (1996) conducted their analysis on data gathered from the Federal prison system. Blacks comprised roughly 25 percent of the inmate populations in the 58 federal facilities included in their sample. In contrast, Blacks typically comprise a larger percentage of the inmate population in state-run facilities.[10] For example, in 1993, Blacks represented roughly 33 percent of the inmate population in federal facilities, while in state-run institutions they comprised nearly 50 percent of the inmate population[11] (Maguire and Pastore 1995). In environments with relatively few Black inmates, it is not likely that the cumulative effect of Blacks will have a significant impact on prison violence.

Summary and Contributions

Research pertaining to the violent tendencies of Black inmates is contradictory in large part due to problematic research designs. Of the six studies using dichotomous group comparisons, only one project had minimal limitations. In that study, Harer and Steffensmeier (1996) found that Black inmates were significantly more violent in comparison to White inmates. Given the methodological considerations made by Harer and Steffensmeier (1996) we can assume that their findings reflect the true racial pattern in prison violence. However, researchers have failed to duplicate a similar pattern in studies measuring race as a continuous variable. None of the three studies assessing the cumulative effect of race provided an adequate assessment of the relationship. Two of the studies considered the percentage of nonwhite inmates instead of the percentage of Black inmates. The third study failed to create an institutional violence rate and gathered data from the federal prison system where Blacks are typically under-represented. Therefore, the literature on prison violence failed to produce a single study concerning the cumulative effect of Black inmates on facility violence rates.

The current study seeks to build on the literature concerning the cumulative effect of race by addressing four limitations of previous research. First, the study examines the effect of the percentage of Black inmates and not just the percentage of "nonwhite" inmates on prison violence. Second, the institution is the unit of analysis for both the independent and dependent variables. Third, the study includes a larger sample of prisons, which are more representative of the average American correctional facility. To achieve this goal the study examines strictly state-run facilities. In 1990, 64 federal adult population confinement facilities housed male inmates exclusively. In that same year, there were 795 such facilities on the state level. Likewise, for 1995 the numbers were 92 federal and 830 state facilities. In 1990 and 1995, federal institutions comprised less than 10 percent of American prisons (*Census of State and Federal Adult Correctional Facilities*, 1990, 1995). Therefore, studies conducted on the state-level produce findings that are more generalizable and paint a more accurate picture of the typical American prison. Fourth, the study provides relative measures of the change in Black inmates and Black prison staff over time. By analyzing three waves of cross-sectional data, the design captures the influence of demographic changes in both the staff and inmate populations on prison violence.[12]

Black Inmates and Prison Whiteness

The second line of argument involving race and prison violence is that not only are Black inmates more violent, but their violence tends to be directed specifically at Whites. Black inmates entering the American prison system bring with them years of rage and frustration directed at the larger system of White oppression (Cleaver 1968; Jackson 1970). Their feelings of racial discrimination are exacerbated within the prison setting where "the very structure of the prison--its walls and bars, its rigid hierarchy, its whiteness--seems designed to foster an image of a racist conspiracy" (Carroll 1982: 184). Black inmates view prison as the next stage of the larger system of White oppression working against them. Therefore, attacking prison whiteness provides the Black inmate the opportunity to vent his anger and frustration "developed through 300 years of oppression against individuals perceived to be representative of the oppressors" (Carroll 1974: 184). As expected, given the history of race relations in the U.S., research indicates that Black inmates engage in *target violence*,[13] with White correctional officers and White inmates being the primary victims of preference.

Research examining target violence usually follows one of two formats. The first format consists of rich ethnographic accounts such as

Irwin's (1980) *Prisons in Turmoil* or Jacob's (1977) *Stateville: The Penitentiary in Mass Society*. Although such texts provide extensive descriptive detail, they reflect one person's observation and assessment of the prison subculture (Wright 1991). The second format consists of empirically generated profiles of prison victims and aggressors. Works of this nature include Lockwood's (1980) *Prison Sexual Violence* or Bowker's (1980) *Prison Victimization*. Although these works quantify important prison relationships, they tend to be rather limited in scope (Wright 1991). Given the variety of research methods employed, the evidence used to support research claims varies from descriptive narratives to quantitative statistics. The literature on target violence divides prison whiteness into two sections: staff whiteness and inmate whiteness.

Prison Whiteness Among Guards

Symbols of Oppression

There are two reappearing subtopics or themes within the literature on target violence involving White correctional officers. The first theme suggests that Black inmates view White correctional officers as symbols of the system of racism working against Blacks in general. This system of racism includes institutions within the American educational, political, and economic structures. Black inmates attribute their failure to succeed in legitimate activities to the system of racism working against them. Glasgow (1980) states that lower-class Blacks view "poverty, unemployment, and the constellation of deprivation in which they are caught is the result not of chance but of deliberate disqualification, deceit, racism, and the use of power by 'the man'" (103). The prison setting presumably removes Black inmates from the source of their failure; therefore, White guards become "a convenient and highly visible symbol of White economic dominance and authority over Blacks lacking the footing to gain equality" (Fox 1982: 65).

For Black inmates, the over-representation of Whites in positions of power within the prison structure reinforces the subordinate position of Blacks found within free society. The consistent image of *White-power* results in the view of White correctional officers as gatekeepers of the larger social system with racist motives and values behind their discretionary judgments (Fox 1982). Skepticism surrounds every use of power by White officers. Blacks interpret the routine enforcement of particular prison rules as acts of racial prejudice (Fox 1982; Carroll 1982). For example, the events leading to the 1967 race riot at San Quentin Correctional Facility began when a White guard in the San Quentin dining room "tried to take a cup of milk from a [Black] prisoner and then gave him a disciplinary report for having the milk" (Irwin 1980: 84). Although this appears to be a rather trivial event, the prisoner's Black coworkers attributed the act to racial prejudice, and their objection to this act began the sequence of events leading up to the riot (Irwin 1980). This example illustrates the sensitivity of Black inmates to discrimination, with the actions of White officers serving as "triggering mechanism[s] for the release of accumulated feelings of racial injustice" (Fox 1982: 64-65). Perceived discrimination in free society and in prison solidifies the Black inmate's notion that the larger social system has conspired to insure his failure. Given that Black inmates view White correctional officers as symbols of this system, White guards are frequently the victims of Black assaults. Furthermore, the lack of cultural understanding between the two groups exacerbates this already strained relationship.

Cultural Ignorance

White correctional officers are primarily from rural areas where interracial contact is infrequent and racial prejudice is prevalent (Williams 1964; Schwartz 1972; Nagel 1973; Fox 1982). Coming from rural areas, many White guards have little to no experience in dealing with Black culture. In his study of Eastern Correctional Institution, Carroll (1974) found that none of the White correctional officers he interviewed admitted to having social contacts with Blacks outside of prison, and for several, their contact with Blacks on the job was the first and only interracial contact in their lives. The White guard has limited knowledge of Black culture, which influences their interactions with their Black coworkers and Black inmates. Fox (1982) found that 1) White guards lacked the flexibility to develop effective working relationships with their Black fellow workers and that 2) many carried either a basic misunderstanding about minorities or harbored feelings of resentment and distrust. Furthermore, Owen (1985) reported that the racial conflict that plagues the inmate population is a mirror image of staff relations. Given the hostile racial atmosphere of the guard subculture, it is not surprising that the majority of Black officers who terminate their employment cite strained relations with White superiors as their reason for leaving (Jacobs and Grear 1977). In contrast, the majority of White officers who terminate their employment cite conflict with minority prisoners as their reason for leaving (Jacobs and Grear 1977).

The White guard's ignorance of Black culture fosters conflict with minority prisoners, which has two negative consequences. First, it contributes to the perpetuation of negative racial stereotypes. For example, Fox (1982: 74) found that "White officers tended to see Black prisoners and social misfits as one in the same because their observation of Black culture has been largely tempered by their direct power and control over convicted offenders." Given that their only interaction with Blacks has been in the form of controlling criminals, White guards do not understand Black culture and behavior. Their lack of understanding results in a developed fear of the *unknown* and subsequently, White guards assume a more aggressive and coercive demeanor towards Black inmates. As such, the second consequence of the cultural gap is the over-reliance on coercion and force in the relationship between White guards and Black inmates rather than human concern and understanding (Fox 1982). In contrast, shared cultural understanding facilitates a more positive relationship between White guards and White inmates. Carroll (1974: 127) observes:

> Moreover, in spite of the moral distance between the respectable White guardians and convicted White criminals, they share many subcultural orientations, and thus the behavior of the White convicts is more easily understood by White staff.

The coercive stance of White guards towards Black inmates is reflective in their tendency to over analyze and excessively regulate Black behavior. For example, research shows that because White guards are more likely to perceive Black inmates as dangerous or threatening, they keep Black inmates under closer surveillance than Whites (Carroll 1982). Due to the closer surveillance, Black inmates receive disciplinary infractions at a greater frequency than White inmates (Carroll 1974; Held et al. 1979). Likewise, Carroll (1974) further found that Black inmates are more likely to 1) have their visitors and cells searched, 2) be denied passes to go from one part of the prison to another, and 3) be prevented from socializing by being told to "break it up" when conversing in small groups.

Black inmates receive a daily round of discretionary decisions, which further confirm their sense of discrimination and victimization. The relative difference in the treatment experienced by the Black inmate fuels their anger and frustration directed towards the larger White system of oppression. Johnson (1976) reports that Black prisoners express such strong concerns about being victims of inequity and abuse by the criminal justice system that many fear being unable to control their anger and resentment at this perceived victimization. In sum, White officers are the frequent victims of Black assaults because their ignorance of Black culture leads to a reliance on more coercive methods of control that subsequently confirm Black feelings of discrimination in American society.

Prison Whiteness Among Inmates

Displaced Aggression

More so than White officers, White inmates are particularly vulnerable to violent outbreaks in their interactions with Black inmates. Three subtopics concerning target violence within the inmate subculture highlight the White inmate's vulnerability to Black aggression. The first theme suggests that due to displaced aggression, White inmates become the scapegoats for Black frustration directed at the larger system of White oppression and White correctional officers. White inmates are forced to interact with Black prisoners who not only feel that the larger White system is responsible for their failure, but who also experience discriminatory treatment daily from White correctional officers. These two factors have significant consequences for the relationship between Black and White inmates. One consequence is that White and Black prisoners remain extremely segregated in all prison activities (Irwin 1980). A second consequence is that there is extreme hatred between these two groups. Irwin (1980) considers the hate and distrust between White and Black prisoners to be the most powerful source of division within the inmate subculture. Despite the highly segregated prison lifestyle, White inmates still manage to absorb a vast majority of the Black inmate's frustration.

Two factors maintain the position of White inmates as scapegoats for Black anger and frustration. First, Black inmates are cut-off from the primary targets of their frustration--the White power structure of free society.[14] Second, the costs are likely too high in assaults against the secondary targets of Black frustration--White prison staff. Although a successful assault against a White officer is likely to bring a Black inmate tremendous status within the inmate subculture, the certainty of retaliation from all officers deters many attempts (Carroll 1974). Challenges to the authority of a prison staff member results in extreme displays of force as a way of re-establishing administrative control of the prison environment (Bowker 1980; Hamm et al. 1991). Inmates who challenge staff authority risk receiving a "tune-up." Marquart (1986; 351) states that tune-ups "consist of verbal humiliation, shoves, kicks, and head and body slaps." Adding to the assault, the guards significantly outnumber inmates during tune-ups, and the guards follow a code of silence similar to that of the police, making prosecution of staff members involved next to impossible (Bowker 1980). Consequently, the certainty of retaliation, coupled with the low probability of punishment to staff members, deters some Black inmates from assaulting White prison staff. However, because of trickled down anger and frustration, the White inmate by default absorbs the consequences for White oppression over Blacks in prison and in free society.

Silberman (1995) quantified the process of displaced aggression in his study on prison violence. Specifically, he assessed the relationship between the degree of expressed hostility towards staff and the actual number of inmate-on-inmate assaults. His results showed that inmates who expressed great hostility toward staff were more than twice as likely to have assaulted another inmate as those who said they had never expressed any sort of anger toward staff. While his findings highlight the displacement process, Silberman (1995) does not incorporate the influence of race in his quantitative analysis. However, during an interview with an inmate, he notes that "when the officer is White and the inmate is Black, resentment may be directed toward White inmates" (53). Carroll (1974) reports a similar finding, when he concludes that in assaulting a White inmate, "the Black aggressor may in some measure be assaulting the White guard on the catwalk" (194). In sum, Black inmates displace their aggression for the general system of White oppression and the prison authority structure onto White inmates.

Lack of Adjustment

The White inmate's lack of adjustment to prison life sustains their position as scapegoats for the Black inmate's anger. Due to their adjustment problems, Black inmates label Whites as weak and easy targets for assault (Carroll 1974). The literature on White inmates suggests a number of psychological and emotional problems experienced during imprisonment. For example, White inmates are significantly more likely to suffer self-inflicted injuries (Johnson 1976; Wright 1989). In terms of suicide, the ultimate form of self-injury, White inmates contemplate this act far more frequently than Blacks. In a study of the Tennessee State Prison, Jones (1976) found that one-third of White inmates considered committing suicide during confinement compared to three percent of Black inmates. Furthermore, Fagan and Lira (1978) found that White inmates demonstrated symptoms of psychological distress, such as confusion, anxiety, depression, and other mood disturbances, more frequently than Blacks. The difficulty separating from free society compounds the psychological problems of White inmates. Johnson (1976: 122) found that White inmates tended to "reside physically in the prison while living psychologically in the free (real) community." In contrast, Black inmates "do easy time" by cutting themselves off from outside ties and worries (Hawkins and Alpert 1989). The indifference of the Black inmate towards outside worries is evident by their greater tendency to follow the inmate code and their deeper submersion into the inmate subculture (Carroll 1974).

Concern with physical safety is also a significant cause of psychological and emotional distress for White inmates. Johnson (1976: 68) found that White inmates were more likely to suffer "fate avoidance," which he defined as the "fear that one is unable to stand up to prison pressure, especially the pressure generated by threats from other inmates." Toch (1977) and Jones (1976) observed similar safety concerns among White inmates. In efforts to achieve some degree of safety, Whites are more inclined to seek removal from the general inmate population. Bartollas and Sieverdes (1981) found that White inmates were more likely to use "flight" rather than "fight" as their method of handling prison challenges.[15] The flight tendency is reflective in the disproportionate number of White inmates housed in protective custody (Carroll 1982; Fox 1982). For example, in a study of several Michigan prisons, Jacobs (1983) found that 75 percent of those seeking protective custody were White. In the absence of protective custody, White prisoners attempt to develop closer ties with guards for support and protection (Fox 1982; Hawkins and Alpert 1989). Whites rely heavily on guards for support because they lack access to group protection. Without a class or ethnic consciousness to rally around, White inmates appear more concerned with "doing their own time" (Carroll 1982). In contrast, Black and Hispanic inmates are group oriented with a focus on "doing group time" (Hawkins and Alpert 1989; Carroll 1974, 1982; Fox 1982).

The individual orientation of White inmates, coupled with their adjustment problems noted above, renders White inmates vulnerable to assaults. Witnessing the problems of their White counterparts, Black inmates view Whites as weak and use the prison environment as an opportunity to reverse the traditional dominance pattern established in the larger society (Hawkins and Alpert 1989; Carroll 1974). Blacks may have lacked the essential skills and requirements necessary for success in free society; however, in the prison subculture the tables of justice have turned. Given their deficiencies, Whites find themselves cast into the "inferior" role.[16] Even in prisons where Whites form the numeric majority, Black inmates still assume the dominant position over the largely disorganized White majority (Hawkins and Alpert 1989). The superior mindset of Black inmates results in their over-representation among the aggressors in prison confrontations, while Whites are more likely to be the victims (Bowker 1980; Bartollas and Sieverdes 1981; Scacco 1982). For example, of the incidents documented by Fuller et al. (1977), 40 percent were interracial and 82 percent of the interracial incidents involved a Black aggressor and a White victim. Likewise, Toch (1977) found that 80 percent of aggressors were Black and 80 percent of victims were White in prison assaults. A White prisoner in

Carroll (1974: 147) illustrates the posture of Black inmates towards Whites:

> They think they're superior and they push us around all the time. Like in the dining hall. If I was late and trying to catch up with a buddy and cut in front of one of them [a Black] I'd probably get piped. But they cut in front of White men all the time and nothing happens...It's the same in the wings. The tier I'm on used to be all White. Now it's 50-50 and it ain't safe for a White to walk along it. If he does, he better walk quick and keep his eyes open.

The inmate testifies to the power structure found within the inmate subculture. In sum, White inmates often assume an inferior role given their inability to adjust to prison life, and their tendency to "do their own time." Because of their inferior status, they become easy targets for Black inmates seeking to demonstrate their superiority.

Sexual Domination

Sexual domination is the ultimate demonstration of supremacy within the inmate subculture. Issues surrounding the sexual domination of Black inmates over Whites constitute the third subtopic found within the literature on target violence. Research on sexual domination focuses on two areas: 1) Demographic studies measuring the background characteristics of aggressors and victims in prison sexual assaults; and 2) theoretical studies explaining sexual assaults in male correctional facilities. Demographic studies, both quantitative and qualitative, consistently show Black inmates over-represented among the aggressors and Whites over-represented among the victims of prison sexual assaults. Since 1968, eleven research projects have studied the topic of prison sexual assault.[17] All of the studies found that Blacks were disproportionately the aggressors and Whites were disproportionately the victims in sexual assaults. For example, Lockwood (1980) found that while Blacks comprised 50 percent of the prison populations, they comprised 78 percent of the aggressors in sexual assaults.

In facilities where Black inmates comprise the numeric minority, they maintain their over-representation among the aggressors in prison sexual assaults. For example, Blacks comprised only 22 percent of inmate population studied by Carroll (1974), but they represented 75 percent or more of the aggressors in sexual assaults. Juvenile detention centers displayed a similar racial pattern in sexual assaults (Bartollas and Sieverdes 1981; Starchild 1990).[18] Despite the compelling statistics, Blacks do not perceive themselves as over-represented among the aggressors in prison sexual assaults. Jones (1976) asked a sample of Tennessee State prisoners to describe the racial profile of most prison rapes. About 93 percent of the White sample in comparison to approximately 5 percent of the Black sample felt that most prison rapes involved a Black aggressor and a White victim. Although denying their aggressor tendency, none of the Black respondents recalled an incident when a White inmate raped a Black inmate (Jones 1976).

Generally, researchers use two theoretical models to explain the observed interracial pattern of prison sexual assaults: masculinity-identification and the power/domination explanation. The masculinity-identification hypothesis states that homosexual rape in prison results from the restriction of social outlets for playing masculine roles (Bowker 1980; Hawkins and Alpert 1989). Masturbation does not alleviate this deprivation and participating in consensual sexual relationships adds to the masculinity threat already present in the prison setting (Bowker 1980). Therefore, one manner in which individuals maintain their manhood is by forcing sex on weaker, more feminine males, which creates a class of inmates against which the aggressor can compare their masculinity (Hawkins and Alpert 1989).

One limitation of the masculinity-identification hypothesis as described by Bowker (1980) and Hawkins and Alpert (1989) is its inability to explain the interracial pattern observed between assault victims and aggressors. According to the masculinity-identification hypothesis, the distribution of victims and aggressors in sexual assaults should be relatively equal across all races. The observations of previous researchers, however, show strong racial patterns in the populations of victims and aggressors. Carroll (1974) makes the connection needed between race and masculinity to explain the interracial pattern observed in prison sexual assaults. According to his argument, Black inmates are overwhelmingly the aggressors in prison sexual assaults due to their emasculation by over 300 years of oppression. Denied the opportunity to demonstrate their manhood in free society, Blacks use the prison setting as the stage for displaying their masculinity. The following quote from Carroll (1974: 181-182) describes the emasculation process endured by Black males and the subsequent consequences:

From the beginning of slavery, White males have been accorded access to Black as well as to White females. At the same time, reciprocal access to White females has been denied to Black males...This caste patterning of sexual relations has had implications for Black males beyond the asymmetrical access to females. More importantly it has degraded the Black male through repeated demonstration of his inability to protect Black

women...In the prison, where the significance of sex is
intensified by the deprivation of heterosexual contact and where
Black and White males live close together, the role of sex in
racial conflict is thrown into sharp relief. In the confines of
prison, the rage of Black males at their psychological
emasculation is vented against White males.

American society has traditionally affirmed masculinity through qualities
such as assertiveness, self-determination, power over others, and the
ability to provide for and protect one's family. These are precisely the
attributes denied to Black males by slavery and the legacy of racism
(Carroll 1974). Consequently, Black males develop an emasculated self-
identity and the predominantly White prison staff, coupled with the
deprivations of prison life, exacerbates the Black male's sense of
emasculation. To counter their feelings of emasculation, Black males
feminize Whites in efforts to confirm their masculinity. The ability to
force another male into a degrading sexual act is thus a symbol of
manhood (Carroll 1974). A Black inmate in the study conducted by
Carroll (1974) describes the significance of race in the process of
masculinity-identification:

To the general way of thinking it's cause we're confined and
we've got hard rocks. But that ain't it at all. It's a way for the
Black man to get back at the White man. It's one way he can
assert his manhood. Anything White, even a defenseless punk,
is part of what the Black man hates. It's part of what he's had to
fight all his life just to survive, just to have a hole to sleep in and
some garbage to eat...It's a new ego thing. He can show he's a
man by making a White guy into a girl.

The strong anti-White sentiment found among Black inmates provides
group support and approval for sexual assaults against Whites. In many
cases, the sexual assault of a White inmate serves as "an initiation rite by
which Black prisoners demonstrate their manhood and blackness to their
peers" (Carroll 1974: 185). In free society, homosexual activity reflects a
lack of manhood. However, the aggressors in prison sexual assaults
maintain their manhood by using force. Bowker (1980: 11) states, "It is
necessary for prison rapists to participate in homosexual activity without
thinking of themselves as homosexuals in order to preserve their
masculine identity." Excessive violence during sexual assaults is a
common solution to the masculinity dilemma (Hawkins and Alpert
1989).
    The second theory of prison sexual assaults suggests that the desire
for power and domination over others are the motivating factors behind

sexual assaults (Hawkins and Alpert 1989). As in free society, prison rape is as much an expression of power and domination as it is sexual (Propper 1981; Rideau and Wikberg 1992; Silberman 1995). Given the deprivations characteristic of prison life, "manhood" is the most valuable possession an inmate owns. Therefore, to lose one's manhood through a homosexual rape attributes a great deal of power to the aggressor. For Black inmates, subjected to White control throughout their life, sexual assault offers them the opportunity to exert symbolic control over a White victim who represents the dominant White power structure of the prison and free society (Silberman 1995). Black domination of Whites leads to the attribution of power to Black inmates. Victimizing Whites brings a degree of balance to the power scale in the minds of Black inmates, as seen in the comments from two inmates at Eastern Correctional Institution:

> It's getting even I guess...You guys [Whites] been cutting our balls off ever since we been in this country. Punking [slang for raping] Whites is just one way of getting even. (Carroll 1977: 422)

> The Black man is just waking up to what's been going on. Now that he's awake, he's gonna be mean. He's been raped-politically, economically, morally raped. He sees this now, but his mind's still small so he's getting back this way. But it's just a beginning. (Carroll 1974: 185)

To bring greater balance to the power scale, Black inmates desire to victimize those Whites who possess a certain degree of power. A successful assault results in the transference of power from the victim to the aggressor. A statement from a Black inmate from Illinois captures this power dynamic:

> In the prison, the Black dudes have a little masculinity game they play. It has no name, really, but I call it whup or fuck a White boy – especially the White gangsters or syndicate men, the bad juice boys, the hit men etc. The Black dudes go out of their way to make faggots out of them. And to lose a fight to a White dude is one of the worst things that can happen to a Black dude... (Robinson 1971: 29)

The more power and status possessed by the White victim, the more power and status awarded to the Black aggressor following a successful assault. In prison, sexually assaulting an inmate who appears feminine in their physical build and demeanor brings very little power and likely raises questions about one's own sexuality (Hawkins and Alpert 1989).

Summary and Contributions

In sum, research indicates that prison whiteness has a significant impact on the violent tendencies of Black inmates. White correctional officers are the frequent victims of Black assaults for two reasons: 1) they symbolize White domination and oppression of Blacks in general; and 2) their ignorance of Black culture results in a more coercive relationship with Black inmates, which fuels feelings of injustice and discrimination among Blacks. Research also indicates that White inmates are the frequent victims of Black assaults for four reasons: 1) displaced Black aggression, 2) the inability of White inmates to adjust to prison life, 3) the affirmation of manhood by Black inmates, and 4) the Black inmate's desire for power and domination.

The current study seeks to build on the previous literature concerning the influence of prison whiteness on Black violence in three ways. First, the study offers a large-scale quantitative assessment of the relationship between prison whiteness and Black violence. With the exception of the literature on homosexual rape, much of the research conducted in this area consists of qualitative case studies of relatively few correctional facilities. In most cases, the narrative given by inmates or the notes gathered by a lone researcher served as evidence to support research claims regarding the influence of race on prison violence. What complicates these findings is the relatively small number of correctional facilities considered. For example, one could easily argue that racial hostility is likely to vary across the United States given the history of racism characteristic of the American south. Therefore, we cannot assume that the patterns of racial violence observed in one facility necessarily apply to all correctional institutions. The second objective of the current study is to conduct a regional comparison of the influence of race on prison violence. Third, the study provides a more recent assessment of the influence of prison whiteness on Black violence. Most of the previous work in this area dates to the 1970's and early 1980's. Subsequently, the racial atmosphere at that time was likely more hostile than it is today (many would perhaps disagree). Therefore, we do not know if prison whiteness is as significant today as it was then in producing Black violence.

Black Inmates and Prison Blackness

Given that the previous literature indicates that prison whiteness contributes to the violent tendencies of Black inmates, the logical research question comes to mind: "What effect does prison blackness have on the violent tendencies of Black inmates?" Prison blackness is similar to the concept of prison whiteness. As such, there are two parts to prison blackness: blackness among both guards and inmates. Analyzing the influence of prison blackness permits one to formulate two additional research questions. First, since Black inmates view White officers as symbols of White oppression, "How does their behavior change when more Black officers are introduced into the correctional facility?" Second, since White inmates often serve as the scapegoats for Black frustration and anger, "What happens to this rage in prisons where Blacks form the overwhelming majority within the inmate population?" Despite the extensive literature on the connection between prison whiteness and Black inmate violence, very little research has examined the influence of prison blackness on Black inmate violence. Subsequently, the literature as it stands does not provide answers to any of the aforementioned questions.

The limited literature in this area focuses almost exclusively on blackness among prison guards. In particular, three studies have examined the influence of Black guards on the prison subculture: Jacobs and Kraft (1978), Fox (1982), and McCorkle et al. (1995). Concerning blackness among inmates, only one study suggests a connection between the percentage of Black inmates and prison violence (Harer and Steffensmeier 1996). All of the studies concerning prison blackness contain methodological problems that prohibit one from answering the questions above. The lack of interest in prison blackness by criminologists is surprising given the nationwide push to recruit more Black correctional officers following the 1971 prison riot at Attica Correctional Facility.

Prison Blackness Among Guards

The Aftermath of Attica

On September 13, 1971, 500 New York State troopers stormed Attica Correctional Facility firing roughly 2200 bullets in nine minutes, ending the four-day prison riot. The aftermath revealed that the state troopers killed 39 individuals (10 hostages and 29 inmates). The disproportionate number of Black inmates killed clearly indicated the significance of race at every stage of the Attica uprising. Blacks represented slightly over 50 percent of the inmate population at Attica. However, all of the inmates killed were Black. Following the riot, New York State officials authorized the McKay Commission[19] to study all events and individuals surrounding the riot to determine its cause.

One major finding by the McKay Commission was the proclamation that prison whiteness was a major cause of the large-scale disturbance. Specifically, the commission testified that the large racial difference between the inmate and staff populations at Attica created a racially hostile atmosphere. At the time of the riot, the inmate population at Attica was 54.2 percent Black, 36.6 percent White and 9.2 percent Puerto Rican and other (McKay Commission 1972). However, in sharp contrast, the prison staff was all White with the exception of one Black civilian teacher and one Puerto Rican correctional officer (McKay Commission 1972). In addition to racial differences, the inmate and staff populations differed drastically in terms of their geographic backgrounds. The Black inmate population was largely urban with 87.8 percent of the Black inmate population originating from one of four metropolitan areas in New York State (New York City at 51.7 percent, Buffalo at 16.5 percent, Rochester at 13.6 percent, and Syracuse at 6 percent). The "all-White correctional staff from rural western New York State" was culturally unprepared to handle the urban Black inmate (McKay Commission 1972: 107). In fact, many of the White officers testified that controlling convicted criminals was their first exposure to Blacks. As a result, the guards and inmates "began with little or nothing in common, and Attica was not a catalyst, which made people want to learn about each other" (McKay Commission 1972: 80).

The cultural gap produced by the drastic differences in the racial and geographic backgrounds of the inmate and staff populations resulted in staff-to-inmate relations based largely on "fear, hostility, and mistrust, nurtured by racism" (McKay Commission 1972: 80). In their landmark report, the commission concluded that (4):

> Above all, for both inmates and officers, "corrections" meant an atmosphere charged with racism... There was no escape within the walls from the growing mistrust between White middle America and the residents of urban ghettos. Indeed, at Attica, racial polarity and mistrust were magnified by the constant reminder that the keepers were White and the kept were largely Black and Spanish-speaking. The young Black inmate tended to see the White officer as the symbol of a racist, oppressive system which put him behind bars. The officer, his perspective shaped by his experience on the job, knew Blacks only as belligerent unrepentant criminals. The result was a mutual lack of respect which made communication all but impossible.

Following the official report issued by the McKay Commission, there was a nationwide push to recruit more minority officers, particularly Blacks. The need for more Black correctional officers was evident in statements and depositions issued by prison reformers,[20] national commissions,[21] and federal judges.[22] The general belief was that the presence of Black correctional officers would alleviate some of the stresses of prison life and foster a less hostile atmosphere.

The tragic events of Attica along with federal pressures for more affirmative action programs forced many prison systems to actively recruit Black officers. For example, in Illinois, "recruitment trailers and sound trucks were sent into the inner city to interview and hire guards" from minority populations (Jacobs 1977: 126). The Illinois initiative was successful in recruiting Black officers to work for the prison system, particularly at Stateville Penitentiary. In 1970, the year before the Attica uprising, there were 38 Black guards at Stateville. In 1972, the year after Attica there were 146 Black guards and the number continued to climb in 1973 when there were 200 Black guards at Stateville (Jacobs 1977). In a matter of three years, the population of Black guards at Stateville increased by 426 percent. Similar patterns of growth among Black prison guards took place across the U.S. Despite the rationale behind hiring more Black officers and the subsequent increase in their numbers, few criminologists have actually studied the impact of Black officers on the prison subculture. The limited literature on prison blackness among guards divides into three arguments considered below.

No Significant Difference "in Theory"

Jacobs and Kraft (1978) test the assumption that replacing veteran White rural prison guards with young Black urban guards would significantly reduce strain and conflict within the prison setting. Their study included survey data gathered from a sample of 238 prison guards from the Stateville and Joliet maximum-security prisons in Illinois. The survey contained background information and attitudinal items measuring racial variations in response to statements about different aspects of prison life.

There were four important findings from the work of Jacobs and Kraft (1978). First, Black guards perceived themselves as having a more positive working relationship with inmates than White guards. In response to the statement "Black guards get along better with inmates than Whites do," roughly 48 percent of Black guards agreed in comparison to about 31 percent of White guards. Second, Black guards preferred to work in parts of the prison where exposure to contact with the inmate population is relatively high. About 23 percent of Black guards preferred to work in the cell houses, while only 7 percent of White guards preferred such assignments.[23] Third, Black guards are more likely to attribute the criminality of minority inmates to the lack of opportunities or racism. For example, 63 percent of Black guards and 41 percent of White guards felt that lack of opportunities was a significant reason for the high representation of minority inmates. Lastly, Black guards were more optimistic about the prospect of rehabilitation. In response to the statement, "Rehabilitation programs are a waste of time and money," 32.8 percent of Black guards strongly disagreed in comparison to 12.4 percent of White guards. Despite the observed attitudinal differences between the Black and White guard populations, Jacobs and Kraft (1978) concluded that, *in theory*, there were no major differences between Black and White officers. As such, state officials should not expect that adding more Black correctional officers would alleviate the stresses of prison life.

Because Jacobs and Kraft's (1978) study neglected to include any measures of prison stress or strain, they are unable to make accurate predictions regarding the likely influence of Black guards. Without such measures, their study merely predicts that given the minor differences observed between White and Black officers, adding more Black officers should not have a significant impact on prison tension. However, Jacobs and Kraft (1978) failed to consider the symbolic impact of Black versus White guards on a prison subculture over-populated with Black inmates.[24] Essentially, their study was nothing more than an exploration of the background and attitudinal differences between White and Black officers. While *in theory* Black guards were no different from Whites, *in reality* the symbolic image of a Black officer has a significant influence on the inmate subculture by changing the Black inmate's perceptions and behavior. Racial tensions perhaps reduce given that Black inmates see other Blacks in position of authority within the prison. The presence of Black guards disrupts the traditional image of the prison guard as a symbol of White oppression.

Effectiveness of Black Officers

Based merely on background comparisons, such as Jacobs and Kraft (1978), White and Black guards should be equally effective in dealing with the inmate population. However, qualitative narratives indicate that Black officers are more effective at handling Black inmates, especially in hostile situations. For example, Fox (1982) found that it was commonplace for White guards to admit their inability to respond effectively to hostile Black prisoners. For this reason, officials often ask Black officers to intervene in potentially volatile situations involving Black prisoners since "Blacks are more effective in dealing with hostile prisoners" (Fox 1982: 74). One White officer interviewed by Fox stated:

> We have several Black sergeants and a Black lieutenant, and simply because they are Black and have grown up in a situation

that's very familiar to most of the inmates, their ability to calm
down a cell hall, especially at a time when there's a Black
uprising or unrest, is incredible. And I think they're needed
very much because they can go in and say a few words like,
"Look you motherfuckers, calm that shit down, the shit stops
now or we'll bring..." And I can say these things, but I have
trouble getting the rap down. They don't, so they're very
effective people.

The statement from the White officer indicates the advantage of Black
guards in being able to use their familiarity with Black culture in
maintaining prison order. Not only does the White officer lack the
familiarity with the language, but there are also certain words and
phrases that when used by White officers assume completely different
meanings. Consequently, White officers scrutinize their choice of words
and their delivery. These limitations undermine the seriousness of their
commands, which may result in the defiance of their orders. Black
officers recognize their symbolic advantage in interactions with Black
inmates, as evident by a comment from Fox (1982: 75):

Like so and so would be on the phone too long, and they would
say, "you go down there and tell him to get off the phone."
They [White officers] expected this guy to blow up, and I'd just
go down there and tell him, "Look here, time's up, and you have
to go," No problem, see, being Black, I really had an edge on
them. They [White officers] are looked at as the "system." I'm
looked at as "what the fuck are you doing here?" I just told
them quite frankly how I felt about the whole thing, "Were I not
here, you would have a harder way to go."

The officer's statement indicates keen awareness of his symbolic
advantage in issuing commands to Black inmates. Because White
officers represent *the system*, their commands issued to Black inmates
evoke feelings of racism and discrimination. In contrast, the commands
issued by Black officers do not carry the undertone of racism and
discrimination, and therefore fail to produce the same effect as
commands issued by Whites. Fox (1982) offers valuable insight
regarding the influence of prison blackness among correctional officers
in curtailing Black violence among inmates. However, he provides
relatively few narratives to support the generalized claim that Black
guards reduce Black inmate violence. The two narratives do not provide
sufficient evidence to form overall generalizations concerning the
influence of prison blackness.

White-to-Black Guard Ratio

One way in which researchers have attempted to quantify the effectiveness of Black officers at maintaining prison order is by considering the ratio of White-to-Black officers in models of prison violence. In a large-scale quantitative study conducted by McCorkle et al. (1995), the researchers consider the influence of Black guards on three measures of prison violence: inmate-on-inmate assaults, inmate-on-staff assaults, and prison riots. The data used for their analysis came from the 1984 and 1995 versions of the *Census of State and Federal Adult Correctional Facilities.*[25] McCorkle et al. (1995) assessed the impact of prison blackness by incorporating the ratio of White-to-Black correctional officers as one of the factors measuring their management model of prison violence. Based on their analysis from a sample of 371 correctional facilities, they found that the White-to-Black guard ratio was the most significant factor in predicting prison staff assault rates, next to security level. Specifically, the higher the ratio of White-to-Black guards the higher the staff assault rate. The ratio of White-to-Black guards was also significant in predicting inmate assault rates. A third finding showed that the inmate-to-guard ratio was not significant in either model of prison violence. This finding, coupled with the first, suggests that the sheer number of correctional officers is not important in predicting prison violence; however, the race of correctional officers is highly significant.

The McCorkle et al. (1995) study has one major limitation. In estimating their models, they failed to control for the influence of inmate race on their observed relationship between the White-to-Black guard ratio and measures of prison violence. For example, it would be important to know if the ratio of White-to-Black guards is more significant in determining staff assault rates in prisons with a relatively large number of Black inmates. Subsequently, as it stands, McCorkle et al. (1995) cannot assess how well the observed relationship holds in environments with relatively large, or small, Black inmate populations. The current study builds on McCorkle et al. (1995) by considering the significance of the interaction between the race of correctional officers and the race of inmates in the production of prison violence.

Prison Blackness Among Inmates

Relative Numbers

Criminologists have neglected to assess the impact of prison blackness within the inmate population on institutional violence rates. Recall the first section of the current literature review presented three studies that attempted to measure the cumulative impact of race on violence rates.

Two of the studies, Ellis et al. (1974) and Gaes and McGuire (1985), examined the proportion of nonwhite inmates, which does not allow for specific statements regarding the influence of Black inmates on prison violence. The third study, conducted by Harer and Steffensmeier (1996), examined only federal correctional facilities where Black inmates typically comprise a smaller percentage of the inmate population. Their study also failed to present a measure of prison violence reflecting the institutional violence rate. Collectively, none of the three studies considered permit one to make statements regarding the influence of prison blackness within the inmate population on prison violence rates, with any degree of confidence.

Despite the lack of adequate empirical research conducted in this area, Harer and Steffensmeier (1996) offer a conceptual model to predict the likely influence of prison blackness on institutional violence rates. The researchers suggest that in prisons where White inmates form the majority, the smaller number of Black inmates may engage in defensive violence to deter hostile attacks by White inmates. Harer and Steffensmeier (1996) further state that in prisons where Blacks form the majority they provide a greater collective deterrent to violence by Whites; subsequently, reducing individual incidents of violence by Black inmates. Using this model, Harer and Steffensmeier (1996) would predict that a high percentage of Black inmates should result in a low institutional assault rate (among inmates), and a low percentage of Black inmates would have the opposite effect. The model proposed by Harer and Steffensmeier (1996) however, focuses primarily on relative numbers and not race. According to their perspective, any racial group that constitutes the numeric minority should have the most significant impact on institutional violence rates.

Summary and Contributions

Research is limited regarding the influence of prison blackness on aggressive behavior within the inmate subculture. Despite the preponderance of evidence indicating a strong link between prison whiteness and Black inmate violence, few researchers have considered the subsequent effect of prison blackness on Black inmate violence. It was not until the 1971 prison riot at Attica Correctional Facility that prison blackness among guards received consideration among prison violence researchers. Since that time, three subtopics have emerged from within this area of literature. The first suggests that "in theory" Black and White officers have no significant differences; therefore, their influence on inmate behavior should be similar. However, the difference is perhaps more in the symbolic image of minority officers. The second theme suggests that Black officers are better at controlling and relating to Black inmates given their familiarity with Black culture. Given their cultural advantage, White guards often ask their Black coworkers to intervene in hostile situations involving Black inmates. The final theme suggests that the ratio of White-to-Black officers has a significant influence on both the staff and inmate assault rates.

There was virtually no literature pertaining to the impact of prison blackness among the inmate population on prison violence rates. This was surprising given the preponderance of cultural studies proclaiming that Blacks, males in particular, adhere more strictly to violence codes. If individual Black males follow violence codes, then a collection of Black males should have a significant impact on the institutional violence rates, since more violence prone individuals will share a limited space. Harer and Steffensmeier (1996) proposed a theory based on relative numbers within the inmate population. However, their theory focuses more on relative numbers and not cultural values.

The current study seeks to build on this area of literature in the following ways. First, the study quantifies the relationship between prison blackness and institutional violence rates. Fox (1982) presented narratives from qualitative interviews to demonstrate the effectiveness of Black officers in controlling Black inmates. Therefore, Black officers should have a reducing effect on prison violence rates in a quantitative analysis. Second, the study assesses the influence of the interaction between Black officers and Black inmates on institutional violence rates. Previous works such as McCorkle et al. (1995) considered the influence of Black officers but neglect to control for the percentage of Black inmates. Third, the study provides the first adequate assessment of the influence of prison blackness among inmates on facility violence rates. The study proposes a theory of Black rage, which predicts a positive relationship between the institutional violence rate and the percentage of Black inmates and a negative relationship between the institutional violence rate and the percentage of Black staff.

[1] Lee Carroll (1982: 194), Race, Ethnicity, and the Social Order of the Prison

[2] John Irwin (1980: 182), *Prisons in Turmoil*

[3] Anonymous White inmate from New York State Department of Corrections interviewed by Daniel Lockwood (1980: 79), *Prison Sexual Violence*

[4] Relative deprivation stresses the perceived discrepancy between achieved and expected status or goals (Davies 1972; Piven and Cloward 1977). Frustration over the failure to reach what one expects to achieve is what produces violent tendencies.

[5] Other researchers have also reported findings consistent with the idea that Blacks have a greater tendency towards violence than Whites for cultural reasons. For example, Wolfgang's (1958) subculture of violence thesis stated that Blacks perceive a slightly derogatory remark differently than Whites. Furthermore, Wolfgang contends that as a cultural expression, Blacks are quick to resort to physical combat as a measure of daring or defense of status and selfhood. Likewise, Bernard (1990) states that Blacks are more likely to perceive their surroundings as being aggressive or dangerous, and consequently they engage in aggressive or violent responses for self-protection.

[6] Three studies report no significant differences between the violent tendencies of Blacks and Whites: Cannon (1994); Erlanger (1974); Shoemaker and Williams (1987). A fourth study by Dixon and Lizotte (1987) contends that Whites are more supportive of violence than Blacks. All of the studies however fail to produce appropriate measures of violence and attitudes favorable towards its use (see, e.g., the review by Luckenbill and Doyle 1989).

[7] Ellis et al. (1974) failed to disclose their rationale for hiring ex-convicts as research assistants. Nor did they state whether the ex-convicts 1) disclosed information regarding their ex-inmate status, or 2) conducted interviews where they were once incarcerated. Without any evidence to dispute the claim that ex-convict interviewers resulted in an inflation of the actual number of prison assaults, we have to assume that it is a possibility.

[8] Wright never presents the actual number of facilities represented by his sample of inmates.

[9] Petersilia ranked the infraction types according to seriousness and issued numeric values that increased with seriousness.

[10] Gaes and McGuire (1985) also analyzed data from the federal prison system; however, they provided no information regarding the percentage of nonWhite inmates.

[11] The data for 1990 and 1995 displayed a similar pattern. For example, in 1990 Blacks accounted for 26.0 percent of federal inmates and 46.9 percent of state inmates. Likewise, in 1995 Blacks accounted for on average 33.5 percent of federal inmates and 50.9 percent of state inmates (Census of State and Federal Adult Correctional Facilities).

[12] Both the staff and inmate populations began to undergo significant demographic changes in the early 1980's. The inmate population became increasingly Black because of the war on drugs, and the staff population became increasingly Black following the push towards affirmative action.

[13] Target violence as used, refers to violence that is racially motivated, particularly those acts involving Black aggressors and White victims. This definition differs from Lockwood (1980). Lockwood refers to potential victims of sexual assaults as targets. As such, target violence is the aggressive reaction of potential victims to the sexual approaches of other inmates.

[14] Thus, prisons are "total institutions:" places where "a large number of like-situated individuals, cut off from wider society for an appreciable period of time, together lead an enclosed, formally administered round of life" (Goffman 1961, xiii). Cutoff from the wider society, the Black inmate has no way of venting his anger at White America.

[15] The fight versus flight norm found within the prison subculture refers to the fact that there are only two options for dealing with inmate challenges. Flight involves admitting defeat and asking for help or retreating to a protective setting. Fight entails publicly attacking one's aggressor. The flight option carries with it several negative consequences, including the loss of reputation and a diminished self-esteem. Also choosing this option leaves one vulnerable to future assaults. The fight option has the positive benefit of bringing one a violent reputation that serves to deter future assault attempts (Toch 1977).

[16] The notions of inferior and superior roles refer to the social hierarchy established by the inmate population. Those inmates more submerged into the inmate subculture and those more equipped for survival in the inmate population have superior status over weaker inmates and those indifferent to the inmate subculture. Consequently, superior inmates assume dominant positions in the prison environment. For example, they often control the market of illicit goods (i.e. drugs, contracts), as well as they tend to be overly aggressive towards the weaker inmates.

[17] See Davis (1968), Irwin (1971), Carroll (1974), Scacco (1975), Jones (1976), Toch (1977), Nacci (1978), Lockwood (1980), Bowker (1980), Wooden and Parker (1983), and Nacci and Kane (1984).

[18] Giallombardo (1966) and Carter (1973) observed a similar interracial pattern in consensual homosexual relationships in female prisons. Blacks were disproportionately "butches" (dominant role) and Whites were disproportionately "femmes" (subordinate role).

[19] The McKay Commission conducted an impartial investigation into the events occurring before, during and after the Attica riot. In conducting their fact-finding mission the committee was granted unlimited access to all information regarding, the inmates, the guards, the daily operations of the facility, the warden, the Governor, etc. Following their 8-month investigation, the commission produced a 533-page report entitled, *The Official Report of the New York State Special Commission on Attica.*

[20] In his argument for the hiring of more minority correctional officers, prison reform activist Herman Schwartz (1972: 50) issued the following statement: "The guard population is drawn from the extremely conservative residents of these rural areas, who become guards for the pension, and often as a second job to a farm or other occupation. These people usually have no sympathy or understanding for the strange urban groups, with their often unfamiliar and often immoral life styles, with their demands and their resentments. Racial prejudice is

often present for the White backlash is particularly powerful among such rural types, even apart from the prison."

[21] In 1973, the prestigious National Advisory Commission on Criminal Justice Standards and Goals observed that: "Black inmates want Black staff with whom they can identify...Correctional agencies must become sensitive to this issue. They should abandon policies and practices that weaken identification between members of these groups and launch programs that capitalize on cultural differences as opportunities to improve their programs rather than as problems to contend with...The need for a role model to admire and emulate is undeniable. All youth need heroes. So do adults. Corrections should provide them among its staff, rather than weed them out. Both White and minority staff must be trained to accept this program goal."

[22] In describing the abuses of the Alabama prison system, Federal District Court Judge Frank Johnson issued the following statement in *Pugh v. Locke* (1976): "The problems posed by understaffing are aggravated by the fact that most of the large institutions are located in rural areas of the state. The guards, drawn largely from the local population, are practically all White and rural in contrast to the predominantly Black and urban inmate population they supervise. A number of witnesses testified that staff members address Black inmates with racial slurs, further straining already tense relations...Defendants shall immediately institute an affirmative hiring program designed to reduce and having the effect of reducing the racial and cultural disparity between the staff and the inmate population."

[23] White guards overwhelmingly preferred to work in the tower (36.3 percent) where there is virtually no contact with the inmate population. In comparison, only 17.5 percent of Black guards would consider the tower as the best prison job.

[24] Fox (1982) makes the same mistake in regards to Hispanic officers versus Black or White officers in controlling Hispanic inmates. Fox (1982) studied organizational and racial conflict at five maximum-security prisons. In his section on racism and sexism, each sample of prison guards responded to the following statement, "Except for language, Hispanic correctional officers are no more effective than Black or White officers in dealing with Hispanic prisoners" (65). His findings revealed that all guard samples across the five prisons tended to agree with the statement. Fox concluded, "Their perspective acknowledges the advantage of Spanish-speaking officers in this situation but does not recognize any additional social or cultural advantages" (66). Like Jacobs and Kraft (1978), Fox (1982) fails to consider the symbolic influence of minority officers on the prison subculture from the inmate's perspective.

[25] This study uses these two versions of the census along with the 1995 edition.

CHAPTER III

Understanding Black Rage

To be Black and conscious in America is to be in a constant state of rage.[1]

Black males have every right to be angry.[2]

What happens to a dream deferred? Does it dry up like a raisin in the sun? ...Or does it explode?[3]

Understanding Black Rage

Black rage is the central concept in the proposed theory of prison violence. Inmate narratives and victimization studies indicate that Black rage against White America is a significant factor in understanding the observed interracial pattern in prison assaults. Previous research on prison violence has failed to consider the importance of Black rage; therefore, in the context of corrections, the concept remains uninvestigated. In order to understand the relationships proposed in the theoretical model, it is essential that the reader become more familiar with the concept of Black rage, particularly in relation to Black males. This section provides answers to three specific questions. First, what are the essential components and properties of Black rage? Second, what historical and contemporary factors encourage Black rage? Lastly, what are some of the societal and interpersonal consequences of Black rage?

Definition of Black Rage

While there is a large body of literature concerning Black rage, few researchers have actually defined the concept. Grier and Cobbs (1968) conducted one of the first systematic assessments of Black rage. Their book defined Black rage as a manifestation of anger resulting from the lack of power. Specifically, Grier and Cobbs (1968: 60) argued that Black males, both individually and collectively, lacked the ultimate form of power, "the freedom to understand and alter one's life." Attributing this lack of power to racism, Black men desire to attack Whites as a conscious attempt to attack those who keep them powerless (Grier and Cobbs 1968). D'Souza (1995) provides a more contemporary definition of Black rage. In contrast to the power explanation offered by Grier and Cobbs (1968), D'Souza (1995) defined Black rage as a response to Black suffering and failure, which is exacerbated by "the irresistible temptation to attribute African-American problems to a history of White racist oppression" (6). While the definitions share similarities, the position stated by D'Souza (1995) reflects the general definition of Black rage found in subsequent research[4] (P. Harris 1997; Gibbs 1994; Hooks 1995; Cose 1993; Peterson 2000).

Lessons from History

The history of White oppression is an essential element in the Black rage definition provided by D'Souza (1995). Despite the temporal distance from slavery, the lynching era, the Jim Crow era, and the enduring Civil Rights Movement, Black males maintain a conscious hold on the lessons learned from their history of interactions with Whites. In particular, history has taught Black males lessons regarding their sense of manhood, the need to suppress rage, the injustice of the criminal justice system, and the cost for expressing rage. Twentieth century Black males carry the lessons learned from history and use them as justifications for their rage. As such, the contemporary Black male is at "one end of a psychological continuum which reaches back in time to his enslaved ancestors." Furthermore, "much of the pathology that we see in Black people had its genesis in slavery" (Grier and Cobbs 1968: 31). Thus, in order to understand the rage of present-day Black males, it is necessary to consider the significance of historical lessons taught to Black males through their interactions with Whites. These historical lessons form the core of the Black man's rage. As such, so long as America is unable to alter its racist past, and history descends from generation to generation, Black males will always have a foundation for rage. "Understanding the historical roots and the current social context" of the rage found in contemporary Black males, "is merely the first step in analyzing its symptoms and its consequences for Black males, their families, their communities, and the broader society" (Gibbs 1994: 132).

Slavery: The Denial of Manhood

The first lesson of history taught Black males that manhood is an earned status and not an ordained right. The struggle to define manhood, for Black males, began during the early days of American slavery. Black males suffered emasculation from their experience with slavery, both psychologically and physically. Their psychological emasculation occurred as they helplessly stood by while White males raped their wives, sisters, and daughters (Dollard 1957; Herton 1965; Grier and Cobbs 1968; Carroll 1974; Morrison 1987). The inability to protect Black women, and the denial of similar access to White women, severely damaged the Black male's psychological sense of manhood. In addition to psychological castration, Black males faced physical emasculation from both slaveholders and their Black slave mothers (Grier and Cobbs 1968; Gibbs 1994). Black mothers during slavery had the difficult task of raising Black males to assume subordinate positions in society. The maternal instinct to be caring and nurturing was countered by the Black mother's recognition that "she must intuitively cut off and blunt his masculine assertiveness and aggression lest these put the boy's life in jeopardy" (Grier and Cobbs 1968). Essentially, Black mothers had to take on the role of the slave master and "treat the child with capricious cruelty, hurt him physically and emotionally, and demand that he respond in an obsequious helpless manner-a manner she knew would enhance his chance of survival" (Grier and Cobbs 1968: 171). Therefore, in order to insure the child's safety, the slave mother repressed the normal signs of manhood in her slave son. For nearly 250 years, Black males, out of fear for their safety, suppressed the normal signs of manhood (i.e. independence, self-confidence, assertiveness, or defiance) through "passive resistance, childlike ignorance, self-denigrating humor, and sullen withdrawal" (Grier and Cobbs 1968; Gibbs 1994: 130).

One longstanding consequence of masculinity suppression is that Black males now engage in a never-ending battle to acquire manhood. For "the Black man, attaining any portion of manhood is an active process," during which he "must penetrate barriers and overcome opposition in order to assume a masculine posture" (Grier and Cobbs 1968: 59). In contrast, for White males, "manhood is an ordained right," granted at "birth by the possession of a penis and White skin" (Grier and Cobbs 1968: 59). The rage in Black males stems partly from their frustration with actively pursuing manhood, while Whites are born with manhood attributions. The manhood deficiencies and struggles of the contemporary Black male are direct side effects of the psychological and physical emasculation of their slave ancestors. The psychological conditions necessary for masculine growth and development have not changed very much since the days of slavery. Despite better jobs, housing, and other signs of external progress, "the American heritage of racism will still not allow the Black man to feel himself master in his own land" (Grier and Cobbs 1968: 60-61).

Lynching: Whites Above the Law

The second lesson of history taught Black males that Whites are above the law in their crimes against Blacks. After the Civil War White males developed alternative measures for controlling Black rage and "keeping the Negro in his place" (Powdermaker 1943: 133). One practice for controlling Black males was lynching. Wright (1990) found that more cases of lynching occurred during the 15-year period immediately following the Civil War (1865-1880) than during any other 15-year period in U.S. history. Conservative estimates for the number of deaths during the "lynching era"[5] range from 2,400 to 4,900[6] (Pinar 2001; Tolnay and Beck 1995). Exact estimates are difficult to obtain, given that many cases included police officers who then erased the event from public record (Feagin and Hernan 1995). However, Black historians, such as Ida B. Wells (1969), estimated that during the lynching era over 10,000 Black lives were lost.

In contrast to the high frequency of Black lynchings, the frequency of convictions for such offenses remained considerably low. Between 1900 and 1930, researchers estimate that only 0.8 percent of lynchings in the United States resulted in a criminal conviction (Chadbourn 1933; Brown 1965). For instance, Florida had the greatest percentage of Black lynchings, yet from 1900 to 1934, there was not a single conviction for lynching (Pinar 2001). Furthermore, as late as the 1930's, only six states had disciplinary statutes prohibiting lynchings (McGovern 1982). Even for states with statutes against lynchings, there was still no guarantee that a lynching would result in a conviction. For example, in August of 1955, Emmitt "Bo" Till, a Chicago teenager visiting a relative in Money, Mississippi, made the fatal mistake of seeming "too familiar" with a White female working in a local grocery store (Gibbs 1996). Days later, the body of the fourteen-year old Emmitt Till surfaced in the Tallahatchie River, bloody and severely mutilated (Gibbs 1996). In spite of eyewitness testimony and an admission of guilt by the store clerks boyfriend, an "all-White, all-male jury acquitted the two defendants after deliberating for sixty-seven minutes" (Gibbs 1996: 256).

The history of unpunished crimes against African-Americans plays a significant symbolic role in the rage of Black males today. Cases such as Emmitt Till's murder and the other numerous unpunished crimes against Blacks, historically confirmed the notion that Whites were above the law in their crimes against Blacks. Thus, in present-day offenses, where Whites and others receive lenient sentences (if punished at all) for crimes against Blacks, it signals a symbolic return to days of slavery, a time when Blacks were merely property. Therefore, the ability of Whites to *beat the system* serves as a constant reminder to African-Americans that very little has changed since the days of slavery. Unlike the past, however, frustration over justice denied in contemporary times is more likely to result in large-scale disturbances, such as the 1992 Los Angeles riots following the acquittals of the White police officers videotaped beating Black motorist, Rodney King.

Convict Leasing: Roots of Injustice

The third history lesson taught to Black males suggests that not only can Whites beat the system, but also that the system is set-up to work against Blacks. The present-day distrust of the criminal justice system, among Blacks, originates from their post-civil war experience. Before the war, there were virtually no Black convicts (Pinar 2001). After the war, the Black prison population grew as more and more states adopted the convict lease system. The convict lease system was a practice by which state officials leased the labor of convicted criminals to private contractors. The leasing system first began in 1858, when Virginia State officials leased Black convicts to work for railroad and canal companies (Pinar 2001). Before the Civil War, Virginia was the only state with a convict lease system; however, after Emancipation, nearly all of the confederate states adopted this practice (Ayers 1984; Mancini 1996; Colvin 1997). The convict lease system was not only profitable for private contractors[7] but it was also profitable for state treasuries. For example, during the 1880's and 1890's, convict labor generated nearly ten percent of the states' annual revenue in Tennessee and Alabama (Ayers 1984; Colvin 1997).

The lucrative economic incentives for the State resulted in false accusations of crimes by Black males and disproportionate sentences for those imprisoned. A Black male defendant convicted of a simple misdemeanor was frequently "sentenced to ten days hard labor for his crime, and three, six or eight months, for cost" (Pinar 2001: 992). The leasing system thrived on the victim's inability to pay court cost, which resulted in forced labor to repay the State. From the inception of the American prison system, socioeconomic status and race played a significant role in determinations of guilt and imposed sentences. A Black newspaper in New Orleans noted that convicted Black offenders received "three days for stealing, and eighty-seven for being colored" (quoted in Ayers 1984: 178).

Black males sentenced to the convict lease system faced conditions comparable to, if not worse than, slavery (Pinar 2001). Convicts were excessively punished and often without pretext. Adding to the deprivation was the constant threat of death due to armed guards "notorious for shooting with little provocation" (Ayers 1992: 126). Under such conditions, the death rate for leased convicts far surpassed the general population. For example, in 1870, 41 percent of Alabama's leased convicts died (Ayers 1984). In addition to the high mortality rate, it was also very common for inmates to disappear "as if the earth had opened and swallowed them" (quoted in Ayers 1984: 226). Furthermore, the mysterious "disappearance of convicts was well known among African-Americans" (Pinar 2001: 1000).

Perceived discrimination, in the present-day criminal justice system, plays an important role in the production of rage in Black males. The perception of injustice, in arrests and sentencing decisions, originates from the early development of the American prison system. The historical facts of the convict lease system support the contemporary image of the "system" as working against Black males. Thus, the antagonistic stance of Black males towards the justice system is somewhat understood given that the "Black man has never known law and order except as an instrument of oppression" (Staples 1982: 41). Moreover, "he can never quite respect laws which have no respect for him" (Grier and Cobbs 1968: 178).

Civil Rights Movement: The Cost for Expressing Black Rage

History has also taught Black males that expressing black rage in a peaceful or militant fashion can mean death. Justified Black rage against racial and economic oppression fueled the civil rights movement of the 1950's and 1960's (P. Harris 1997). Despite the one common goal of equality for Blacks, there were two diametrical forces within the Black community working to achieve justice. On one side, there was the Reverend Dr. Martin Luther King Jr. and his devoted followers of the principle of non-violent civil disobedience. Dr. King used Christian doctrines and the influences of Mohandas Karamchand Gandhi and Henry David Thoreau to convince his followers to channel their rage into nonviolent, peaceful protest. The belief among his followers, that God created them for freedom, instilled a rebellious spirit in Black Christians, which empowered them to fight nonviolently and risk death for equality (Cone 1991). Dr. King successfully defused the violent tendencies of Black rage and persuaded thousands of African-Americans to channel these feelings in positive directions. For example, Black rage provided the fuel that "kept the young men and women of the Student Nonviolent Coordinating Committee (SNCC) warm as they filled the jails of the south" (P. Harris 1997: 145).

Malcolm X and his more militant followers represented the other force at work during the civil rights struggle. Contrary to the nonviolent, turn the other cheek approach preached by Dr. King, Malcolm X encouraged his followers to practice self-defense and to seek equality by any means necessary. In contrast to Dr. King's Christian notion of loving thy brother unconditionally, Malcolm X followed his Muslim belief in "an eye for an eye and a tooth for a tooth" (Cone 1991). At a speech in November of 1964, Malcolm defined the Muslim religion as one that "teaches you if someone steps on your toe, chop off their foot," and he insured the crowd that he carried his religious axe with him at all times (quoted in Brietman 1970: 140). Malcolm's self-defense philosophy encouraged his followers to use their Black rage not only to point out injustice but also for protection in their struggle for equality. Consequently, Malcolm's teachings fired "the imaginations of Black men all over the world," as he "articulated Black rage in a manner unprecedented in American history" (Grier and Cobbs 1968: 200; West 1993: 95).

In sum, two diametrical forces supported the civil rights movement. Black rage was an essential element in both forces. Dr. King suppressed and channeled Black rage in positive directions through colorful speeches such "I Have a Dream," while Malcolm X encouraged Black rage with speeches such as "The Ballot or The Bullet." The untimely and questionable deaths of both Dr. King and Malcolm X taught African-Americans that peaceful or militant displays of rage could result in death. Grier and Cobbs (1968: 206) state that Dr. King's death "grew out of that large body of violent bigotry America has always nurtured-that body of thinking which screams for the blood of the radical, or the conservative, or the villain, or the saint." They later concluded that to the extent that Dr. King "was Black and was calling America to account, his days were numbered by the nation he sought to save" (Grier and Cobbs 1968: 206). Both statements easily apply to Malcolm X as well. The mysteries behind their deaths, and the other lessons learned from history, have a significant effect on the rage of contemporary Black males.

Contemporary Significance of History

White Americans acknowledge the historical oppression inflicted upon Blacks; however, most fail to see the contemporary significance of these events (D'Souza 1995). As such, many perceive racism as flourishing today, not in American society, but in the imagination of Black activists (Mayer 1992; Lichtenberg 1992). The general belief among Whites is that "systemic oppression came to a halt with the civil rights era of a generation ago" (D'Souza 1995: 9). In contrast, for many Blacks, racism is not outdated but a continuing force that brutally limits their current position and aspirations (D'Souza 1995). The discrepancy concerning the contemporary significance of White oppression stems from the inability of White Americans to understand the lingering psychological consequences of oppression. The fact that the consequences are internal to the Black experience contributes to the discrepancy, but White Americans have also "developed a high skill in the art of misunderstanding Black people" (Grier and Cobbs 1968: 210). The current study contends that two psychological consequences from the history of Black oppression significantly influence present-day Black rage: belief in conspiracy theories, and the victim mentality.

Conspiracy Theories

Conspiracy theories are prevalent among groups that have endured malicious assaults by outsiders in their past (Farmer 1992; Knopf 1975; Turner 1993). In his provocative book, *Two Nations*, Andrew Hacker (1992) raised the question "Can this nation have an unstated strategy for annihilating Black people?" Based on Black history, most contemporary Blacks would answer this question in the affirmative (Sasson 1995). For many, the history of Blacks in America is "an indictment of the criminal justice system, a coordinated effort, sanctioned by the state and local governments and enforced by their police surrogates, to deprive a whole segment of Americans of their rights to life, liberty, and the pursuit of happiness" (Gibbs 1994: 235). Events, such as the documented history of slave families being destroyed, unsolved public lynchings, and unpunished murders and assaults on civil rights demonstrators, encourages Black belief in conspiracy theories. Blacks have historically explained their oppression in terms of their world-view as an oppressed and powerless people (Turner 1993). As such, they inevitably "perceive those in power as manipulative and completely Machiavellian in their motivations to maintain the status quo of the White majority at all cost" (Gibbs 1996: 236).

The conspiracy theories found within the Black community cluster around four major categories (Gibbs 1996). First, contamination and disease theories suggest that the U.S. government uses Blacks as victims or guinea pigs to test out new viruses or spread diseases in a vulnerable population (Gibbs 1996). Theories of this nature gained popularity in July 1972 when reports surfaced about the Tuskegee Syphilis Study.[8] The Tuskegee scandal was so powerful that when news of the AIDS epidemic appeared, many Blacks attributed the disease to a government conspiracy (Turner 1993; Gibbs 1996). Professor Leonard Jeffries, Chairman of the Black-studies program at City College of New York, stated that the possibility of "AIDS coming out of a laboratory and finding itself localized certainly has to be looked at as part of a conspiratorial process" (quoted in Sykes 1992: 214). Furthermore, in late 1990, a New York Times/CBS poll of 1,047 individuals found that 29 percent of the Black respondents endorsed the theory that "AIDS was deliberately created in a laboratory in order to infect Black people" (quoted in Sykes 1992: 213).

Second, there are conspiracy theories of government involvement in crime and drugs. Such theories suggest that the government has deliberately flooded the Black community with drugs in order to increase criminal activity (Gibbs 1996). For instance, 60 percent of the Black respondents in the New York Times/CBS survey supported the claim that "the government deliberately makes sure that drugs are easily available in poor Black neighborhoods in order to harm Black people" (quoted in Sykes 1992: 213). The crime and drug theories often appear in tandem with the hypothesis that the police and the criminal justice system target young Black males for the specific purpose of weakening the Black family and destroying potential resistance (Gibbs 1996). Indiana University Professor Coramae Richey Mann offered support of this position in her book, *Unequal Justice: A Question of Color*. Mann (1993) suggests that the criminal justice system was intentionally racist as part of a larger plan devised by the White male capitalist elite to maintain its hegemony since the means of economic and political control used in the past are no longer morally acceptable.

The third type of conspiracy theory suggests that the U.S. government systematically attacks Black leaders and civil rights organizations. The New York Times/CBS poll found that 77 percent of the Black respondents felt that the government deliberately singles out Black officials "in order to discredit them in a way it doesn't do with White officials" (quoted in Sykes 1992: 213). For example, despite substantial evidence, many Blacks remain convinced that a government-led conspiracy is responsible for the deaths of Dr. King and Malcolm X (Gibbs 1996). The fact that the FBI heavily watched both leaders encourages the conspiracy notion. More recently, the general belief in governmental conspiracies against Black leaders prompted the re-election of Marion Barry as Mayor of Washington, DC, after an FBI sting operation caught Mr. Barry smoking crack cocaine. Blacks felt that Marion Barry was "entrapped by a racist federal justice system that targets Black politicians for persecution" (Robinson 1995: 95). African-Americans' belief in conspiracy theories is also one of the factors believed to be responsible for the acquittal of O.J. Simpson (Gibbs 1996).

The fourth type of conspiracy theory suggests that the U.S. government has supported the racial and cultural genocide of African-Americans. Theories in this area claim that the government "has supported Ku Klux Klan lynchings, police killings of Blacks, forced sterilization and involuntary birth control as a means of eradicating or decimating the Black population and destroying Black culture" (Gibbs 1996: 237-238). The typology of conspiracy theories in the Black community is quite extensive.[9] Some of the conspiracy theories contain elements of historical facts, while others are fabrications. Regardless of the authenticity of each theory, the high prevalence of such notions circulating in the Black community undoubtedly influences how African-Americans view the world.

The main consequence of conspiracy notions is that African-Americans develop a cultural paranoia. Grier and Cobbs (1968) defined cultural paranoia as the process in which Blacks treat all Whites as a potential enemy unless proven otherwise, and every social system as an adversary until personal experience proves differently. The paranoia is worse for Black males, since they can never predict how others will react to them. In some instances, they may "be treated as an 'invisible man,' as an object of curiosity, as a symbol of aggression, as a token of affirmative action, or simply as a human being" (Gibbs 1994: 136). Given the uncertainty, Black males in America must "develop a profound distrust of his White fellow citizens" and "be more sensitive to the motives of the people around them" (Grier and Cobbs 1968: 160,177). Failure by the Black man to protect himself against physical hurt, cheating, slander, and humiliation, will result in "a life of such pain and shock as to find life itself unbearable" (Grier and Cobbs 1968: 178). A side effect of cultural paranoia is that Blacks become race conscious, which necessitates anger. Peterson (2000) described the process by which race consciousness fosters anger:

> To be a member of a racial group is to always be on guard against slights and insults. One must cultivate a super-sensitivity to racism, and react with great fury whenever one perceives it. An "us-against-them" mentality results, and one's individuality begins to recede behind a wall of racial anger and personal hostility that is poisonous to the person. Happiness and anger cannot coincide, and the person infected with race consciousness is inevitably going to harbor hostility against those who he thinks have not treated his group with sufficient deference and respect. (Peterson 2000: 21-22)

The oppressive history of African-Americans significantly influences contemporary Black males by shaping their psychological framework for viewing the world. Notions of conspiracy theories, cultural paranoia, and race consciousness enhance Black rage. The belief among African-Americans that Whites and the government are conspiring against them produces cultural paranoia, in which Blacks treat all Whites and institutions as the enemy until proven otherwise. Cultural paranoia requires that Blacks remain extremely race conscious in all of their interactions. The anger associated with race consciousness intensifies

Black rage. Black rage intensifies because it gives "one the illusion of power and retribution, and makes one feel as though they are fighting back against a perceived offense" (Peterson 2000: 24).

Victim Mentality

The perceived offense committed against African-Americans began in 1619 at Jamestown, Virginia, and lasted approximately 246 years. American slavery, or the "Black holocaust," as referred to by Robinson (2000) was "the most heinous human rights crime visited upon any group of people in the world over the last five hundred years" (216). The crime America committed resulted in the country becoming "rich and powerful in large measure on the backs of Black laborers," without compensating Blacks for their service (Grier and Cobbs 1968: 205; Robinson 2000). In fact, the revenue generated from cotton produced by slaves exceeded the revenue produced by all other American exports combined (Taylor, Y. 1999). Talks of compensating Blacks for slavery first surfaced during the Civil War when presumably, Abraham Lincoln promised Northern Blacks "forty acres and a mule" for their contributions to the Union Army. This notion spread throughout the country such that, "by the time of Lee's surrender the belief that forty acres and a mule would be given to each former slave was firmly planted in the newly emancipated African-Americans' minds" (Turner 1993: 42).

When the promise of forty acres and a mule failed to materialize, ex-slaves viewed the situation as the U.S. government reneging on its commitment (Turner 1993). Instead of issuing reparations, "America followed slavery with more than a hundred combined years of legal racial segregation and legal racial discrimination" (Robinson 2000: 230). The subsequent denial of reparations and the Jim Crow era of American racism compounded the initial crime of slavery. Many contemporary African-Americans view this combination of factors as a justification for their fixation to a victim mentality. For example, Black conservative Jesse Lee Peterson (2000: 16) effectively stated that "of all the groups in America vying for victimhood, it is only African-Americans who can legitimately make the claim that in American history they have been systematically and continuously persecuted." White Americans often sustain the victim mentality among Blacks through their tendency to "encourage passivity by rewarding those Black folks who whine, grovel, beg, and obey" (Hooks 1995: 18).

In addition to the tendency of certain leaders to encourage victimhood, the psychology behind the victim mentality is appealing to African-Americans for a number of other reasons. First, there is power in seeing oneself as a victim. According to Steele (1990), victimization metamorphoses into power via innocence. Steele (1990: 5) defined innocence as a "feeling of essential goodness in relation to others and, therefore superiority to others." Individuals who view themselves as innocent believe they are entitled to power. Furthermore, Steele (1990: 5) contends that the "racial struggle in America has always been primarily a struggle for innocence." African-Americans believe their history of oppression justifies their claims for innocence and power. In many ways, the Civil Rights Movement strengthened the position of African-Americans by encouraging White guilt. Dr. King effectively manipulated southern White racism, the media, and the practice of nonviolent civil disobedience, in portraying the innocence of African-Americans and their entitlement to push for equality. Consequently, the 1964 Civil Rights Act not only insured equality under the law, but also served as "an admission of White guilt" (Steele 1990: 78-79). If White America was guilty, Black America was subsequently innocent and justified in their demands for power based on the history of racism.

The admission of guilt that came with the Civil Rights Act of 1964 granted contemporary African-Americans the authority to "play the race card." Robinson (1995: 36) defined playing the race card as "a form of power used by Blacks to gain moral authority over White people who are presumed guilty of some racial infraction." The race card is similar to the joker in a deck of cards. The joker is the wild card that maintains power over all other cards and can strengthen a weak hand of cards. As such, regardless of the merits of a particular position or point of view, once the race card is introduced, all other issues are compromised (Robinson 1995). Since race "remains a source of White shame," the goal in playing the race card is to put Whites in touch with their collective guilt (Steele 1990: 4). The race card is a power move that attempts "to freeze the 'enemy' in self-consciousness" (Steele 1990: 4). For example, U.S. Supreme Court Justice Clarence Thomas played the race card during his Senate confirmation hearings by referring to the process as a "hi-tech lynching reserved for uppity Blacks" (quoted in Robinson 1995: 37). His comments visibly shook the White liberal Senators. Clarence Thomas, effectively "exercised his moral superiority as a Black man" by reminding "the Senators…that they were White males, who at the very least had some guilt to bear vis-à-vis Black men" (Robinson 1995: 21-22).

One negative consequence of obtaining power, via playing the race card, is that it traps the recipient into the role of the victim. In his book *A Nation of Victims,* Charles Sykes (1992: 18) contends that victimhood "debilitates its practitioners by trapping them in a world of oppressive demons that they cannot by definition, control." Therefore, playing the race card brings "victim power" which "binds the victim to his victimization by linking his power to his status as a victim" (Steele 1990:

14). For example, Clarence Thomas gained power temporarily during the Senate hearings but in the end, he lost power. His comments solidified the notion that he was an affirmative action candidate, and by playing the race card, he "tacitly requested that the Senate Judiciary Committee vote for him because of his race" (Robinson 1995: 38). Playing the race card taints Black progress by attributing Black success to victim power. This reinforces victimhood and the victim mentality.

In addition to the illusion of power, some African-Americans embrace victimhood because it provides a blanket excuse for their failures. The "impulse to flee from personal responsibility and blame others" for our failures is "deeply embedded within the American culture" (Sykes 1992: 14-15). In our society, victims are not responsible for their condition. Therefore, by claiming a victim status, the individual absolves themselves of personal responsibility for their condition (Robinson 1995; Steele 1990; Prager 1998). As such, the problem with many African-Americans and the crutch of victimhood is that "all problems are seen as coming from outside the self" (Robinson 1995: 22). For some Blacks, "the victim mentality is so strong," that "they are reluctant to find fault in the behavior of any Black person, no matter how blatant the behavior" (Robinson 1995: 94). For example, in 1993 Colin Ferguson, a Jamaican immigrant, boarded a Long Island commuter train and murdered several people out of anger at Whites and (in his words) "Uncle Tom Negroes." After the shooting, a *National Law Journal* survey showed that 68 percent of Blacks believed that White racism caused Ferguson's actions (D'Souza 1995). The understanding being that because he was a victim of racism, Ferguson was somehow not responsible for his actions.

The denial of personal responsibility for one's actions has one major consequence: it forever traps the individual in the victim mentality, which necessarily produces anger. Victims regard themselves as having no control over their life; essentially, "Whatever happens in their lives happens *to* them, not *by* them" (Prager 1998: 78). Consequently, the loss of control produces an angry disposition that renders happiness impossible (Prager 1998). Happiness becomes impossible since a natural product of victimhood is self-pity. Furthermore, self-pity is an addictive drug that can render a person destructive to self and others (Prager 1998). Increasingly, it becomes easy for an individual to "wallow" in self-pity, which paralyzes one from taking control of their situation. In regards to others, the more people perceive that they have no control over their life, the angrier they become and the more likely they are to lash out at others (Prager 1998). Sykes (1992: 16) coined the phrase "victimspeak" to describe the process by which victims lash out at others. He states, "Victimspeak is the trigger that permits the unleashing of an emotional and self-righteous response to any perceived slight" (16). Victimspeak generally conveys anger and rage since its natural tone is one of assertions of prerogatives and demands for reparations (Sykes 1992).

In sum, the history of African-Americans, from slavery to the enduring civil rights struggle, significantly influences the mindset of contemporary Black males. Two specific consequences of history are the belief in conspiracy theories and the perpetuation of a victim mentality. Conspiracy theories contribute to Black rage by forcing Black males to be extremely race-conscious in their interactions with Whites, which fosters an "us-against-them" demeanor. The victim mentality contributes to Black rage by further trapping Black males into a state of victimhood. The aspects of victimhood that make this position appealing, i.e. the illusion of power and the denial of personal responsibility, also reinforce the victim status. The notion of conspiracy theories and the victim mentality form the foundation of Black rage. However, other contemporary societal factors aggravate the rage found in present-day Black males.

Contemporary Sources of Rage

The interaction between the psychological effects of history and several present-day conditions intensifies the level of rage found in contemporary Black males. Based on his history in America, every Black man harbors the potential for rage and anger (Grier and Cobbs 1968). Some individuals are able to successfully process the grueling facts of the Black man's history in America, and not succumb to its psychological consequences. Others, however, hold on to this history and use it as fuel for their notions of government-led conspiracies and as a justification for their victim mentality. Regardless of whether or not contemporary Black males can sufficiently look beyond their history, several present-day factors produce and encourage Black rage. For the Black man trapped in *the cage of history*, present-day conditions exacerbate their level of rage. For those outside *the cage of history*, present-day conditions provide sufficient justifications for the production of Black rage. The discussion below considers the influence of only four contemporary sources of rage in Black males.[10]

Breakdown of the Black Family

The demise of the Black family gained considerable notoriety in 1965 following the release of Daniel P. Moynihan's policy paper, *The Negro Family: the Case for National Action*. In describing the problems confronting the Black family, Moynihan noted that 25 percent of all Black families were female-headed. While the relatively high figure stirred a great deal of controversy among Blacks and Whites, since the Moynihan Report, the condition of the Black family has deteriorated even more. By 1980, the percentage of female-headed Black families had risen to 43 percent, and by 1990, the figure was well over 50 percent (U.S. Census 1980, 1990). Although the high rate of divorce in America frequently bears the blame for the increasing number of female-headed households, in the Black community the problem stems more from a lack of marriage all together. For example, in 1960, 56 percent of Black males, age 20 to 24 were "never married"; by 1990, this figure increased to 85 percent (U.S. Census 1960, 1990). The low marriage rate for young Black males results from their high rates of unemployment, incarceration, and mortality (Taylor 1994). Given the detrimental state of Black males, Black women, especially young Black women, face a shrinking pool of "marriageable men" (Wilson 1987).

Therefore, it is no surprise that the growth rate for the number of Black children born out of wedlock parallels the change in the percentage of Black female-headed households. In 1965, 25 percent of Black children in America were born out of wedlock (Moynihan 1965); by 1980, this figure was at 50 percent. Still on the incline, the figure grew to roughly 64 percent by 1990, and is now at an all-time high of nearly 70 percent (U.S. Census 1980, 1990; Peterson 2000). The lack of two-parent families in the Black community significantly increases the poverty rate. For example, the 1990 census reported that 45 percent of all Black children live in families with incomes below the poverty line. Consequently, children in Black female-headed families are five times as likely to be welfare-dependent than those in intact Black families (Gibbs 1988). Research also shows that female-headed family structures have a negative impact on the economic status and opportunities for all Black youth; however, this family structure is particularly detrimental for Black males (Children's Defense Fund 1986).

Anger among Black males is a significant consequence of child rearing in female-headed families. Interpersonal psychologists H.S. Sullivan (1953) described anger as a reaction to early separation from a nurturing parent. Because of separation, as the child matures, they evoke angry feelings in situations where their emotional security is threatened (Sullivan 1953). In challenging situations, Black males reared in female-headed households vent anger at their absent fathers for their failure to provide models of appropriate masculine behaviors and positive models of identification. According to Black conservative Jesse Lee Peterson, "When 60 to 70 percent of Black boys grow up without fathers to be their moral models and disciplinarians, rage and violence are not surprising" (quoted in Robinson 1995: 31). Based on his personal background and experience as a counselor to Black youth, Peterson concludes that Black males abandoned by their fathers are likely to be angry individuals. In describing his personal battle with rage, Peterson writes:

> The anger and fury I carried around with me everywhere I went-which, for many years, I directed at White people-was primarily the product of being abandoned by my father. I hated and resented him for leaving me; I hated and resented my mother for hating him; and I hated and resented both of them together for not succeeding as a family. It was my fragmented and troubled family life that was the basic source of my hostility and discontent. As a young man, I translated that into racial rage because that gave me a feeling-however false-of self-control and power. By hating White people and being angry at America, I avoided the pain of facing my resentment of my parents, and my hurtful awareness of how they failed me. I missed not having a father to love me and nurture me into manhood. In his place, I accepted hostility toward others, particularly Whites-those who my community had taught me were the origin of my suffering as a Black man in America. (Peterson 2000: 25)

Peterson's (2000) testimony depicts the manner in which resentment towards the absent Black father spills over into anger directed at others, White Americans in particular. The tragic reality of the relatively high rate of female-headed households, within the Black community, is that significantly more Jesse Lee Petersons exists who face conditions more oppressive than two decades ago.

Marginal Status in Education

In addition to the demise of the Black family, marginal status in education further contributes to rage among Black males by decreasing their legitimate economic opportunities. Over the past 2½ decades, some researchers proclaimed that "African-Americans made stunning progress" in education (Mason 1999: 160). Consider for example, the fact that the median number of years of schooling between Blacks and Whites has decreased significantly, as well as racial differences in standardized test scores, and high school completion rates (Mason 1999). However, neatly concealed by inclusive statements about the educational progress of African-Americans is the fact that Black males lag significantly behind their female counterpart. Subsequently, failure to disaggregate the racial category into Black males and Black females conceals the true patterns of Black progress in education. While Blacks have made significant educational gains over the past 2½ decades, this progress is largely the result of advances by Black females. For example, the percentage of Black males completing high school and attending college is significantly less than the percentage of Black females (Bennett 1991). In which case, statements about the increasing rate of African-Americans enrolled in higher education most often reflect increasing Black female rates. Figures 3.1 to 3.4 disaggregate according to gender data presented in the *Digest of Education Statistics 2001*, published by the U.S. Department of Education. The figures present the total number of Black students enrolled at various levels of higher education, and clearly illustrate the influence of Black females on the progress of African-Americans in higher education.

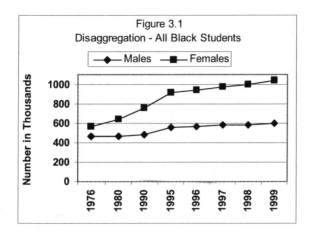

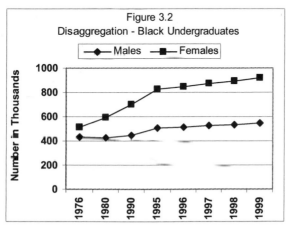

Figures 3.1 to 3.4 indicate that 1) Black females comprise the majority of Black students across all higher education levels and 2) the rate of

growth is greater for Black females than Black males. In fact, during many periods where the number of Black males decreased or remained relatively stable, the number of Black females significantly increased.

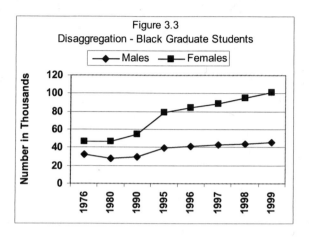

These figures, along with the finding of Bennett (1991) that Black females also comprise the majority of African-Americans graduating from high school, paint a disturbing picture regarding the marginal status of Black males in education. Not only are Black males significantly behind White males and females in educational attainment, but they are also surpassed by their cultural counterpart, the Black female. To comprehend the disadvantaged position of Black males in higher education requires consideration of the detrimental forces working against Black males at earlier stages of the education process.[11]

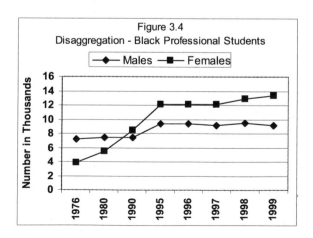

Black Males and Identification with Academics

The low level of educational attainment among Black males often reflects a lack of identification with academics, which prevents Black males from incorporating scholastic achievement as an important part of their self-concept (Osborne 1999). Furthermore, research indicates that a lack of identification with academics causes or contributes to poorer scholastic performance (Osborne 1997; Osborne and Rausch 2001). When an individual does not identify with a certain domain, such as academics, interactions and feedback from that domain have little effect on the individual's self-esteem (Osborne 2001). Identification with academics is therefore a necessary condition for learning. Students who identify with academics "should be more motivated to succeed and persist longer in the face of failure because their self-esteem is more strongly influenced by academic performance" (Osborne 1999: 557). On the other hand, for the non-identified student, good academic performance is not intrinsically rewarding, just as poor academic performance is not intrinsically punishing, which leaves non-identified students little intrinsic incentive to expend effort in academic endeavors (Osborne 1999). Three factors inherent in U.S. society prevent Black males from identifying with academics and contributes to their disadvantaged position in educational statistics: 1) stereotype threat (Steele 1992, 1997), 2) cultural ecology (Ogbu 1992), and 3) the cool pose (Majors and Billson 1992).

The fear of giving a wrong answer or appearing foolish in class creates a certain level of anxiety for all students. However, this anxiety level is greater for Black males since negative group stereotypes concerning their academic ability plague American culture (Steele 1992, 1997). "For these individuals, a wrong answer is not only personally damaging but also confirms the negative group stereotype" (Osborne 1999: 557). Under the stereotype threat hypothesis, Steele (1992, 1997) argues that as a self-protective measure, minority students sometimes devalue or reduce their identification with academics. Academic aversion reduces the stereotype-induced anxiety and allows students to be no longer concerned with evaluation in the academic domain (Epps 1970; Katz and Greenbaum 1963).

The cultural ecological perspective, proposed by Ogbu (1992), suggests that Black males fail to identify with academics because they view education as a system controlled by the group that subjugated and oppressed them and their ancestors. The study of group dynamics teaches that involuntary minorities tend to develop social or collective identities in opposition to the social identity of the dominant group (in the case of the U.S., Whites). As such, school and scholastic achievement are seen as inappropriate aspects of "proper" African-American identity (Fordham and Ogbu 1986). The desire to avoid identification with academics intensifies when Black males' witness that even those among them who succeed in school are not fully accepted or rewarded in the same fashion as White students (Osborne 1999). Accordingly, the peer pressure and the cultural pressure not to "act White" (Fordham and Ogbu 1986) serve as formidable forces against identification with academics among Black males.

The cool pose, offered by Majors and Billson (1992), reaffirms the cultural opposition perspective suggested by Ogbu (1992). The cool pose is a ritualized approach to masculinity that allows Black males to cope and survive in the face of oppression and racism (Majors and Billson 1992). "Black males learn early to project this façade of emotionless, fearlessness, and aloofness to counter the inner pain caused by the damaged pride, poor self-confidence, and fragile social competence that results from their existence as a member of a subjugated group" (Osborne 1999: 558). In the context of school, the cool pose is problematic because it often leads to flamboyant, nonconformist behavior that frequently elicits punishment. Majors and Billson (1992) further contend that the cool pose is incompatible with the good student image, which requires a close identification with academics. Hence, the coping strategy adopted by Black males for handling their placement in a stigmatized group opposes identification with academics.

Educator Perceptions and Expectations of Black Males

While the cool pose and other aspects of non-identification protect the self-concept of Black males, these activities negatively influence the perceptions and expectations of educators, which further reinforce the disadvantaged position of Black male students. Researchers have long noted that teachers often carry negative perceptions of Black male students (Clark 1965; Irvine and York 1993; Foster 1995; Garibaldi 1991). For example, in a survey of public school teachers in New Orleans, Garibaldi (1991) found that 60 percent of the teachers polled did not expect their Black male students to go to college. Furthermore, Foster (1995: 66) analyzed both educator and non-educator perceptions of Black males and concluded that for many educators, negative Black male stereotypes serve as the "inner meaning context" for which to interpret Black language and behavior. Subsequently, the over reliance on stereotypes for interpreting Black male language and behavior contributes to their disproportionate expulsion, suspension, special education placement, and general discipline in the school setting. Consider for example, the fact that certain school districts have suspended Black male students for "walking in an insolent manner"

(Breinin 1981). With such culturally arbitrary suspension criteria, it is not surprising that Black males are disproportionately suspended and expelled from school.[12]

Negative perceptions or stereotypes about Black males not only influence disciplinary matters but they also affect the academic performance of Black male students. Studies have shown that a student's academic performance often parallels teacher expectations (Clark 1965; McKenzie 1991; Davis and Jordan 1994). If the teacher expects the student to perform well, this usually turns out to be the case, and vice versa. Therefore, the negative expectation of teachers in regards to Black males predisposes these individuals to academic failure. When teachers do not expect a student to learn, they adopt more of a custodial and disciplinary mindset, as opposed to a nurturing educator (Epps 1995). The teacher's emphasis on discipline has a negative influence of Black male achievement (Davis and Jordan 1994). "The time teachers spend handling disciplinary problems is time taken away from instruction;" consequently, Black male achievement suffers (Davis and Jordan 1994: 585). Despite their position as a facilitator of learning, teachers often do not take responsibility for the school failure of Black males. Irvine and York (1993) found that teachers tended to attribute the failure of Black students to their parents' inadequacies and deficiencies or the student's personal traits and characteristics. The academic failure of Black male students has the added disadvantage of increasing their likelihood of special education placement.

Special Education Placement

Tragically, for many Black males "the special education process begins on the first day of their school careers" (Harry and Anderson 1994: 610). Consequently, a significant factor in the marginal status of Black males in education is their disproportionate placement rate into special education programs. Two landmark legislative acts, designed to promote equality and opportunity in education, have ironically produced detrimental effects for Black males. First, there was the 1954 U.S. Supreme Court decision in *Brown v. The Board of Education* which ended legal segregation in public schools but, inadvertently forced "diversity reluctant" school districts to develop alternative methods of segregating students. Second, there was the passage of the Education for all Handicapped Children Act[13] (EHA) in 1975, which mandated specialized services for disabled students who could not benefit from regular educational curriculum and instruction. Essentially, the EHA required either separate classrooms or separate facilities for students with learning disabilities. Thus, the stipulations of the EHA, in conjunction with the subjective decisions in determining which students exhibit learning disabilities, provided diversity reluctant school districts a cover for racial segregation[14] (Prasse and Reschly 1986). Despite court rulings, such as *Larry P. v. Riles (1979)*, the over-representation of Blacks in special education has continued unabated. For example, in 1993, nationwide Blacks comprised 16 percent of the school-age population but represented 27 percent of those in special education for Serious Emotional Disturbances (SED). Furthermore, 76.4 percent of the Black students diagnosed with SED were males.[15]

The preponderance of Black males in special education is more prevalent when considering mild disabilities.[16] Mild disabilities, such as SED, have a more subjective identification process than serious special education categories. To identify a child with mild disabilities, school officials (primarily teachers) are required to make subjective judgments about whether a student has academic or social deficits in comparison to other students (Gardner and Miranda 2001). In which case, the degree of racial homogeneity among public school teachers increases the likelihood that Black males will receive erroneous special education placements. According to Cook and Boe (1995), 87 percent of general education teachers in public schools are White. Moreover, McIntyre and Pernell (1985) found that "teachers tend to recommend students for special education placement who are racially dissimilar from themselves" (112). Stevens (1981) found a similar relationship regarding the importance of student race on the special education referral, assessment, and placement decisions. Consequently, the cultural disconnection between the teacher and the student increases the referral rate for Black male students to special education.

The education obstacles presented above, along with others not considered, support the marginal status of Black males in education. These obstacles combine to produce a series of detrimental consequences for both Black males and females. One such consequence is that gaps in the academic performance of Black and White students appear as early as age 9 and persist through age 17 (U.S. Department of Education 1995). Another consequence is that Black children are more likely to be below the modal grade for their age than White children (U.S. Department of Education 1995). Perhaps the most significant consequence is the tendency among Black males to lower their expectations, degrade their scholastic ability, and substitute compensatory items for positive self-regard and sense of achievement (Hare and Castenell 1985; Irvine 1990). Furthermore, the marginal educational status of Black males serves as a contemporary source of Black rage by limiting their legitimate economic opportunities.

Marginal Status in Employment

The disadvantaged position of Black males in education affects their marginal status in employment. Most urban researchers would agree that Black males experience significantly more employment difficulties than any other racial group (Stoll 1998). Given this fact, many observers of Black culture intuitively attribute the socioeconomic problems plaguing the Black community to the high rates of unemployment among Black men. For instance, the problems created by high Black male unemployment rates were key features in the "Tangle of Pathology" described by Moynihan (1965) in his controversial report. However, in spite of early warnings from researchers such as Moynihan, the economic disparity between Black males and their White counterparts has steadily crept upwards since the 1950's, with a dramatic jump during the early 1970's (Welch 1990). In fact, even during the expansionary business cycle of the mid-1980's, the employment gap between Black and White males continued to widen (Simpson 2000). Moreover, "despite what is widely considered to be the most favorable labor market conditions in thirty years, Black male unemployment rates remain double White rates" (Cherry 1999: 31). Unfortunately, the racial disparity in unemployment rates is greatest among young Black males.

While, in general, Black employment rates have historically been more sensitive to fluctuations in the business cycle (Cherry 1999), this is especially true for young Black males. For more than any other group, the unemployment rate of young Black males rises and falls disproportionately during business expansions and contractions. Using data from Jacobs and Abu-Aish's (2000) *Handbook of U.S. Labor Statistics*, Figures 3.5-3.8 present average male unemployment rates by race across various age categories.

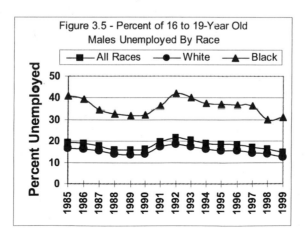

Figure 3.5 - Percent of 16 to 19-Year Old Males Unemployed By Race

As indicated by Figure 3.5, from 1985 to 1999 Black males age 16 to 19 had an unemployment rate that was on average over twice as high as their White counterparts. The average unemployment rate for 16 to 19-year old Black males was 35.94 percent, in comparison to 15.47 percent for White males. The rates peaked for both racial groups during the economic contraction of 1992. However, despite general hard times, the disparity between the racial groups was greatest in 1992, suggesting that when jobs become scarce, the exclusionary status of young Black males from the labor force increases. Also disturbing was the fact that as of 1999, the rate of unemployment for young Black males was increasing while the rates for Whites and all other races were declining.

In the next age demographic, those 20 to 24-years old, the overall unemployment rates reduced; nevertheless, a similar racial disparity appeared.

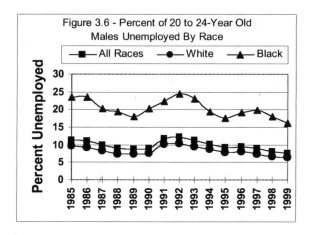

Among this slightly older age demographic, the average Black male unemployment rate was 20.33 percent, versus 8.35 percent for White males. Although the gap between the racial groups narrowed, Black males still occupied a select disadvantage in the labor force. The unemployment rate for Black males differed significantly not only from their White counterparts but also from all races. In which case, during the formative years of adulthood, from the late-teens to mid-twenties, Black males face disproportionate exclusion from legitimate employment opportunities.

From age 25 to 34 (Figure 3.7), the unemployment rate for Black males fell to an average of 10.92 percent. This was nearly a 10-percentage point reduction in comparison to the average rate for Black males age 20 to 24 during this same period. However, despite their progress, Black males were still unemployed at a rate over twice as high as White males (10.92 versus 4.93 percent). Furthermore, during periods of economic growth, such as 1996 when the unemployment rates for White and other males age 25 to 34 fell, the rate for Black males actually increased. This supports the thesis that "strong impediments to Black male employment growth may exist even when labor demand is quite strong" (Cherry 1999: 33).

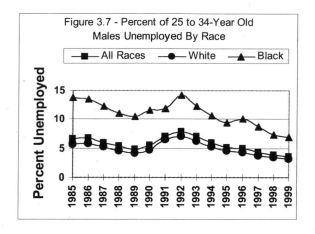

Figure 3.7 - Percent of 25 to 34-Year Old Males Unemployed By Race

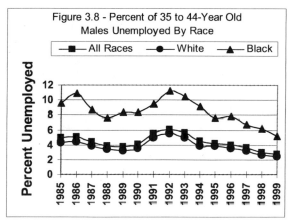

Figure 3.8 - Percent of 35 to 44-Year Old Males Unemployed By Race

Among the oldest age category, 35 to 44, the average unemployment rate for both White and Black males fell to single digits at 3.84 and 8.49 percent respectively. Although the overall unemployment rates for individuals age 35 to 44 were much lower than the previous age groups, the same racial disparity appeared as in all of the previous figures. Hence, we can conclude that regardless of the age demographic, from

1985 to 1999, Black males faced unemployment at rates significantly higher than White males and all races in general. In addition, both the absolute and relative rates of unemployment were far greater for a young Black male, which has tremendous implications for a number of problems plaguing the Black community (Massey and Shibuya 1995). Unfortunately, the multiplicity of causes offered to explain the unemployment gap renders the search for a uniform solution next to impossible.

Causes of the Employment Gap

Explanations for the employment difficulties of Black males have focused on a variety of topics, such as the inaccessibility of transportation to jobs (Kain 1968; Kasarda 1983, 1989, 1990); the increasing employment of White females (Rolison 1993); and the use of informal recruitment mechanisms for the replenishment of labor (Scott 1988; Waldinger 1986). Throughout the literature on Black male unemployment, three themes consistently appear. The first area of research suggests that an economic credential deficiency among Black males largely explains their disadvantaged position in employment statistics. For instance, research overwhelmingly indicates that the combination of low levels of educational attainment and the increasing demand for skilled employees, contributes significantly to the economic disadvantage of Black males (Blackburn et al. 1990; Simpson 2000). Consider the fact that during the expanding market economy of the 1980's lower average levels of educational attainment (Bound and Freeman 1992) and lower standardized test scores (Jencks and Peterson 1991) left Black males "ill-prepared to meet the higher level occupation skills requirements that characterized the expanding sector" (Simpson 2000: 329). In addition to a lower quantity of education, lower quality of education also contributes to the economic disadvantage of Black males. For example, Maxwell (1994: 249) found that "the main source of the Black-White wage differential [was] the racial difference in the quality rather than the quantity of schooling." Other researchers have also noted the detrimental effect of poor quality educational institutions on racial disparities in the labor market (Boozer et al. 1992; Card and Krueger 1992a, 1992b).

    A second often cited reason for the economic problems confronted by Black males, addresses the relocation of job opportunities to suburban areas. Researchers describe the detrimental effects of geographic relocation as the "spatial mismatch hypothesis" (Stoll 1998). The basic premise of the mismatch hypothesis holds that the moving of jobs to the suburban ring in conjunction with discriminatory housing practices, which restrict Black residential choices to the central city,[17] contributes significantly to the low level of Black employment (Kain 1968). Thus, spatial mismatch raises the Black male unemployment rate by creating an oversupply of Black workers relative to the number of jobs remaining in the central city (Stoll 1998). Compounding the effects of the deconcentration of jobs in the central city is the even more detrimental influence of deindustrialization. For instance, from 1978 to 1982, the Los Angeles economy lost roughly 70,000 manufacturing jobs due to plant closings, most of which were concentrated in predominantly Black communities (Soja et al. 1983). Thus, massive deconcentration negatively affects the economic status of Black males as well as massive deindustrialization (Wilson 1987; Johnson and Oliver 1991). Both factors contribute to the spatial mismatch by removing jobs from places with high concentrations of Black males.

The third explanation for the marginal economic status of Black males' focuses on the fact that employers often hold negative perceptions about this disadvantaged group (Braddock and McPartland 1987; Culp and Dunson 1986; Kirschenman and Neckerman 1989; Wilson 1996). In perhaps the most comprehensive study to date on this topic, Wilson (1996) analyzed qualitative data obtained from 170 employers in the Chicago area concerning their attitudes towards race and employment. The study found that 74 percent of White employers and 80 percent of Black employers expressed negative views regarding the job-related traits of inner-city Blacks. Furthermore, although inner-city Blacks in general faced negative perceptions, both Black and White employers reserved their harshest criticisms for Black males (Wilson 1996). For instance, concerning the dependability of Black males, one White employer noted:

> Number 1...they're not dependable. They have never been taught when you have a job you have to be there at a certain time and you're to stay there until the time is finished. They may not show up on time. They just disappear for an hour or two at a time. They'll call you up and say, "Ahhh, I'm not coming in today"...

Several employers echoed similar negative comments about Black males on a variety of character traits such as the inability to take orders, poor verbal and written language skills, lack of a stable employment history, and laziness (Wilson 1996). A White suburban employer summed the general attitude towards Black males up best:

> It's not every case but the experiences that I've had is the fact that they're not willing to set themselves straight, put 100%

effort into their job and try to develop and build with a
company. The experiences that I've run into with it is that they
develop bad habits, I guess is the best way to put it. Not
showing up to work on time. Not showing up to work.
Somewhere down the road they didn't develop good work
habits. (Wilson 1996: 119)

Thus, given the general negative perception of Black males, many
employers seeking to diversify their staff population, in terms of African-
American representation, are more inclined to hire Black females. In part
due to the shortcomings of the Black male, one employer effectively
noted "inner-city Black women have a need to work" that "translates in
many cases into a very responsible employee" (Wilson 1996: 124). The
employer goes on to state, "Certainly the education can still be a
problem, but...I certainly think they don't suffer the same problems that
a Black male would have in terms of getting a job" (Wilson 1996: 124).
Hence, the preference for Black females intensifies the marginalized
economic status of Black males. Furthermore, the fact that Black males
are also more threatening to employers is a contributing factor in the
preference for Black females (Wilson 1996).

The executive director of an inner-city charity succinctly captured
the fear factor when he noted, "People are afraid of Black men" (Wilson
1996: 125). Another employer included in Wilson's (1996) study
suggested that the perceived fear of Black males resulted partly from the
fact that "Black men present a particularly menacing demeanor to White
men." Moreover, because of the fear evoked:

When many companies hire Black males, they hire the most
complacent, the least aggressive, the most eunuchish type they
can get because they don't want to have some crazy, who's
going to become some kind of warmonger, running around the
company and spatting. They hire the ones that are most
acceptable, and sometimes they're not necessarily the brightest
or the most capable (Wilson 1996: 125).

According to research by Taub (1991), employers perhaps have just
reasons for their fear of Black males. In a study comparing Black and
Mexican males, Taub (1991) found that Blacks were much more hostile
with respect to low paying jobs. In addition, Black males were less
flexible in terms of taking assignments or tasks not included as part of
their job description, and were less willing to put forth additional effort
for the same low wages (Taub 1991). Part of the Black males' hostile
attitude stems from their greater sense of "honor" which often results in
their seeing the work, pay, and treatment from bosses as insulting and

degrading (Taub 1991). Thus, "Inner-city Black men grow bitter and resentful in the face of their employment prospects and often manifest or express these feelings in their harsh, often dehumanizing, low-wage work settings" (Wilson 1996: 144).

In addition to the production of inner rage and anger, the marginal economic status of Black males has one other noteworthy consequence as well. A high level of joblessness encourages the development of "alternative" means of survival (Wilson 1987; Sullivan 1989; Jankowski 1991; Anderson 1999). Denied legitimate employment opportunities, many Black males rely on "hustling" for financial support. Hustling involves doing whatever is necessary to make money (Hicks-Barlett 1991). Furthermore, hustles can be both legal and illegal, and transpire in the formal and informal economy (Hicks-Barlett 1991). However, the profit margins witnessed from illegal activities, combined with the disappearance of legitimate jobs makes criminal activity more attractive to marginalized Black males (Moss and Tilly 1991; Viscusi 1986). Unfortunately, the tendency to engage in illegal activities for survival, or whatever reason, contributes significantly to the level of contact between Black males and the American criminal justice system; the arena where Black males face perhaps the greatest disadvantage.

Discrimination in the American Criminal Justice System

A presumption of racially biased punishment in the American criminal justice system is common among Black males. Racial disparities in the percentage of Black males arrested, incarcerated, condemned to death row, or under the general control of the criminal justice system contributes to the belief that punishment in America is racially biased. African-Americans use the disproportionate number of Black males under the control of the justice system as further evidence of a government-led conspiracy against Blacks. For example, Mann (1993) proposed a quasi-Marxist conspiracy theory that accused the American criminal justice system of being intentionally racist as part of a larger plan to subjugate Blacks. While Mann's theory is perhaps unfounded, statistical facts about the American criminal justice system contribute to the perpetuation of the Black male's belief that punishment in America is racially biased. Consider the following statistics:

❖ From 1965 through 1992, the average annual arrest rate per 100,000 inhabitants was 3,305 for Blacks and 648 for Whites (Maguire and Pastore 1995).

❖ The lifetime risk of arrest for Blacks in many urban areas is as high as 80 percent (Donziger 1996).

❖ As of 1997, one in four Black males between the ages of eighteen to twenty-nine years old were under the control of the criminal justice system, i.e. prison, jail, probation, or parole. In comparison, only one in sixteen White males and one in eleven Hispanic males, in the same age group, were under such control (U.S. Department of Justice 1997).

❖ In 1997, the number of Black males incarcerated in prison or jail (715,051) was significantly higher than the number enrolled in institutions of higher education (572,500) (U.S. Department of Justice 1997; U.S. Department of Education 2001).

❖ Based on the current rate of incarceration, by the year 2020, 63.3 percent of all Black males in the U.S. between the ages of 18-34 will be in prison (Donziger 1996).

❖ Black males born in 1991 have a 29 percent chance of incarceration at some point in their lifetime. The figure for White males is 4 percent, and 16 percent for Hispanic males (Bonczar and Beck 1997).

❖ Black males comprise roughly 43 percent of those condemned to death row (NAACP Legal Defense and Educational Fund 2000).

Victimization data, such as the National Crime Victimization Survey (NCVS) confirm that Black males have a higher rate of offending for a variety of crimes. However, even for crimes where Blacks have a low rate of offending, the cumulative effects of race on processing through the justice system solidify the perception of racially biased punishment in America, particularly against Black males. Despite the relatively high rate of crime by Black males, three facts about the American criminal justice system perpetuate the notion of discrimination and subsequently increase Black rage: police brutality, racial profiling, and racially biased processing.

Police Brutality

One of the greatest sources of rage in contemporary Black males, fostered by the American criminal justice system, is the constant threat of becoming a victim of police brutality. Decades of police brutality in the Black community fostered a culturally ingrained fear and distrust of the police, as well as overall anxiety. Testifying to this anxiety, California Assemblyman Curtis Tucker noted that, "When Black people in Los Angeles see a police car approaching, they don't know whether justice will be meted out or whether judge, jury and executioner is pulling up behind them" (Stevenson 1991: A16). Research indicates that race is a significant factor in predicting police use of force (Locke 1996; Geller and Toch 1996; Stycos 1994). For instance, a 1991 study of 650 officers with the LAPD revealed that racial prejudice among officers was a significant determinant of whether an officer used excessive force (Christopher Commission 1991). Furthermore, Worden (1996) argued that the quickness with which officers resort to even reasonable force against Blacks suggests that officers adopt a more punitive or coercive approach to Black suspects than Whites. Consequently, interactions between African-Americans and the police induce anxiety and foster negative perceptions of the police within the Black community.

Researchers consistently report that African-Americans hold more negative perceptions of the police than their White counterparts. In fact, since 1950 over twenty studies have found that African-Americans hold a less favorable attitude towards the local police than Whites.[18] For example, a Gallup survey revealed that among White citizens 59 percent perceived the police as "very high or high" on honesty and ethical standards. In contrast, only 32 percent of Black citizens gave the police such ratings on both qualities (Maguire and Pastore 2000). Likewise, Blacks also have less reported confidence in the ability of the police. The Gallup survey further found that only 38 percent of Blacks had a "great deal" of confidence in the police, in comparison to 59 percent of Whites.

Perhaps White Americans view the police more favorably by virtue of their inexperience with police brutality and harassment. In *Race and Getting Hassled by the Police*, Browning et al. (1994) found that 47 percent of Blacks and 10 percent of Whites reported being "personally hassled" by police; and 66 percent of Blacks and 12.5 percent of Whites reported being "vicariously hassled" by police. In regards to police brutality, 28 percent of Whites perceived police brutality as a problem in their area compared to 53 percent of Blacks (Maguire and Pastore 2000). The inexperience of White Americans with police brutality also likely influences their tendency to support the use of force by police officers. For example, in response to the question, "Are there any situations you can imagine which you would approve of a policeman striking an adult male citizen?" White respondents answered "yes" 76 percent of the time in comparison to 56 percent for Black respondents (Maguire and Pastore 2000).

The pessimistic attitude towards the local police by African-Americans stems largely from their historical and contemporary over-representation among the victims of police brutality. The limited available research on police and the use of force consistently shows a disproportionate number of African-Americans among the victims in cases of both fatal and non-fatal displays of force by the local police. The lack of systematic police data prohibits researchers from adequately assessing the true extent of police brutality.[19] Consequently, many of the data sets used to address police brutality are relatively small. For example, in his book, *Police and the Use of Force*, Vance McLaughlin (1992) examined the Savannah Police Department and found that Blacks were by far the most common victims in situations involving the use of force by police. More specifically, McLaughlin (1992) found that Blacks accounted for roughly 76 percent of the victims in altercations requiring the use of force by police. McLaughlin (1992) further found that Black males were the most common targets of police force, representing 61 percent of the victims in all cases of police force. The research of Lersch and Feagin (1996) showed an even more dramatic interracial pattern in police brutality cases. Lersch and Feagin (1996) conducted their study of police brutality by analyzing newspaper accounts of violent police-citizen altercations over a 16-month period. Their data showed that African-Americans were the victims in violent encounters between the police and citizens in 86 percent of the cases.[20] Furthermore, the police officers were White in 93 percent of the violent altercations between citizens and police (Lersch and Feagin 1996).

In addition to their over-representation among the victims of general police brutality, Black males are significantly more likely to suffer fatal injuries at the hands of police. For example, from 1920 through 1932, White police officers killed 54 percent of the 749 Blacks killed by a White person in the South and 68 percent of those killed in other regions (Myrdal 1944). The number of African-Americans *assassinated* by a police officer reached an all time high during the 1960's and 1970's when Blacks were shot and killed at a ratio of 8:1 in comparison to Whites (Walker et al. 1996). Police justified many of their assaults on Black life under the guise of the *fleeing felon rule,* which permitted White officers "to act on their prejudices" (Walker et al. 1996: 92). The fleeing felon rule "allowed police officers to shoot to kill, for the purpose of arrest, any fleeing suspected felon. The rule gave police officers very broad discretion; they only had to suspect that the person had committed a felony" (Walker et al. 1996: 92). The fleeing felon rule drew considerable criticism following the shooting death of 15-year-old, Edward Garner. On October 3, 1974, two Memphis police officers shot and killed Garner, a Black male, for fleeing with a stolen purse containing $10. His parents later sued and in *Tennessee v. Garner,* the

U.S. Supreme Court declared that the fleeing felon rule violated Fourth Amendment protection against unreasonable searches and seizures (Walker et al. 1996).

Following the 1985 decision of the U.S. Supreme Court, which declared the "fleeing felon rule" as unconstitutional, police departments adopted the "*defense of life rule*." The new standard limited police shootings to situations that posed a threat to the officer's life or some other person (Walker et al. 1996). Despite the change in standards, the death rate for Black males, at the hands of White police officers, remains relatively high. The change in standard shifted the disproportionate representation of Black males among police fatalities to the category of *justifiable homicides* in police statistics.[21] The following examples illustrate the volatile nature of interactions between Black males and White police officers:

❖ In February 1999, four White New York City police officers killed West African immigrant Amadou Diallo, in the doorway of his apartment building. As Mr. Diallo reached for his identification, the police officers fired over 40 rounds of ammunition. The officers later claimed that they thought Mr. Diallo was reaching for a weapon.

❖ In July 2000, a White police officer in Sacramento, California fatally wounded Donald Venerable, a 33-year-old Black male. Although Mr. Venerable stated that he was unarmed, the officer shot the suspect when he misidentified Mr. Venerable's cellular phone as a gun.[22]

❖ In January 2000, two White police officers in Rhode Island killed Cornel Young Jr., an off-duty, out-of-uniform, Black police Sergeant. Sergeant Young was attempting to control a domestic dispute at a local restaurant when the two White police officers arrived and demanded that he drop his gun. Despite proclamations of his officer status, the two White officers opened fire on Sergeant Young for refusing to drop his gun.

The examples illustrate the tendency of police officers to "shoot first and ask questions later" when approaching Black suspects. The first two examples illustrate the slight degree of provocation required for a White police officer to resort to fatal violence when interacting with a Black male suspect. The relatively insignificant inducements needed to incite violence in some White police officers has resulted in many Black parents socializing their children, Black males in particular, on the proper behavior and demeanor during police interactions. For example, a Black social worker interviewed by Harris (1999: 24) reported that she plans to give her son the following speech, once he is old enough to drive:

> The police are supposed to be there to protect and to serve, but you being Black and being male, you've got two strikes against you. Keep your hands on the steering wheel, and do not run, because they will shoot you in your back. Let them do whatever they want to do. I know it's humiliating, but let them do whatever they want to do to make sure you get out of that situation alive. Deal with your emotions later. Your emotions are going to come second—or last.

Delivering the same message, but to a much larger audience, is police Sergeant Delacy Davis, who travels the country informing African-Americans on, *"What to do when stopped by the police."* As a representative of the grassroots organization, *Black Cops Against Police Brutality* (B-CAP), Sergeant Davis has appeared on the Oprah Winfrey Show, Maury Povitch, Ricki Lake, ABC Nightline, BET's Tavis Smiley, Hardball, FOX Files, and the CBS Morning Show (www.b-cap.org/bcap_media.html).

The case of Sergeant Cornel Young demonstrates the vulnerability of all Black males to police brutality regardless of age, education, or occupation. Sadly, the death or assault of a Black police officer at the hands of their fellow White counterpart is not a rare occurrence. Consider the following examples:

❖ 1989 Long Beach, CA – Donald Jackson, a Black off-duty police officer, is thrown through a glass window by White police officers after he decides to document the manner in which White officers harass Black youth. An NBC-TV camera crew was following Officer Jackson at the time and recorded the incident.

❖ 1992 New York, NY – Two White police officers shot and severely wounded Derwin Pannell, an undercover transit officer, without warning. Officer Pannell was in the process of detaining a suspect guilty of "farebeating" when the incident occurred.

❖ 1992 Nashville, TN – Two White police officers severely beat Reggie Miller, an on-duty undercover cop. Ironically, the two White officers worked in the same police station and on the same shift as Officer Miller.

❖ 1994 New York, NY – Desmond Robinson, an undercover transit officer, was shot several times in the back by a White police officer who mistook Officer Robinson for a robbery suspect.

❖ 1997 Miami, FL – Major Aaron Campbell was wrestled to the ground, hit with pepper spray, and arrested, after he was pulled over for an illegal lane change and having obscured tags. Major Campbell identified himself as a Metro-Dade Police Officer at the start of the altercation.

❖ 2001 Oakland, CA – William Wilkins, an undercover Black police officer, died from gun shot wounds inflicted by several "rookie" White police officers. Officer Wilkins was in the process of making an undercover arrest in a high crime area when the other officers arrived on the scene and opened fire without warning.

These six examples merely scratch the surface of the total population of Black officers beaten or fatally wounded by White police officers. In New York City alone, 23 Black officers have suffered fatal wounds and 18 have endured severe assaults by fellow officers since 1941 (Wilson 1996). Retired NYPD detective, Roger Abel, who is currently writing a book about police-on-police violence, proclaims that not one White officer has ever been shot by a Black officer[23] (Wilson 1996). Given the statistics, it is not surprising that Black police officers express distrust towards their White counterparts,[24] and often attempt to separate themselves from traditional police practices.[25]

The examples of brutality against Black police officers and the formation of groups such as *Black Police Officers Against Police Brutality* (B-CAP) inflames Black rage on two fronts. First, the highly publicized cases of violence against Black officers solidify the notion among Black males that everyone is a potential victim of police brutality. Regardless of their age, education, or even occupation, Black males are always one stop away from being a victim of police brutality (Payne 1992). The inability of Black males to earn respect as they climb the educational or occupational ladder of success intensifies their rage towards the dominant White structure, as they realize their entrapment in a game that they cannot win. Second, the formation of separatists' Black police organizations, and their subsequent statements about police injustice and brutality, confirms the suspicions of Black males that the criminal justice system is their adversary. Black police officers provide the Black community with an inside connection to the "system." The fact that Black officers, such as Donald Jackson in Long Beach, CA observed an injustice so great that he was willing to risk his life to document police harassment of Black citizens speaks volumes in the Black community. Individuals such as Officer Jackson and organizations such as B-CAP and NBPA testify to the notion that injustice and discrimination are integral parts of the American criminal justice system. Essentially, these groups confirm the suspicions of African-Americans concerning the notion that the system treats them unfairly and justifies their subsequent rage.

In addition to the manners mentioned above, police brutality also intensifies Black rage due to the low probability that the offending officer(s) will receive any form of punishment. A study conducted in the early 1990's by *The Gannett News Service*, examined the 100 worst police brutality lawsuits in America and found that the officers responsible for the violence were rarely disciplined, much less fired (Payne 1992). Of the 185 police officers involved in the cases analyzed by *The Gannett News Service*, only five lost their jobs. In contrast, 19 either received promotions or got better jobs with other police departments.[26] Lersch and Feagin (1996) reported a similar pattern when they found that roughly 13 percent of the brutality cases in their sample resulted in an official punishment. Under the guise of "justifiable homicides" or the charge of "resisting arrest," many of the cases of brutality against Black males go unpunished.

The probability of punishment against police officers involved in brutality cases remains low for two reasons. First, many of the cases are transitory and occur out of the public eye (McLaughlin 1992). Subsequently, the only eyewitness is usually a fellow officer. Unfortunately, the police officer "code of silence" and informal punishments against "ratting" insure that victimized Black males do not receive justice (Robinson 1995). The code consists of one simple rule: "an officer does not provide adverse information against a fellow officer" (Christopher Commission 1991: 168). In his book, *Violence and the Police*, Westley (1970) found that police departments have a tendency to regard the public as the "enemy," particularly when under attack or criticism, at that time the pressure is even greater to maintain a code of silence. Moreover, Westley (1970) found that officers were eagerly willing to lie to cover up misconduct by fellow officers. Consequently, the "code of silence" not only reduces the probability of punishment, but also reduces the likelihood that citizens will report cases of brutality altogether.[27]

The second factor reducing the probability of punishment in police brutality cases is the reluctance of jurors to convict guilty officers, regardless of the evidence. In one case analyzed by Lersch and Feagin (1996: 43), "two officers admitted on the stand that they had beaten a car theft suspect, and that something inside them had 'just snapped'."

Despite their admission, the jury failed to find the officers guilty of police brutality (Freed 1991). This example and the many highly publicized cases of White police officers beating the system in cases of brutality against Black males, inflames Black rage. The deadly riots that followed the acquittal of the four police officers involved in the Rodney King beating, demonstrated the manner in which the denial of justice in the face of blatant brutality can trigger Black rage into a violent frenzy. In a more recent example, in April 2001, Cincinnati experienced three nights of Black rage and frustration over the shooting death of 19-year-old Timothy Thomas, an unarmed Black male with minor warrants for several misdemeanors and traffic violations. Violence erupted when news of Mr. Thomas' death first circulated throughout the Black community, and later in September 2001, when a jury found the White officer accused of killing Mr. Thomas not guilty of negligent homicide. Numerous cities across the United States have experienced violent displays of Black rage similar to the situation in Cincinnati. Repeatedly, the Black community finds itself infuriated by the alarming rate at which the police brutalize Black males and the subsequent denial of justice in the American court of law.

Racial Profiling

The preponderance of Black males among the victims of police brutality results largely from their frequent contacts with law enforcement officers. While many of the interactions between Black males and the police stem from legitimate criminal investigations, vast majorities of these encounters eventuate from racial profiling. Callahan and Anderson (2001: 2) define racial profiling as the police "practice of stopping and inspecting individuals who are passing through public places...where the reason for the stop is a statistical profile of the detainee's race or ethnicity."[28] Although some government and law enforcement officials adamantly deny the existence of racial profiling, the experiences of Black males since the 1960's tell a different story. In 1968, the Kerner Commission reported that one of the major complaints within the Black community was the police "stopping of Negroes on foot or in cars without obvious basis" (303). Over three decades later, a joint survey conducted by the *Washington Post*, Harvard University and the Henry J. Kaiser Family Foundation observed a similar pattern in police behavior. The survey revealed that nearly 52 percent of all Black males and 25 percent of all Black females felt the police had unfairly stopped them because they were Black ("Black Men Say," 2001). Similarly, a public opinion poll conducted by Harris Interactive found that 36 percent of Blacks and only 14 percent of Whites answered yes to the question, "Are you sometimes afraid that the police will stop and arrest you when you are completely innocent, or not?" (Maguire and Pastore 2000).

As indicated by the opinion polls, Black males are keenly aware of the predisposed guilt associated with Black skin in police investigations. In order to understand the extent of the bias against Black males in police investigations, one must comprehend two essential aspects of police work. First, a large proportion of police arrests result from proactive investigations. In proactive investigations, police initiate inquiries at their own discretion, unlike in reactive investigations where the police respond to calls from citizens for service (Walker et al. 1996). Second, officers maintain a great deal of discretion in conducting their police activities. "Most police officers work most of the time without direct supervision. Their discretionary decisions, thus, are not generally open to review by supervisors" (Reiss 1974: 181). Away from the watchful eye of a supervisor, and in some cases under the direct orders of a superior,[29] police apply their discretionary power in a racially discriminatory fashion, under the guise of conducting proactive criminal investigations.

The combination of proactive investigations and unregulated discretionary power allow the police to incorporate racial and class stereotypes as built-in parts of police work. Officer training encourages police to be suspicious and to look for criminal activity. Consequently, they rely on visual cues such as dress, demeanor, context, gender, age, and most importantly race, in developing "a perceptual shorthand to identify certain kinds of people" as suspects (Skolnick 1994: 44-47). Race is perhaps the most significant factor on the list of "clues," since "for many Americans, crime has a Black face" (Armour 1994: 787). For instance, a 1990 study conducted by the University of Chicago found that 56 percent of Americans believe that Blacks are "violence prone" (Smith 1990). Furthermore, Cole (1999) suggests there is no reason to suspect the police will vary significantly from the public in their racial attitudes. In fact, a study by Bayley and Mendelson (1969) compared the attitudes of police officers and regular citizens in Denver, CO, and found that police officers were slightly more prejudice than the community as a whole. A year before the Denver study, the NAACP issued the following statement in an amicus brief to the Supreme Court (Maclin 1998: 387):

> Police attitudes toward working class Negro youths and young adults are often based on the concept of the Negro as a savage, or animal, or some being outside of the human species. Therefore, the police expect behavior from Negroes in accordance with this concept…Because of the police officers' conception of the Negro male, he frequently feels that most

Negroes are dangerous and need to be dealt with as an enemy even in the absence of visible criminal behavior.

Many would perhaps argue that police attitudes have changed significantly since the 1960's, especially given that more minorities are now working as police officers. However, research shows that the police perception of African-Americans may not have changed at all. Consider for instance, the 1991 study of 650 police officers with the LAPD, conducted by the Christopher Commission. The Commission (1991: 69) found that "racial bias on the part of officers toward minority citizens currently exists and contributes to a negative interaction between police and the community."[30] Furthermore, consider the frightening similarities between the statement issued by the NAACP in the 1960's, and legal researcher, Robin K. Magee in 1994:

Black men are often labeled and treated as criminal by police, even where no criminal activity is suspected...Police perceive Blacks as more prone to criminal activity. They find Blacks more dangerous and, in other ways, easier prey for police excesses.

Consequently, the infusion of racial prejudice into police work predisposes officers to reach the general conclusion in criminal investigations that "Black + Male = Usual Suspect."

The preconceived racial stereotypes by police officers subject a significant number of law-abiding Black males to criminal treatment. While it is true that Black males receive arrests and convictions for a disproportionate amount of violent crime, it is also true that in any given year only about 2 percent of all African-Americans are arrested for committing any crime.[31] Therefore, a police officer relying on racial prejudice and stereotypes to guide their investigations is likely to stop and harass far more innocent Black males than guilty (Cole 1999; Harris 1998). The inability of White police officers to "catch the clues that distinguish law-abiding young men from those who are up to no good" fosters the harassment of young Black males (Hacker 1992: 128).

The criminal treatment endured by innocent Black males is the primary force behind contemporary discussions of racial profiling. Much of the discussion focuses on racial profiling in regards to pre-textual traffic stops or "Driving While Black" (DWB).[32] Debates concerning racial profiling have centered on pre-textual traffic stops, primarily because the experience affects Black males of all social classes and demographic backgrounds.[33] Accordingly, as Black males with occupational status and legal expertise became the victims of pre-textual traffic stops, the issue received more media attention and brought about some institutional changes.[34] However, the racial profiling debate often neglects to include police discretion in "stop and frisks," which may be the most common form of encounter between the police and Black males, particularly in lower class, inner-city communities (Harris 1994). The exclusion of stop and frisks victims from the debate on racial profiling is ironic given that many of the legal issues surrounding pre-textual traffic stops developed in court cases involving stop and frisk situations. Subsequently, the discussion that follows considers the legal basis of racial profiling as it relates to both stop and frisks and pre-textual traffic stops, since both are important sources of rage in contemporary Black males.

The Law and Racial Profiling

Any adequate discussion of the legal basis of racial profiling must begin with a consideration of America's continuing war on drugs. Standard explanations for racial profiling focus on institutional racism. However, the practice grows primarily from an array of "tangible sources, all attributable to the war on drugs" (Callahan and Anderson 2001: 2). Statistical evidence and qualitative testimonials clearly indicate that drug crimes are the exclusive focus of investigation in most racial profiling cases (Callahan and Anderson 2001). Furthermore, "the war on drugs has almost become synonymous with policing the African-American community and Black males" (Weatherspoon 1994: 23). For instance, according to a report written by David Harris (1999) for the American Civil Liberties Union (ACLU), today Blacks constitute 13 percent of all drug users in the U.S. Yet, they represent 37 percent of those arrested on drug charges; 55 percent of those convicted; and 74 percent of all drug offenders sentenced to prison. The reliance of law enforcement agents on racist drug-courier profiles largely explains the disproportional number of Blacks sentenced for drug offenses. Harris (1999: 3) insightfully notes that "five times as many Whites use drugs" but "because the police look for drugs primarily among African-Americans and Latinos, they find a disproportionate number of them with contraband. Therefore, more minorities are arrested, prosecuted, convicted, and jailed, thus reinforcing the perception that drug trafficking is primarily a minority activity." This self-fulfilling prophecy allows many White drug dealers and users to go unapprehended, since these individuals fail to fit the drug-courier profile.

Paul Markonni, a Drug Enforcement Administration Special Agent, assigned to surveillance duty at the Detroit Metropolitan Airport (Harris 1999), developed the first drug-courier profile in the early 1970's. The initial profile included only behavioral traits. However, with the emergence of crack cocaine in the 1980's, "skin color alone became a major profile component" in airport inspections (Harris 1999: 7). For example, in 1990, a police officer working at the Memphis International Airport testified that at least 75 percent of those followed and questioned at the airport were Black[35] (*United States v. Taylor* 1992). Slowly, reliance on drug-courier profiles expanded into train stations, bus terminals, and ultimately general law enforcement (Cole 1999). In 1986, "Operation Pipeline" of the Drug Enforcement Administration (DEA) facilitated the spread of racial profiling into police work. The operation was a highway drug interdiction program, which trained officers to use pre-textual traffic stops as a means to search for drugs in vehicles. To date, the program has trained approximately 27,000 officers from 48 states (Harris 1999).

With more and more law enforcement agencies involved in the war on drugs, the courier profile has developed into a "hodgepodge of traits and characteristics so expansive that it potentially justifies stopping anybody and everybody" (Cole 1999: 47). Essentially, the inclusive nature of the various profiles provides law enforcement officers "a ready-made excuse for stopping whomever they please" (Cole 1999: 49). Unfortunately, the available research and data on stop and frisks, and pre-textual traffic stops, indicates that the police are far more likely to use this unfettered discretion against Black males. Sadly, the U.S. Supreme Court has sanctioned this discretionary power with a series of opinions dating back to the late 1960's.

Stop and Frisks

Since 1968, several court cases have combined to provide the police absolute power over Black males.[36] In particular, two combined court cases produce the abusive police power displayed in stop and frisk encounters between the police and Black males. Before 1968, a police officer could not stop and frisk a suspect without "probable cause" that the suspect was involved in criminal activity. However, after *Terry v. Ohio,* justification for a "stop and frisk" shifted from "probable cause" to "reasonable suspicion."[37] In *Terry v. Ohio,* the U.S. Supreme Court ignored the tension-creating effects[38] of stop and frisks, and ruled that a police officer may detain and search a suspect without probable cause if he has "reasonable and articulable suspicion" that "criminal activity may be afoot and that the persons with whom he is dealing maybe armed and dangerous" (392 U.S. 1 1968). The Court further stated that mere suspicion and inarticulable hunches would not justify a stop and frisk (392 U.S. 22 1968). Nonetheless, since the *Terry* decision, "the Court has exhibited increasing deference to the judgments of police officers in its interpretation of the reasonable suspicion standard"[39] (Davis 1997: 429).

The Court's decision in the *United States v. Cortez* legalized judicial deference to the judgment of police officers, and provided the police with unquestionable power in their intrusive stops of Black males. In the *Cortez* decision, the U.S. Supreme Court directly instructed the lower courts to defer to the judgment of police officers in defining what constitutes reasonable suspicion. The Court's opinion stated that "when used by trained law enforcement officers, objective facts, meaningless to the untrained, can be combined with permissible deductions from such fact to form a legitimate basis for suspicion of a particular person and for action on that suspicion" (449 U.S. 419 1981). The *hands-off* stance of the Supreme Court in defining what constitutes reasonable suspicion granted police officers the power to create their own subjective guidelines for detecting suspicious behavior.

Although in theory the stop and frisk rule is color-blind, in practice, race, directly and indirectly, is the primary factor used by officers to define suspicious behavior. The stop and frisk rule creates a double standard by "extending a wide degree of discretion to police officers in settings where race and class considerations frequently play a significant role" (Cole 1999: 43). For instance, Harris (1994) details several cases where police officers have used an individual's presence in a "high crime area" or a "drug activity location" as justification for a stop and frisk. Unfortunately, these high crime areas tend to be inner-city neighborhoods populated largely by Blacks and Hispanics. In addition to location, evasive behavior also serves as clear evidence of reasonable suspicion, warranting a stop and frisk (Harris 1994). Consequently, the police combine location and evasive behavior to produce sufficient evidence for reasonable suspicion. This deduction creates a double standard. First, by merely living in high crime neighborhoods, Black males already have one "reasonable suspicion strike" against them (Cole 1999; Harris 1994). Second, Black males are more frequently the victims of undesirable police treatment, and are therefore "naturally more likely to want to avoid contact with the police"; since, "they wish to avoid harassment, baseless stops and frisks, and even more extreme actions, such as beatings, at the hands of the police" (Harris 1994: 680). Thus, contrary to the belief that only those guilty of a crime have reason to avoid the police, the statistics on police brutality and wrongful convictions indicate that Black males have multiple justifications for avoiding *officer friendly*.

Police consideration of location and evasive behavior brings us full circle. Lower class Black males are likely to find themselves in high-crime areas simply because of where they live and work. If they "choose to avoid the police—a choice they have the constitutional right to make—the police may stop them" (Harris 1994: 680). Not surprisingly, this combination produces an over-representation of Black males among those stopped and frisked. A San Diego Field Interrogation study found that although Black males comprised 4.8 percent of the population in that area, they represented nearly 47 percent of those singled out for stop and frisks (Boydston 1975). Furthermore, a 1989 study of Boston police officers revealed patterns of Black males and females "being stopped and questioned without any basis for suspicion, threatened by the officers if they asked why they were being stopped, and subjected to highly intrusive, embarrassing strip searches in public" (Walker et al. 1996: 101). The practice of routinely stopping Black males for forcible stops and intrusive frisks facilitates hostility and distrust towards the police, and "no doubt contributes to the pervasive sense among African-Americans that the criminal justice system is biased against them" (Cole 1999: 47).

Pre-textual Traffic Stops

Stop and frisk encounters occur primarily in high crime areas or other public places notorious for drug trafficking, such as train stations or bus terminals. As such, only small segments of the total population of Black males experience such encounters; specifically, those trapped in the lower class and inner-city residential areas. Pre-textual traffic stops, on the other hand, affect Black males of all socioeconomic backgrounds and geographic locations. A pre-textual stop is "any stop in which a police officer pretends to stop an individual for one reason so that he may investigate them for another" (Davis 1997: 426). The vast majority of pre-textual stops involve police officers detaining motorists for alleged traffic violations in order to discover clues of other victimless crimes, most commonly drug offenses.

Traffic violations are inevitable given the plethora of detailed regulations in state vehicle codes (Harris 1998; Salken 1989). States have traffic regulations for every conceivable aspect of vehicle operation. Thus, "even the most cautious driver would find it virtually impossible to drive for even a short distance without violating some traffic law" (Harris 1998: 560). Subsequently, given the sheer volume, police officers cannot issue traffic citations for every observed violation (Davis 1997). Such strict adherence to the law would require that police officers spend 99 percent of their time enforcing vehicle codes. Therefore, given the large pool of traffic violations, police officers use their discretionary power in deciding which infractions warrant a citation.

In theory, police officers consider only objective evidence pertaining to vehicle codes in making traffic stops. However, in practice, race is a significant determinant in police decisions to conduct vehicle stops (Leitzel 2001). Consider for instance, the 1992 study on police discrimination directed by ABC's 20/20. The experiment involved two groups of young men, one White and one Black, driving through Los Angeles on successive evenings. Both groups drove identical cars and took identical routes at identical times. Under the watchful eye of ABC News cameras, the police stopped and questioned the Black group on several occasions, while the police passed the White group sixteen times without showing any interest (Cole 1999).

The racial disparity in traffic stops would not be displeasing if, in fact, research showed that Blacks were worse drivers than Whites. There is, however, no empirical evidence to support this claim (Maclin 1998). On the contrary, Michael A. Fletcher (1996) argued in *"Driven to Extremes; Black Men Take Steps to Avoid Police Stops,"* that Black males make conscious and meticulous efforts to follow traffic laws in order to reduce police contact. Despite, perhaps, paying greater attention to traffic details, the results from two violator surveys suggests that strict adherence to vehicle codes does not necessarily result in fewer traffic stops. The plaintiffs in *Wilkins v. Maryland State Police* found that of the motorists violating a traffic law along a stretch of Interstate 95, 17.5 percent were Black, and 74.7 percent were White. However, Black motorists drove 73 percent of the vehicles stopped and searched by state troopers. A similar survey conducted by the defense attorneys in *State v. Pedro Soto* revealed that Blacks accounted for 15 percent of those observed speeding on a New Jersey turnpike, yet made up more than 46 percent of those stopped by the New Jersey State Police (Cole 1999). Thus, the frequency of traffic infractions, alone, is unable to account for the disproportionate number of Black motorists stopped by the police.

The police tendency to use race as a proxy for criminality provides a more plausible explanation for the racial disparity in traffic stops. Harris (1998: 559) states that the "disproportionate use of traffic stops against African-Americans indicates that police are using race as a proxy for the criminality or general criminal propensity of an entire racial group." In order to comprehend the proposed connection between race as a proxy for crime and the predominance of Blacks among traffic offenders, one must understand the significance of traffic stops in police work. Traffic stops provide police officers with a guise to conduct unwarranted criminal investigations. Although the stop in and of itself does not grant the police the authority to conduct a full-scale search of a vehicle, the stop usually begins a chain of events heading in the direction of a search.[40] Furthermore, the police are well aware of the investigative power of traffic stops.[41] The investigative latitude of traffic stops provides police officers a legally sanctioned avenue for exploring the preconceived racial stereotype that Black males are more likely to be involved in criminal activity, particularly drug offenses.

In due course, the empirical evidence suggests that police officers stop and search Black motorists far out of proportion to their representation among the total population of drivers (Harris 1998, 1999; Maclin 1998; Davis 1997; Larrabee 1997). Consider for instance, the results of a 1992 investigation conducted by *The Orlando Sentinel.* Police cars in Volusia County, Florida are equipped with video cameras mounted on the dashboard. As such, officers routinely videotaped traffic stops. Under Florida's Public Records Law, *The Orlando Sentinel* received 148 hours of videotape, covering 1,084 traffic stops. The tapes revealed that while 5 percent of the drivers were minorities, nearly 70 percent of those stopped were Black or Hispanic, and more than 80 percent of the cars searched were driven by Blacks and Hispanics[42] (Curtis 1992; Brazil and Berry 1992). Statistical evidence from North Carolina, Texas, New Jersey, Maryland, Colorado, and Illinois display similar patterns in the ratio of Black drivers to the total population of drivers stopped and searched (Harris 1999; Larrabee 1997; Maclin 1998).

Along with the mere racial disparity, two additional factors indicate the pre-textual nature of traffic stops involving Black males. First, citations for traffic violations are rarely given. In the study done by *The Orlando Sentinel,* only nine, or less than one percent, of the 1,084 cases analyzed resulted in a traffic ticket.[43] The fact that Black motorists rarely receive citations for traffic violations, but the police search their vehicles for contraband and illegal substances, clearly highlights the ulterior motives behind many traffic stops involving African-Americans. Second, there are significant differences in the number of citations issued to Black motorists by police officers on normal patrol duty and those assigned to specialized drug units. For example, in North Carolina, the State Police Special Emphasis Team, which targets drug offenders, issued significantly more traffic citations to Black males traveling Interstates 85 and 95 than normal state troopers patrolling the same areas. The Special Emphasis Team issued 45 percent of its tickets to Black males, compared to 24 percent by the state troopers[44] (Neff and Stith 1996). The commander of the drug team proudly issued 60 percent of his traffic citations to Black males (Maclin 1998). The investigative power of traffic stops largely explains the obsession of drug units with traffic violations.[45] Traffic stops allow police officers to detain and search individuals who fit the drug-courier profile under the legal guise of traffic enforcement. Subsequently, police abuse of this practice has raised constitutional issues concerning unreasonable searches and seizures.

The 1996 U.S. Supreme Court decision in *Whren v. the United States* addressed the constitutionality of pre-textual traffic stops. In a controversial decision, the U.S. Supreme Court ruled that such stops did not raise Fourth Amendment concerns. The Court stated that a traffic violation constitutes "probable cause" and legally warrants an observing officer to stop the vehicle (*Whren v. U.S.*, 116). Furthermore, "the rule applies even if no reasonable officer would have made the stop to enforce the traffic laws, and even if the stop was only a pretext to enable the officer to investigate a mere hunch or intuition" (Harris 1998: 556). The *Whren* decision essentially sanctioned the practice of pre-textual traffic stops by granting police officers virtually unlimited authority to stop and search any vehicle they want (Harris 1999). The ruling allows "officers who have no more basis for suspicion than the color of a driver's skin to make a constitutional stop" (Cole 1999: 39). With the Court's ruling and our society's fixation on race as a proxy for crime, Black males will continue to be the primary victims of the legalized discretionary power exercised by the police. Understandably, pre-textual stops produce many negative consequences for Black males and the legal system as a whole.

Pre-textual traffic stops undermine the integrity of the criminal justice system by further intensifying feelings of distrust and disrespect towards the legal system and its agents. Despite police assumptions, Black males can detect when an officer has pulled them over for illegitimate reasons. This becomes obvious once the officer asks if they are carrying drugs or guns, and seeks consent to search the vehicle (Harris 1999). "If the stop was really about the enforcement of the traffic code, there would be no need for a search" (Harris 1999: 25). Consequently, pre-textual traffic stops reinforce the perception among Black males that the police view them as criminals, who deserve singular scrutiny and treatment as second-class citizens[46] (Maclin 1998; Cole 1999). Such treatment undoubtedly produces anger towards the police. Expectedly, the police are the object of widespread hatred in the Black community, primarily due to the aggressive patrol practices used against Blacks. Consider for instance, the rage of Aaron Campbell, a Black off duty police officer pulled over on a pre-textual traffic stop in 1997:

> The majority of the people they are searching and humiliating are Black people. That's why I was so angry. I went from being an ordinary citizen and decorated officer to a criminal in a matter of minutes (Harris 1999: 11).

The degrading experience of police detention and treatment as a criminal for no reason other than your race provokes Black rage and destroys the integrity of the judicial system. Racial profiling further deters minorities from cooperating with the police in criminal investigations, and causes minority jurors to question the testimony of police officers serving as witnesses in court cases (Harris 1999; Leitzel 2001). Likewise, some researchers contend that the *sea of hostility*, which exists between the police and minority citizens, encourages minority jurors not to convict minority criminal defendants (Leitzel 2001). In sum, racial profiling produces a series of negative consequences for both the individual victim and the legal system as a whole. Moreover, "discriminatory police stops are the first in a chain of racially lopsided decisions by officials in the criminal justice process" (Davis 1997: 442).

Racially Biased Processing

The "lopsided" representation of Black males from arrests through incarceration indicates the significance of race on case processing in the American criminal justice system. From its inception, African-Americans have viewed the justice system skeptically, as insinuated by the historical and contemporary proclamations that the system blatantly discriminates against Blacks. Empirical research frequently supports the allegations of racial discrimination in the justice system. Focusing strictly on sentencing, Zatz (1987) reviewed six decades of discrimination literature, and concluded that the justice system has progressed from overt discrimination to more subtle forms of racial bias against minorities. Some researchers contend that these "subtle" forms of racism explain a substantial part of the prevalence of Black males in prison (Spohn et al. 1981; Kempf and Austin 1986; Unnever and Hembroff 1988; Austin et al. 1994; Crutchfield et al. 1994). In perhaps the most comprehensive examination of discrimination in the justice system, the *Harvard Law Review* published a provocative legal series entitled *Developments in the Law* (1988) (hereafter *Developments*). This authoritative journal examined every aspect of the justice system, from arrest through the death penalty, and concluded that discrimination against Blacks exists at practically every stage. While the *Developments* found some instances of overt racism, much of the behavior described in the series reflects "unconscious racism" as defined by Lawrence (1987). Given the moral shift of the 1960's and 1970's against racism, and the sentencing guidelines of the 1980's, many researchers contend that overt discrimination is no longer the greatest nemesis of Black males in the justice system. Instead of the open, blatant forms of racism confronted in the past, Black males today are more likely to face unconscious racism in the American criminal justice system[47] (Lawrence 1987; Johnson 1988).

Unconscious Racism

According to Lawrence (1987), Americans share a common historical and cultural heritage, in which racism has played, and continues to play, a dominant role. Lawrence (1987) further contends that racism is such a universal aspect of the American culture that we irrationally attached significance to race at both the conscious and unconscious levels. In addition, as "our society has more recently embraced an ideal that rejects racism as immoral," much of the behavior that produces racial discrimination results from unconscious racial motivations (Lawrence 1987: 323). There are two explanations for why racism persists on the unconscious level. First, according to Freud's psychoanalytic theory, "the human mind defends itself against the discomfort of guilt by denying or refusing to recognize those ideas, wishes, and beliefs that conflict with what the individual has learned is good or right" (Lawrence 1987: 317). Incidentally, the newfound moral stance against racism within our culture results in cognitive dissonance when individuals encounter internal racist ideas. The mind excludes racism from our consciousness, since it conflicts with the societal ethic and our basic understanding of right and wrong (Lawrence 1987). Second, cognitive psychology theorists contend that our culture transmits both direct and subliminal beliefs and preferences that we process as explicit lessons. The messages conveyed through cultural "transmitters," such as the media, parents, and peers, order and shape individual perceptions of the world (Lawrence 1987). The infectious power of racism over the American culture renders all such cultural transmitters as consciously or unconsciously influenced by racist beliefs. Racism is such a universal aspect of the American culture that explicit verbal instructions are unnecessary. The message "is likely to be transmitted by tacit understandings" (Lawrence 1987: 323). For example, in our society, a child does not need to receive verbal instruction that Blacks are inferior; he or she learns that lesson by observing others. Furthermore, since tacit understandings are rarely articulated, they "are less likely to be experienced at a conscious level" (Lawrence 1987: 323).

In the absence of personal experience or confirmation of the fact, these tacit understandings become ingrained cultural stereotypes. One such stereotype, mentioned earlier, pertains to the American tendency to use race as a proxy for criminality.[48] When police officers and other agents of the justice system make decisions based on these stereotypes, both consciously and unconsciously, the result is discriminatory treatment towards Black males. Because the transmission of such stereotypes is more likely to take place in a subliminal fashion, one can learn, internalize, and use these "lessons" without an awareness of their source (Lawrence 1987). Consequently, the absence of conscious thought about the stereotype renders the perceived racist 100 percent confident that their decisions stemmed from objective considerations of tangible facts unrelated to race. However, race influences the decision at the unconscious level. Therefore, even the most thorough investigation of conscious motives fails to uncover the race-based stereotypes that influence justice decisions (Lawrence 1987). In which case, "government officials will always be able to argue that racially neutral considerations prompted their action" (Lawrence 1987: 319).

Nonetheless, agents of the justice system "are not immune from our culture's racism, nor can they escape the psychological mechanisms that render us all, to some extent, unaware of our racist beliefs" (Lawrence 1987: 380). Consequently, ingrained tacit understandings about Black males and Black culture influence police behavior and significantly contribute to the series of conscious and unconscious racially lopsided decisions throughout the justice process. Research shows that as Black males progress through the justice system from arrest to incarceration, they encounter harsher treatment than Whites (Developments 1988; Kempf 1992). The cumulative effect of racial discrimination is the topic of consideration in the proposed study. In assessing racial discrimination at later stages of justice processing, such as sentencing, the discussion begins with a consideration of biases at earlier stages, beginning with arrest.

Race and Police Discretion

Any discussion of racial discrimination (both conscious and unconscious) at later stages of the justice process must first address the correlation between race and punishment at the initial point of entry into the system.[49] Discretion, and ultimately discrimination, in the judicial system begins with the arbitrary nature of police investigations. Proactive criminal investigations provide police officers a tremendous amount of discretionary power. An essential aspect of this power is the authority to decide when to execute lawful stops and arrests. Intrinsically linked to the *when* question is the issue of deciding *who* warrants detention. Legally, an officer must observe objective facts that establish sufficient grounds for reasonable suspicion or probable cause that criminal activity is afoot before arresting an offender. However, the U.S. Supreme Court has routinely upheld race as a legitimate factor in detaining a suspect.[50] Furthermore, it is not unusual for police officers to admit, casually, that race was a factor when the officer decided to follow, detain, search, or arrest a suspect (Hepburn 1978; Smith et al. 1984; Johnson 1983). The combination of racial stereotypes, and the police autonomy to enforce laws at their own discretion, is a significant factor in explaining the racial disparities observed at later stages of the justice process.

Much of the discrimination literature focuses on the sentencing stage and attempts to explain the large racial disparity in incarceration (see

Zatz 1987). However, the key to understanding the disparity in incarcerations is to comprehend the disparity and discrimination at earlier stages of the process. Drug offenses provide the best illustrative example of the cumulative effects of racial discrimination in the justice system. In addition, since the 1980's, no policy has contributed more to the incarceration of Black males and increased the racial disparities in incarceration than the war on drugs (Mauer 1995). To demonstrate how police discrimination affects later stages of justice processing, consider Figures 3.9 and 3.10, constructed using data from the 1997[51] versions of the *National Household Survey on Drug Abuse, Survey of State and Federal Inmates*, and the *FBI Uniform Crime Report*.

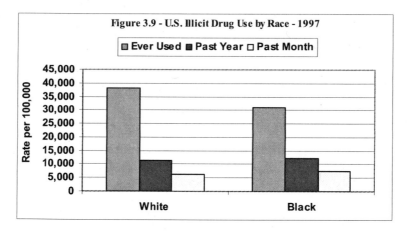

Police officers abuse their discretionary power when they fail to detain or arrest Whites who commit crimes for which Blacks are frequently prosecuted (Davis 1998). For instance, the *National Household Survey on Drug Abuse* has routinely found that the distributions of illicit drug use between Whites and African-Americans are relatively equal.[52] Yet Blacks comprise a disproportionate percentage of drug arrests, convictions, and incarcerations. Figure 3.9 illustrates the similarities between the distributions of illicit drug use according to race. Among those having ever used drugs, the rate of usage was significantly higher for Whites, while Blacks were slightly more likely to have used within the past year or month. At any rate, both distributions are relatively equal and indicate a high prevalence of drug use among both Whites and Blacks. Furthermore, given that there are significantly more Whites than Blacks in America, the comparable rates indicate that far more Whites use drugs than Blacks (Mauer 1995). However, the statistics on arrests and incarcerations for drug offenses paint a different picture.

Although the distributions of illicit drug use between races are relatively equal, and despite the fact that far more Whites used drugs, Figure 3.10 illustrates that Blacks are arrested at nearly four times the rate of Whites for drug offenses.[53] Per 100,000, there were 1,659 Blacks arrested for drug offenses in comparison to 424 Whites. Two factors explain much of the racial disparity in arrest for drug offenses. 1) Police patrol lower class inner-city areas more frequently. Blacks largely populate these locations and drug activity tends to take place in "open air drug markets" (Mauer 1995: 148). Drug deals in suburban White neighborhoods take place behind closed doors and are therefore not readily identifiable to passing police (Mauer 1995). 2) Police are more inclined to use investigative tactics, such as stop and frisk or pre-textual traffic stops against Blacks in efforts to search for drugs. As such, because the police stop a disproportionate number of Blacks using these tactics, they find a disproportionate number of Blacks with drugs or drug paraphernalia. Conscious and unconscious racist ideas or stereotypes are essential factors that perhaps lead police to focus their efforts on one particular racial group, or minorities in general. This suggestion is consistent with prior research indicating a racial disparity against minorities in police arrest (Dannefer and Schutt 1982; Petersilia 1983; Miller 1992; Tonry 1995; Walker et al. 1996; Donziger 1996).

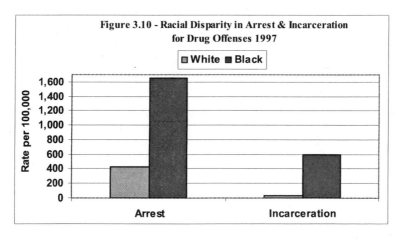

Figure 3.10 - Racial Disparity in Arrest & Incarceration for Drug Offenses 1997

The discretionary power of police officers in conjunction with racist ideals (both conscious and unconscious) taints the initial point of entry into the criminal justice system with a layer of racial discrimination. The initial level of racial disparity brought in by the police passes into other stages and magnifies. Figure 3.10 further illustrates the disproportionate number of Blacks incarcerated for drug offenses. The 4-to-1 ratio of

Black-to-White arrest for drug offenses grows to nearly an 18-to-1 ratio
at the stage of incarceration. Per 100,000, there were 592 Blacks
incarcerated for drug offenses in comparison to 33 Whites. Donziger
(1996) analyzed the 1992 versions of the *National Household Survey on
Drug Abuse, Survey of State and Federal Inmates,* and the *FBI Uniform
Crime Report* and reported virtually identical rates of incarceration for
drug offenses.   Considering the disproportionate number of Blacks
arrested for drug offenses, it seems logical to expect a similarly
disproportionate distribution of Blacks incarcerated for drug offenses.
However, the widening disparity from arrest to incarceration indicates
discrimination against Black offenders.[54] The findings from Austin and
Allen (2000) support the claim that the justice system discriminates
against minority offenders in drug cases. Austin and Allen (2000) found
that drug arrests provided a rather weak explanation of racial disparity in
court commitments for drug offenses.[55] Overall, when Austin and Allen
(2000) compared the arrest rates for the FBI's eight index crimes along
with other assaults and drug offenses, the arrest rates only explained 39
percent of the disproportionality in incarcerations. In which case, "much
room is therefore left for the influence of nonlegal variables, including
racial discrimination, on commitment to prison" (Austin and Allen 2000:
208).

In sum, based on the *National Household Survey on Drug Abuse,* far
more Whites are eligible for drug arrests. Unfortunately, the
investigative tactics of police officers focus almost exclusively on Blacks
and other minorities, which subsequently encourage self-fulfilling
prophecies that reinforce negative racial stereotypes about who commits
crime (Donziger 1996; Developments 1988). As seen in the example
using drug offenses, the low rate of Whites arrested reflects lower rates
of stops and searches, and not lower rates of offending. Discriminatory
police practices generate racially lopsided arrest statistics, which the
police then turn around and use as further evidence of the increased
criminal propensity of Black males. Such cyclical thinking perpetuates
discrimination in the justice system and has direct implications on
incarceration rates; particularly, for victimless crimes that require
proactive investigations. The discussion below briefly describes the
manner in which subsequent agents of the justice system deepen the
initial disparity created by the police, by either supporting an officer's
discriminatory decisions or introducing their own conscious and
unconscious racism.

Race and Prosecutorial Power

With the exception of potentially testifying in court, police power over
criminal processing begins and ends at the arrest stage. The American

prosecutor, on the other hand, has discretionary power and influence at every stage of the justice process, including arrest[56] (Davis 1998). In describing the scope of the prosecutor's power, Justice Jackson of the U.S. Supreme Court insightfully noted that "the prosecutor has more control over life, liberty, and reputation than any other person in America" (Davis 1969). The prosecutor's power stems from his direct control over two essential aspects of the criminal justice process: the charging decision and the terms of plea-bargain negotiations. After the police initiate an arrest, the prosecutor decides whether sufficient evidence exists to file formal charges against the suspected offender, and determines the number and seriousness of the charges filed[57] (Walker et al. 1996). In the case of serious crimes, 13 states require that a grand jury determine whether there is probable cause of guilt to file formal charges against an offender (Davis 2001). However, since most grand jurors are ordinary citizens without legal expertise, the prosecutor essentially controls the process (Davis 2001; Leipold 1995). The decision to file, dismiss, upgrade, or downgrade charges against an offender rest solely with the prosecutor. The charging decision is the most important point in the justice process since Federal and State sentencing guidelines require various mandatory sentences based on the specifics of the charges filed. The charging decision predetermines the length, nature, and severity of the sentence the offender receives (Davis 2001). Unfortunately, for minorities, with the exception of selective prosecution challenges, which are extremely difficult to sustain, there is very little public or judicial scrutiny of the prosecutor's decisions (Davis 1998).

In addition to the charging decision, the prosecutor also controls the terms of plea bargain negotiations between the offender and the court (Davis 1998). Plea-bargaining is a process in which the defendant pleads guilty to a certain offense in exchange for a reduction in criminal charges or a sentence recommendation to the judge[58] (Brosi 1979; Sanborn 1986). In the typical plea arrangement, the prosecutor offers to dismiss the most serious charge, or charges, in exchange for a guilty plea to a less serious offense by the defendant (Davis 1998). By accepting the plea agreement, the defendant forfeits his right to trial, where there is an increased probability of a more serious conviction and a longer prison sentence (Davis 1998). The prosecutor makes the decision to offer a plea agreement and controls the terms of a plea arrangement. Defense attorneys may attempt to negotiate the best possible offer for their clients; however, ultimately, the arbitrary power of the prosecutor controls the plea bargaining process (Davis 1998).

Along with police arrest, "the arbitrary use of prosecutorial discretion greatly exacerbates racial disparities in the criminal process"

(Davis 1998: 20). Because of both conscious and unconscious racism, prosecutors often make seemingly race-neutral decisions that have a racially discriminatory impact against Blacks and other minorities. Regardless of whether this impact is intentional or unintentional, research shows that prosecutors, in exercising their discretionary power, unfairly discriminate against minorities. Spohn et al. (1987) found that Black and Hispanic males were significantly less likely than White males to have felony charges rejected or dismissed by the prosecutor. Instead of issuing a charge reduction, prosecutors frequently overcharge minority defendants (NMAC 1980). Overcharging is "a prosecutorial practice of initially indicting a defendant with the most serious charge – one that is usually unsustainable" (Mann 1993: 182). The stiffer sentence that comes with the more serious charge then serves as leverage to induce a guilty plea on a lesser charge in minority cases (NMAC 1980: 210).

Prosecutors further discriminate against Blacks by increasing the seriousness of the charges filed when the victim in the alleged crime is White. For example, LaFree (1980) found that Black males arrested for raping White women had a higher likelihood of receiving felony charges than Black males arrested for raping Black women or White men arrested for raping White women. Several other studies report similar charge upgrades for crimes involving Black offenders and White victims (Radelet 1981; Myers and Hagan 1979; Radelet and Pierce 1985; Bowers and Pierce 1980).

Perhaps the most compelling evidence of prosecutorial discrimination pertains to the death penalty. Of the 38 states that currently allow executions, *none* have mandatory laws that *require* the death penalty in any particular case (LaFave and Scott 1986). The decision to seek the death penalty rests solely on the discretion of the prosecutor (Johnson 1994). Somewhat predicted, based on the prior charging disadvantages of Blacks, research shows that prosecutors are more likely to seek the death penalty for serious crimes involving Black offenders and White victims. In perhaps the most comprehensive study of capital punishment, Baldus et al. (1983) found that prosecutors sought the death penalty in 70 percent of cases involving Black defendants and White victims; 32 percent of cases involving White defendants and White victims; 15 percent of cases involving Black defendants and Black victims; and 19 percent of cases involving White defendants and Black victims.

Along with racial bias in the prosecutor's charging decision, research also indicates discrimination against minorities in the plea bargaining process. Farnworth et al. (1991) studied defendants convicted of the same offense (possession of marijuana) where each offender had a prior record. Their study revealed that White males were significantly more likely to have their charges reduced or receive probation while Hispanic and Black males were more likely to receive jail or prison sentences; despite committing the same offense and having comparable criminal records. Humphrey and Fogarty (1987) reported a similar finding among burglary defendants who pled guilty. Minority burglary defendants were 20 percent more likely to receive imprisonment than Whites, although all pled guilty. The racial discrepancy in imprisonment rates for similarly situated offenders stems from the fact prosecutors often offer better deals to Whites.[59] The advantageous position of Whites in the plea bargaining process received considerable attention following a 1991 study conducted by *The San Jose Mercury News*. After examining nearly 700,000 criminal cases from California, covering nearly a decade, the study concluded that at virtually every stage of the plea-bargaining process, Whites were more successful than Blacks. Specifically, the study found that Whites were better at getting charges dropped; getting cases dismissed; avoiding harsher punishment; avoiding extra charges; and having their criminal records wiped clean (Schmitt 1991). Although the inability of minority defendants to obtain private counsel is partially to blame for their disadvantaged position, much of the discrepancy stems from unconscious stereotyping and deliberate discrimination (Donziger 1996). Consider the comments from a California public defender explaining the discrepancy in plea bargain deals:

> If a White person can put together a halfway plausible excuse, people will bend over backward to accommodate that person. It's a feeling, you've got a nice person screwing up as oppose to the feeling that this minority person is on a track and eventually they're going to end up in the state prison. It's an unfortunate racial stereotype that pervades the system. It's an unconscious thing. (quoted in Donziger 1996: 113)

Rarely are prosecutors as vocal, much less aware, of the manner in which their subconscious racial beliefs influence their decisions. Such racist ideals, no doubt, combine to produce bias against Black males in both the charging decisions and in plea bargain negotiations. The discretionary power of the prosecutor compounds the initial disparity in police arrest. Unfortunately, for Black males, the trend of disadvantage continues throughout the criminal justice process.

Race and Pretrial Detention

The arbitrary power of judges in formulating decisions regarding pretrial detention solidifies the already disadvantaged position of Black males in justice processing. After the prosecutor files formal charges against a suspect, the judge decides whether to release or detain the accused while pending trial (Goldkamp and Gottfredson 1979). In theory, judges consider "objective" criteria surrounding the offense and the offender to determine their probability of not appearing at trial, and the possible danger they pose to society (Goldkamp 1985; Katz and Spohn 1995). Following consideration of the objective facts, the judge faces three options concerning the pretrial status of the accused (Katz and Spohn 1995). 1) Do the circumstances surrounding the offense and the offender warrant releasing the accused on their own recognizance? 2) If release on recognizance is not an option, will the offender receive detention without bail? 3) Given the opportunity to post bail, what is the appropriate bail amount? Although the law requires judges to ponder only objective criteria in matriculating through the three options, research demonstrates that subjective factors, such as race, often influence their assessment (Bynum 1982; Patterson and Lynch 1991; LaFree 1985; Ayres and Waldfogel 1994; Petee 1994).

Release on recognizance grants the accused liberation from jail without posting a cash bond. Essentially, the defendant secures release following a mere promise to appear at trial (Harmsworth 1996; Eskridge 1983). The recognizance decision takes into account a variety of factors believed to asses the likelihood of appearance at trial and the safety risk posed to the community by the offenders' pretrial release (Goldkamp and Gottfredson 1985). These factors measure residential and employment stability, offense seriousness, criminal history, and evidence of prior incidents of failure to appear in court (Gottfredson and Gottfredson 1988; Hall et al. 1984). Despite the apparent objective nature of the consideration factors in recognizance decisions, the frequency with which judges deny minorities release on recognizance suggests racial discrimination. For example, Bynum (1982) found that Blacks and Native Americans were less likely to receive release on recognizance than non-minority offenders with similar characteristics. Likewise, Petee (1994) found a significant relationship between race and release on recognizance after controlling for offense seriousness, number of prior convictions, prior failures to appear in court, current probation or parole status, living arrangements, and employment status. The results of Petee's study (1994) suggests that net of all other controls, "nonwhite" offenders faced significantly lower odds of being released on their own recognizance. The disadvantaged position of minorities in recognizance decisions extends into bail deliberations.

Once the judge denies the accused release on recognizance, he or she then decides if the offender will receive detention without bail. Under the bail system, the judge assigns a monetary figure based on the specifics of the offense. The accused secures release by paying the court 10 percent of the judge's imposed amount (Thomas 1976). The accused has a vested financial interest in returning to trail, since the bail deposit is refundable upon their appearance in court (Thomas 1976). Subsequently, failure to appear results in a forfeit of the bail deposit (Inciardi 1984). During the formative years of the bail system, all defendants received the opportunity to post bail and judges simply determined the bail amount. However, in 1984, 34 states and the federal government enacted legislation giving judges the right to deny bail to defendants deemed dangerous (Goldkamp 1985). The new legislation also allowed judges to deny bail when "the defendant poses such a risk of flight that no condition or combination of conditions will reasonably assure the defendant's presence at trial" (Doyle et al. 1997: 316). Granting judges the authority to detain suspects before trial, based on their perceived risk of flight and dangerousness, introduced significant opportunities for racial discrimination in pretrial detention. Essentially, "if judges stereotype African-Americans as less reliable and more prone to violence than Whites, they will be more inclined to detain African-Americans and release Whites, irrespective of their more objective assessments of risk of flight or dangerousness" (Katz and Spohn 1995: 164).

Unfortunately, much of the literature on detainment without bail focuses on the general change in detention rates that resulted from the sweeping legislative reforms of 1984 (Katz and Spohn 1995). These studies fail to consider the demographic factors influencing detainment without bail decisions. The few studies that do consider the variables influencing detainment decisions indicate that racial discrimination is perhaps a major factor in the judge's decision process. For example, Feeley (1979) found that Blacks were 15 percent more likely than Whites to be required to post bail, despite being 6 percent less likely to flee. Reporting a similar finding, Seron et al. (1997) conducted a series of interviews with members of the criminal defense bar and found a "general perception" that minorities received bail opportunities less frequently than Whites. To explore the issue further, the Annual Survey of American Law commissioned Dr. David Bositis to examine pretrial detention rates for the Second Circuit, using data provided by the Statistics Division of the Administration Office of the U.S. Courts. Bositis (1997) controlled for a variety of factors and found that there remained "a residual, unexplained difference in pretrial detention rates based on race and ethnicity" (Doyle et al. 1997: 320). Furthermore, federal data from the two years surrounding the legislative changes of 1984 illustrate the discriminatory impact of detainment without bail on African-Americans. In 1983, the year before federal legislation granted judges the power to detain suspects based on their perceived risk of flight and dangerousness, judges in the federal system detained only 1.7

percent of Black offenders. In 1985, the year after the legislative change, judges detained 19.1 percent of Black offenders (Mann 1993).

Closely tied to the detainment without bail decision is determination of the actual bail amount. Setting the bail amount is intrinsically different from the first two pretrial issues considered by the judge. In deciding between release on recognizance and detainment without bail, the judge has only two options (Goldkamp and Gottfredson 1979). However, in determining the amount of bail, the judge has a wider range of options and subsequently greater latitude to allow racist beliefs and ideals to influence bail amount decisions. In exploring this possibility, the National Minority Advisory Council on Criminal Justice found that minorities were significantly more likely to receive 1) legal maximum bail settings; 2) extremely high bails for minor offenses; 3) over-charges at arrest that carried higher bails; and 4) multiple charges, with bail imposed at the legal maximum for each separate charge (NMAC 1980: 204). Likewise, a 1991 study by *The Hartford Courant* reported a similar disadvantage for minorities in bail amounts. Based on analysis from 150,000 cases, the study found that Black and Hispanic males paid, on average, double the bail of White males for similar offenses. The discrepancy widened in drug cases where Black and Hispanic males received bail amounts four times higher than their White male counterparts (Ewing and Houston 1991). Further analysis of Connecticut criminal court data revealed that judges were attempting to "systematically 'overdeter' Black and Hispanic defendants from fleeing after release on bail by setting bail at seemingly unjustified high levels" (Ayres and Waldfogel 1994: 986).

In efforts to curtail the subjective nature of bail amounts, many states require judges to follow a bail schedule. The bail schedule contains a list of all charges and the dollar amount corresponding to each offense category (Hall et al. 1984; Patterson and Lynch 1991). In theory, the bail schedule should minimize discrimination by establishing rules related to offense seriousness that are equally applicable to all defendants (Patterson and Lynch 1991). The problem with bail schedules is that judges maintain the authority to impose bail amounts above or below the prescribed guideline. The slim research on diversions from bail schedules, suggests that race is a significant factor. For example, Patterson and Lynch (1991) found that judges circumvented the guidelines at different rates according to the race of the offender. Specifically, they reported that Whites and minorities were equally likely to receive bail amounts over the prescribed guidelines; however, Whites were significantly more likely to receive bail amounts under the required minimum (Patterson and Lynch 1991).

In sum, the three factors: release on recognizance, detainment without bail, and actual bail amounts; significantly reduce the likelihood of pretrial release for minority offenders. In dissecting the inclusive minority category, researchers have found that discriminatory treatment towards criminal defendants may be restricted primarily to Black males (Katz and Spohn 1995; Spohn et al. 1985). For example, Katz and Spohn (1995) found that Black males were significantly less likely than White males, White females, and Black females to secure release before trial. The inability of Black males to secure pretrial release produces a *spillover effect* into other processing decisions.

Pretrial detention produces several negative consequences for Black males as they proceed through the justice system. First, local jails indiscriminately mix defendants awaiting trial with convicted felons and other violent offenders. Subsequently, each year, dozens of detainees are beaten, raped, and murdered (Inciardi 1984). Second, detained offenders are unable to assist in the preparation of their case. Confinement limits their ability to locate evidence and witnesses, as well as complicates access to legal counsel (Mann 1993). Third, pretrial detention stigmatizes the offender in the few cases that make it to trial (Levine et al. 1986). Detained offenders enter the courtroom in handcuffs, wearing jail issued clothing, and accompanied by an armed bailiff. All of these factors "may influence the judge's or jury's opinion concerning the defendant's guilt" (Patterson and Lynch 1991: 40). Fourth, sentence severity is significantly higher for detained offenders. Research has routinely shown that in comparison to released defendants, detainees face disadvantages at the indictment and conviction stages, as well as receive more harsh sentences (Walker et al. 1996; Foote 1954; Farrell and Swigert 1978; Wheeler and Wheeler 1980; Unnever 1982; Albonetti 1991; Petersilia 1983). Finally, pretrial detention in deplorable jail conditions coerces defendants into plea negotiation in order to settle the matter more rapidly (Inciardi 1984). On the contrary, when the defendant secures pretrial release, it severely handicaps the prosecutor in plea negotiations, since the defendant feels less pressure to plead guilty (Lizotte 1978). Consequently, Lizotte (1978: 572) found that in efforts to dispose of cases quickly, both public defenders and private attorneys "may be less inclined to help their clients make bail." Those individuals with the endurance to withstand the pressure to accept a plea bargain and the confidence to assert their right to trial face yet another discrimination obstacle in the jury process.

Race and the Jury Process

The sixth amendment of the U.S. Constitution grants those accused of a crime the right to a "speedy and public trial, by an *impartial jury* of the State and district wherein the crime shall have been committed"[60] (emphasis added). However, for nearly two centuries, what constituted an impartial jury was largely a panel of White, male, upper class Americans.[61] It was not until 1975 that the U.S. Supreme Court in *Taylor v. Louisiana* determined that in order for a jury to be considered impartial, the initial panel of eligible jurors must represent a "fair cross-section of the community." To the detriment of Black males, the initial selection process for jury panels in conjunction with the use of peremptory challenges during *Voir Dire* and juror misconduct during deliberations, often combine to inhibit the constitutional right of minority offenders to an impartial jury trial.

From the inception of the jury system, racial minorities have not received equal representation on juries in the United States. Before the mid-twentieth century, the disadvantaged position of Blacks on jury panels received formal sanctioning by the laws of several states. For example, at issue in *Strauder v. West Virginia* was a state statute that specifically limited jury service to "White males who are [at least] twenty one years of age" (quoted in Serr and Maney 1988: 3). Despite the removal of such overt forms of racial discrimination in the jury process, minority under-representation continues today in large part due to the minority filter that plagues every level of the current selection system. Most states used selection processes that severely limit minority participation at each stage of the process from generating the initial source list to the final jury panel (Developments 1988). In creating the initial source list, most states and the federal government rely on list generators that inadvertently increase the relative odds of low minority representation. For example, many jurisdictions rely on lists of registered voters, property tax rolls, or automobile registrations, to generate the initial source list of jurors (Walker et al. 1996). The problem with these seemingly objective lists is that in many jurisdictions, minorities are significantly less likely than Whites to be registered voters, own an automobile, or possess taxable property (Walker et al. 1996). Consequently, the initial pool of jurors over-represents White middle and upper class Americans, while severely under-representing racial minorities. Figure 3.11 presents a brief illustration of the jury selection process and demonstrates the manner in which the system filters out potential minority jurors from the jury pool at every stage.

After generating the source list, judicial officials construct the qualified jury wheel based on responses to mailed questionnaires. Because Blacks and other minorities are more likely to be renters instead of homeowners, their high degree of residential mobility decreases the likelihood that they will receive the jury questionnaire (Fukurai 1985; Fukurai et al. 1991). Subsequently, when minorities fail to receive questionnaires due to relocation or neglect to return the qualification questionnaires, they are systematically eliminated from jury service in future cases within that particular geographic region (Fukuria et al. 1991). Even minorities who secure the questionnaire and a certified summon to the courthouse for potential jury placements are still likely to receive exemptions from jury duty because of economic hardship. Van Dyke (1977) estimated that about 60 percent of those who return jury questionnaires request exemption due to economic hardship. The presiding judge decides whether to grant request for exemption, and most courts concede all requests (Developments 1988). In which case, "the hardship loophole exacerbates the under-representation of nonwhites who are disproportionately poor and cannot afford to lose wages" because of jury duty (Developments 1988: 1564; NMAC 1980).

Figure 3.11 - Jury Selection Process: Racial Filtering

Following the hardship loophole, the next stage in the jury filter is statutory venire qualifications. At a minimum, most jurisdictions require that potential jurors be U.S. citizens who are able to read, write, speak, and understand English, as well as live in the judicial district for a certain period of time (Developments 1988). While these qualifications surely "limit minority participation in certain areas of the country,"[62] they are not as subjective as key man characteristics once used by many states (particularly in Southern U.S.). For example, a key man characteristic listed in the Arkansas venire qualifications stated that jurors had to possess "good character, approved integrity, sound judgment, reasonable information, and good behavior" (Benokraitis and Griffin-Keene 1982: 432). Consequently, attorneys removed many Blacks who reached the courthouse from the pool of qualified jurors due to a perceived lack of intelligence or some other statutory venire qualification (Benokraitis and Griffin-Keene 1982).

The few potential minority jurors, who manage to survive through the previous levels of the selection process, have an increased probability of removal from the jury pool during Voir Dire. Voir Dire (pronounced vwar deer) is a French term meaning to speak the truth. Legal officials refer to the process during which judges and attorneys review prospective jurors to determine their fitness to serve on a particular jury trial as Voir Dire. During Voir Dire, judges and attorneys ask prospective jurors a series of questions to assess their strong personal and political biases. When respondents show strong biases, they may be removed from the jury panel for cause.

In addition to removal for cause, attorneys may also strike potential jurors from the selection pool by using peremptory challenges. Peremptory challenges allow attorneys to remove jurors without explanation[63] (Developments 1988). All 50 states and the federal courts permit several peremptory challenges to both the prosecutor and the defense attorney. Usually, both sides receive the same number of challenges, with the number increasing with the severity of the charges filed (Developments 1988). The use of peremptory challenges is a very common practice within the jury selection process. In fact, peremptory challenges remove almost one-third of all prospective jurors (Hans and Vidmar 1986). Although the objective goal of peremptory challenges is to insure an impartial jury, the subjective nature of the challenges introduces significant opportunities for racial discrimination. Research has routinely found that prosecutors remove Blacks from jury panels using peremptory challenges at rates far greater than for Whites[64]: Walker et al. (1996); Turner et al. (1986); *United States v. Carter* (1975); *United States v. McDaniels* (1974); Rose (1999). After the use of peremptory challenges, the final jury panel is established. Typically, because of the aforementioned obstacles, the "jury consists of White, middle class, middle aged persons whose beliefs and cultural attitudes mirror those of the dominant (White) political and economic structure" (NMAC 1980: 207). Peremptory challenges offer such discriminatory power that a former trial court judge wrote an article advocating the abolition of peremptory challenges and referred to the practice as "the last best tool of Jim Crow" (Hoffman 1997: 827).

What are the consequences of low minority representation on jury panels for Black males accused of a criminal offense? There are three major consequences for Black male offenders on trial before all White or predominantly White juries. First, without the broad range of social experiences that a diverse panel could provide, juries often lack the tools necessary to evaluate effectively the facts presented (Sperlich and

Jaspovice 1975; Johnson 1985; Van Dyke 1977). In which case, "An all-White jury simply may not understand the language involved in the case and may act on this misunderstanding to the detriment of a minority defendant" (Developments 1988: 1559; Hans and Vidmar 1986). The second consequence of low minority representation on jury panels is that it increases the odds of discriminatory behavior or statements during jury deliberations. For example, in *Tobias v. Smith* (1979), one juror instructed the remaining panel to ignore the problems with identifying the defendant because "you can't tell one Black from another. They all look alike"[65] (quoted in Developments 1988: 1595). Thus, to the detriment of the minority defendant, racist statements during deliberations "render the juror's perception of all evidence and events at trial unreliable" (Developments 1988: 1595). Consequently, the punishment netted to a Black defender may be more a product of racial prejudice instead of an objective evaluation of the evidence presented.

The third disadvantage to Black offenders, sentenced by all White or predominantly White juries is that they face a greater risk of receiving unjust verdicts. Given that Black defendants often receive absurd sentences with less-than-convincing evidence, it appears "racial prejudice still sometimes seems to sit as a thirteenth juror" (Levine 1992, quoted in Walker et al. 1996: 136). Numerous studies illustrate the impact of racial prejudice on jury verdicts: *American Criminal Law Review* 1980; Johnson 1985; Hans and Vidmar 1986; Lipton 1979; Starr and McCormick 1985; Wishman 1986. For example, Johnson (1985) found that White jurors, in empirical and mock trials, were more likely to convict minority defendants. It is not surprising that "in a system in which largely White juries predominate, nonwhite defendants are more likely than White defendants to be found guilty and to be punished severely" (Developments 1988: 1560).

In many cases, the race of the victim systematically biases the jury's verdict. Research indicates that White jurors often find the testimony of minority victims less persuasive; consequently, they are less committed to seeing justice done in their case (Klein and Creech 1982; Miller and Hewitt 1978). The influence of race of the victim bias is particularly strong in cases involving the death penalty, with juries more likely to impose the death penalty in Black offender/White victim cases (Bowers and Pierce 1980; Baldus et al. 1983). In sum, there were three major disadvantages for Black male offenders sentenced by all White or predominantly White juries: lack of social experiences required for effective evaluation of evidence; racist behavior and statements during deliberations; and consequently more severe and unjust sentences. A fourth consequence discussed in the next section deals with the increased odds of receiving a wrongful conviction.

Race and Wrongful Convictions

Miscarriages of justice occur when innocent Black males receive erroneous convictions for crimes, which they did not commit. Given the illusion of justice in the American court system, the typical citizen prefers to believe that the police, prosecutors, judges, and juries are always correct in their determinations of guilt (Gershman 1993). However, the rate of errors within our irreproachable system of justice is perhaps higher than many would care to admit. While precise estimates for the rate of wrongful convictions are difficult to compute,[66] researchers attempting to quantify the phenomenon have reported rates ranging from relatively few cases each year up to 20 percent of all convictions (Huff et al. 1986). For example, Huff et al. (1986) surveyed a sample of 353 criminal justice officials in Ohio, extending from judges to chief of police, to determine their perception of how frequently wrongful convictions occur. Only 6 percent of survey respondents believed that wrongful convictions never occurred. The vast majority of respondents (72 percent) believed that wrongful convictions occurred in less than 1 percent of cases, and approximately 20 percent believed that the rate of wrongful convictions was between 1 and 5 percent. The rates may appear rather low, however, when considering the high volume of cases processed annually by the justice system, this amounts to a rather large number of erroneous convictions. Assume for example, that based on the work of Huff et al. (1986) the true rate of wrongful convictions is 0.5 percent (a rather conservative estimate). If the estimate is reasonable, roughly 4,990 of the 997,970[67] felony convictions in state courts in 1996 involved wrongful convictions!

More disturbing than the sheer volume of justice mishaps is the degree of racial homogeneity among the victims of wrongful convictions. Previous research on discrimination in justice processing has focused primarily on arrest, sentencing, and the administration of the death penalty (Walker et al. 1996; Barnes and Kingsnorth 1996; Spohn et al. 1981, 1982; Bowers 1984). Researchers, however, have devoted little attention to the influence of racial bias in cases where innocent Black males receive erroneous convictions. Despite the small volume of literature in this area, ample evidence reveals that the disadvantaged position of Black males found in the aforementioned sections of the criminal justice system continues in cases involving miscarriages of justice (Parker et al. 2001). For example, Bedau and Radelet (1987) examined 350 cases of wrongful convictions and found that 40 percent involved Black defendants. Other researchers have reported a similarly strong concentration of African-Americans among the victims of wrongful convictions (Radelet et al. 1996; Huff et al. 1996; Holmes 2001; Ost 1987). Research further indicates that the rate of wrongful convictions for African-Americans increases significantly when the alleged crime is a capital offense. According to statistics from *The Death Penalty Information Center,* as of August 2002, Blacks represented roughly 42 percent of those released from death row by determination of innocence.[68]

The high concentration of African-Americans among the victims of wrongful convictions results from a variety of factors. Researchers generally agree that the primary cause of wrongful conviction is eyewitness error (Huff et al. 1986, 1996; Rattner 1988). Eyewitness misidentification accounts for significantly more cases of wrongful conviction than all other justice mishaps combined. For example, in June 2000, *The Center on Wrongful Convictions* at Northwestern University analyzed the 67 then-known DNA exonerations in the U.S. and Canada, and found that roughly 76 percent of these cases involved inaccurate eyewitness testimony. Furthermore, in nearly 38 percent of the 86 total exonerations included in the Northwestern study, eyewitness testimony was the only evidence against the defendant (Warden 2001). The Northwestern study examined only capital offenses; however, the deleterious influence of eyewitness error exists across all crime categories. Rattner (1988) for example, found that of 205 wrongful convictions for crimes ranging from murder to arson, roughly 52 percent resulted from eyewitness misidentification.

Sadly, justice officials are very much aware of the high probability of error involved in cases centered on eyewitness testimony. Huff et al. (1986) found that nearly eight out of ten justice officials ranked eyewitness error as the leading cause of wrongful convictions. The relative odds of mistaken eyewitness identifications are significantly higher in cases involving defendants and witnesses from different racial groups. Such scenarios further homogenize the victims of wrongful convictions since "Blacks are more likely to be victimized by erroneous cross-racial identification than are Whites" (Parker et al. 2001: 121). The tragic story of Lenell Geter demonstrates the ease with which faulty eyewitness identifications perpetuate the worst nightmare of every Black male in America:

Lenell Geter, a young Black engineer employed in the Dallas area, is at work one day when a fast food restaurant is robbed 50 miles away. A White woman tells of Geter's "suspicious" habit of reading and feeding ducks in the park near her home. Several witnesses to the crime identify Geter from photographs, even though their previous descriptions of the robber bore little resemblance to Geter. Geter's coworkers testify that he was at work when the robbery occurred. There is no physical evidence linking Geter to the crime. Nonetheless, Geter is convicted and sentenced to life in prison. Following intense national publicity, including a feature on CBS's *60 Minutes*, Geter is finally released[69] (see McBride 1987).

Cross-racial identifications are so controversial that Elizabeth Loftus, a leading expert on eyewitness identification, concluded: "It seems to be a fact…that people are better at recognizing faces of persons of their own race than a different race" (quoted in Parker et al. 2000: 121). Unfortunately, the heightened probability of error in cross-racial identification is rarely the only factor contributing to the high rate of wrongful convictions for Black males.

Often the injection of error into the justice process by eyewitness misidentifications, such as in Lenell Geter's case, is fostered by societal pressure on criminal justice agents for the quick apprehension of alleged offenders. Media coverage intensifies public pressure on the justice system to punish someone for known offenses (Huff et al. 1986). Consequently, the public is seemingly always under the impression that crime is out of control. This notion tends to result in a great public outcry against criminals and an increased pressure towards arrest, conviction, and incarceration, particularly for violent and drug crimes. Although such pressure may potentially create a justice system more responsive to the social values of the larger public (Huff et al. 1986), it also offers an increased potential for error. For example, injustice frequently results when citizens apply pressure on justice agents to produce guilty verdicts against Black males where there is at least reasonable doubt concerning the offender's guilt (Huff et al. 1986). Thus, while public pressure may reflect the general sentiment regarding social and criminal justice, it may also "reflect public vengeance and fears, easily manipulated by demagogues who are ready and willing to oblige" (Huff et al. 1986: 531).

Black males are particularly vulnerable to public vengeance and fears given their tendency to serve as *easy targets* for high profile or unsolved criminal offenses. In criminal cases where public sentiment demands an immediate justice response, Black males are extremely susceptible to pressure convictions, which are subsequently more likely to be wrongful convictions. In the minds of many Americans, crime and Black males are synonymous (Russell 1998). Largely due to media sensationalism, most Americans wrongly believe that Blacks are responsible for committing the majority of crimes (Russell 1998). Consequently, the culturally engrained image of Black males as deviance prone individuals has become so deeply embedded into our collective conscious that when the typical American thinks about crime, they picture a "criminalblackman"[70] (Russell 1998). Widespread belief in the myth of the "criminalblackman" provides society with a believable scapegoat for both real and imaginary crimes. The myth has become so strong and used so frequently that Comedian Paul Mooney has devoted an entire routine to the phenomenon. In his act entitled "1-900-Blame-A-Nigger,"[71] Mooney humorously depicts the tendency of White Americans to scapegoat Blacks for crimes they commit. Mooney jokingly stated:

> Didn't some White man in Boston shoot his pregnant wife and then shot his-self, crying, "Oh niggers did it." Always trying to blame some niggers. That's why I'm gonna start a new ad, "900-Blame-A-Nigger." So when White folks get into trouble, just call my agency. "[Hello] Blame-A-Nigger. I just pushed my mother down the stairs. I don't want to go to jail. Send a nigger over here."

Although presented as part of comedy routine, Mooney's comments contain a frightening element of truth when considering the literature on racial hoax.

A racial hoax occurs "when someone fabricates a crime and blames it on another person because of his race or when an actual crime has been committed and the perpetrator falsely blames someone because of his race" (Russell 1998: 70). While both Whites and Blacks concoct racial hoax, the phenomenon overwhelmingly involves White victims fabricating offenses by Black males. Russell (1998) examined 67 known racial hoaxes that occurred between 1987 and 1996. The sample of hoaxes ranged from lesser-publicized local fabrications to international stories such as the 1994 Susan Smith allegations. In roughly 75 percent of the hoaxes analyzed by Russell (1998), Black males were the perpetrator of preference. In 94 percent of the racial hoaxes where Black males were the alleged perpetrators, the accused was White, and 34 percent of the White-on-Black hoaxes resulted in the arrests, detention, or questioning of innocent Black males.[72] Those who accuse Black males of alleged crimes ranged in social status from doctors, judicial officials, and even police[73] (Russell 1998). Furthermore, "The fact that so many White-on-Black hoaxes are successful indicates society's readiness to accept the image of Blacks as criminal" (Russell 1998: 77). American culture has internalized the myth of the "crimInalblackman" to such deep seeded levels that Black males serve as easy and believable targets for both real and imaginary crimes. The inability of Black males to protect themselves against such allegations contributes significantly to the rate of wrongful convictions.

Research shows that Black males' frequently lack the legal, political, and economic resources necessary to protect themselves against erroneous convictions (Parker et al. 2001). Without financial resources and other forms of social capital, such as established connections with affluent individuals, Black males are often unable to secure the resources necessary for proving their innocence against unjust prosecutions (Parker et al. 2001). Subsequently, differential access to the resources necessary to achieve vindication further magnifies the racial differences in wrongful convictions (Parker et al. 2001: 118). However, even with equal access to resources, Black males must confront unethical police and prosecutors, the last contributing factors to the high rate of wrongful convictions among Black males.

Huff et al. (1986) ranked police and prosecutorial errors as the second and third most frequently contributing causes to wrongful convictions. Contrary to the officer friendly image, research shows that police officers are not above engaging in unethical behavior to secure arrests and convictions. The problem is that often times, this unethical behavior directly results in the conviction of an innocent Black male. For example, in the early 1990's, a group of police officers from North Philadelphia (a predominantly Black neighborhood) admitted to planting evidence and lying to support false convictions (Cole 1999). The investigation ultimately led to the conviction of several officers and the reversal of over fifty criminal convictions obtained on the strength of the officer's testimony (Cole 1999). In addition to planting evidence, research indicates that police officers also induce false confessions (Leo 2001) and fabricate informants (Zimmerman 2001) in order to secure convictions.

Police-induced false confessions have always been a leading cause of wrongful convictions in the U.S. (Bedau and Radelet 1987; Borchard 1932; Leo and Ofshe 1998). While precise estimates of the phenomenon currently do not exist,[74] "social science literature has established that such confessions occur with troubling regularity and are highly likely to lead to unjust deprivations of liberty" (Leo 2001: 44-45). Once the police secure a false confession, the alleged offender receives more harsh treatment at every stage of the criminal process (Leo 1996; Ofshe and Leo 1997). Equally damaging is the police practice of fabricating informants. Police often fabricate informants in efforts to bolster warrant applications or improve the strength of evidence against an alleged offender (Curriden 1995; G. Taylor 1999). False confessions and fabricated informants serve as flawed evidence in criminal proceedings. Often, the corruption injected by the police goes undetected by the prosecutor. However, even when detected, there is still no guarantee that justice will prevail.

Although legally and ethically required to turnover all available evidence to defense attorneys,[75] the prosecutor often suppresses information that could potentially help to establish an offender's innocence. Prosecutors maintain superior resources as well as early involvement with the police in criminal investigations. Such resources invariably lead to the accumulation of "evidence that may cast doubt on a defendant's guilt" (Gershman 1993: 510). Neglecting to reveal this information, whether inadvertently or intentionally, increases the odds of a wrongful conviction by denying defense attorneys the opportunity to prepare adequately for their client's case.

Prosecutors also contribute to the rate of wrongful convictions through the plea-bargaining process. After experiencing the deplorable conditions of jails across the U.S., many alleged offenders desire immediate removal from such environments. Those prosecutors aware of the defendant's sense of urgency in securing pre-trial release use this desire as leverage during the plea-bargaining process. Accordingly, when the prosecutor offers immediate release from jail in exchange for a guilty plea, "with nothing more consequential than a minor criminal record," innocent Black males, unfamiliar with "institutional culture" and unable to make bail, may find it extremely difficult to resist such offers (Huff et al. 1986: 530). The odds of innocent Black males accepting deals of this nature are particularly high when the individual resides in a community where criminal records are a common occurrence and subsequently not highly stigmatizing (Huff et al. 1986: 530). Thus, many innocent Black males perhaps plead guilty to crimes that they did not commit in efforts to avoid pretrial detention in deplorable jails.

Prosecutors further maintain an advantaged position in more serious cases involving relatively weak evidence. In such cases, the prosecutor's ability to overcharge, in conjunction with the racial bias of the jury system, often induces Black males "to enter a plea of guilt and accept a certain but slight penalty rather than run the risk of a more serious conviction" (Farrell and Swigert 1978: 446). Research has shown that prosecutors are more inclined to overcharge minority defendants (NMAC 1980). By overcharging offenders frequently with charges that would not hold at trial, the prosecutor creates the *illusion of a deal* for minority defendants. In which case, when the prosecutor presents the option of pleading guilty to *one* of the charges filed or going to trial on all *five* charges filed, many Black males accept the plea. The prosecutor uses two facts about jury trials as leverage in these cases; 1) juries tend to convict minority defendants on less stringent evidence[76], and 2) juries generally sentence minority defendants to longer prison terms[77]. Therefore, when prosecutors confront innocent Black males and present plea-bargains as *take it or leave it deals*, many offenders, out of fear of the jury system, accept a plea[78] (NMAC 1980).

In sum, the combination of eyewitness error, societal pressure on justice agents, the myth of the "criminalblackman," and misconduct by police and prosecutors, significantly increases the rate of wrongful convictions among Black males. Black males vindicated from a wrongful conviction endure severe humiliation and frequently lose their family and career opportunities, all with little or no compensation for such suffering[79] (Huff et al. 1986). In addition, wrongfully convicted offenders frequently endure the harsh conditions of jail and prison for prolonged periods during the appeals process. For example, Warden (2001) reported that in cases of exoneration where eyewitness testimony was the only evidence against the accused, the average time between arrest and exoneration was 95 months (just short of 12 years). Such injustice diminishes the confidence of the Black community in the fairness of the justice system and forever enrages the victims of wrongful convictions. As stated by Wilbert Lee, a Black man twice convicted by all-White juries of murdering two White gas station attendants and 12 years later exonerated of all charges: "I am bitter, and I will be until the day I die."[80]

Summary of Historical and Contemporary Sources of Rage

The preceding discussion considered the influence of a variety of historical and contemporary factors in the maintenance and production of Black rage. Historically, the lessons taught to Black males predispose one to anger and rage given the propensity to adopt a victim mentality, believe in conspiracy theories, and function with a heightened level of race consciousness. In terms of contemporary social factors, such as the breakdown of the Black family, marginal status in education and employment, and discrimination in the criminal justice system, each of these elements individually contributes to the production of anger in Black males. However, the individual level of anger associated with each factor in isolation is not likely to produce noticeable consequences. Moreover, given the intrinsic connection between all of these elements, summing the cumulative spells of anger paints a not-so-promising picture regarding the potential level of rage concealed within many Black males. In his Third Law of Motion, the great physicist Sir Isaac Newton stated that "for every action, there is an equal and opposite reaction." Thus, we can expect that the rage produced within Black males will eventually surface with detrimental interpersonal and societal consequences.

Consequences of Black Rage

Research shows that black rage contributes to a variety of behaviors, both negative and positive. Contrary to intuition, Black rage is not always destructive. For instance, several famous Black authors vividly described their ability to channel anger and rage into insightful and forceful books about race relations (see Hooks 1995; or McCall 1995). Furthermore, "Black people have always tapped into their rage to achieve in the sciences, in the arts, in the law, and in their daily struggle" (P. Harris 1997: 145). In fact, productive rage often receives credit as being the fuel behind the civil rights movement, the force behind the eloquence of Malcolm X, and the subject matter of which Maya Angelou turned into eloquent poetry and prose (P. Harris 1997). However, despite the positive displays of Black rage, the mass media often chooses to portray only the negative images of Black rage. This is "usually personified by angry young Black males wreaking havoc upon the 'innocent'" which subsequently teaches "everyone in the culture to see this rage as useless, without meaning, destructive" (Hooks 1995: 18). Moreover, destructive displays of rage do not necessarily result in Black males assaulting innocent Whites. For instance, Black rage also produces negative physical and mental health consequences for Black males. Thus, destructive displays of Black rage transpire both internally and externally. The current study considers two internal consequences of Black rage, physical and mental health problems, and one external consequence, the increasing phenomenon of Black-on-White crime.[81]

Black Rage and Physical Health

Data from epidemiological research, community health surveys, and experimental studies, have demonstrated a strong relationship between rage in Black males and physical health problems. The relationships are not always direct. However, there is general agreement that many health problems in Black males "are caused by or exacerbated by high levels of chronic anger, hostility, and anxiety that are suppressed and denied emotional expression" (Gibbs 1994: 134; Tarvis 1989; Williams et al. 1985). For example, epidemiologists have routinely shown that Black males have higher rates of hypertension than White males (Myers 1990). Furthermore, experimental studies on hypertension have demonstrated a direct connection between suppressed rage and high blood pressure symptoms in Black males (Harburg et al. 1973; Myers 1990). Hypertension increases the prevalence of heart disease among Black males. Consequently, the five leading causes of death for Black males age fifteen to twenty-four are homicide, accidents, suicide, cancer, and heart disease (U.S. Department of Health and Human Services 1985).

The increasing rate of suicide among Black males further indicates the physical health problems suffered because of suppressed rage. According to the Bureau of the Census (1990), from 1960 to 1990, the suicide rate for young Black males tripled. "Suicide is conceptualized psychodynamically as a response to anger turned against the self" (Gibbs

1994:129). As such, the increase in suicide rates among Black males "indicates a growing inability...to cope constructively with their overwhelming feelings of anger and rage" (Gibbs 1994: 129; Gibbs 1988; Hendin 1969).

Rage and anger further contribute to the high death rate among Black males by encouraging unhealthy behaviors believed to alleviate stress. In 1985, the U.S. Department of Health and Human Services conducted an official report on the health of Blacks and other minorities. The report concluded that many of the premature deaths among Black males are due to "high-risk health behaviors," including alcohol and substance abuse. Furthermore, that same year, Williams et al. (1985) summarized several studies suggesting that smoking and substance use serve as means for Black men to alleviate tensions and to withdraw from their stressful daily reality.

Black Rage and Mental Health

In addition to physical health problems, rage in Black males also severely affects their mental health. The subliminal messages conveyed to Black males during early adolescence establish a firm foundation for future mental health problems. Pierce (1970) coined the phrase "micro-aggression" to describe the constant assaults on the self-esteem of all Blacks in America. The detrimental effects of these societal assaults are worse for Black males. From early adolescence, "Black boys daily receive subtle and overt messages that they are expected to be unsocialized, unmotivated, and undisciplined" (Gibbs 1994: 135). Teachers, as well as parents, reinforce these messages (Reed 1988; Peters 1981). Consequently, at an early age, many Black boys internalize negative views of themselves as "dumb, deviant, disturbed, disadvantaged, and dysfunctional, the five d's that society has attributed to them and to their families" (Gibbs 1994: 135; Gibbs 1988; Gibbs and Hines 1989). Young adulthood reinforces the internalized attributions through differential and discriminatory treatment from various social agencies (i.e. the police). Black males endure tests of their mental stability daily by functioning in a society that subjects them to rage-producing conditions, while simultaneously teaching them to suppress their negative feelings.

In her book, *Killing Rage*, Bell Hooks (1995) suggests that, "to perpetuate and maintain White supremacy, White folks have colonized African-Americans," and a part of that colonizing process has been teaching Blacks to repress their rage (14). Hooks (1995) further contends that Blacks in America have always had to learn how to "choke down" their rage. The fears of punishment, both formal and informal, as well as the potential economic exile, provide added incentive for Black males to choke down rage (Powdermaker 1943; Hooks 1995). However, despite pressures to suppress their rage, the Black male's anger eventually manifests itself in a variety of detrimental symptoms, attitudes, and behaviors (Grier and Cobbs 1968; Poussaint 1983). Psychiatrists and clinicians have long noted that repressed anger is a major symptom of psychological problems in Black males (Gibbs 1988; Grier and Cobbs 1968; Pierce 1970; Poussaint 1983; Staples 1982). Black males may seek treatment for a variety of mental conditions; however, "anger is a common symptom that is never far from the surface and often the underlying cause of their emotional distress" (Gibbs 1994: 135). The Black male's mental health problems are not always apparent given that many Black males erect "elaborate defense mechanisms and develop dysfunctional behaviors in order to prevent their rage from overwhelming them and causing them constant distress" (Gibbs 1994:135).

Black Rage and Black-on-White Crime

One important external consequence of Black rage is the influence of this concept on interracial crime. Despite increasing evidence of the role of Black rage in crime production, "Criminologists are loath to speak openly on race and crime for fear of being misunderstood or labeled racist" (Sampson and Wilson 1995: 2). Consider for instance a comment made by Black rapist and author Eldridge Cleaver (1968: 14) in his provocative book, *Soul On Ice*:

> Rape was an insurrectionary act. It delighted me that I was defying and trampling upon the White man's law, upon his system of values, and that I was defying his women – and this point, I believe, was the most satisfying to me because I was very resentful over the historical fact of how the White man had used the Black woman. I felt I was getting revenge.

Cleaver's poignant statement reveals the fact that certain crimes have an ideological component, which represents an explosion of hatred by Black males against their oppressor (Agopian et al. 1974: 93). Curtis (1974: 78) echoed a similar point by interpreting the rape of White women by Black men as "the penultimate way for a Black male to serve up revenge on his White male oppressor." In fact, a number of researchers have suggested that certain crimes, in particular rape, which involve a Black offender and a White victim, are due in large part to Black rage (Poussaint 1966; Herton 1965; LaFree 1982; Wilbanks 1985). Statements such as those made by Cleaver and Curtis indicate that for Black offenders, there is a "socially created drive" to victimize Whites

(O,Brien 1987: 819). In support of this "socially created drive" hypothesis, research on interracial crime reveals that Blacks are far more likely to victimize Whites, than Whites are to victimize Blacks.

To illustrate this point, Figure 3.12 presents the racial breakdown of the offenders and victims in all single offender/single victim homicides from 1982 to 1999 using the FBI's *Uniform Crime Report.*

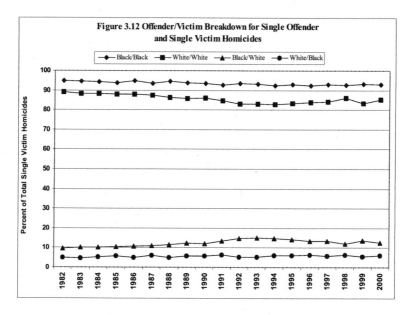

Figure 3.12 Offender/Victim Breakdown for Single Offender and Single Victim Homicides

While the vast majority of homicides involved offenders and victims of the same race, in the case of interracial homicides, Blacks are far more likely to murder Whites than vice versa. Each year, approximately 93.5 percent of all Black homicides were "Black-on-Black," and roughly, 85.5 percent of all White homicides were "White-on-White." However, on average, 12.5 percent of all White homicide cases involved a Black offender, in comparison to roughly 5.5 percent of all Black homicide cases involving a White offender. Thus, even when examining homicides, which are notoriously intraracial, the increased tendency of Black offenders to victimize Whites, in comparison to the opposite, becomes evident.

Research concerning the interracial dynamics of a variety of other crimes reveals an even stronger preference of Black offenders to seek out White victims (Chilton and Gavin 1985). For example, Black offenders chose White victims more frequently than White offenders chose Black victims in 23 of the 24 studies of rape reviewed by LaFree (1982), and in 7 of the 8 studies reviewed by Katz and Mazur (1979). Furthermore, the interracial dynamic holds when considering robbery, rape, and assault based on the National Crime Victimization Survey (Wilbanks 1985).

To demonstrate the tendency of Black offenders to choose White victims, consider a few summary statistics on interracial violence:

- ❖ Each year of the approximately 1,700,000 interracial violent crimes involving Blacks and Whites, 90 percent are committed by Blacks against Whites (Taylor and Whitney 1999).

- ❖ Blacks are 50 times more likely than Whites to commit individual acts of interracial violence and 250 times more likely than Whites to partake in multiple-offender or group interracial violence (Taylor and Whitney 1999).

- ❖ Approximately 56 percent of all violent crimes committed by Blacks involve a White victim, while only 2-3 percent of violent crimes committed by Whites involve a Black victim (Taylor and Whitney 1999).

- ❖ In gang-related assaults, violent Black-on-White incidents are 21 times more likely to occur than the reverse (Krupey 1997).

- ❖ In gang-related robberies, Black-on-White incidents are 52 times more likely to occur than the reverse (Krupey 1997).

- ❖ A Black male is 64 times more likely to rape a White woman than a White man is to rape a Black woman (Krupey 1997).

The National Crime Victimization Survey and the FBI's *Uniform Crime Report* served as the sources for the summary statistics presented above. However, the trend appears even when considering the FBI's *Hate Crime Statistics*. The 1990 *Hate Crime Statistic Act* mandated that the FBI collect national statistics on criminal acts motivated by bias based on race, ethnicity, religion, sexual orientation, or multiple forms of bias. In 1997, there were 9,861 hate crimes, according to FBI statistics; of that number 5,898 involved crimes motivated by racial bias. There were 718 Blacks charged with anti-White hate crimes, in comparison to 2,336 Whites charged with anti-Black hate crimes. Thus, although more Whites committed anti-Black hate crimes, given the sheer differences in the overall population sizes, when computing the hate crime rates per 100,000, the rate for Blacks was twice as high (Taylor and Whitney 1999).

Given that multiple sources indicate the potential significance of Black rage on interracial crime and violence, as suggested by the tendency of Black offenders to select White victims, the question becomes, "What happens to Black rage upon incarceration"? The current study proposes that the same Black rage that wreaks havoc in the free society produces detrimental outcomes within the confines of the American prison, particularly for White correctional staff. Chapter III has defined black rage, and proposed several historical and contemporary factors that likely contribute to the continued production of racial hostility within Black males. It is only through such holistic analysis that criminologists can begin to understand the totality of background baggage and animosity that the Black inmate carries within. Criminologists must move beyond the mere observation that Black inmates significantly increase prison violence as suggested by Carroll (1974), Harer and Steffensmeier (1995), and Silberman (1995), and attempt to understand *why* this is so. Furthermore, this new exploration requires that criminologists step back to examine what has likely transpired in the Black inmate's life before incarceration. In stepping back, the naïve criminologist is likely to see that Black rage and its historical and contemporary sources are factors that every Black male carries from birth through adulthood, and subsequently, will be there with him upon his arrival to the American prison.

[1] James Baldwin – Quoted in P. Harris (1997: 1), *Black Rage Confronts the Law*

[2] Jewelle Taylor Gibbs (1994: 140), Anger in Young Black Males: Victims or Victimizers

[3] "A Dream Deferred," in *The Collected Works of Langston Hughes*, Edited by Arnold Rampersad (2001)

[4] Hooks (1995) offers an example of the criticism launched at the definition of Black rage offered by Grier and Cobbs (1968). Hooks (1995) accused Grier and Cobbs of using "their Freudian standpoint to convince readers that rage was merely a sign of powerlessness." Consequently, "they did not urge the larger culture to see Black rage as something other than sickness, to see it as a potentially healthy, potentially healing response to oppression and exploitation" (Hooks 1995: 12).

[5] Tolnay and Beck (1995) defined this period as the five decades between the end of Reconstruction and the beginning of the Great Depression (1882-1930).

[6] For variation in lynching estimates, see Brown (1975), Harris (1984), Hall (1979), Zangrando (1980) or Cutler (1905).

[7] J.S. Hamilton acquired substantial wealth leasing Mississippi convicts for a monthly fee of $1.10 each, and then subleasing the inmates to contractors for $9.00 per month per convict (Oshinsky 1996; Woodward 1951; Colvin 1997).

[8] The Tuskegee Syphilis Study was a government sanctioned research project that began in 1932. In the study, 399 rural, uneducated Black men received Syphilis injections that remained untreated for forty years. The study proposed to investigate the effects of untreated Syphilis on their health and overall functioning. The men were perfectly healthy before the study. The researchers deceived the subjects into thinking that they had the disease and needed treatment. Federal hearings in 1972 revealed that the researchers never obtained informed consent from the subjects (Gibbs 1996).

[9] For a thorough discussion on Black conspiracy theories, see *I Heard It Through the Grape Vine* by Patricia Turner (1993).

[10] These four sources are by no means intended to be an exhaustive list.

[11] While there are numerous issues faced by Black male students, the current discussion only considers the three most thoroughly researched; lack of identification with academics, negative teacher perceptions, and special education placement.

[12] For example, the African-American Male Task Force (1990) conducted an evaluation of the Milwaukee Public Schools, and discovered that between 1978-1985, 94.4 percent of all students expelled from school were Black. The report further revealed that during the 1989-1990 academic year, nearly 50 percent of all Black male students received a suspension at some point in time, despite only comprising roughly 28 percent of the citywide student population.

[13] Officials later renamed the Education for all Handicapped Children Act (EHA) as the Individuals with Disabilities Education Act (IDEA).

[14] For example, the judge in *Larry P. v. Riles (1979)* ruled that the mechanism used for placement into California's special education classes revealed an "unlawful segregative intent" (Dent et al. 1991). In the district from which the

lawsuit originated, Blacks comprised approximately 29 percent of the student population, but 66 percent of the students in Educable Mental Retardation (EMR) classes (Harry and Anderson 1994).

[15] For a complete discussion on the disproportionate representation of Blacks and more specifically Black males across a variety of special education categories, see Harry and Anderson (1994).

[16] For more serious special education categories, where a medical diagnosis is required, Blacks have a representation proportional to their percentage in the general student population (National Academy Press 2002).

[17] While Blacks have increasingly moved to the suburbs since the 1970's, "housing market discrimination has largely kept Blacks and to a lesser extent Latinos' residential locations concentrated in the central city" (Stoll 1998: 2225). See also Yinger (1995) and Massey and Denton (1993). Furthermore, Blacks in the suburbs are largely restricted to the outer rim that borders the central city (Kain 1985).

[18] For more recent examinations of this topic, see Smith et al. (1991); and Jones-Brown (2000).

[19] There are very few police departments that systematically record and process cases of police brutality and/or citizen complaints. Consequently, "good secondary data" sources are not available for adequately studying the problem of police brutality. However, in some studies involving large-scale assessments of police brutality, *the powers that be* have censored the results. For example, following the 1991 Rodney King incident, the Christopher Commission conducted a detailed examination of police brutality in the Los Angeles Police Department. This was "the first comprehensive and impartial review of a major police department...since the 1973 Knapp Commission that studied New York City" (Lersch and Feagin 1996: 35). After their extensive study, the Christopher Commission issued the vague conclusion that the LAPD did not perform the task of law enforcement in a fair and non-discriminatory manner for citizens of LA. The Commission judged the specific findings of the study as "too sensitive" for public viewing. Therefore, the Commission stored the more sensitive material in the archives of the University of Southern California and ordered that the records remain sealed for 20 years (see "College to be given archives of a study on police brutality," *New York Times* 08-27-91). The U.S. Justice Department made a similar decision following their six-year, nationwide examination of police brutality. The purpose of their study was to investigate regional patterns of abuse and to determine if certain departments had high rates of complaints. Over the six-year period, the Justice Department received 48,000 complaints against officers, and formally investigated 15,000. Although the study concluded in 1991, the document is not available to researchers or the public, despite pressure from the Black members of Congress for its release (Lersch and Feagin 1996). In which case, "the intentional withholding of the findings of the report has increased Black suspicions about the insensitivity of the governmental response to police brutality at the national level" (Lersch and Feagin 1996: 35; Bishop 1991).

[20] White citizens were the victims in five out of the 130 cases. Interestingly, three of the five White victims were in the company of an African-American at the time of the police encounter (Lersch and Feagin 1996).

[21] From 1976 to 1998, police nationwide killed 8,578 suspects. Despite representing roughly 13 percent of the U.S. population, African-Americans represented 42 percent of the victims in police homicide cases (Hulsey 2001).

[22] In similar stories, in Pennsylvania in 1996, police beat Johnny Gammage to death, after officers claimed the suspect reached for a weapon. The item later turned out to be a cellular phone. Likewise, in Chicago in 1999, police fatally wounded Latanya Haggerty after they mistook her cellular phone as a weapon.

[23] Lersch and Feagin (1996) reported a similar finding when their analysis of 130 cases of violent police-citizen interactions, failed to produce a single case that involved a White citizen as a victim of excessive force by a Black officer. Likewise, of the 168 cases of police force examined by McLaughlin (1992) only four involved a Black officer and a White citizen.

[24] "D.C. Black Cops Don't Trust Fellow White Cops," *Jet Magazine*, March 11, 1976, p.5.

[25] For example, in September 1994 the National Black Police Association (NBPA) sent a letter to then U.S. Attorney General Janet Reno complaining about "...the continuing trend that appears to have gained momentum over the past five years-an aggressive criminal assault on the African-American community." The letter stated that the NBPA believed the trend was directly "related to the notion that African-American males are criminals, due in part to police profiles" (quoted in Gibbs 1996: 252-253).

[26] For Example, in Louisville, KY, in March 2000 two White officers who shot an unarmed Black teenager to death received departmental awards for "Exceptional Valor" in the confrontation. Subsequently, the mayor of Louisville fired the police chief the day after the chief issued the awards to the two officers (The Associated Press March 4, 2000).

[27] The Police Services Study found that in a sample of over 12,000 citizens from three metropolitan areas, only 30 percent of those who believed they had a reason to complain about a police officer actually filed a complaint. Almost half of the subjects who did not file a complaint believed the complaint "would not do any good" (Whittaker 1982: 45-46).

[28] Some researchers have chosen to use the term "racially biased policing" as oppose to "racial profiling." For example, Fridell et al. (2001) contend that the term "racial profiling" conjures an array of negative emotions for both police and citizens. Therefore in their report, which was coincidentally funded by the Police Executive Research Forum, Fridell et al. (2001) defined "racially biased policing" as the process in which law enforcement officers "inappropriately consider race or ethnicity in deciding with whom and how to intervene in an enforcement capacity" (5). Their definition is essentially a play on words that describes the basic process of "racial profiling" used by subsequent researchers.

[29] For example, in a lawsuit against the Police Department in Avon, Connecticut, several current and former police officers testified that top Avon officials had long tolerated the practice of targeting Blacks and Hispanics. The

supervising sergeant of the Avon Police Department instructed his officers to find a reason to stop Black and Hispanic motorists driving through Avon (Trotta 1994).

[30] The Mollen Commission (1994) found a similar pattern of racial discrimination towards minorities, primarily Blacks, in a 1994 investigation of five precincts in New York. Likewise, internal investigations as part of a criminal deposition, in 1995 found severe racial discrimination against Blacks by the police in Philadelphia (Gibbons 1995).

[31] Each year 97.9 percent of Blacks and 99.5 percent of Whites are not arrested for committing a crime (*Developments in the Law* 1988).

[32] This is a commonplace expression within the Black community, which describes the race-based suspicions confronted by Black and brown motorists (Russell 1999). Although the phrase has appeared for years in magazines and newspapers directed towards African-Americans, references to "DWB" now appear in Esquire, Newsweek, TIME, and even introductory criminology textbooks (Harris 1999; Seigel 2006). For more on "DWB" and related experiences of African-Americans see Russell (1999).

[33] Black males from all lifestyles, have testified to their experience with racial profiling in pre-textual traffic stops. For a more thorough discussion of the indiscriminant nature in which police harass Black males across economic, education, and general background characteristics, see Harris (1999:9-17), Payne (1992), Cole (1999:24-25) or Jamison (1992).

[34] For example, current discussions of racial profiling largely began in 1993 when Maryland State Police (MSP) detained and searched, Robert L. Wilkins, a Black attorney, for no apparent reason. The ACLU filed a class-action lawsuit on behalf of Mr. Wilkins, and won a $50,000 settlement, which included a court decree ordering the MSP to keep demographic records of all motorists stopped by the MSP to monitor future patterns of discrimination (Larrabee 1997).

[35] Similar statistics presented at a U.S. House Ways and Means Committee hearing in 1999 indicated that Black women are 20 times more likely to be searched for drugs by airport customs officials than White women (Zaslavsky 1999).

[36] For a thorough discussion on U.S. Supreme Court cases and police power see Davis (1997), Harris (1994 and 1998), Maclin (1998), or Cole (1999).

[37] The shift to reasonable suspicion made it easier for police to stop and frisk a suspect since this standard requires less evidence than probable cause.

[38] Less than one year before the *Terry* decision, both the Kerner Commission (1968) and the President's Commission on Law Enforcement (1967) observed that stop and frisks practices were a major sources of frustration and civil disorder within Black communities.

[39] See Harris (1994) for a brief summary of the *Terry* decision and the subsequent cases, which used *Terry* as a precedent.

[40] For a discussion on the legal boundaries of police during traffic stops, and the sequence of events that grant officers the legal right to conduct further investigations see Harris (1998: 568-576) or Davis (1997: 426 footnote 6).

[41] For instance, consider the statements issued by officers dating back to the 1960's (Tiffany et al. 1967, 131-133):

"You can always get a guy legitimately on a traffic violation if you tail him for a while, and then a search can be made."

"You don't have to follow a driver very long before he will move to the other side of the yellow line and then you can arrest and search him for driving on the wrong side of the highway."

"In the event that we see a suspicious automobile or occupant and wish to search the person or the car, or both, we will usually follow the vehicle until the driver makes a technical violation of a traffic law. Then we have means of making a legitimate search."

[42] The disparity is perhaps even greater, given that police officers have the discretion to turn off the camera. For instance, Harris (1999) found that officers turned off the camera in the pre-textual stop and search of Rossano Gerald, a Black U.S. Army Sergeant First Class, traveling through Oklahoma. Unfortunately, there is no available data on how often police turn off the camera and in what types of cases.

[43] Data from Eagle County, Colorado, reveal a similar pattern. There 400 Blacks and Hispanics were pulled over and searched for alleged traffic violations, but none received a traffic citation (Jackson 1995).

[44] Professor Phil Meyer of UNC-Chapel Hill was the statistical expert who analyzed the data. In his final report to state officials, Professor Meyer noted, "this is a wildly improbable difference…something other than chance is causing it" (Neff and Stith 1996).

[45] As an illustrative example, consider the case of Sergeant James Perry of the High Country Drug Task Force in Eagle County, Colorado. In 1988, Sergeant Perry arrested three Black males traveling with 20 pounds of cocaine in their vehicle. However, the district attorney threw out the case since Perry stopped the motorists solely based on a drug-courier profile. Once judicial officials in Colorado decided that racist justifications were no longer sufficient to warrant police stops, officers shifted to using traffic violations as a cover. Before the incident, Perry's log routinely cited "criminal investigation" as the reasons for his stops. After the incident, "traffic violations" became the primary reasons for his stops. A district court judge in *United States v. Laymon* reviewed Perry's records and commented on his newfound interest in traffic violations. The judge noted, "If Perry's own records are to be construed literally, Perry went from being a Drug Task Force Officer who went for days at a time without ever concerning himself with any traffic violations, to a drug enforcement officer obsessed with traffic enforcement."

[46] Consider the following statement issued by Black police officer, Don Jackson: "The African-American finds that the most prominent reminder of his second class citizenship are the police…Operating free of constitutional limitations, the police have long been the greatest nemesis of Blacks, irrespective of whether *we* are complying with the law or not" (Jackson 1989).

[47] I do not contend that overt discrimination against minorities no longer exists within the justice system. It is possible, and quite likely that in some non-

progressive areas of the United States Blacks and other minorities face justice treatment reminiscent of the pre-civil rights era. However, as a whole, I contend that the overt discrimination of the past has metamorphosed into unconscious discrimination against Blacks and other minorities.

[48] Recall the statement by Armour (1994: 787) noting that "for many Americans crime has a Black face," and the 1990 University of Chicago study indicating that 56 percent of Americans believe that Blacks are violence prone (Smith 1990).

[49] Inflation of the number of minority arrests by discriminatory police practices will cause "an overestimation of explained racial disproportionality at later processing stages" (Austin and Allen 2000: 205). Inflated arrest statistics also exaggerate the differences that might exist between crime patterns for Whites and Blacks (Developments 1988).

[50] See Davis (1998) at footnote 66.

[51] The example uses 1997 since that year reflects the most recently available data on all three sources, collectively.

[52] Donziger (1996) found that the distributions of illicit drug use are relatively equal for Whites, Blacks, and Hispanics.

[53] In 1993, *USA Today* reported that in some cities the rate of drug arrests for Blacks was at as much as 50 times the rate of White arrests for drug offenses (Meddis 1993).

[54] Some might contend that far more Blacks sell drugs than Whites and perhaps this explains the widening disparity from arrest to incarceration. However, a 1997 report from the National Institute of Justice found that Whites are frequently involved in selling drugs. After studying drug transactions in six cities, the researchers concluded, "respondents were most likely to report using a main source of their own racial or ethnic background" (Riley 1997: 1).

[55] Specifically, they found that the drug arrest rate, in Pennsylvania for 1995, accounted for only 19 percent of the disproportionality in incarceration rates for drug offenses, which subsequently left 81 percent of the disproportionality to other factors, one of those being racial discrimination (Austin and Allen 2000).

[56] The prosecutor evaluates police arrests to determine if sufficient grounds exist for criminal charges. In some instances, prosecutors may exercise their discretion by declining to prosecute those cases where inappropriate or illegal considerations of race influenced the police decision to initiate an arrest. For example, Petersilia (1983) found that in California prosecutors were more likely to release Blacks without filing formal charges following arrest, indicating that the police were more likely to arrest Blacks on less stringent evidence (Walker et al. 1996). Over-turned police arrest, however, are the exception and not the rule, since prosecutors rely on the police to prosecute their cases successfully (Davis 1998). Therefore, it is not in the prosecutor's best interest to confront the police with allegations of racial discrimination. In which case, the prosecutor typically supports police arrests regardless of the potential influence of race on the officer's decision to detain a suspect.

[57] See Walker et al. (1996: 132) for a discussion of the formal reasons a prosecutor may choose to file or reject charges.

[58] Guilty pleas save the justice system both time and money. Therefore, prosecutors are motivated to offer plea agreements; in some jurisdictions as many as 90 percent of criminal cases end in guilty pleas (Hollander-Blumoff 1997).

[59] The sentences of two state prisoners, one Black and one White, who entered the California prison system best illustrates the disadvantage of minorities in plea bargain negotiations. Each offender had a prior nonviolent conviction, and both currently faced three counts of burglary and one count of receiving stolen goods. Both offenders did not use a weapon and both agreed to plea bargains. The Black offender received convictions on all four of the original charges and received an eight-year prison sentence. While the White offender had three charges dismissed by the prosecutor, a conviction on one count of burglary and received a sixteen-month sentence (example taken from Donziger 1996: 112).

[60] From "Amendments to the Constitution" at:
http://www.house.gov/Constitution/Amend.htm.

[61] See Diperna (1984) noting that until the mid-twentieth century, jury lists in most jurisdictions contained only the names of affluent White males.

[62] Developments 1988: 1564.

[63] In 1986, the U.S. Supreme Court in *Batson v. Kentucky* ruled that attorneys could no longer use peremptory challenges to strike minority jurors solely because of race. The *Batson* decision required that prosecutors be able to offer race-neutral explanations when questioned about the removal of minority jurors. However, many judicial officials including then Supreme Court Justice Thurgood Marshall criticized the decision for not going far enough and potentially opening the gate for even more discrimination in jury selection. Specifically, Justice Marshall argued in his dissent, that "any prosecutor can easily assert facially neutral reasons for striking a juror, and trial courts are ill-equipped to second guess those reasons" (quoted in Serr and Maney 1988). Sadly, the inability of trial judges to detect hidden racism in prosecutorial strikes has resulted in their acceptance of almost any explanation offered by the prosecutor. For example, in *United States v. Cartlidge*, the prosecutor struck a potential jury because they avoided eye contact with the prosecutor. See Serr and Maney (1988), and Melilli (1996) for a full depiction of the range of explanations offered by prosecutors for peremptory strikes.

[64] Prosecutors assume that minority jurors will side with minority defendants, based on their shared experiences or culture (Walker et al. 1996). Consequently, in most of the court cases where prosecutors use their peremptory challenges to remove potential Black jurors, the defendant was also Black. For example, in 1990, prosecutors used all of their peremptory challenges to eliminate Blacks from the jury that would try Marion Barry, the Black mayor of Washington D.C., on drug charges (Walker et al. 1996).

[65] In other examples, a juror in *Smith v. Brewer* (1978) strutted around the jury room imitating a Black minstrel. Equally derogatory, in *State v. Shillcut* (1984) a juror remarked, "Let's be logical, he's Black, and he sees a seventeen year old White girl – I know the type" (Developments 1988: 1595). The true extent of racism during jury deliberations is difficult to measure, since the only way the

public or court officials ever find out about such behavior is for jury members to come forward after the trial, which rarely happens.

[66] Much of the literature on wrongful convictions consists of individual case histories, such as Dreyfus or the Scottsboro Boys, which do not allow researchers to make accurate generalizations about the true extent of the problem.

[67] Figure obtained from *Felony Sentences in State Courts, 1996* (see Brown et al. 1999). This subsequently was the most recent year of data available.

[68] These figures are updated regularly and are published on the website for *The Death Penalty Information Center.* (www.deathpenaltyinfo.org)

[69] Story reported as told in Huff et al. (1986) pages 524-525.

[70] Russell (1998: 3) coined the phrase "criminalblackman" to describe the manner in which many Americans incorrectly assume that most Black men are criminals.

[71] Walter Watson, "Comedian Paul Mooney Uses Humor to Attack Racism," September 23, 1995, *National Public Radio*, Transcript #1979-7.

[72] In the case of the 1989 hoax by Charles Stuart in Boston, the police invaded Mission Hill, a mostly Black neighborhood in Boston, rounding up innocent Black males for a police line-up.

[73] In 1995, a Delaware State trooper provided police with a vivid description of a Black teenager who allegedly shot her in the arm. Following a two-month investigation, the trooper confessed to fabricating the story in order to cover up the fact that she accidentally shot herself in the arm with her service revolver (Russell 1998: 77).

[74] Most false confessions "are likely to go unnoticed by researchers, unacknowledged by police and prosecutors, and unreported by the media" (Leo 2001: 45). Consequently false confessions are rarely discovered. The documented cases likely represent only the tip of a much a larger iceberg (Leo 2001).

[75] See *Brady v. Maryland* (1963) and *ABA Standards for Criminal Justice* (1992).

[76] See Levine (1992).

[77] See Johnson (1985), Hans and Vidmar (1986), Lipton (1979), Starr and McCormick (1985), and Wishman (1986).

[78] Gregory (1978) observed this coercive effect in social psychological experiments where he found that innocent defendants were more likely to accept plea bargains when faced with a large number of charges or a relatively high probability of severe punishment.

[79] Only 15 states and the federal government have established compensation funds for the victims of wrongful convictions, but these vary significant in how the victim is compensated. For example, in Virginia those wrongly convicted receive 90 percent of the state's annual per capital income (roughly $30,000) for up to 20 years of imprisonment. In Alabama, the wrongfully incarcerated receive a minimum of $50,000 per year of incarceration, while in New Jersey such indivudals receive up to $20,000 per year or twice their preprison salary, whichever is greater (Seigel 2006).

[80] Quoted at http://www.cnn.com/US/9807/13deathrow.restitution/

[81] These three items do not represent the totality of negative consequences that result from Black rage.

CHAPTER IV

Building the Theoretical Model

In modern times, the term scapegoat has been used to describe a relatively powerless innocent who is made to take the blame for something that is not his fault.[1]

Although the victim is "innocent" his place in the social structure does have something to do with his being victimized.[2]

Aggression demands action and can thus free the frustrated from this sense of helplessness and can endow the aggressor with some sense of purpose and achievement in the form of discharge of tension.[3]

Black Rage is Real

The current chapter takes as its starting point the fact that Black rage is a *real* concept, with *real* causes and *real* consequences. One of the major consequences of Black rage, outlined at the end of Chapter III, was the observed effect of this factor on interracial violence. The rage produced by the irresistible temptation to link Black failure and suffering to some form of White oppression is often manifested in the form of aggressive acts against White Americans. However, despite the strength of the literary evidence regarding the significance of Black rage, previous works failed to detail concisely how the progression from rage-to-violence transpires. The current chapter proposes a conceptual model designed to explain the rage-to-violence progression among Black males in prison. Relying heavily on psychological concepts, such as ruminations, cognitive neoassociation, frustration-aggression, and displaced aggression, the current chapter expounds the proposed theory by defining the mechanisms by which Black rage likely produces violent outcomes in the prison environment.

I argue that Black rage produces detrimental outcomes in the prison environment, particularly in regards to staff assaults, because of the historical and contemporary significance of racism. For this reason, those who perceive systematic racism as outdated and question the lingering effects of historical racism[4] will undoubtedly question the futility of a Black rage perspective. However, it is hopeful that Chapter III convinced the naysayer of the increasing forms of covert racism confronted by African-Americans. These covert acts of racism serve as constant reminders to African-Americans that racism has not disseminated, but rather has taken on new forms. Thus, the first step in constructing a systematic model of Black rage involves outlining the methods in which historical and contemporary acts of racism (both overt and covert) influence the cognitions of Black males, which subsequently influence their behavior. The literature on ruminations offers a potential explanation for the inability of African-Americans to *let go* of racism.

Ruminations

Martin and Tesser (1989) defined ruminations as conscious thoughts directed toward a given object for an extended period. Although ruminations can be both positive and negative, much of the literature focuses on negative reoccurring thoughts. Due to their similarity with other processes, ruminations are often lumped with additional forms of intrusive thought, such as cognitive factors in the production of anxiety (Tallis et al. 1994), obsessional thoughts (Rachman and Hodgson 1980), and negative automatic thoughts (Beck 1976). Ruminative thought is an important topic of investigation, given that repetitive and unwanted thoughts are major symptoms of a number of mental disorders, and may potentially instigate and maintain some disorders, such as depression (Beck 1983; Ellis 1962; Nolen-Hoeksema 1987; Pysczynski and Greenberg 1987). In addition to the increased potential for mental illness, through cognitive neoassociation, ruminations can produce emotional states that predispose one to aggressive or violent behavior. Before explaining the significance of ruminations in the proposed theory of Black rage, the text presents a brief discussion on some of the general features of ruminative thoughts.

Ruminations differ from ordinary memories given their automatic and intrusive nature. While we can somewhat control *normal memories* by recalling and storing such information at will, "ruminations intrude, anytime and anywhere" (Gold and Wegner 1995: 1246). For instance, ruminations can occur in the absence of environmental cues instigating recurring thoughts (Tait and Silver 1989). A second distinguishing feature of ruminations is their tendency to focus on past events. By virtue of the past-oriented focus of ruminations, we typically are unable to alter or change the events for which we cannot seem to forget (Gold and Wegner 1995). Consequently, ruminative thoughts are often counterproductive and, at times, even pointless (Martin and Tesser 1989; Gold and Wegner 1995). A third essential feature of ruminations is the inability to suppress such thoughts. Because ruminations tend to be counterproductive, there is a strong conscious desire to control such thoughts. However, "evidence from studies on thought suppression suggests that the suppression of unwanted thoughts may in fact fuel the very emotions and thoughts we are trying to avoid" (Gold and Wegner 1995: 1245).

Wegner (1992) effectively described two cognitive processes that negatively influence conscious attempts to suppress ruminations. The first process involved in trying to suppress a particular rumination is the "controlled distracter search," which is a conscious, attention-demanding search for thoughts other than the unwanted thought. The second process involves what Wegner (1992) referred to as an "automatic target search," which is a relatively less attention-demanding process that searches for any sign of the unwanted thoughts. The simultaneous operation of both processes causes the suppressed thought to become hyper-accessible. As described by Gold and Wegner (1995: 1253):

> The suppressed thought becomes the focus of an intensive automatic search process that operates without conscious attention. This process can make the unwanted thought ironically return to mind, especially when the search for distracters is sidetracked.

Also working against the ability to forget certain thoughts is the "suppression-induced rebound effect." When a distracter fails to suppress an undesired thought, it becomes permanently associated with the rumination one is trying to avoid (Gold and Wegner 1995). Furthermore, each time a distracter fails, i.e. the rumination returns, "people try again to distract themselves, often-times by picking another distracter" (Gold and Wegner 1995: 1254). In the end, "when we try desperately to not think of something, we end up creating associations between the unwanted thought and all the various distracters, which in turn serve as cues to remind us of the unwanted thought at a later time" (Gold and Wegner 1995: 1254).

Black Rage and Ruminations

In the context of the proposed theory of Black rage, I contend that for many African-Americans, the history of slavery, the enduring civil rights struggle, and the general subjugation to White oppression, produces a negative rumination involving *racism*. Despite lacking first-hand experience with historical racism, the everlasting stories and images provide more than sufficient cognition for the development of negative ruminations. For instance, even among contemporary African-Americans, artifacts such as the horror stories of the middle passage; images of the police with water hoses and dogs viciously assaulting civil rights demonstrators; and photos of the grossly mutilated body of 12-year old Emmitt Till, create lasting images of racism. As such, many African-Americans find themselves unable to completely suppress, or forget, the harsh treatment endured by their ancestors. Accompanying the recurrent thoughts of historical racism are often feelings of anger and rage. Contemporary bouts with overt and covert racism fuel the intense rage associated with ruminations regarding historical racism. Through the process of cognitive neoassociation, contemporary racial experiences can trigger the negative memories, feelings, motor responses, and physiological reactions associated with the emotionally charged reaction to ruminative thoughts regarding slavery, lynching, Jim Crow Laws, etc.

Cognitive Neoassociation

The theory of cognitive neoassociation begins with the basic premise that emotional states involve a collection of feelings, thoughts, memories, and expressive-motor reactions (Berkowitz 1993). Given the interconnection between the items comprised in an emotional state, activation of any one component will tend to activate the other parts of the network. Furthermore, in developing the theory of cognitive neoassociation, Berkowitz (1993) proposed that unpleasant events are likely to make people hostile and aggressive by initiating negative affect. "Negative affect is the unpleasant feeling state elicited in a reflexive and automatic way by aversive conditions" (Geen 2001: 32). Berkowitz (1993) argued that negative affect lowers human inhibitions against aggressive behavior by producing anger through cognitive neoassociation, which subsequently leads to "aversively stimulated aggression."

When experiencing negative affect brought on by aversive conditions, humans encounter two immediate and simultaneous tendencies (Berkowitz 1993). First, there is a *fight* response, which includes aggression-related tendencies and the experience of rudimentary anger. Second, there is a *flight* response, which includes escape-related tendencies and the expression of rudimentary fear. If the latter tendency is stronger than the former, the result will be inhibition of aggressive behavior and manifestation of the *anger-in* response (Berkowitz 1993). However, if the propensity towards aggression is stronger than the flight tendency, then due to cognitive neoassociation, the individual is likely to display their anger through aggression against the source of their negative affect.

Black Rage and Cognitive Neoassociation

Concerning the proposed theory of Black rage, cognitive neoassociation provides two mechanisms for understanding the emotions displayed by contemporary African-Americans in response to overt and covert forms of racism. First, when confronted with a perceived display of racism, the emotional reaction chosen significantly influences the likelihood of aggressive behavior. For instance, if an individual becomes enraged or angered over a racist act, they instantly tap into the cognitions, feelings, and expressive behaviors cognitively associated with that mood state. Furthermore, the cognitive neoassociation model predicts that angry feelings (or negative affect) are more likely to produce "aversively stimulated aggression."

The cognitive neoassociation perspective also offers a mechanism for understanding the rage of African-Americans based on historical displays of racism. For instance, if the historical treatment endured by African-Americans evokes a particular mood state, then contemporary displays of racism are likely to evoke similar feelings given their cognitive link to the past. Case in point, when confronted with aversive stimuli, such as a perceived display of racism, this encounter is likely to trigger ruminative thoughts regarding historical racism. Reflecting on historic facts, such as slavery and the civil rights movement, by way of cognitive neoassociation, brings forth the cognitions, emotions, and expressive behaviors associated with those events. Thus, if an individual cognitively links historical displays of racism with feelings of anger and rage, then reflecting on these memories following a perceived display of racism, should evoke similar feelings. In which case, relatively minor displays of racism may evoke dual levels of anger. On one level, there is anger cognitively associated with the perceived offense, and on the other level, there is residual anger brought on by the cognitive connection between the racist act and historical racism. With a higher degree of anger, the propensity towards aggression significantly increases. However, to understand precisely how anger produces aggressive behavior requires examination of other psychological principles, such as the frustration-aggression hypothesis proposed by Dollard et al. (1939).

Frustration-Aggression Hypothesis

A group comprised of psychologists, sociologists, and anthropologists first constructed the frustration-aggression hypothesis in efforts to explain the "universal causal relationship between frustration and aggression." The proposed hypothesis by Dollard et al. (1939) reflected a learning theory adaptation of Freud's (1920) idea that anger and aggression were instinctive responses to frustrated impulses. Specifically, Dollard et al. (1939) stated that frustration produced a readiness or instigation to aggressive behavior. The researchers defined frustrations as "the interference with the occurrence of an instigated goal-response at its proper time in the behavior sequences" (Dollard et al. 1939: 7). After experiencing frustration, the hypothesis predicts that aggressive tendencies may be "temporarily compressed, delayed, disguised, displaced, or otherwise deflected from their immediate and logical goal" but "not destroyed" (Dollard et al. 1939: 2). The strongest, and perhaps most controversial, statement surrounding the hypothesis pertained to the stipulation that some form of frustration always preceded aggression. Today, ample research has demonstrated that frustration is neither necessary nor a sufficient condition for aggression (Averill 1982). However, despite the lack of a universal cause and effect relationship between frustration and aggression, the hypothesis, as proposed by Dollard et al. (1939), provides an ideal model for detailing the process of displaced aggression, which is the central concept in the proposed theory of Black rage.

The frustration-aggression hypothesis proposed by Dollard et al. (1939) suggests two important psychological processes paramount in the theory of Black rage. The first principle notes that despite the deterrent effect of a potential target, once a situation generates frustration, these feelings remain intact until the selection of an outlet for expression. Dollard et al. (1939) proclaimed that the basic variable deterring aggressive acts was the anticipation of punishment. Explicitly, Dollard et al. (1939) stated, "the strength of inhibition of any act of aggression varies positively with the amount of punishment anticipated to be a consequence of the act" (33). The researchers also noted that the anticipation of failure effectively deterred aggressive behavior. Thus, the lack of a suitable target for expressing aggression, or insurmountable difficulties in carrying out an aggressive act, also reduces the strength of the causal relationship between frustration and aggression. Regardless of the reason for restraining from aggressing against the initial source of frustration, the essential point is that these feelings of frustration never dissipate until released in some form.

The second essential principle presented in the frustration-aggression hypothesis stated that "the greater the degree of inhibition specific to a more direct act of aggression, the more probable will be the occurrence of less direct acts of aggression" (Dollard et al. 1939: 40). Strong inhibitions against direct aggression forces one to change either the object of aggression or the form of aggression. Changes in the object of aggression (i.e. displaced aggression) are the primary concern of the Black rage theory. Figure 4.1 summarizes the chain of events, suggested by Dollard et al. (1939), concerning frustration, aggression, and displacement.

As illustrated by Figure 4.1, during the initial frustrating event, the pivotal factor in the decision to aggress is the perceived likelihood of punishment, as indicated by the power possessed by the primary target of aggression.

Figure 4.1 Graphic Summary – Frustration, Aggression, and Displacement[5]

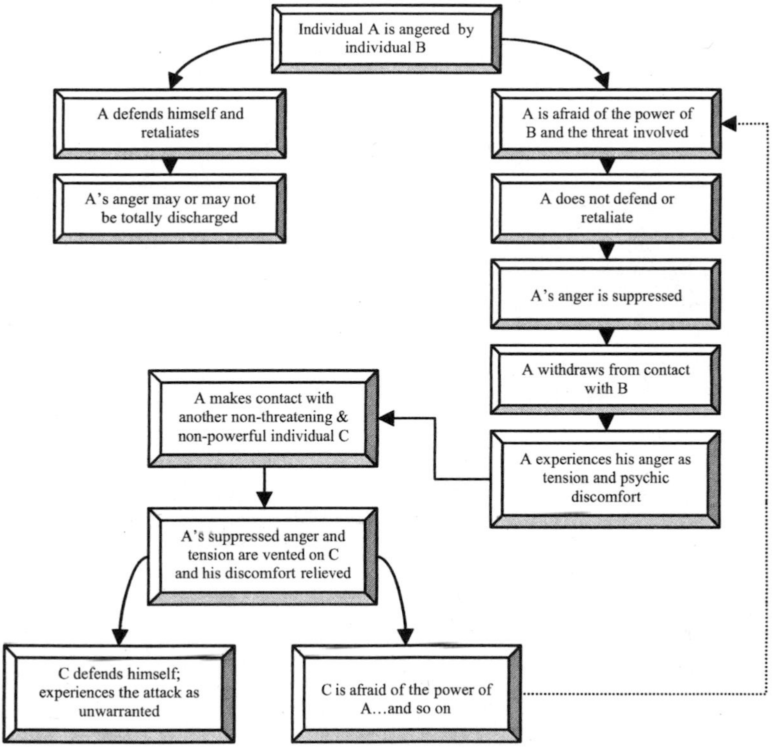

The decision to avoid aggressing against the primary target does not dissipate the initial level of frustration. Instead, the feelings reside internally until a more suitable, less powerful target becomes available. Once the aggressor locates an available target, they displace their frustrations and release the internal, psychic tension and turmoil, created by refraining from aggressing against the initial provocateur. Although the causal model is rather simplistic and not without criticism (Douglas 1995), it provides a template for the theory of Black rage. For instance, re-examine Figure 4.1 while letting person A = Black males, person B = the "system" (White oppression) and person C = White prison staff. The frustration-aggression hypothesis provides a mechanism for understanding the production of black rage and its eventual displacement.

Black Rage and Frustration-Aggression

The frustration-aggression hypothesis would suggest that Black rage would inevitably seek expression in some form or another. For instance, Chapter III detailed multiple forms of expression for Black rage, which included both internal and external variations.[6] Internally, Black rage significantly influences both the physical and mental health of Black males. Lack of an expressive avenue for Black rage contributes to many detrimental conditions disproportionately effecting Black males, such as hypertension, psychotic disorders, and suicide. Externally, the presence of black rage significantly influences Black-on-Black violence, as well as Black-on-White violence. Thus, as prescribed by the frustration-aggression hypothesis, once the production of black rage occurs, these feelings remain active until an eventual avenue for expression emerges. With an accessible avenue or target, the probability of displaced aggression significantly increases.

Displaced Aggression

Conceptually, displaced aggression is the process of deflecting aggression from a primary target, which was the source of initial frustration onto another target that has likely done nothing to provoke the aggressor, or at most has committed some minor offense (Geen 2001). Miller (1941) proposed three more common reasons for the displacement of aggression: (1) the provoking agent is unavailable, (2) the source of frustration is intangible, and (3) the aggressor fears retaliation or punishment from the provoking agent. Although the concept of displaced aggression offers tremendous promise in terms of understanding interracial violence, researchers in criminology and other disciplines have neglected to incorporate this factor into explanatory models of violence.

Following the release of *Frustration and Aggression* by Dollard et al. (1939), the concept of displaced aggression witnessed a dramatic surge in academic interest. Nonetheless, shortly thereafter, subsequent interest sharply declined (Marcus-Newhall et al. 2000). In fact, contemporary psychology textbooks consider displaced aggression an obsolete principle.[7] The lack of academic interest in the concept is tragically ironic, given the prevalence of displaced aggression observed on a daily basis. For instance, "the irate motorist who is angered by heavy traffic on a motorway and responds by swearing at or threatening another driver is displacing his aggression to a single individual who is not responsible for his irritation" (Geen 2001: 38). Many critics of displaced aggression allege that the concept is difficult to test empirically and that studies examining the concept have serious validity issues.[8] On the contrary, Marcus-Newhall et al. (2000) reviewed 49 studies on the topic of displaced aggression and concluded that the evidence for such aggression was very much reliable. Marcus-Newhall et al. (2000) also found significant relationships between three moderator variables and displaced aggression.

The first moderator variable was the strength of the initial provocation that produced feelings of frustration and anger. The strength of the initial provocation inversely related to the amount of displaced aggression (Marcus-Newhall et al. 2000). Despite the counterintuitive nature of this finding, it actually conforms to fundamental processes governing human judgment (Campbell 1956; Helson 1964). Since judgments are comparative, "the nastier the provocation, the nicer the displaced aggression target appear[s] by comparison, and consequently the less aggression displaced onto him or her" (Marcus-Newhall et al. 2000: 680). However, when the target commits a triggering action, the stronger the initial provocation, the stronger the amount of displaced aggression (Miller and Marcus-Newhall 1997).

The second moderator variable in the process of displaced aggression pertained to the degree of negativity within the environment in which the interaction between the target and the aggressor transpired. Research indicates that the more negative the interaction environment, the greater the magnitude of aggression displaced onto the target (Marcus-Newhall et al. 2000). This further suggests the importance of cognitive neoassociations by indicating that negative interaction settings cognitively associate with aggressive behavior. Thus, "cognitive cues that are associated with negative affect can be expected to exacerbate the effect of a negative interaction setting and further increase the likelihood of displaced aggression" (Marcus-Newhall et al. 2000: 683). Along with situational aggression cues, there may also be negative cues inherent to the target of aggression. For instance, Carlson et al. (1990) found that when the target of displaced aggression was an out-group member or a disliked other, these factors served as negative cueing properties and thereby increased the level of displaced aggression. Both types of negative cues, i.e. those inherent to the environment and those inherent to the target, are essential in the current examination of the proposed theory of Black rage. On one hand, the interaction between the target and the aggressor takes place in perhaps the most negative of all environmental settings (prison). On the other hand, the preponderance of White staff members serves as an inherent negative cue for Black inmates, which increases the likelihood of displaced aggression.

The third moderator variable concerns the degree of similarity between the initial provocateur, the aggressor, and the target of displaced aggression. Miller (1948) suggests that three factors influence the choice of a target for displaced aggression: (a) the strength of aggressive instigation; (b) the strength of inhibitors against direct retaliatory aggressive behavior; and (c) *the similarity of alternative targets to the original provocateur* [emphasis added]. The closer the similarity between the provocateur and the target in terms of personal demographics and position, the greater the amount of displaced aggression. However, the provocateur and the target will not match exactly, since the same factors that kept the aggressor from venting against the initial provocateur are likely still in operation in the case of a mirror image target. Thus, "a target with moderate similarity to the provocateur will be preferred" (Marcus-Newhall et al. 2000: 673).

Research further indicates that high levels of similarity between the aggressor and the target reduce the level of displaced aggression (Marcus-Newhall et al. 2000). This finding lends further support to a central prediction of the Black rage theory. The theory predicts that in the prison environment, frustrated Black males are more likely to vent against White prison staff as oppose to Black prison staff. Marcus-Newhall et al. (2000) suggests that this is the case primarily because of the degree of racial similarity between the aggressor and the target.

In addition to the three moderator variables noted by Marcus-Newhall et al. (2000), other researchers have noted unique elements of displaced aggression paramount to the proposed theory of Black rage. For instance, Johnson (1961) observed that the process of selecting a displacement target is never purely random or irrational; rather there is at least a symbolic connection between the target and the frustrations of the aggressor. On this matter, Johnson (1961: 597) noted, "Although the victim is 'innocent' his place in the social structure does have something to do with his being victimized." Similarly, in "The Stimulus Qualities of the Scapegoat," Berkowitz and Green (1962: 293) found that "the object serving as the target for the intolerant person's aggression usually has certain stimulus qualities for this person, and that objects not possessing these characteristics are less likely to be attacked." Consequently, for Black inmates, violence against White prison staff is likely to produce internal rewards as well as symbolize an attack against the larger system of White oppression. A quote from *Power and Innocence: A Search for the Sources of Violence* by Rollo May (1972: 82) captures the internal rewards likely apparent in Black inmate assaults against White prison staff:

> In its typical and simple form, violence is an eruption of pent-up passion. When a person (or group of people) has been denied over a period of time what he feels are his legitimate rights, when he is continuously burdened with feelings of impotence which corrode any remaining self-esteem, violence is the predictable end result. Violence is an explosion of the drive to

destroy that which is interpreted as the barrier to one's self-esteem, movement, and growth.

Therefore, for Black inmates, an assault against a Black staff member is not likely to produce the same amount or type of internal reward that comes with assaulting a White staff member. In which case, White staff members are the victims of preference in aggressive displays by Black inmates given the internal gratification and the racial similarity between White staff and the larger "system" of oppression.

In addition to the factors noted above, also increasing the odds of Black violence against White staff is the threshold effect of displaced aggression. Buss (1961) and Worchel (1960 and 1966) described the threshold effect as the process by which the inability to respond to an initial frustration lowers the level of inhibition against future aggression. Hence, if a Black male fails to aggress following an initial frustrating event, i.e. a perceived experience with racism, their odds of displacing their aggression significantly increases in future situations, regardless of the intensity level of future provocations. In which case, there is the potential for relatively minor offenses to spark a wrath of rage far out of proportion to the frustration generated by the actual offense. For instance, with a lowered threshold, an individual may behave aggressively after a certain event because of the psychic turmoil created by not aggressing in a similar past situation, and not necessarily because of the anger produced by the current event.

Ruminations, Cognitive Neoassociation, and Displaced Aggression

Collectively, the various psychological concepts presented here are highly complimentary and suggest a powerful conceptual foundation for the theory of Black rage. Both ruminations and cognitive neoassociations support the concept of displaced aggression by providing mechanisms for which a lowered threshold might occur (Marcus-Newhall et al. 2000). For example, based on the suppression theory offered by Gold and Wegner (1995), if an individual experiences a frustrating event and attempts to suppress this thought, they actually force anger-related feelings and emotions to become more accessible. This increased accessibility to angry feelings lowers the aggression threshold in future provocations that are of trivial intensity (Marcus-Newhall et al. 2000). Furthermore, "When ruminating about an initial provocation, cues signaling similarity between a target and the initial provocateur may simultaneously make a target appear more negative and deserving of aggression" (Marcus-Newhall et al. 2000: 684). Thus, a Black inmate ruminating about a racist encounter with a White police officer is more apt to aggress against a White correctional officer, given the tendency to draw similarities between the two.

Cognitive neoassociations also lower the threshold for displaced aggression given that initial provocations generate frustrations that induce negative affect (Marcus-Newhall et al. 2000). For a variety of aforementioned reasons, the angered individual may not aggress against the initial provocateur. However, the associated network of emotions, memories, and expressive behaviors evoked by the initial event remain in place. In which case, when encountering situations similar to the initial provocation through the process of cognitive neoassociation, the negative affect induced by prior events lowers the threshold for displaced aggression.

Black Rage in Action

Sadly, incidents of Black-on-White violence, resulting from the combination of the psychological principles described above, occur at a greater frequency than many scholars and media outlets would care to admit (Krupey 1997; Taylor and Whitney 1999). The manifestation of Black rage through the channels of ruminations, cognitive neoassociation, and displaced aggression often combine to produce detrimental outcomes for innocent White citizens. Consider for instance, the following three examples:

❖ In October 1989, in Kenosha, Wisconsin a group of young Black males became consumed with rage and hate after watching the film *Mississippi Burning*, which depicted members of the Ku Klux Klan inflicting violence on Blacks in the South during the civil-rights era. To alleviate their frustrations, the group decided to "move on some White people" and as a result savagely beat 14-year old Gregory Riddick, leaving him with permanent brain damage. (Krupey 1995: 201)

❖ On January 14, 1995 a carload of Blacks murdered 19-year old Michael Westerman of Guthrie, Kentucky, after the group became enraged by the Confederate flag flown from the victim's pickup truck. (Krupey 1995: 202)

❖ On March 20, 1995, two Black males were carrying on a conversation while walking down through the streets of Monessen, Pennsylvania. The two males repeatedly used the word "Nigger," throughout their conversation. At one point, they passed 39-year old Valerie Johnson who was walking with her 3-year old son. After hearing the males use the word "Nigger,"

Ms. Johnson's son innocently repeated the word. This however, outraged the two Black males and consequently the two physically assaulted Ms. Johnson on two different occasions that day, both in the presence of her son. Injuries suffered during the second assault caused Ms. Johnson's death three days later on March 23, 1995. (Krupey 1995: 203)

In all three examples, an event transpired that triggered ruminative thoughts about slavery and the general history of Black subornation to Whites. Through cognitive neoassociation, the perpetrators reflected on negative ruminations and tapped into the anger and rage associated with Black oppression. Once this aggression reached the surface, the Blacks in the stories above displaced their anger onto individuals who symbolically represented the larger system of White oppression. This study contends that the progression from rage-to-violence detailed in these three examples occurs in a similar fashion within the confines of the American prison system, but with less provocation.

Theory of Black Rage – Model Construction

Using the psychological principles detailed above, this study proposes a theory of Black rage designed to explain interracial violence and aggression. The theory purports that Black males possess a certain degree of anger and rage at the larger system of White oppression, stemming from several historical and contemporary factors. Historical and contemporary sources of rage provide an abundance of aggressive energy for displacement onto individuals perceived to represent the larger system of White oppression. The theory proposes that ruminations about the harsh treatment endured by African-Americans, and cognitive neoassociation regarding the negative affect induced by events such as slavery, increase the propensity of Black males to displace aggression onto innocent Whites. Although the current study examines the theory in the context of prison violence, the processes and variables described offer tremendous explanatory power in terms of other interracial patterns observed in crime and violence statistics. Figure 4.2 presents the conceptual model designed to capture the effect of Black rage on staff assaults in the prison environment.

The model begins with the basic assumption that Black males have a positive influence on the staff assault rate, as suggested by previous literature on prison violence (Carroll 1974; Harer and Steffensmeier 1996; Silberman 1995). The remainder of the model partitions the influence of Black inmates on the staff assault rate based on the presence of Black rage and the racial breakdown of the staff population. As indicated by the contemporary sources of rage presented in Chapter III, by the time a Black male reaches the confines of the American prison, they have ample material for the development of rage against the larger system of White oppression. The combination of anger over factors such as the historical treatment of Blacks, race consciousness, absence of fathers, marginal educational and economic status, along with discrimination in the American criminal justice system, significantly increases the potential for the importation of Black rage into the prison environment. While the sources detailed in Chapter III were merely suggestive, the research findings of Carroll (1974 and 1977), Robinson (1971), Fox (1982) and Silberman (1995) confirm the importation of racial hostility into the correctional facility by Black inmates.

Figure 4.2 – Graphic Summary: Black Rage and Prison Violence

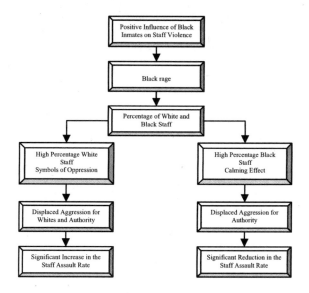

Building from the importation of black rage into the correctional facility, Figure 4.2 suggests that the racial breakdown of the staff population mediates the influence of black rage on the staff assault rate. In facilities with a high percentage of White correctional officers, Black inmates are likely to view these individuals as symbols of oppression. As noted by Fox (1982: 65), in the prison environment, White guards become "a convenient and highly visible symbol of White economic dominance and authority over Blacks lacking the footing to gain equality." Thus, through ruminations about slavery and racism in general, as well as the process of cognitive neoassociation, Black inmates are more likely to displace their aggression for the larger system of White oppression onto White prison staff. Furthermore, as a natural response to confinement, inmates develop a certain sense of opposition to the staff population. In which case, displaced aggression towards White staff occurs for both racial and authoritative reasons. With dual frustrations released by Black inmates, the theory predicts that a high percentage of White staff, in conjunction with the importation of Black rage, will significantly increase the staff assault rate.

The theory predicts the opposite effect for facilities with a relatively high percentage of Black prison staff. The lack of racial similarity between Black staff and the larger system of White oppression should eliminate a significant proportion of the Black inmate's rage. With more Black staff members, there is perhaps less of a tendency to ruminate about slavery and other contemporary displays of overt and covert racism. In the absence of these negative ruminations, the negative affect cognitively associated with such memories remains suppressed. The reason being that Black inmates in American prisons have likely progressed through social structures from school, to employment, to the justice system, where from their disadvantaged position they have equated White with authority. As such, the presence of Black staff members disrupts the general image of the prison setting as another arena in which Whites control and oppress Blacks. Therefore, the theory predicts that a higher percentage of Black staff will have a calming effect on the violent tendencies of Black inmates, as indicated by a significant reduction in the staff assault rate. The presence of Black staff will not eliminate the aggressive tendencies of Black inmates altogether, given their residual displaced aggression for authority figures.

Empirical Assessment

As in most research endeavors involving secondary data analysis, it was not possible to test all aspects of the proposed theoretical model. Specifically, data limitations prohibited direct measurement of Black rage and displaced aggression. However, in addition to the previous literature, there are two core observations that would suggest the presence of the Black rage. First, the observation that Black inmates significantly increased the staff assault rate would serve as a proxy indicator of the general level of anger and rage imported into the correctional facility by Black inmates. Second, the observation that the percentage of Black staff effectively counters the positive influence of Black inmates on the staff assault rate would suggest that with more Black staff, a certain proportion of the Black inmate's rage dissipates, due to the lack of a racial connection between prison staff and the large system of White oppression. Essentially, Black staff should significantly decrease the staff assault rate, while Black inmates should have the opposite effect on the staff assault rate. In part due to data limitations and in part due to problems with multi-collinearity, I operationalized the Black rage perspective using the percentage of Black inmates, the percentage of Black staff, and the ratio of White-to-Black staff.

[1] Aronson (1980: 202), *The Social Animal* (Third Edition)

[2] Johnson (1961: 597), *Sociology: A Systematic Introduction*

[3] Douglas (1995: 115), *Scapegoats, Transferring Blame*

[4] Throughout this chapter, the term "historical racism" refers to the more overt forms of racism found in the past such as slavery, Jim Crow Laws, etc.

[5] Chart duplicated using the terms presented by Douglas (1995: 113).

[6] Not all forms of expression involving Black rage are negative. For instance, notable Black author, Bell Hooks, channeled her rage induced by a racist encounter on an airline flight into her provocative book, insightfully titled *Killing Rage*. There are also numerous biographical accounts of Black athletes and entertainers who credit the ability to productively channeling their rage as a contributing force in the success of their career.

[7] Marcus-Newhall et al. (2000) conducted a content analysis of 122 psychology textbooks written during the period from 1900-2000 to determine the average amount of text devoted to displaced aggression. Their results found that other than during the five-year period immediately following the release of *Frustration and Aggression* (1939), scholars have devoted very little attention to the concept of displaced aggression.

[8] On this matter Marcus-Newhall et al. (2000: 680) noted, "scholars do not appear to view it as a well-established and empirically validated phenomenon in need of additional research."

CHAPTER V

Data Summary and Statistical Design

They are called wise who put things in their right order.[1]

Some people hate the very name statistics, but I find them full of beauty and interest. Whenever they are not brutalized, but delicately handled by the higher methods, and are warily interpreted, their power of dealing with complicated phenomena is extraordinary. They are the only tools by which an opening can be cut through the formidable thicket of difficulties that bars the path of those who pursue the Science of man.[2]

Brief Data Summary

To test the proposed theory of Black rage, I analyzed data from the 1984, 1990, and 1995 versions of the *Census of State and Federal Adult Correctional Facilities*. The Bureau of Justice Statistics sponsored each version, while the Bureau of the Census administered the questionnaires and recorded the data. Earlier versions of the census appeared in 1974 and 1979[3]. The three editions used in the current analysis included 903 state institutions in 1984: 1,287 state and federal facilities in 1990: and 1,500 state and federal facilities in 1995. The 1990 edition was the first volume to include federal and private facilities. However, only those private facilities under contract to house primarily state or federal prisoners were included. In addition, the 1974, 1979, and 1995 versions of the census included companion surveys designed to describe the background and demographic characteristics of inmates housed in state and federal prisons. Although both data sources contain rich amounts of correctional information, the survey neglects to consider staff demographics and other elements essential to testing the proposed theory of Black rage. Furthermore, given that the census includes the total population of correctional facilities, its inclusive scope renders the studies findings more generalizable to all correctional settings.

By surveying the entire population of correctional facilities, in conjunction with persistent follow-up, research officials ensured that sampling bias did not contaminate the *Census* results. To survey the entire population of correctional institutions, researchers first contacted every facility registered with the *American Correctional Association* (ACA). Researchers captured non-registered ACA facilities by requesting that representatives from each state's Department of Adult Corrections update the facility list for their respective state. Moreover, to capture federal facilities not registered with the ACA, in both 1990 and 1995 representatives from the Federal Bureau of Prisons received requests to update the census list as well. After establishing the total population of adult correctional facilities for each year, census officials narrowed the population list based on four conditions. Specifically, the census included only institutions: 1) Administered and staffed by state or federal employees[4], 2) housing primarily state or federal prisoners, 3) physically, functionally, and administratively separate from other facilities, and 4) operational on the reference date.[5]

Following the generation of the facility list, census officials mailed questionnaires to the entire population of state and federal adult correctional facilities. Two to three months after mailing the initial questionnaires, non-respondents received a follow-up questionnaire.[6] Facilities that remained non-responsive after the second attempt received reminder telephone calls from census officials. The persistent follow-up resulted in a final response rate of 100 percent for all three editions of the census.

The census questionnaire requested information regarding facility characteristics, racial demographics of the staff and inmate populations, correctional programs, inmate work assignments, and prison disturbances (i.e. assaults and riots). The variables measuring the demographic characteristics of the staff and inmate populations were one-day counts from the aforementioned reference dates. The variables measured as annual rates or percentages referred to the fiscal year, which typically began on July 1 and ended on June 30.[7] Prior to submission for public access, Bureau of Justice officials examined the data for internal consistency, illegitimate skip patterns, and illegally coded values. As the final step in cleaning the data, research officials at the Interuniversity Consortium for Political and Social Research (ICPSR) re-coded data irregularities as missing values.

Sample Selection

In efforts to eliminate non-relevant institutions, I did not use the total population of facilities included in the original versions of the census. The three factors used to narrow the sample sizes included: sex of inmates housed, type of institution, and facility operation. First, only correctional facilities that housed male inmates, exclusively, were included in the sample. Despite their increasing numbers, females comprise a relatively small percentage of the U.S. prison population. For example, every year from 1925 through 1993, females comprised less than five percent of all state and federal prisoners in the United States (Maguire and Pastore 1995). Furthermore, violent activities are less likely to occur in female facilities. Consider for example that in 1995, the average number of assaults in male facilities was 39 in comparison to only 16 in female institutions (U.S. Department of Justice[8] 1995).

Institution type was the second factor used to narrow the study sample. Each survey respondent indicated the various functions of their institution. The options for facility functions included adult population confinement, boot camp, reception/diagnostic center, drug and alcohol treatment, work release, youthful offenders, and medical treatment. In several cases, facilities reported multiple functions. Only those facilities indicating adult population confinement as one of their functions were included in the study sample. Facilities not classified as confinement institutions perhaps lack the deprivation and inmate stress level characteristic of the typical U.S. prison, which subsequently renders prison violence less likely to occur in these *abnormal* prison settings.

Facility operation was the third factor used to narrow the study samples. Facility operation refers to the level of administrative control: state, federal, private, or local authority. Only those facilities administered and staffed by state employees were included in the sample, for three reasons. A) The 1984 version of the census only provided information on state institutions. Therefore, in efforts to keep the samples comparable across all three years, the 1990 and 1995 samples excluded federal and private facilities. B) The number of federal and private adult correctional facilities was relatively small across years. For example, in 1995, local, private, and federal officials operated 117 adult population confinement facilities that housed only male inmates[9], in comparison to 821 such facilities controlled by state authorities (USDJ 1995). The data for 1990 displayed a similar distribution (USDJ 1990). In both years, state institutions comprised over 85 percent of all correctional facilities housing male inmates exclusively. C) Black inmates typically comprise a higher percentage of the inmate population in state facilities. In 1995, Blacks comprised roughly 51 percent of the inmate population in state prisons, and only 34 percent of the inmate population in federal facilities (USDJ 1995). Given the racial demographics of the inmate population, state facilities represent the ideal setting for testing the proposed theory of Black rage. Table 5.1 illustrates the change in the sample size with each restriction.

Table 5.1 – Sample-Narrowing Summary

Factor	1984	1990	1995
Total Initial Population	903	1,287	1,500
Narrowing – Sex of Inmates Housed	771	1,098	1,279
Narrowing – Facility Function	579	953	1,064
Narrowing – Facility Operation	579	795	826
Final Sample Size	**579**	**795**	**788***

*38 additional facilities were removed from 1995 for extreme missing values

Analytical Designs

Given the inclusive scope of the census, as well as the presence of unique identifiers in the 1990 and 1995 versions, the data analysis includes both cross-sectional and longitudinal approaches. The cross-sectional analysis involved the estimation of truncated regression models to test the proposed theory of Black rage within each wave of the census. Since each edition included the total population of adult male prisons, the cross-sectional analysis provided a large scaled examination of the proposed theory. Subsequently, the large number of observational units permitted the formulation of more accurate generalizations of the studies' findings. However, because cross-sectional designs are inherently static, the direction of the causal relationship is not always clear and, furthermore, such approaches are not well suited for the study of processes and change (Finkel 1995; Singleton and Straits 1999). Therefore, as a supplement to the cross-sectional analysis, I included longitudinal statistical models using the 1990 and 1995 versions of the census.

Both the 1990 and 1995 editions of the census included the facility name for each institution. The facility name provided a unique identifier that allowed for the linkage of facilities across the two waves of the census.[10] The initial merge of the two data sets using SPSS (Statistical Package for the Social Sciences) resulted in the pairing of 411 facilities.[11] This sample of facilities, however, only reflected the number of institutions whose names appeared verbatim in 1990 and 1995. Close examination of the data revealed that in several cases, SPSS failed to pair facilities with minor variations or alterations in the facility name. For example, in 1990, one facility recorded its name as "A.C. WAGNER YOUTH CORR. INST," while in 1995 this facility recorded its name as "YOUTH CORRECT INST. A.C. WAGNER." In another case, the name reported in 1990 was "APALACHEE CORRECT INSTIT" and the name reported in 1995 was "APALACHEE CORRECTIONAL

INSTITUTIO." In either example, because the names did not match exactly, SPSS failed to merge the two observations. Therefore, in efforts to pair facilities with slight variations in the reported names, and ultimately increased the sample size for the longitudinal data set, I visually compared the 795 facility names reported in 1990 with the 826 facility names reported in 1995. For previously unpaired visual matches, three different sources provided verification of the likelihood that the two facility names represented the same institution.

First, information from the 1990, 1991, 1995, and 1996 editions of *The Directory of Juvenile and Adult Correctional Department, Institutions, Agencies, and Paroling Authorities.*[12] provided evidence pertaining to the likelihood of facilities being the same. Each edition of the directory provided facility demographics, as well as personnel characteristics and contact information, such as the facility address, and telephone number. Similarities in the directory information served as the first indication that two facilities were the same. Second, the directory information, in conjunction with the variables presented in the data sets, such as construction year and the design capacity, were used to vigorously examine all presumed matches. Unique factors within each edition of the census allowed for facility comparison from data set to data set, as well as from the data sets to the *ACA Directory*. Lastly, on a few rare occasions, the internet provided evidence regarding facility linkages. For example, information provided at http://www.prisons.com/calendar/ confirmed the suspicion that some time between 1990 and 1995, the "Kansas State Prison" changed its name to "Lansing Correctional Facility." Documentation of this change subsequently was not available from the information presented in either data set or the *ACA Directory.*[13]

In all, I conducted 130 queries to determine if previously unmatched facilities using SPSS were in fact the same institution. In the vast majority of the queries, the discrepancy between the two data sets was merely a misspelling of the facility name, with the most common mistake being inconsistent abbreviations. Appendix A provides a detailed list of all of the facility names included in the queries and the subsequent decisions to either include or exclude the facility from the study sample. Appendix B presents the research notes, which formed the basis of the inclusion/exclusion decisions. The 130 queries resulted in 122 *fairly confident* facility matches across the two data sets. The additional 122 institutions, along with the original 411 paired by SPSS, raised the total sample size to 533 for the longitudinal data analysis. The vigorous and time-consuming task of researching presumed facility matches increased the sample size by roughly 30 percent.

To protect against any biasing effects, I examined descriptive statistics for the subsequently matched facilities to examine for any irregularities. The 122 facilities matched through subsequent research efforts included facilities from 36 of the 46 states represented by the longitudinal sample. Roughly, 21 percent of the subsequently matched prisons were located in Florida, followed by 10 percent from Virginia, 8.4 percent from Pennsylvania, and 7.6 percent from Michigan. There was a relatively equal distribution of the remaining subsequently matched facilities throughout the other 32 states. Once more, Florida had the greatest percentage of prisons matched by subsequent efforts when considering the total number of prisons within each state included in the longitudinal sample. For example, of the 533 facilities included in the longitudinal sample, 32 were from Florida, and of this number, 87.5 percent (or 28) were included following additional research efforts. For Pennsylvania, the 11 matched facilities represented 84.6 percent of those prisons from Pennsylvania included in the longitudinal sample. Mississippi had the third highest percent of matched facilities included in the sample with 55.6 percent. However, this state only had nine facilities included in the longitudinal sample. In terms of security level, the matched prisons represented 36 percent of the 136 maximum-security facilities in the longitudinal sample; 26 percent of the 223 medium-security facilities; and 13 percent of the 183 minimum-security facilities.[14] The subsequently matched facilities did not appear uniquely different from the overall sample, in which case the influence of potential biasing effects should be minimal.

Measurement and Operationalization

Dependent Variable

Prison violence was the dependent variable in the current research project. Each version of the census included violence indicators for the reference year in question. However, the wording used in the violence items differed across the three editions. In 1984, respondents provided the number of inmate assaults on staff and other inmates; the questionnaire included no extra instructions. In contrast, the 1990 respondents provided the number of "major incidents," including sexual assaults, recorded for the reference year. The instructions also included an attached note to "exclude tickets, official warnings, and other minor incidents." The 1995 version requested the number of inmate-inflicted physical or sexual assaults against prison staff or other inmates. The differences in wording created the potential for the 1990 and 1995 versions to include more serious forms of assaults (i.e. physical and sexual), while the 1984 edition may include other less violent forms of assault, such as verbal altercations. Nonetheless, given the nature of the census process, the violence measures are highly comparable across the three years.[15] Using these measures, the study attempts to deduce the factors significantly related to changes in the rate of inmate-on-staff assaults.

Each version of the census included a direct count variable measuring the number of inmate-on-staff assaults for a one-year period. Because direct frequencies do not account for variations in facility size, I converted the raw assault numbers into rates based on the total population of high-risk prison staff.[16] To illustrate the dilemma, consider two facilities reporting 50 inmate-on-staff assaults for 1990. Based strictly on the raw frequencies, both facilities would appear similar in their levels of staff violence. However, if one facility had a staff population of 250 while the other had a staff population of 1000, the overall violence level for the two facilities is significantly different given the variations in staff population size. Therefore, we cannot directly compare facilities until standardizing the raw frequencies as rates based on the total populations of high-risk prison staff.[17]

The staff violence rate reflects the number of inmate-on-staff assaults per 100 high-risk staff members, as opposed to the entire prison staff. Following the advice of a former correctional officer, the staff assault rate excluded certain staff members who, based on their job descriptions, had minimal contact with the inmate population (M. Karpos, personal communication, Spring 1999). Among the various employment roles within the prison structure, particular individuals were at greater risk of assault by virtue of their job description and duties. Hence, for a more precise measure of staff violence, researchers should calculate staff assault rates based on the number of individuals in frequent contact with the inmate population. Measures of the staff assault rate based on the entire population of prison staff likely underestimate the true violence level by including a number of individuals, who have virtually no physical contact with the inmate population. Table 5.2 presents average staff assault rates for those facilities with at least one reported assault across the three utilized versions of the census. The table illustrates that the staff assault rate varies as a function of how one defines the staff population. Simple difference of means analysis revealed that all of the dichotomous comparisons within any particular year were significant at $\alpha = 0.01$.

It appears that assault estimates, based on the entire population of prison staff, underestimate the rate of staff assaults; while excessively conservative approaches, such as examining strictly correctional officers, who by far have the most persistent contact with the inmate population, overestimates the rate of staff assaults. Therefore, in efforts to minimize potential biasing effects, I used as a compromise between the two extremes, the rate of assaults per 100 high-risk staff members.

Table 5.2 – Variations of the Average Staff Assault Rate

Variations	1984	1990	1995
Assaults per 100 Total Staff	5.76	5.89	5.42
Assaults per 100 High Risk Staff	6.60	7.36	8.20
Assaults per 100 Correctional Officers	8.26	9.00	10.06

Independent Variables

The chosen independent variables measure three theoretical models of prison violence: the importation, deprivation, and management perspectives. The process proposed by the theory of Black rage is an extension of the importation model. Although Chapters III and IV described the theory of Black rage in detail, the following discussion serves to clarify the rage perspective by deepening the readers' understanding of the importation model. The deprivation and management models are included as theoretical controls. The inmate assault rate, region, and security-level were also included as additional controls, since research has shown a significant correlation between these factors and violence against prison staff. The description below presents each perspective and the factors used to operationalize the essential concepts.

Importation Model

Irwin and Cressey (1962) developed the importation model, which states that the inmate subculture and its violent orientation are the result of inmate characteristics transported into the correctional facility. Specifically, Irwin and Cressey (1962) argued that lower class offenders import sub-cultural values and attitudes regarding violence into the prison environment that subsequently shape the inmate subculture. An important assumption in Irwin and Cressey's (1962) theory was the notion that the prison structure could not successfully remove the earlier socialization of the entering inmate. Therefore, criminologists wanting to understand the violent inmate subculture must consider the inmate characteristics transferred into the prison (Hawkins and Alpert 1989). Irwin and Cressey's (1962) finding countered the traditional explanation of inmate violence, which described prisons as schools of violence where aggression was a normal reaction to the oppressive conditions of the prison structure. Essentially, the importation model shifted the blame for prison violence from the institution to the individual. Since the initial work of Irwin and Cressey (1962), researchers have examined a variety of pre-prison factors to determine their significance in predicting prison violence and/or adjustment to prison life. For example, researchers have considered variables measuring pre-prison social conditions, such as education level, marital status, and work history (Thomas 1977; Jaman et al. 1971; Myers and Levy 1978; Clemmer 1958; Coe 1961; Jaman 1972; Flanagan 1983). Other researchers have considered prior criminal history, substance abuse, or personality dysfunction (Light 1990; Gaes and McGuire 1985; Watman 1966; White 1980).

I tested the importation model by hypothesizing that the interaction between Black rage and the racial demographics of prison staff had a significant impact on the staff assault rate. Previous studies have neglected to include both staff and inmate demographics simultaneously in their prediction models. Comprehending and predicting prison violence requires an understanding of all of the elements involved, i.e. the aggressor, the victim, and the situation. Since violence is a product of the interaction between all three elements (Gibbs 1981), it is inadequate for researchers to study prison violence, particularly assaults against prison staff, by merely considering the influence of inmate or situational characteristics. I used three variables to measure the importation model and, more specifically, the theory of Black rage: the percentage of Black inmates, the percentage of Black staff, and the ratio of White-to-Black staff. Table 5.3 briefly defines each variable and describes the measurement of each factor.

Deprivation Model

The deprivation model states that prison violence is a natural product of the stressful and oppressive conditions found within the prison. Researchers contend that prison-created deprivations, such as isolation from relatives, restriction of time and mobility, heavy surveillance, and exposure to arbitrary rules, foster negative inmate behavior that is functional for survival (Goffman 1961; Hawkins and Alpert 1989). The deprivation model implies that prisons are *total* institutions where pre-prison socialization is insignificant in shaping inmate behavior within the institution. Given the structural orientation of the deprivation theory, tests of this model largely examine institutional level factors and attempt to explain variations in facility violence rates, as opposed to individual violence rates.

The factors used to operationalize the deprivation model typically measure absolute or relative deprivation. In the context of prison, *absolute deprivation* refers to the structural aspects of the facility that directly contribute to the oppressive nature of the inmate subculture. Measures of absolute deprivation include variables such as crowded living conditions, restriction of contact with the free world, lack of rehabilitation programs, stringency of rule enforcement, and loss of privacy. Research has shown significant correlations between each of these factors and prison disturbances (Barak-Glantz 1985; Cooke 1989; Ellis et. al. 1974; Feld 1977; Gaes and McGuire 1985; Silberman 1988; Light 1990). *Relative deprivation* refers to the discrepancy between an individual's expectation and actual achievement (Davies 1972; Piven and Cloward 1977). With the routine nature of prison life, any sudden change in facility rules, or the unexpected loss of inmate privileges, disrupts inmate expectations and may lead to violence out of frustration (Kratcoski 1988).

I build on the deprivation model by improving the factors used to measure prison deprivation. Previous researchers have failed to reach consensus regarding the importance of the deprivation model due in large part to limitations in operationalizing the concept. For example, Gaes and McGuire (1985) concluded that the deprivation model was "implicated" in their study, but clearly not as important as the crowding variable in determining violence rates. This conclusion is problematic given that other researchers, such as McCorkle et al. (1995), defined crowding as a measure of deprivation. In addition to miss-categorizing essential factors, such as crowding, previous studies have also included poor measures of deprivation. For example, Gaes and McGuire (1985) measured deprivation with three factors: average percentage of time remaining on an inmate's sentence, the staff-to-inmate ratio, and the percentage of staff who were correctional officers. The first variable, the percentage of time remaining on the inmate's sentence, does not necessarily imply that the facility is oppressive, while the second and third variables measure management issues and not prison deprivation. I measured the deprivation model using three variables: the crowding rate, inmate-housing arrangements, and a computed deprivation score.

Management Model

The management model states that prison violence, both individual and collective acts, result from failed prison management. The management model shifts the blame for prison violence onto prison administrators. This approach contrasts with the deprivation and importation models where the inmates and facility characteristics were to blame for prison violence. Failed prison management provides inmates with the opportunity to engage in violent activities. Good administrators (i.e. those who maintain order) are able to limit violence opportunities by effectively managing their facilities and controlling the inmate's time (Gaes and McGuire 1985). While there is some agreement on what constitutes good prison management, exactly what reflects failed prison management varies among researchers. For example, DiIulio (1987) considers failed prison management to consist of the following actions: security lapses, high staff turnover, lack of discipline among guards, unlocked doors, unsearched inmates, and crowds not quickly dispersed.

Table 5.3 – Summary of Variables

Variable	Description	Measurement
Dependent Variable		
Staff Assault Rate	The number of assaults against facility staff per 100 high-risk staff members.	Divide the number of staff assaults by the number of high-risk staff members. Multiply the ensuing decimal by 100.
Importation Model		
Percent – Black Inmates	The percentage of Black inmates reported on the reference date in question.	Divide the number of Black inmates by the total inmate population. Multiply the ensuing decimal by 100.
Percent – Black Staff	The percentage of Black staff reported on the reference date in question.	Divide the number of Black staff members by the total staff population. Multiply the ensuing decimal by 100.
White-to-Black Staff	The number of White staff members per each Black staff member.	The total number of White staff members divided by the total number of Black staff members.
Deprivation Model		
Crowding Rate	The percentage over or under the average facility capacity.	Average the rated and design capacities. Subtract the average capacity from the inmate population. Divide by the average capacity. Multiply by 100.
Cell Arrangements	The type of inmate housing arrangement (i.e. single vs. multiple inmates per cell).	1 = Inmates housed exclusively in single-cells 0 = Inmates housed in other arrangements
Deprivation Score	The number of conditions for which the facility is under federal court order.	Description presented in footnote[18]
Management Model		
Male-to-Female CO's	The number of male correctional officers per each female correctional officer.	The total number of male correctional officers divided by the total number of female correctional officers.
Percent – CO's	The percentage of the total staff that are correctional officers.	Divide the number of correctional officers by the total staff population. Multiply the ensuing decimal by 100.
Index – Racial Variation	The degree of racial homogeneity within the staff population.	Description presented in footnote[19].
Additional Controls		
Inmate Assault Rate	The number of assaults against inmates per 100 inmates.	Divide the number of inmate assaults by the inmate population. Multiply the ensuing decimal by 100.
Region	The geographic region for each facility.	Regions were assigned according to the Census Bureau[20]: 1 = South, 2 = West, 3 = Northeast, and 4 = Midwest.
Security Level	The overall security-level that best describes each facility.	1 = Maximum Security 0 = Medium or Minimum Security

Other researchers have considered variables such as the ratio of treatment staff to inmates (Harer and Steffensmeier 1996), the ratio of White-to-Black guards (McCorkle et al. 1995), facility size (Sylvester et al. 1977), and the frequency of changes in prison rules (Bidna 1975). With the exception of McCorkle et al. (1995), previous studies testing the management model have considered structural and procedural variables, but have neglected to include staff demographics among the management factors. In addition to procedural decisions, prison administrators also make staffing choices that directly influence the demographics of the staff population, which subsequently influences prison violence. In the present study, I operationalized the management model using three variables. The first measure provided an assessment of racial diversity within the staff population using the index of qualitative variation (IQV), created by Simpson (1949) and later refined by Mueller and Schuessler (1961). The IQV estimates the likelihood that two observations drawn at random from a population are from different categories on a chosen qualitative variable (Healey 2002). I used IQV to create a direct measure of racial diversity among prison staff, index of racial variation (IRV). The second and third variables used to measure the management model included the ratio of male-to-female correctional officers, and the percent of the staff population that were correctional officers.

Data Strengths and Limitations

Ideal for Proposed Research Question

The data presented in the *Census of State and Federal Adult Correctional Facilities* are ideal for answering the proposed research question for four reasons. First, unlike comparable data sources, the census provides racial demographics for both the inmate and staff populations. Previous studies of prison violence have primarily used the individual as the unit of analysis and based their findings on primary data collected through field observations and/or survey instruments (Wright 1989; Ellis et al. 1974; Carroll 1974; Silberman 1995). Although such data sources tend to possess a rich amount of variables describing inmate characteristics, they lack indicators of staff demographics. Equally restrictive are studies from secondary data sources, with a rich amount of variables, describing structural aspects of the prison environment, but neglecting to include staff demographics (Gaes and McGuire 1985). In the proposed theory of Black rage, both inmate and staff race are essential variables. Therefore, the census represents the best available secondary data source for researchers wanting to assess the impact of both inmate and staff racial demographics, simultaneously, on prison violence.

Second, the census data permits regional comparisons of the effect of Black rage on prison violence. An important component of the Black rage definition offered by D'Souza (1995) was the history of White oppression over African-Americans. White oppression over Blacks has traditionally been greatest in the American south. Consequently, based on America's racial history, I hypothesize that the tendency of Black inmates to view White guards as symbols of oppression is greater in the American south. In which case, the influence of Black officers on prison violence should vary according to region. The demographic and geographic data provided by the census permits an examination of the proposed relationship between region, Black rage, and Black guards.

Third, the census is ideal for addressing the proposed research question because of the ability to control for competing theories of prison violence. The plethora of variables contained within the census allows the analysis to control for the deprivation and management models of prison violence. One of the underlying objectives for the current study is to demonstrate the significance of Black rage on prison violence and, in the process, weaken the criticisms launched at the importation model.[21] Despite numerous studies demonstrating the significance of the importation model, researchers remain highly critical of this perspective. In the current study, I test the importation model on a large-scale with better measures of this concept. With a more thorough research design, I hypothesize that the relative significance of the importation model will be evident.

Lastly, the census is ideal for the proposed research question given the ability to link facilities across the 1990 and 1995 editions. Although the sample size of the longitudinal data set is somewhat smaller than that used in the cross-sectional analysis, having dependent observations in the longitudinal data set allows for the assessment of change in the independent variables on prison violence. Conducting repeated measures analysis on a dependent sample controls for random variation within the population of facilities across time. This additional level of control provides more powerful analysis than the simple cross-sectional approach. For example, by linking the facilities across the five-year interval, for each institution we can assess the influence of the change in the percentage of Black prison staff on the subsequent change on the staff assault rate. Also possible with observations measured from dependent samples at different points in time, is the ability to isolate the proper ordering of the independent and dependent variables used to suggest a cause and effect relationship.

Gaps in Previous Data Sources

In addition to being ideal for the proposed research question, the census data also addresses three gaps in previous data sources. First, the census provides a large-scale quantitative assessment of the relationship between displaced aggression, Black rage, and Black guards. Both Carroll (1974 and 1977) and Silberman (1995) suggested that Black anger towards White correctional officers frequently transforms into assaults against White inmates. Carroll (1974) supported his claims regarding displaced aggression with qualitative narratives, while Silberman (1995) quantified the relationship. Silberman (1995) found that inmates, who expressed hostility towards staff, were more than twice as likely to have assaulted another inmate, as opposed to those who never expressed any sort of anger towards staff. Although Silberman (1995) succeeded in quantifying the relationship between staff frustrations and inmate violence, he failed to include the influence of race on the process of displaced aggression. Nevertheless, his qualitative statements suggest that Black inmates assault White inmates because of their anger towards White staff.

The findings from Carroll (1974) and Silberman (1995) indicate that increasing the number of Black guards may reduce prison violence. Fox (1982) offered qualitative support for this claim. Through quotes from staff narratives, Fox (1982) presented affirmations from both White and Black officers acknowledging the ability of Black guards to control the rage of Black inmates. Fox (1982), however, did not quantify this relationship, and later researchers have failed to do so as well.[22] The data provided in the census offers a large-scale quantitative assessment of the qualitative relationship suggested by Carroll (1974 and 1977), Silberman (1995), and Fox (1982). While the census data cannot precisely measure the qualitative relationships specified, it can approximate these effects by incorporating staff and inmate racial demographics into the proposed model of prison violence. Based on the qualitative findings, the theory predicts that staff assault rates will be higher in prisons with a high concentration of Black inmates and a high concentration of White staff. Likewise, the theory predicts that prisons with a high concentration of Black inmates and a high percentage of Black staff will have lower staff assault rates.

The second gap addressed by the census data concerns the unit of analysis used in prior data sources. The census data used the institution as the unit of analysis. Many prison violence studies, such as Carroll (1974) and Silberman (1995), used the individual as the unit of analysis. However, "assaults are relatively infrequent occurrences in an inmate's institutional life and thus individual data would have to be collected over a prohibitively lengthy period" (Gaes and McGuire 1985: 42).

Furthermore, tracking inmates over a prolonged period is not only expensive, but also extremely difficult given the frequency of inmate housing changes, both intra- and inter-institutionally (Gaes and McGuire 1985). Consequently, researchers using the individual as the unit of analysis typically base their findings on a relatively small sample of prison assaults.[23] With a limited number of assaults, it is difficult to discern any true patterns in prison violence. Some criminologists, such as Harer and Steffensmeier (1996), and Gaes and McGuire (1985), recognized the limitations of individual-level data, and consequently incorporated the institution as the unit of analysis. Nonetheless, neither project allowed for conclusive statements regarding the influence of Black inmates on prison violence since both samples included only federal facilities. Conclusions based on atypical samples prohibit the researchers from generalizing to a larger segment of the prison population. The census data uses the institution as the unit of analysis and includes state facilities, which are more representative of the typical American prison.

Lastly, the census is superior to previous data sources because it includes a wider section of the total population of adult correctional facilities. With the exception of McCorkle et al. (1995), whose sample included 371 state prisons, prior studies had sampling limitations. Because of these limitations, the conclusions were generalizable to only a small segment of the total population of correctional facilities. The most common sampling problems were relatively small inmate sample sizes (Wright 1989), analysis based on single prisons (Silberman 1995; Carroll 1974), or atypical facilities comprising the study sample (Harer and Steffensmeier 1996; Gaes and McGuire 1985). The census includes the total population of state correctional facilities, which significantly reduces the likelihood of sampling bias. Therefore, the conclusions drawn from the census data are safely generalizable to a much larger segment of the American prison population.

Limitations

Although the census data are ideal for the proposed research question and fill several gaps from previous data sources, there are two limitations of the data set. First, the census does not measure all of the components in the proposed theory of prison violence. Specifically, the census lacks direct measures of concepts, such as displaced aggression and sub-cultural norms, which are included as elements of the theory of Black rage. Given the high degree of complexity proposed by the theory of Black rage, it is unlikely that any secondary data source would provide measures of all of the important concepts. However, the census does permit tests of the core prediction of the Black rage theory. The core prediction of the Black rage theory suggests that manipulating the race of correctional officers should significantly change the dynamics of violence against prison staff, in particular, in facilities with a high percentage of Black inmates. Findings confirming this prediction would indicate the potential significance of Black rage and suggest new directions for prison violence theories. As such, the current project is an adventure in theory development. I hope that the exploratory analysis will deepen our understanding of prison assaults and direct future researchers interested in understanding prison violence, through primary data, towards previously unconsidered factors.

The second limitation of the census data is that it does not provide information regarding the demographics of assault victims or aggressors. An important assumption of the Black rage theory is the conception that White prison employees are the primary targets of the Black inmate's rage. However, without information on assault victims or aggressors, the relationships can only be "suggested" through systematic analysis. Because the census lacks demographic information on prison assaults, the analysis must prove two relationships in supporting a theory of Black rage. A) The analysis must demonstrate that the percentage of Black inmates has a significant impact on the staff violence rates. B) The direction of the influence of Black inmates on staff assault rates should vary according to the racial demographics of the staff population. For example, the relationship between Black inmates and staff violence should be strong and positive in prisons with a high percentage of White staff. On the other hand, the relationship between Black inmates and staff violence should be negative and weak in prisons with a high percentage of Black staff. The census provides data to allow for adequate examinations of both A and B. Establishing these two relationships will permit generalized conclusions regarding the demographics of victims and aggressors in prison assaults.

In sum, the census is ideal for answering the proposed research question for four reasons. 1) The data includes measures of both staff and inmate race. 2) The data permits regional comparisons for the effect of Black rage. 3) The data allows one to control for competing theories of prison violence. 4) The data allows for longitudinal analysis on a dependent sample of prisons. In addition to being ideal for answering the proposed research question, the census data also addresses three gaps from previous data sources. 1) It quantifies important qualitative relationships found by previous researchers. 2) It uses the institution as the unit of analysis. 3) It includes a wider section of the total population of adult correctional facilities. Focusing on theory development, and deducing essential relationships through systematic analysis, minimizes the effects of the two limitations of the census data.

Statistical Methodology - Cross-sectional Data Analysis

The nature of the dependent variables included in the cross-sectional analysis required special care in choosing a statistical technique for conducting the analysis. By definition, staff assault rates are count variables that cannot assume negative values. Each rate must be a positive integer greater than or equal to zero. Furthermore, since prison assaults are not a guaranteed occurrence over a one-year period, a substantial number of respondents reported zero staff assaults across each census year. For instance, in 1984, 42.3 percent of the sampled prisons reported zero staff assaults. Likewise, in 1990 and 1995, 45.5 and 37.2 percent of the sampled prisons reported zero staff assaults, respectively. Hence, each year, roughly 42 percent of the sample facilities reported zero assaults against prison staff. Because of the relatively high number of reported zero values, the distribution of prison assault rates was negatively skewed for each year. Most of the observed values were concentrated between the ranges of zero to three assaults per year for each measure of the dependent variable. As an illustrative example, Figure 5.1 presents the shape of the distribution of staff assault rates for 1984. According to the graph, roughly 78 percent of the facilities sampled in 1984 had an inmate assault rate between 0 and 4.82. The distribution of staff assault rates across each year resembled the pattern displayed in Figure 5.1. The non-normal distribution of prison assault rates required the use of more advanced statistical techniques, such as estimating TOBIT models, in conducting the analysis.

Figure 5.1
Distribution of Staff Assaults Rates for 1984

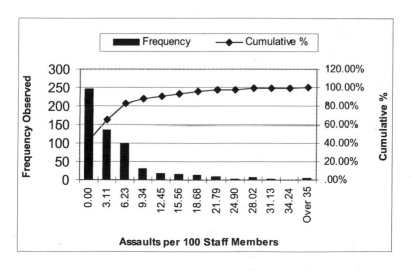

TOBIT Model

Economists developed the TOBIT model to analyze data with censored or truncated values on the dependent variable. James Tobin (1958) observed that the distribution of household expenditures on durable goods had a significant number of cases concentrated around the lower limit, zero dollars spent. To handle such non-normal distribution, Tobin (1958) developed a regression model ideal for estimating relationships with limited dependent variables. The model proposed by Tobin (1958) was a hybrid of the PROBIT regression model and traditional ordinary least squares (OLS) regression. However, the TOBIT model builds on its predecessors by allowing researchers to analyze information that neither PROBIT nor OLS regression, separately, would allow (Witte 1980). More specifically, the TOBIT model expands the PROBIT model in two ways. 1) Since more information is available in the TOBIT model, (i.e. known values on the dependent variable) estimates of the coefficient values (β's) are more efficient (Long 1997). 2) It is possible to estimate the variance of the dependent variable in the TOBIT model, whereas in the PROBIT model, censored values complicate estimates of the variance for the dependent variable (Long 1997).

The TOBIT model expands OLS regression by improving the precision of coefficient estimates for truncated or censored data. Using OLS regression techniques, researchers have two options for analyzing data with limited values on the dependent variable. 1) Estimate truncated regression models, which exclude the zero values from the analysis. Long (1997), however, demonstrated how truncated regression models overestimate the intercept coefficient and underestimate the slope coefficient. Furthermore, truncated regression models produce inconsistent estimates due to correlations between the independent variables and the error terms (ϵ). 2) Estimate censored regression models, in which the censored observations are included in the analysis as zero values. While the censored regression model includes all of the observed data, this process underestimates the intercept and overestimates the slope coefficient (Long 1997). In sum, findings based on censored or truncated data, analyzed by conventional OLS regression techniques, are inaccurate due to violations of the OLS regression assumptions of normality and homoscedastic distribution of the error terms (Witte 1980).

In contrast to truncated or censored OLS regression models, the TOBIT procedure uses all observations, both those at the limit (0) and those above the limit, to estimate the parameters and predict the regression line (McDonald and Moffitt 1980; Long 1997; Amemiya 1984). The TOBIT procedure accommodates truncated distributions, by using maximum likelihood estimation to calculate two separate equations for predicting values of the dependent variable. The two equations estimated by the TOBIT procedure are as follows:

$$\text{if } X\beta + \varepsilon \leq 0, \text{ then } Y = 0 \qquad \text{Equation (1)}$$
$$\text{if } X\beta + \varepsilon > 0, \text{ then } Y = X\beta + \varepsilon \qquad \text{Equation (2)}$$

Where $X\beta$ = the independent variables multiplied by the appropriate TOBIT coefficient

       ε = the normally distributed error term

       Y   = the predicted value on the dependent variable

The first equation predicts the influence of the independent variables on the probability of the dependent variable being limited (i.e. equal to zero). The second equation estimates the effect size of the independent variables on the observed values of the dependent variables for the non-limited responses.

Interpreting the Effects of TOBIT Models

Given the complexity of the TOBIT procedure, interpreting TOBIT coefficients is not as simple as interpreting OLS regression coefficients. In general, each independent variable in the TOBIT model has two types of effects (Roncek 1992). 1) The effect of the independent variable on the values of the dependent variable for non-limited cases (non-zero). For example, this effect would consider the influence of the percentage of Black inmates, on the staff assault rate for institutions with at least one staff assault reported. 2) The second effect obtained from the TOBIT coefficients describes the influence of the independent variables on the probability of having a non-limited value for cases with limited values on the dependent variable (equal zero). For example, this effect would consider the influence of the percentage of Black inmates, on the probability of having a staff assault for prisons that reported zero staff assaults. These two effects parallel the structure of the TOBIT model.

Decomposing TOBIT Coefficients

Researchers often misinterpret the TOBIT model coefficients. The problem with interpretation emerges because the ordinary TOBIT output provides only one unstandardized coefficient for each of the independent variables. In their original form, it is not clear how one coefficient can represent two different effects. Therefore, researchers make the common mistake of simply interpreting TOBIT coefficients as the effect of the independent variable on the dependent variable for cases that are above the limit (Roncek 1992). In contrast, however, the ordinary TOBIT coefficient provides a measure of the effect of the independent variable on the latent (unobserved) dependent variable (Roncek 1992). Decomposition of ordinary TOBIT coefficients is necessary in order to produce the two effects specified by the TOBIT equations (McDonald and Moffit 1980; Roncek 1992). The following decompositions produced the desired effects of the independent variables on the dependent variables:

Above the limit $= \beta_i * [1 - \{z * f(z)/F(z)\} - f(z)^2/F(z)^2]$ Equation(3a)

At the limit $= \beta_i * [f(z)/\sigma]$ Equation(3b)

Where β_i = the unstandardized TOBIT coefficients for each independent variable
    $F(z)$ = the proportion of cases above the limit
    $f(z)$ = the ordinate of the normal curve at the z-score associated with $F(z)$
    z = the z-score for the area under the normal curve [based on $F(z)$]
    σ = the standard deviation of the error term

In addition to the main two effects specified above, TOBIT coefficients are also capable of describing the fraction of the total effect of an independent variable that is attributable to being above the limit (McDonald and Moffit 1980). The quantity inside the brackets of equation (3a) measures this effect.

Standardizing TOBIT Coefficients

The unstandardized TOBIT coefficients prohibit one from directly comparing the relative effects of each independent variable. In order to make relative comparisons, the research must standardize the TOBIT coefficients. Standardized coefficient values required two steps: 1) Divide each unstandardized TOBIT coefficient by the standard deviation of the error term and 2) multiply the ensuing value by the standard deviation of the corresponding independent variable (Roncek 1992). The standardized TOBIT coefficient "behaves reasonably for models with dependent variables having a large number of cases at the limit (zero), and a wide variation of values on the independent variables" (Roncek 1992: 506). Converting the coefficients to standardized measures permits comparisons of the overall significance of each independent variable, relative to all other factors. The ability to compare factors is essential for assessing the merits of the Black rage theory against the effects of the deprivation and management models of prison violence.

Testing for Significant Effects

The TOBIT model estimates relationships on non-normal distributions. Therefore, the TOBIT output does not provide indicators of significant effects commonly associated with normal distributions, such as "t" or "z" test ratios. While standardizing the coefficients permits one to directly compare the effects of factor "A" with the effects of factor "B," standardization does not tell if the effects of either factor were significant. "Quasi t-ratios" served as indicators of significant effects for each of the independent variables. Amemiya (1973) found that the ratio of the unstandardized TOBIT coefficients to the standard errors for the coefficient estimates is normally distributed asymptotically under the null hypothesis that the associated coefficient is zero. The distribution of the "quasi t-ratio" is approximately normal for finite sample sizes (Amemiya 1973). Once created, each ratio is interpreted similar to the traditional t-ratio (e.g. any ratio $>=$ to the absolute value of 1.96 is considered significant at $\alpha = 0.05$).

Statistical Methodology - Longitudinal Data Analysis

With the proclamation that "change rather than stability is the norm" (Wohlwill 1973: 23), researchers have frequently criticized static concepts and cross-sectional data models for failing to capture the degree to which observed relationships result from developmental processes (Finkel 1995). For example, Liker et al. (1985: 80) argued, "the complex interaction of changing humans in changing environments is not thought to be captured adequately by simple relationships among variables at a point in time." To address this dilemma, I analyzed panel data and explicitly incorporated change into the model designs in efforts to enhance the empirical assessment of the factors associated with change in facility violence rates. The analysis of panel data permitted stronger causal statements regarding the influence of X on Y (Finkel 1995). In order to establish a true cause and effect relationship, the researcher must satisfy the three conditions of causality (Menard 1991): 1) X and Y must co-vary: 2) X must precede Y in time: and 3) the relationship must not be spurious. While cross-sectional TOBIT analysis can provide information regarding the first stipulation of covariation, the models' usefulness in addressing the other two causal requirements is much more limited (Finkel 1995). Assessments of variables measured at a single point in time make it difficult to establish the temporal order of X and Y, in which case there is always the possibility that Y caused X.

Furthermore, since spurious associations in cross-sectional analysis can only be tested by including extra factors as statistical controls, there is always the possibility that some *unmeasured* factor explains the observed relationship between X and Y. Panel data, however, allows for stronger causal statements given the ability to meet and verify all of the necessary conditions for establishing cause and effect relationships (Finkel 1995). Nonetheless, the ability to estimate statistical models based on panel data provides a powerful compliment to the cross-sectional TOBIT analysis, and ultimately provides a more thorough assessment of the proposed theory of Black rage.

One of the major advantages of panel data is the ability to model change. Panel data provides measures of variables for each unit of analysis at multiple points in time (Finkel 1995). Therefore, it is possible to use information about prior, as well as current, values in constructing and estimating causal models (Finkel 1995). For example, having past and current values of an independent variable X permits estimation of the influence of X at time 1 (X_1) on the subsequent change in the dependent variable Y (ΔY or $Y_2 - Y_1$). In addition, panel data offers the potential to construct a measure of change in X (ΔX or $X_2 - X_1$) between waves and model Y_2 or ΔY as a function of X_1, X_2, ΔX, or some combination of these variables (Finkel 1995). Since the power of panel analysis stems largely from the estimation of change, it is necessary that the reader be aware of the frequent criticisms and concerns surrounding change scores.

How Do We Best Measure Change?

While researchers tend to agree on the superiority of panel analysis over cross-sectional designs, there is little agreement on the best method for measuring change. As indicated by the volumes of literature written on the subject of change measurement,[24] the topic is of considerable interest to researchers, and the proposed solutions have not been universally accepted (Burr and Nesselroade 1990). Much of the controversy within the literature deals with the quantitative struggle among researchers to specifying the proper model for measuring change. For example, Dubois (1957) suggested the use of residualized change scores that attempt to predict what the observed change in the dependent variable would have been had everyone started out equal on the independent variable (see also Rogosa et al. 1982). In contrast, Tornqvist et al. (1985) suggested the use of a "base-free" standardized measure of change. With base-free measures, the mathematical properties of the natural log eliminate between-occasion differences in metric scores (Burr and Nesselroade 1990). Constructing base-free measures of change avoids the issue of which value (time 1 or time 2) to use as the base to calculate relative change.

Many of the change score methods mentioned above spawned from criticisms of perhaps the simplest method of measuring change, and coincidentally, the most controversial,[25] the raw difference score (Burr and Nesselroade 1990). Using the raw difference score method, change is simply the difference between values at time 2 and time 1:

$$\Delta Y = Y_2 - Y_1 \qquad \text{Equation (4)}$$

Where ΔY = the difference score
Y_2 = the value of the dependent variable at time 2
Y_1 = the value of the dependent variable at time 1

The criticisms against the statistical properties of difference scores center on three major issues; validity concerns, the unreliability of change scores, and the pitfall of regression towards the mean.

Change Scores and Validity

The most fundamental objection to difference scores stems from validity concerns. At issue is whether the proposed measures (Y_2 and Y_1) reflect the same attributes at time 2 and time 1. For example, changes in the measurement instruments, such as survey design or interview format, from time 1 to time 2 may result in the measurement of very different attributes[26] (Bereiter 1963). In which case, a pure raw difference score may be misleading. As a check for internal validity in the obtained scores, researchers can compute bivariate correlations between time 1 and time 2 scores to assess the strength of the relationship between both measures. Thus, high correlations indicate consistency in measurements, while a low correlation caste doubt on the similarity of measures at time 1 and time 2 (Burr and Nesselroade 1990). As such, researchers desire to maximize the correlation between time 1 and 2 scores; however, this has the added problem of decreasing the reliability of the difference score.

Change Scores and Reliability

Within the change score literature, closely tied to questions concerning validity are statements regarding the unreliability of difference scores. In change score analysis, reliability refers to the ratio of true variance to observed variance (Burr and Nesselroade 1990). All individual scores are comprised of two components:

$$Y_1 = Y_T + Y_E \qquad \text{Equation (5)}$$

Where Y_1 = the observed score at time 1
Y_T = the true score component of Y_1
Y_E = the error component of Y_1

The reliability of observed scores reflects the amount of error variance relative to the amount of true variance in the scores (Burr and Nesselroade 1990). The equation for the reliability of a difference score involves time 1 and time 2 reliabilities, and the correlation between time 1 and time 2 scores. In its simplest form, Allison (1990) expressed the reliability equation as: [27]

$$\frac{\rho_Y^2 - \rho_{12}}{1 - \rho_{12}} \qquad \text{Equation (6)}$$

Where ρ_Y^2 = the common reliability between Y_1 and Y_2

ρ_{12} = the correlation between Y_1 and Y_2

A number of researchers have statistically proven that change scores have surprisingly low reliability, even in cases where Y_1 and Y_2 have high reliability.[28] For example, Allison (1990) effectively demonstrated that if the correlation term is positive, which it usually is, then the reliability of the change score must be less than the ρ_Y^2. Consider the case where $\rho_Y^2 = 0.7$ and $\rho_{12} = 0.6$, then the reliability of the change score is only 0.25 (Allison 1990). This numerical demonstration supports the observation by Lord (1956: 429) that "difference scores tend to be much more unreliable than the scores themselves." In addition, further manipulation of the values plugged into equation (6) reveals that as the correlation between Y_1 and Y_2 increases, the reliability of the change score decreases (Campbell and Kenny 1999). This observation is counterintuitive, given that researchers desire a high correlation between Y_1 and Y_2 to ensure that they are in fact measuring the same concept at two different points in time (Bereiter 1963).

The low reliability of change scores deterred many researchers from change analysis until Overall and Woodard (1975) showed that in some cases, the lower the reliability of change scores, the greater the power to detect intervention effects. Specifically, Overall and Woodard (1975: 85) found that "the loss in reliability due to calculation of difference scores is not a valid concern because the power of tests of significance is maximum when the reliability of the difference scores is zero." Continuing to debunk the myth that change scores are unreliable, Rogosa (1995) found that when individual differences in true change exist, change scores are in fact very much reliable. In cases where true change progresses at about the same rate for all individuals, "the low reliability of the difference score properly reveals that you can't detect individual differences that ain't there" (Rogosa 1995: 13). Other researchers have successfully demonstrated the reliability of change scores under various conditions (Zimmerman and Williams 1982; Sharma and Gupta 1986;

Maxwell and Howard 1981). Consequently, many researchers no longer view the low reliability of change scores as a problem in statistical analysis. In fact, some researchers, such as Allison (1990), have concluded that the low reliability of change scores is irrelevant for the purpose of causal inference.

Change Scores and Regression Towards the Mean

With the "unreliability-invalidity dilemma"[29] somewhat resolved, attention turns to the third criticism against change scores: the inevitability of regression towards the mean. In the context of change scores, regression towards the mean refers to the fact that there is often a negative correlation between ΔY and Y_1 (Burr and Nesselroade 1990). Figure 5.2 presents a graphic depiction of regression towards the mean using hypothetical values from the 1995 and 1990 versions of the census as an example.

Figure 5.2
Illustrative Example of Regressions Towards the Mean

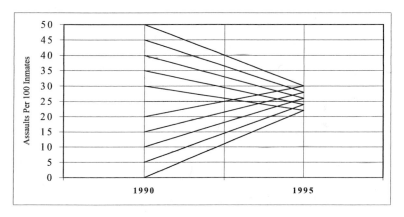

The pattern displayed in the graph depicts regression towards the mean, which is also known as the *Galton Squeeze* (Campbell and Kennedy 1999) and the *Law of Initial Values* (Lacey and Lacey 1962; Wilder 1957). In either case, we would expect that high violence rates in 1990 are associated with lower rates in 1995, a result that produces a negative change score; whereas low violence rates in 1990 are associated with higher rates in 1995, and a positive change score. The overall pattern implies a negative correlation between initial standing and change[30] (Campbell and Kennedy 1999). In regards to why regression towards the mean tends to occur, Burr and Nesselroade (1990: 11) provide a concise and common explanation:

> In terms of measurement error, persons with low time 1 scores or values received them in part because of negative error components and the mean error for this subgroup would also be negative. Differencing values across two times would tend to show a mean error score of zero and, thus, a gain in score or value from time 1 to time 2. The reverse would hold for persons with high initial scores and the scores of both groups would demonstrate regression towards the mean.

The problem created by regression towards the mean is that if any variable is highly correlated with Y_1, it will tend to have a spuriously negative relationship with changes in the dependent variable (Markus 1979). In which case, given the almost universal phenomenon of regression towards the mean this concept is one of the most frequently cited problems associated with difference scores.[31]

How Do We Correct for Regression Towards the Mean?

The pitfalls of the regression effect require special consideration when attempting to specify models of change. The central issue revolves around how best to control for Y_1, the initial value on the dependent variable. If the goal of panel analysis is to show that *X causes Y*, "there is supposedly great merit in examining the relationship between X and Y_2 while 'controlling' for Y_1" (Allison 1990: 94). Controlling for Y_1 allows one to rule out the opposing hypothesis that *Y causes X*, as well as greatly reducing the risk of spurious relationships (Allison 1990). Failure to control for Y_1 interferes with our ability to discover other variables that are significantly associated with change. For example, neglecting to control for Y_1 may produce many variables that relate to change ($Y_2 - Y_1$) only because they relate to Y_1 (Lord 1963). Hence, controlling for Y_1 examines the impact of other explanatory variables on change with the influence of Y_1 effectively partialed out (Lord 1963). Despite the apparent logic behind the need to control for Y_1, researchers remain divided on the appropriateness of including Y_1 as an additional control variable.

Models of Change in Panel Data Analysis

The battle over what to do with Y_1 has produced two distinct camps concerning the appropriate models for estimating change with panel data. On one side, there are researchers, such as Allison (1990) and Liker et al.

(1985), utilizing a first differences model, under which Y_1 does not appear as a statistical control on the right-hand side of the estimation equation. Researchers from this camp believe that including Y_1 among the control variables: 1) produces biased parameter estimates (Liker et at. 1985); 2) tends to underadjust for prior differences (Allison 1990); and 3) is frequently unjustifiable using statistical arguments such as regression towards the mean (Liker et al. 1985). On the other side of the debate, there are researchers such as Finkel (1995), Duncan (1969), and Kessler and Greenberg (1981) contending that unbiased change models are not possible without including the lagged endogenous variable Y_1 among the right-hand side controls. Researchers refer to equations that include Y_1 among the control variables as static-score or conditional change models (Finkel 1995). Using static-score models, Y_2 regresses on both Y_1 and X. Experts from this camp believe there are four reasons why the lagged endogenous variable should appear as a statistical control. First, there may be substantive reasons for assuming that Y_1 is a cause of either Y_2 or ΔY. Second, contrary to their rival camp, static-score proponents contend that the first differences model produces biased results to the extent that the explanatory variable X_1 or ΔX correlate significantly with Y_1. Third, accounting for Y_1 serves to control, at least partially, for omitted variables that influence ΔY. Lastly, the lagged endogenous variable may be included in order to estimate other theoretically relevant parameters of interest.[32] Based on the persuasive arguments presented by both sides, I estimated change with models from both camps.

Model of First Differences

The first differences model regresses the quantity $Y_2 - Y_1$ on changes in the independent variables X and Z:

$$\Delta Y = \Delta \beta_0 + \beta_1 \Delta X + \beta_2 \Delta Z + \Delta \varepsilon \qquad \text{Equation (7)}$$

Liker et al. (1985) proclaims that the first differences model has two noteworthy advantages over static-score models of change. 1) The equation differences out unmeasured and unchanging causes of the outcome measure that may be associated with measured dependent variables. For example, "if the Z variables are unmeasured and unchanging, yet important contributors to the explanation of Y, then the difference equation removes the contaminating effect of Z" (Burr and Nesselroade 1990: 15). Essentially, these permanent individual effects drop out completely through the differencing process (Finkel 1995). 2) The model eliminates measurement error biases under certain conditions. For example, the difference equation negates the deleterious effects of measurement error when there is perfect autocorrelation (i.e. $^r\varepsilon_1\varepsilon_2 = 0$). Even in cases where there is a positive, yet imperfect, autocorrelation (i.e. $^r\varepsilon_1\varepsilon_2 > 0$ but < 1), the difference equation will yield a smaller bias in effect of measurement error (Burr and Nesselroade 1990). Finkel (1995: 5) suggests a third general advantage of the first differences model. 3) "The approach models the individual change in variables directly, as oppose to cross-sectional analyses in which estimates of the 'changes' in an independent variable on 'change' in a dependent variable are based solely on interunit variations at one point in time." Although the first differences model can estimate parameters from panel data, it contains the highly unlikely and restrictive assumption that Y_1 does not influence Y_2 or ΔY (Finkel 1995).

Static-Score Model

Unlike the model of first differences, the static-score model accounts for initial values of Y_1 by including this factor among the control variables. As a general rule, "whenever the present state of the dependent variable (or change in the dependent variable) is determined directly from past states, inclusion of the lagged dependent variable in these situations is necessary to specify the model properly" (Finkel 1995: 8). Consequently, having lagged values of both X and Y provides the researcher with critical additional information, however, the proper method of specifying the effects of these variables is not always obvious. In its most basic form, researchers estimate the static-score model using the following equation (Plewis 1985):

$$Y_2 = \beta_0 + \beta_1 X_2 + \beta_2 Y_1 + \varepsilon_2 \qquad \text{Equation (8)}$$

This model predicts Y_2 from its earlier value Y_1 and from the value of the independent variable X at time 2. An added benefit of the static-score model is that when X is not constant and provides measures from multiple points in time, the effects of X_1, ΔX, and many other possible lag values of X may also be included in the model (Finkel 1995). Along with multiple options concerning specification of the independent variable, equation (8) also allows for manipulation of the dependent variable. For example, the model can reflect the change in the dependent variable over time (ΔY), in which case the equation becomes (Finkel 1995):

$$\Delta Y = \beta_0 + \beta_1 X_2 + (\beta_2 - 1)Y_1 + \varepsilon_2 \qquad \text{Equation (9)}$$

An alternate variation considers the situation where X has both a lagged and an instantaneous effect on Y_2. For example, in a study of stressful life events on an individual's psychological well being, present and past life events may influence one's current psychological state (Finkel 1995). The appropriate model for capturing lagged and instantaneous effects is as follows:

$$Y_2 = \beta_0 + \beta_1 X_1 + \beta_2 Y_1 + \beta_3 X_2 + \varepsilon_2 \qquad \text{Equation (10)}$$

Finkel (1995) presents several static-score model variations. However, the final choice between models is a function of the length of time between panel observations, and the different theoretical assumptions about the nature and timing of the causal lag from X to Y (Finkel 1995). For example, "if the time lag necessary for X to influence Y is sufficiently long but still shorter than the time between panel waves, then a lagged effects model will be more appropriate, where Y_2 is a function of Y_1 and X_1 (Finkel 1995: 13).

[1] Saint Thomas Aquinas, quoted in *Statistics* by Richard J. Larsen and Morris L. Marx (1990: 166).

[2] Sir Francis Galton, quoted in *Statistics* by Richard J. Larsen and Morris L. Marx (1990: 273).

[3] The study excludes the 1974 and 1979 versions given their lack of comparable violence measures with the later editions.

[4] The 1995 version also included facilities staffed by local or private employees. This was the first version of the census to include facilities under joint authority (e.g. state and local officials).

[5] June 29th was the reference date for the 1990 version, and June 30th was the reference date for the 1984 and 1995 editions.

[6] In 1995, instead of sending a follow-up questionnaire, census officials sent a reminder to non-respondents via a fax.

[7] For Michigan, Alabama, and the District of Columbia, the fiscal year was from October 1 through September 30. For New York, the fiscal year was April 1 through March 31, and for Texas, the fiscal year was September 1 through August 31.

[8] Hereafter referred to as USDJ.

[9] The specific breakdown of the 117 non-state controlled male adult population confinement facilities was as follows: local authority (9), private contractor (16), and federal officials (92).

[10] Linking the facilities across the two editions does not violate any promise of confidentiality or anonymity since the names appear in the data sets as presented at the ICPSR web address, which subsequently is a public site. Furthermore, I did not attempt to deduce facility names; names appeared as reported in the original data sets.

[11] Meaning that, of the 795 facility names reported for 1990 and the 826 facility names reported for 1995, only 411 matched perfectly when using the merge function in SPSS.

[12] Recall this was the same source utilized by Bureau of Justice officials in generating the initial population list for the census.

[13] I speculated that these facilities were same after noticing that both had the exact same address and contact information listed in the *ACA Directory*. Both facilities also had similar values on unique variables within the data sets.

[14] The 1995 variable values provided the descriptive statistics for the subsequently matched prisons.

[15] Based on the time lag of the census process, the odds are high that the reported assault values reflect the number of disciplinary reports written. Respondents provided the number of assaults for the entire year. The easiest and most convenient measure of assaults for the year is the number of disciplinary reports. Subsequently, research shows correctional officers often reserve formal punishment (disciplinary reports) for more serious offenses. Therefore, the likelihood of an over saturation of minor assault incidents within the 1984 edition is relatively small.

[16] Rates reflect the number of actual occurrences of some phenomenon divided by the total number of possible occurrences per some unit of time (Healey 2002).

[17] High-risk staff members were those individuals working as correctional officers, prison administrators, or rehabilitation and treatment staff. Across all three years of the census, individuals within these employment roles comprised on average 86 percent of the total population of prison employees.

[18] Each respondent stated the number of conditions for which their facility was under Federal Court Order. The ten conditions considered pertained to crowding, medical facilities, recreation, contact policies, fire hazards, education programs, counseling, food service, discipline procedures, and segregation practices. The deprivation score reflects the number of conditions for which each facility was under court order. The scores varied from 0-10, with zero indicating no court orders, and ten indicating court orders for all ten conditions.

[19] The index of racial variation (IRV) is essentially the same scale as the standard index of qualitative variation (IQV), however the final coefficients were multiplied by 100. The IRV provided a measure of racial diversity within the staff populations for each sample. The index was created by first estimating the diversity coefficient (D); $D = 1 - \Sigma P_i^2$. Where P_i = the proportion of cases in the ith category. In the current project P_1 = proportion of Whites, P_2 = proportion of Blacks, P_3 = proportion of Hispanics, P_4 = proportion of Asians, P_5 = proportion of Native Americans, P_6 = proportion of "others." After creating the diversity coefficients, standardizing the values permitted comparisons across years. The values were standardized by estimating the following equation: IRV = [K/(K-1)] * (D), where K = the number of categories. I multiplied the coefficients by 100 after standardizing for ease of interpretation in the regression models. Subsequently, the maximum value on the IRV was 100, which occurred when a given prison staff spread evenly across all racial categories. The minimum value of zero occurred when all members of a prison staff fell into a single racial category. For a technical description of the IQV, the foundation of the IRV, see Agresti and Agresti (1978), Amemiya (1963), or Labovitz and Gibbs (1964).

[20] According the Census Bureau, South = AL, AR, FL, GA, KY, MS, TX, OK, TN, SC, NC, WV, VA, MD, LA, DC, DE. West = AK, AZ, CA, CO, HI, ID, MT, NV, NM, OR, UT, WA, WY. North Central (Midwest) = IL, IN, IA, KS, MI, MN, MO, NE, ND, OH, SD, WI. Northeast = CT, ME, MA, NH, NJ, NY, PA, RI, VT.

[21] McCorkle et al. (1995) were highly critical of the importation model, claiming that the perspective 1) could not explain collective acts of prison violence, and 2) offered prison officials no implications for governing prison. I contend, however, that the influence of race in prison riots, most notably the 1971 Attica uprising, refutes the first claim of McCorkle et al. (1995) (see also Montgomery 1994). Furthermore, the growing trend among prison officials, especially in California, to segregate known gang rivals, refutes their second claim (Irwin 1980). This practice indicates that prison officials can better govern their facilities by understanding the background characteristics of the inmates under their jurisdiction. The current project further offers implications for governing prisons by suggesting that hiring more minority correctional officers may potential reduce prison violence by controlling the rage of Black inmates.

[22] McCorkle et al (1995) quantified the influence of Black guards on prison violence through their variable measuring the White-to-Black guard ratio. However, they failed to control for the influence of inmate race.

[23] For example, Chapter II revealed that Carroll (1974) based his findings regarding the violent tendency of Black inmates on a sample of 15 violent assaults.

[24] See Burr and Nesselroade (1990), Harris (1963), Gottman (1995), Collins and Horn (1991), and von Eye (1990) for testaments to the volumes of research devoted to the study of change.

[25] See Bereiter (1963); Bohrnstedt (1969); and Cronbach and Furby (1970).

[26] For example, in the section describing the dependent variables in the current chapter, I mentioned how the slight variations in the wording used by census officials could perhaps prevent direct comparisons of the samples of assaults across the three waves. However, based on the retroactive nature of the census, this likelihood of a biasing effect due to wording is very small.

[27] Rogosa (1995), Linn and Slinde (1977) include simple tables used to find the reliability of change scores.

[28] See Kessler (1977); Bereiter (1963); Cronbach and Furby (1970); Furby (1973); Humpreys (1961); and McNemar (1958)

[29] Phrase borrowed from Bereiter (1963).

[30] It is also possible to obtain a zero correlation between change and initial status, known as the Overlap Hypothesis, which dates back to Anderson (1939) and Bloom (1964). In addition, a positive correlation between change and initial status, known as a "fanspread," results from increasing variances over time (Rogosa 1995). However, by far the most commonly observed and most thoroughly researched pattern is that of a negative correlation between change and initial status.

[31] See Bohrnstedt (1969); Clarke et al. (1959); Cronbach and Furby (1970); Hummel-Rossi and Weinberg (1975); Labouvie (1982); Lytton et al. (1973); Nesselroade et al. (1980); Thorndike (1942); Vockell and Asher (1973); and many others.

[32] Interested readers should see Finkel (1995) for a more elaborate discussion of the four benefits of the static-score model in comparison to the first differences approach.

CHAPTER VI

Cross Sectional Models and Prison Violence

Chance is always powerful. Let your hook be always cast; in the pool where you least expect it, there will be a fish.[1]

Chance is nothing; there is no such thing as chance. What we call by that name is the effect which we see of a cause which we do not see.[2]

Statistics means never having to say you're certain.[3]

Descriptive Statistics

Given the two distinct types of data analysis, this study presents the empirical findings in two separate chapters. The current chapter considers the data analysis for the cross-sectional TOBIT models estimated using the three versions of the census. Chapter VII presents ordinary least squares regression and TOBIT estimates using the panel data set created by merging the 1990 and 1995 editions of the census. The analysis for the current chapter included estimated TOBIT models on each version of the census collectively, as well as regional comparisons across the three editions.

To assist the reader in interpreting the patterns observed in the TOBIT analysis as well as to provide an elaboration of the three study samples, general descriptive statistics precede the presentation of the TOBIT models. Tables 6.1(a-c) present descriptive statistics for the control, independent, and dependent variables included in the study. The specific design of Table 6.1 includes overall averages by year for the interval-ratio level factors, followed by average comparisons across the four geographic regions.

On average each year, nearly 50 percent of the facilities analyzed were located in the Southeast region of the U.S. In addition, roughly 25 percent of the facilities in each sample were maximum-security prisons. Not presented in Table 6.1 are the frequency distributions for the cell type variable across each of the three samples. In 1984 and 1990, approximately 20 percent of the sampled facilities housed inmates exclusively in single-cell arrangements. In the 1995 data sample, only 13.8 percent of facilities housed inmates in such arrangements. The average staff assault rate reached a high of roughly 4 assaults per 100 staff members in 1990. The average staff assault rates for 1984 and 1995 were virtually identical at 3.81 and 3.83 per 100 staff members.

Table 6.1(a) – Descriptive Statistics by Year, 1984

Variables	Overall Sample	Region			
		South	West	Northeast	Midwest
	N = 579	N = 282	N = 94	N = 93	N = 110
Staff Assault Rate	3.81	3.97	2.58	4.39	3.92
Inmate Assault Rate	3.66	3.73	2.67	4.94	3.23
% Black Inmates	44.04	53.43	21.73	40.25	42.25
% Black Staff	15.74	22.83	6.056	12.65	8.44
White-to-Black Staff	18.61	9.68	19.92	37.75	27.40
Average Crowding Level	4.03	2.40	4.45	9.03	3.60
Deprivation Score	1.32	1.63	1.63	0.65	0.82
Male-to-Female CO's	18.98	15.89	12.29	32.43	18.04
% Correctional Officers	69.71	73.14	68.04	65.73	65.72
Index of Racial Variation	32.75	39.71	35.11	24.57	19.84

Table 6.1(b) – Descriptive Statistics by Year, 1990

Variables	Overall Sample	Region			
		South	West	Northeast	Midwest
	N = 795	N = 354	N = 135	N = 133	N = 173
Staff Assault Rate	4.02	3.23	2.97	6.07	4.87
Inmate Assault Rate	2.81	2.83	2.16	3.99	2.37
% Black Inmates	46.85	57.19	23.77	44.96	45.16
% Black Staff	18.99	28.47	6.98	16.28	11.03
White-to-Black Staff	19.06	9.24	19.30	35.98	27.73
Average Crowding Level	9.01	3.81	4.24	19.59	15.24
Deprivation Score	1.31	2.16	1.07	0.18	0.62
Male-to-Female CO's	11.03	10.20	7.99	19.77	7.64
% Correctional Officers	66.48	69.68	66.20	64.65	61.56
Index of Racial Variation	36.59	44.20	40.89	29.25	23.30

Table 6.1(c) – Descriptive Statistics by Year, 1995

Variables	Overall Sample	Region			
		South	West	Northeast	Midwest
	N = 788	N = 400	N = 102	N = 120	N = 166
Staff Assault Rate	3.83	3.00	3.06	5.08	5.43
Inmate Assault Rate	2.43	2.14	3.20	3.22	2.06
% Black Inmates	50.93	60.08	21.73	46.43	50.05
% Black Staff	19.76	29.59	7.02	9.94	11.03
White-to-Black Staff	20.29	9.42	29.68	41.26	28.36
Average Crowding Level	11.93	4.73	13.29	16.75	24.95
Deprivation Score	0.88	1.16	0.80	0.47	0.57
Male-to-Female CO's	9.91	7.05	6.44	26.84	6.51
% Correctional Officers	71.75	73.30	71.51	70.93	68.75
Index of Racial Variation	36.66	44.24	42.45	23.58	24.28

Appendix C, Tables 1-3 present bivariate correlation matrices for the dependent, independent, and control variables used to conduct the data analysis. To protect against biased or inefficient estimates of the dependent variables, it is important to insure that multicollinearity among the independent and control variables is not a problem. Assessing the values of the bivariate, Pearson's correlation coefficient is the first step in the multicollinearity diagnostic process. If two variables are highly correlated, then simultaneously including both factors into any regression model could potentially produce biased and inefficient estimates of the dependent variable. One important caution to bear in mind when interpreting the correlation matrices is the sensitivity of measures of association to large sample sizes. With a large sample, relatively small coefficient values may read significant. For this reason, some of the bivariate relationships indicated as significant correlations in Tables 1-3 did not necessarily introduce bias when included simultaneously in the empirical regression models.[4] The discussion on the correlation matrices only considers those coefficients greater than or equal to the absolute value of 0.40.

There were six noteworthy correlations found consistently among the three data samples. First, based on the simple bivariate correlations, the best predictor of the staff assault rate was the inmate assault rate. For instance, computing the coefficient of determination for the 1995 data (Table 3) revealed that the inmate assault rate explained over 20 percent of the sample variance in staff assault rates.[5] Second, there was a mildly strong and positive correlation between the percentage of Black inmates and security level. The higher percentage of Black inmates detained in maximum-security facilities partially explains this correlation. Third, there was also a mildly strong and positive correlation between the percentage of Black staff and security level, largely due to the relatively higher percentage of Black staff employed in maximum-security prisons. Fourth, there was a very strong positive relationship between the index of racial variation (IRV) and the percentage of Black staff. The high coefficient indicated that diversity among prison staff was largely a factor of increasing the percentage of Blacks and not all minorities. For instance, in 1984, (Table 1) the percentage of Black staff explained nearly 58 percent of the sample variance on the IRV. Fifth, there was a strong negative correlation between the IRV and the ratio of White-to-Black staff. Given that high values on the IRV indicate a high level of racial homogeneity, it explains the inverse relationship between this factor and the ratio of White-to-Black staff. Lastly, there was a strong positive relationship between the percentage of Black inmates and the percentage of Black staff. The correlation between these two variables ranged from 0.55 to 0.59 across the three data samples. The strong correlation between these two variables stems from the fact that Blacks, in general, tend to be highly concentrated in certain geographic areas. Thus, areas with a high concentration of Black citizens are subsequently likely to have high concentrations of Black prison staff and inmates. Although, Appendix C flags the six correlations mentioned above as statistically significant, neither of the associations introduced problems of multicollinearity in the TOBIT analysis.

Interpreting the TOBIT Analysis[6]

Because of the dual structure of the TOBIT equation, it was necessary to separate the differing effects regarding the influence of the independent variables on the staff assault rate into two separate tables. For each year, the first table provides the estimated effect size of the independent variables on the observed values of the dependent variable (Y) for the non-censored observations (Y > 0). Non-censored observations are those prisons with at least one reported staff assault. For instance, in 1984, 334 of the 579 included prisons had a reported staff assault; therefore, the coefficients and effects specified in Table 6.2 assess the impact of the independent variables on this sample of 334 prisons. Interpretation of the independent variable effects for non-censored cases is essentially the same as the interpretation of such effects when using ordinary least squares regression. The value underneath the "Effect" column of each respective model presents the influence of a one-unit increase in the independent variable on the subsequent value of the dependent variable (staff assault rate).

In contrast, the second table for each year presents effect size estimates for the influence of the independent variables on the probability of the dependent variable being limited (i.e. equal to zero). For instance, Table 6.3 provides the influence of each independent variable on the probability of a staff assault for the 245 censored observations in the 1984 sample (cases where Y = 0). For ease of interpretation, I converted the influence of each independent variable on the probability of a staff assault into percentages. The values reported underneath the "Effect" column of each model reflect the percentage change in the probability of a staff assault associated with a one-unit increase in the independent variable. The two effects described in both tables parallel the structure of the TOBIT model.

In addition to specifying the dual effects of the TOBIT model, I standardized the TOBIT coefficients, obtained from E-views, using the process outlined by Roncek (1992).[7] The Analogue-Standardized TOBIT Coefficient (ASTC) "behaves reasonably for models with dependent variables having a large number of cases at the limit (zero), and a wide variation of values on the independent variables" (Roncek 1992: 506). When these conditions are satisfied, the ASTC resembles the standardized values obtained for ordinary least squares regression estimates, with coefficient values that range from −1.00 to +1.00. Converting the coefficients to standardized measures was essential for assessing the merits of the Black rage theory against the effects of the deprivation and management perspectives on prison violence.

To provide for a comparison among theoretical paradigms, Tables 6.2, 6.4, and 6.6 include log-likelihood ratios in order to assess the "model fit" for each group of independent variables. The p-values associated with each log-likelihood ratio are included in parentheses. Model 1 presents the influence of the control variables on the staff assault rate. Models 2-4 sequentially add variables from the deprivation, management, and importation perspectives to the original control model. The log-likelihood ratio provides an indication of which model contributes most to our ability to explain variation in staff assault rates. Model 5 included all 3 theoretical paradigms simultaneously to examine the explanatory power of each perspective when considering all factors cumulatively.

Staff Assault Rates Across Time

1984 Findings

Table 6.2 considers the influence of the independent variables on the staff assault rates for the non-censored observations in the 1984 data sample. In all of the models, the variables were included, as detailed in Table 5.3 (on page 157), with the exception of the region variable which was recoded into a binary factor set equal to one if the facility was located in the Southeast, and equal to zero if the facility was located in any other region. Estimating model 1 revealed that the inmate assault rate and security level had significant effects on the staff assault rate. The effect size for the inmate assault rate in model 1 suggests that an inmate assault rate of 25 per 100 produced a 5.25 ($\approx$ 5 assault) increase in the staff violence rate. While high inmate assault rates tended to increase the staff assault rate, being maximum-security decreased the staff assault rate. For instance, being a maximum-security prison, on average, decreased the staff assault rate by 2.60. In model 2, cell type was the only deprivation variable that had a significant effect on staff violence. Housing inmates exclusively in single-cell arrangements increased the staff assault rate by 3.31. Given the standardized coefficient values, cell type explained more variation in staff assaults than security level or the inmate assault rate.

With the introduction of the management variables in model 3, region became significant; indicating that being located in the Southeast significantly lowered the staff assault rate. The percentage of correctional officers was the only management factor with a significant effect on staff violence. The fact that each additional unit increase in the percentage of correctional officers increased the staff assault rate by 0.13 supports the general notion that increasing the opportunities for violence (more guards vulnerable to assault) ultimately produces higher staff assault rates. In addition, although the effect size for the percentage of correctional officers appears relatively small, considering the fact that the average prison in the 1984 sample had 69.71 percent of its prison staff as correctional officers, this variable contributes significantly to the staff assault rate. For a facility with 69.71 percent correctional officers, the subsequent staff assault rate would increase by 9.06 (69.71 * 0.13). The slightly higher log-likelihood ratio for model 3 suggests an improved fit between the management variables and prison violence over the deprivation factors.

The strong influence of the inmate assault rate fell from significance in model 4, which introduced the importation variables used to operationalize the black rage perspective.

Table 6.2 - 1984 ASTC and Independent Variable Effects on Staff
Assault Rates – Non-Censored Cases (N = 334)

Control Variables	Model 1		Model 2		Model 3		Model 4		Model 5	
	ASTC	Effect	ASTC	Effect	ASTC	Effect	ASTC	Effect	ASTC	Effect
Inmate Assault Rate	0.27 *	0.21	0.27 *	0.21	0.41 **	0.34	0.18	0.14	0.30 *	0.25
Security Level	-0.27 **	-2.60	-0.26 *	-2.42	-0.30 **	-3.06	-0.23 *	-2.19	-0.23 *	-2.37
Region	-0.15	-1.22	-0.13	-1.02	-0.28 *	-2.52	-0.38 **	-3.22	-0.37 **	-3.27
Deprivation Variables										
Cell Type			0.33 **	3.31					0.16	1.74
Crowding Level			0.06	0.01					-0.18	-0.04
Deprivation Score			0.18	0.24					0.04	0.05
Management Variables										
Percent CO'S					0.36 **	0.13			0.16	0.06
Male-to-Female CO's					0.13	0.03			0.07	0.01
Index - Racial Var.					0.02	0.00			0.14	0.03
Importation Variables										
Percent Black Inmates							0.60 ***	0.12	0.69 ***	0.15
Percent Black Staff							-0.09	-0.02	-0.24	-0.06
White-to-Black Staff							0.21	0.02	0.22	0.02
LL Ratio (P-value)	13.21 (0.0042)		25.30 (0.0003)		26.62 (0.0002)		34.16 (0.0000)		41.42 (0.0000)	

* = ASTC Significant at α = 0.05   ** = ASTC Significant at α = 0.01
*** = ASTC Significant at α = 0.001

As predicted by the black rage theory, the percentage of Black inmates
had a very strong and positive effect on the staff assault rate. Each
additional unit increase in the percentage of Black inmates increased the
staff assault rate by 0.12. Hence, if a facility had 50 percent Black
inmates, their predicted staff assault rate increased by 6.5 assaults per
100 staff members. Furthermore, in relation to the control variables, the
percentage of Black inmates was far more significant in explaining staff
assault rates (ASTC = 0.60). Although the magnitude of the coefficients
for the percent of Black staff and the ratio of White-to-Black staff were
not significant, the coefficient signs suggested relationships that
supported the proposed theory. Under the theory of black rage, the
percentage of Black inmates should increase the staff assault rate, while
the percentage of Black staff should decrease the staff assault rate. Also
predicted by the theory is that the higher the ratio of White-to-Black staff
members, the higher the predicted staff assault rate. However, while the

coefficient signs observed in models 4 and 5 conform to the theory, only the effect of Black inmates was significant.

Also evident in model 4 was the improved collective fit of the importation variables over the management and deprivation factors. The importation variables increased the log-likelihood ratio by 20.95, in comparison to the 12.09 and 13.41 improvements for the deprivation and management models, respectively. In addition, none of the deprivation or management factors produced a significant effect on the staff assault rate in model 5, where all of the perspectives were simultaneously included. Collectively, the percentage of Black inmates was the most significant factor in predicting staff assault rates among the non-censored observations for the 1984 data sample.

Table 6.3 - 1984 Independent Variable Effects on the Probability of a Staff Assault – Censored Cases (N = 245)

Control Variables	Model 1 Effect	Model 2 Effect	Model 3 Effect	Model 4 Effect	Model 5 Effect
Inmate Assault Rate	0.76	0.75	1.13	0.48	0.82
Security Level	-9.31	-8.81	-10.12	-7.68	-7.93
Region	-4.37	-3.71	-8.34	-11.31	-10.91
Deprivation Variables					
Cell Type		12.05			5.80
Crowding Level		0.04			-0.13
Deprivation Score		0.86			0.17
Management Variables					
Percent CO'S			0.42		0.19
Male-to-Female CO's			0.09		0.05
Index - Racial Var.			0.01		0.10
Importation Variables					
Percent Black Inmates				0.43	0.50
Percent Black Staff				-0.08	-0.21
White-to-Black Staff				0.07	0.08

Model 5, from Table 6.3, details the effects of the independent variables on the probability of a staff assault for the 245 censored observations in the 1984 data sample. The results showed that security level and region significantly reduced the probability of a staff assault. For instance, being a maximum-security prison decreased the probability of a staff assault by 7.93 percent. Likewise, being located in the Southeast decreased the probability of a staff assault by 10.91 percent.

The inmate assault rate, cell type, and the percentage of Black inmates were the only three factors that noticeably increased the probability of a staff assault. Among the censored observations, the probability of a staff assault increased by 0.82 percent per each unit increase in the inmate assault rate. Thus, if a facility had 25 assaults per 100 inmates, this increased their probability of a staff assault by 20.5 percent. Each additional unit increase in the percentage of Black inmates increased the probability of a staff assault by 0.50 percent. Although the effect appears relatively small, consider the fact that if 50 percent of a prison's inmate population is Black, this characteristic alone increased their probability of a staff assault by 25 percent. Hence, in actuality, the influence of Black inmates on the staff assault rate was quite significant.

1990 Findings

Table 6.4 presents the model summaries for the 434 non-censored observations from the 1990 data sample. All three of the control variables in model 1 were highly significant, with the inmate assault rate having a slightly larger effect based on the ASTC values. A one-unit increase in the inmate assault rate produced a 0.60 increase in the staff assault rate. In which case, having an inmate assault rate of 25 per 100 increased the staff assault rate by 16. Likewise, being maximum-security increased the staff assault rate by 6.49, while being located in the Southeast significantly decreased the staff assault rate by 2.27. The effect of the security variable reversed from 1984 to 1990, in large part due to the dramatic increase in the average staff assault rate in maximum-security prisons during the six-year period. Collectively, the control model for the 1990 sample produced a considerably higher log-likelihood ratio than in 1984 (216.00 versus 13.21), indicating a much better model fit for the control variables in the 1990 data analysis.

The deprivation variables in 1990 produced a pattern similar to the 1984 analysis, where all of the factors had a positive impact on the staff assault rate but only the cell type variable was significant. Housing inmates exclusively in single-cell arrangements increased the staff assault rate by 2.62. In single-cell arrangements, inmates spend less time in contact with other inmates; in which case, when angered or frustrated, inmates are perhaps more likely to vent in the form of assaults against facility staff. The deprivation variables improved the overall model fit, unlike the management variables (model 3) where the log-likelihood ratio actually decreased below the base control model. The percentage of correctional officers was, again, the only significant management variable. However, in 1990, the percentage of correctional officers significantly decreased the staff assault rate. For instance, if a prison had

75 percent correctional officers, their predicted staff assault rate decreased by 4.5, versus a reduction of 3 assaults per 100 staff members if the facility staff was only 50 percent correctional officers.

Table 6.4 - 1990 ASTC and Independent Variable Effects on Staff Assault Rates – Non-Censored Cases (N = 434)

Control Variables	Model 1		Model 2		Model 3		Model 4		Model 5	
	ASTC	Effect	ASTC	Effect	ASTC	Effect	ASTC	Effect	ASTC	Effect
Inmate Assault Rate	0.56 ***	0.60	0.55 ***	0.59	0.60 ***	0.63	0.56 ***	0.61	0.56 ***	0.61
Security Level	0.52 ***	6.49	0.44 ***	5.43	0.43 ***	5.23	0.49 ***	6.20	0.37 ***	4.59
Region	-0.22 ***	-2.27	-0.17 **	-1.77	-0.21 ***	-2.20	-0.35 ***	-3.73	-0.27 ***	-2.89
Deprivation Variables										
Cell Type			0.20 ***	2.62					0.12 *	1.53
Crowding Level			0.09	0.02					0.01	0.00
Deprivation Score			0.09	0.15					0.09	0.15
Management Variables										
Percent CO'S					-0.14 *	-0.06			-0.18 **	-0.08
Male-to-Female CO's					0.02	0.01			-0.04	-0.02
Index - Racial Var.					0.10	0.02			0.09	0.02
Importation Variables										
Percent Black Inmates							0.20 **	0.05	0.28 ***	0.07
Percent Black Staff							0.03	0.01	-0.11	-0.03
White-to-Black Staff							0.05	0.01	0.04	0.00
LL Ratio	216.00		232.28		205.01		221.31		212.59	
(P-value)	(0.0000)		(0.0000)		(0.0000)		(0.0000)		(0.0000)	

* = ASTC Significant at α = 0.05   ** = ASTC Significant at α = 0.01
*** = ASTC Significant at α = 0.001

Concerning the importation variables, the percentage of Black inmates was, again, the only significant variable in predicting the staff assault rate. Although the sign of the coefficients for the percentage of Black inmates and the ratio of White-to-Black staff were in directions supportive of the black rage theory, the slight, but positive, influence of Black staff on the staff assault rate was counter to expectations (model 4). In the cumulative model, the sign of the coefficient for the percentage of Black staff reversed in the direction predicted by the Black rage theory; however, the ratio of White-to-Black staff had virtually no impact on the staff assault rate. In which case, as in the 1984 analysis, the importation coefficient signs were in the direction indicating the significance of Black rage; then again, the minimal effects of the percent of Black staff and the lack of an effect for the ratio of White-to-Black staff offered little support for the proposed theory.

Unlike the 1984 analysis, the cumulative model managed to produce at least one significant effect from each perspective. Cell type, percent of correctional officers, and the percent of Black inmates were the non-control variables with significant effects in model 5. While the impact of cell type on the staff assault rate decreased once controlling for each perspective, the effects of both the percentage of correctional officers and the percentage of Black inmates strengthened. In fact, after the inmate assault rate and security level, the percentage of Black inmates was the next most significant factor. Overall, in terms of which paradigm most improved the ability to predict staff assaults in the 1990 analysis, the deprivation variables, driven primarily by the effect of cell type, made the greatest contribution to the log-likelihood ratio. This perspective subsequently was weakest in the 1984 analysis, where the importation model offered more explanatory power.

Table 6.5 examines the influence of the independent variables on the probability of a staff assault for the 361 censored observations in the 1990 data sample.

Table 6.5 - 1990 Independent Variable Effects on the Probability of a Staff Assault – Censored Cases (N = 361)

Control Variables	Model 1 Effect	Model 2 Effect	Model 3 Effect	Model 4 Effect	Model 5 Effect
Inmate Assault Rate	1.18	1.17	1.26	1.18	1.19
Security Level	12.81	10.74	10.46	11.95	8.96
Region	-4.49	-3.50	-4.39	-7.20	-5.64
Deprivation Variables					
Cell Type		5.18			2.99
Crowding Level		0.04			0.00
Deprivation Score		0.30			0.30
Management Variables					
Percent CO'S			-0.11		-0.15
Male-to-Female CO's			0.02		-0.03
Index - Racial Var.			0.05		0.04
Importation Variables					
Percent Black Inmates				0.10	0.14
Percent Black Staff				0.01	-0.05
White-to-Black Staff				0.01	0.01

The three control variables produced noticeable changes in the probability of a staff assault across all five models. Based on the cumulative model, each additional increase in the inmate assault rate increased the probability of a staff assault by 1.19 percent. Hence, if a facility had an inmate assault rate of 25 per 100, this increased their probability of a staff assault by 29.75 percent. As well, maximum-security prisons had an almost 9 percent higher probability of experiencing a staff assault, and housing inmates exclusively in single-cell arrangements increased the probability of staff assault by roughly 3 percent. Region was the only variable that produced a noticeable decrease in the probability of a staff assault (-5.64). Interestingly, the decreasing effect of the region variable was greatest in model 4, where the importation factors were included. This suggests that controlling for differences in the Black/White dynamic between the guard and inmate populations further decreased the probability of a staff assault in the Southeast.

1995 Findings

Table 6.6 presents the coefficient and effect size estimates for the 495 non-censored observations from the 1995 data sample. As in the 1990 data analysis, each of the control variables remained highly significant across all five models. In addition, the log-likelihood ratio for the 1995 control model was considerably higher than in 1984 or 1990. The inmate assault rate and security level continued to exert strong and positive influences on the staff assault rate. However, the strength of both effects observed in 1990 diminished slightly in the 1995 analysis. For instance, in 1990, being a maximum-security prison increased the staff assault rate by 4.59, while in 1995 this variable increased the staff assault rate by 2.92. The influence of region on the staff assault rate remained consistently negative across all three years of data analysis. Furthermore, the direct impact of being located in the Southeast steadily decreased across time. For example, being located in the Southeast decreased the staff assault rate by 3.27 in 1984, by 2.89 in 1990, and by 1.56 in 1995 (see model 5 in each table).

Cell type was the only deprivation variable with a significant influence on the staff assault rate across the three years of analysis. Similar to the region effect, the impact of housing inmates exclusively in single-cell arrangements steadily decreased over time. For instance, single-cell arrangements increased the staff assault rate by 3.31 in 1984, by 2.62 in 1990, and by 1.64 in 1995. Table 6.6 further revealed a slightly significant and positive influence of the crowding variable on the staff assault rate. However, the effect size was relatively small, given that each additional unit increase in the percent over-crowded only increased the staff assault rate by 0.01. Nonetheless, the influence of the crowding variable, observed in model 2, vanished in model 5 after controlling for other factors. The inclusion of the deprivation variables improved the likelihood ratio by 16.36, which suggests a slight improvement in our ability to explain variation in staff assault rates over the pure control model.

Table 6.6 - 1995 ASTC and Independent Variable Effects on Staff
Assault Rates – Non-Censored Cases (N = 495)

Control Variables	Model 1		Model 2		Model 3		Model 4		Model 5	
	ASTC	Effect	ASTC	Effect	ASTC	Effect	ASTC	Effect	ASTC	Effect
Inmate Assault Rate	0.58 ***	0.48	0.58 ***	0.47	0.57 ***	0.47	0.58 ***	0.47	0.59 ***	0.46
Security Level	0.54 ***	3.77	0.49 ***	3.36	0.53 ***	3.68	0.47 ***	3.21	0.44 ***	2.92
Region	-0.26 ***	-1.59	-0.21 ***	-1.24	-0.26 ***	-1.62	-0.32 ***	-1.91	-0.27 ***	-1.56
Deprivation Variables										
Cell Type			0.19 ***	1.64					0.14 **	1.21
Crowding Level			0.11 *	0.01					0.06	0.01
Deprivation Score			0.09	0.11					0.07	0.09
Management Variables										
Percent CO'S					-0.09	-0.03			-0.11	-0.03
Male-to-Female CO's					0.04	0.01			0.01	0.00
Index - Racial Var.					0.04	0.01			0.09	0.01
Importation Variables										
Percent Black Inmates							0.19 **	0.03	0.23 ***	0.03
Percent Black Staff							-0.13	-0.02	-0.20 *	-0.03
White-to-Black Staff							-0.01	0.00	0.00	0.00
LL Ratio (P-value)	290.99 (0.0000)		307.35 (0.0000)		290.31 (0.0000)		286.21 (0.0000)		301.99 (0.0000)	

* = ASTC Significant at α = 0.05   ** = ASTC Significant at α = 0.01
*** = ASTC Significant at α = 0.001

Model 3 illustrates that none of the management variables had a significant impact on the staff assault rate. In fact, the log-likelihood ratio for model 3 is less than that for the basic control model (290.31 versus 290.99). While the percentage of correctional officers was significant in 1984 and in 1990, the other two management variables failed to reach significance across any of the data samples. Likewise, the percentage of Black inmates was the only significant importation factor across all three years of analysis. In 1995, despite the significant coefficient for the percentage of Black inmates, the importation variables lowered the log-likelihood ratio, indicating a weaker model in terms of explaining variation in staff assault rates. The sign of the importation coefficients in model 5 offered the best support for the Black rage theory across any of the cumulative models.

Model 5 suggests that while the percentage of Black inmates significantly increased the staff assault rate, the percentage of Black staff significantly decreased the staff assault rate. This dual relationship is the core assumption of the Black rage theory. The assumption suggests that although Black inmates have a positive and significant influence on the staff assault rate (as evident in all of the models), the percentage of Black staff can effectively counter the positive influence of Black inmates on staff violence. Model 5 shows that each additional unit increase in the percent of Black inmates increased the staff assault rate by 0.03, while each additional unit increase in the percent of Black staff decreased the staff assault rate by the same amount. Thus, if a facility maintained exactly equal Black representation within the staff and inmate populations, they could potentially negate the positive influence of Black inmates on staff violence. The coefficient signs for the importation variables suggest the importance of the Black rage perspective; however, the ratio of White-to-Black staff had virtually no effect on the staff assault rate. After decomposing the unstandardized TOBIT coefficient, each additional unit increase in the ratio of White-Black staff had no effect on the staff assault rate (see both model 4 and 5).

As indicated by Table 6.7, each of the control variables had a far greater influence on the probability of a staff assault among the 1995 censored observations than in the 1984 or 1990 data sample. Consider for instance, the finding that the probability of a maximum-security prison experiencing a staff assault was 8.96 percent higher than medium or minimum-security facilities in 1984, versus 21.05 percent higher in 1995. The influence of the inmate assault rate on the likelihood of a staff assault increased substantially from 1984 to 1995. In 1984, a one-unit increase in the inmate assault rate increased the probability of a staff assault by 0.82 percent, whereas, in 1995, each additional inmate assault increased the likelihood of a staff assault by 3.31 percent. In which case, if a facility had an inmate assault rate of 25 per 100, this increased their odds of experiencing a staff assault by 82.75 percent. Counter to expectations, being located in the Southeast decreased the probability of a staff assault by 10.91 percent in 1984, by 5.64 percent in 1990, and by 11.23 percent in 1995. The fact that the Southeast consistently had a lower average staff assault rate than the other regions combined partially explains this finding.

Table 6.7 - 1995 Independent Variable Effects on the Probability of a
Staff Assault – Censored Cases (N = 293)

Control Variables	Model 1	Model 2	Model 3	Model 4	Model 5
	Effect	Effect	Effect	Effect	Effect
Inmate Assault Rate	3.27	3.25	3.23	3.29	3.31
Security Level	25.90	23.35	25.24	22.66	21.05
Region	-10.93	-8.64	-11.09	-13.48	-11.23
Deprivation Variables					
Cell Type		11.37			8.72
Crowding Level		0.09			0.05
Deprivation Score		0.79			0.65
Management Variables					
Percent CO'S			-0.17		-0.22
Male-to-Female CO's			0.06		0.02
Index - Racial Var.			0.04		0.09
Importation Variables					
Percent Black Inmates				0.20	0.24
Percent Black Staff				-0.13	-0.20
White-to-Black Staff				-0.01	0.00

Cell type displayed a similar jump in significance from 1990 to
1995. In 1990, housing inmates exclusively in single-cell arrangements
increased the probability of a staff assault by 2.99 percent, while in 1995
such cell arrangements increased the probability of a staff assault by 8.72
percent. Although the percentage of Black inmates and the percentage of
Black staff produced equal effects for the non-censored observations, the
percentage of Black inmates had a slightly greater impact on the
likelihood of a staff assault for the censored observations. In 1995, each
additional increase in the percentage of Black inmates significantly
increased the probability of a staff assault by 0.24, while each additional
increase in the percentage of Black staff decreased the likelihood of a
staff assault by 0.20,

Summary. Black Rage and the Staff Assault Rate Across Time

Although the coefficient signs collectively across the three years of data
analysis suggest relationships supportive of the Black rage theory, overall
there was minimal support for the proposed perspective. The positive
influence of Black inmates on the staff assault rate was the only

importation factor that consistently produced a significant effect in the predicted direction. Furthermore, the ratio of White-to-Black staff had no effect on the staff assault rate in 1990 and 1995 (see Tables 6.4 and 6.6, model 5). The 1995 analysis offered the strongest support for the Black rage perspective. In the 1995 analysis, the percentage of Black inmates and the percentage of Black staff both produced significant effects in the direction that would support the proposed theory of Black rage. While the theory of Black rage appears to offer little to no improvement in our ability to explain staff assaults when assessing data nationally, perhaps the model is more significant within various regions of the United States. An essential argument of the Black rage theory is that the history of racism plays an imperative role in the production of violence in American prisons. Furthermore, since this history has traditionally varied across regions of the U.S., analyzing the census data collectively may potentially mask significant regional effects concerning the proposed paradigm. To explore this possibility, the discussion that follows dissects each data sample according to region, and estimates the effects of each of the theoretical perspectives on the staff assault rate.

Staff Assault Rates Across Region and Time

Southeast Region

Table 6.8 presents the analogue standardized TOBIT coefficients (ASTC) and the estimated effect sizes for the independent variables on both the censored and non-censored observations for the Southeast region across each data sample.[8] In the Southeast region, the inmate assault rate was the most significant factor in terms of predicting staff violence (based on the ASTC values). Each additional increase in the inmate assault rate increased the staff assault rate for non-censored observations by 0.17 in 1984, by 0.58 in 1990, and by 0.64 in 1995. In addition, being maximum-security significantly increased the staff assault rate by 5.33 in 1990 and by 2.44 in 1995. Various factors from each of the three paradigms fell in and out of significance across the three years. The most consistent finding was that housing inmates exclusively in single-cell arrangements resulted in a 1.91 increase in the staff assault rate in 1984, and a 2.04 increase in 1995.

Counter to the theory of Black rage, many of the coefficient signs in the Southeast were in directions opposite to prediction by the theory. For instance, contrary to the cumulative analysis in the previous tables, the percent of Black inmates had no effect on the staff assault rate in the Southeast. In fact, all of the coefficients for the percent of Black inmates were negative. Although the coefficients were not significant, this would suggest that the higher the percentage of Black inmates, the lower the staff assault rate. Even more, the percentage of Black staff in 1990 significantly increased the staff assault rate, and the coefficient for 1984 was also positive, however not significant. The ratio of White-to-Black staff continued to have no effect on the staff assault rate. The estimated effect size for this variable across each year was not significantly different from zero.

Table 6.8 - Independent Variable Effects on Staff Assault Rates –
Southeast Region

Control Variables	Non-censored Cases						Censored Cases		
	1984 Sample		1990 Sample		1995 Sample		1984	1990	1995
	ASTC	Effect	ASTC	Effect	ASTC	Effect	Effect	Effect	Effect
Inmate Assault Rate	0.34***	0.17	0.40***	0.58	0.76***	0.64	1.17	0.04	2.38
Security Level	-0.10	-0.62	0.34***	5.33	0.37***	2.44	-4.24	0.35	9.09
Deprivation Variables									
Cell Type	0.24**	1.91	-0.01	-0.23	0.19**	2.04	13.04	-0.02	7.60
Crowding Level	0.16	0.03	0.18	0.07	0.17*	0.03	0.18	0.00	0.10
Deprivation Score	0.23**	0.20	0.05	0.09	0.01	0.01	1.33	0.01	0.05
Management Variables									
Percent CO'S	0.32**	0.08	-0.02	-0.01	-0.02	-0.01	0.57	0.00	-0.03
Male-to-Female CO's	0.16	0.02	-0.27*	-0.16	-0.13	-0.06	0.15	-0.01	-0.22
Index - Racial Var.	0.29	0.04	-0.42**	-0.14	0.10	0.02	0.27	-0.01	0.06
Importation Variables									
Percent Black Inmates	-0.14	-0.02	-0.05	-0.02	-0.03	-0.01	-0.17	0.00	-0.02
Percent Black Staff	0.06	0.01	0.36**	0.12	-0.15	-0.02	0.07	0.01	-0.07
White-to-Black Staff	-0.03	0.00	-0.06	-0.01	0.10	0.01	-0.02	0.00	0.04

* = ASTC Significant at $\alpha = 0.05$ ** = ASTC Significant at $\alpha = 0.01$
*** = ASTC Significant at $\alpha = 0.001$

Based on the log-likelihood ratios for the individual paradigm models (see Appendix C, Table 4), across each year, the deprivation variables provided the largest contribution to our ability to explain variation in staff assault rates in the Southeast. Other than the control variables, the deprivation factors were also the only variables with a noticeable impact on the probability of a staff assault for the censored observations. For instance, in 1984, single-cell arrangements increased the probability of a staff assault by 13.04 percent and by 7.60 percent in 1995. In addition, for 1984, each additional increase in the deprivation score produced a 1.33 percent higher probability of a staff assault. In which case, facilities under federal court order for all ten conditions of confinement that comprised the deprivation score had a 13.3 percent higher probability of experiencing a staff assault.

West Region

Table 6.9 provides regional analysis for both the censored and non-censored observations for the West region across each data sample. Unlike in the Southeast, the inmate assault rate and security level had minimal effects on the staff assault rate among the non-censored cases, with the exception of the slightly significant coefficients observed for 1995. There were no consistently significant factors for any of the three paradigms across the three years of analysis. The most significant factor persistently changed throughout the West across years. In 1984, the most significant factor was the ratio of male-to-female correctional officers; in 1990, the deprivation score was most important; and in 1995, the index of racial variation was most significant.

Based on the log-likelihood ratios for the individual models (see Appendix C, Table 4), there were two important theoretical findings in the West. First, the log-likelihood values were relatively low in comparison to all other regions across each year. This suggests a poor model fit between the variables considered in the present study and the ability to explain variation in staff assault rates observed in the West. Thus, although there were sporadic significant findings, overall in the West, there were other, non-included factors more important than those considered in the current analysis. Second, despite the lower log-likelihood values, the deprivation model was the most significant paradigm within each year. Recall this perspective was also superior in the findings from the Southeast region.

While the two control variables had no impact on staff violence for the non-censored observations, both factors substantially influenced the probability of a staff assault for the censored cases. For instance, in 1995, each additional increase in the inmate assault rate increased the likelihood of a staff assault by 1.85 percent, and being maximum-security increased the chances of staff assault by 18.42 percent. In addition, for 1995, cell type dramatically increased the potential for a staff assault among facilities in the West. Housing inmates exclusively in single-cell arrangements increased the probability of a staff assault by 33.30 percent. The increasing percentage of inmates housed in single-cell arrangements from 1984 to 1995 in the West region partially explains the fluctuation in the effect of the cell type variable. Other factors with consistently noticeable influences on the probability of a staff assault included: deprivation score, ratio of male-to-female correctional officers, and the percentage of Black inmates.

Table 6.9 - Independent Variable Effects on Staff Assault Rates –
West Region

Control Variables	Non-censored Cases						Censored Cases		
	1984 Sample		1990 Sample		1995 Sample		1984	1990	1995
	ASTC	Effect	ASTC	Effect	ASTC	Effect	Effect	Effect	Effect
Inmate Assault Rate	0.38	0.11	0.10	0.03	0.43 *	0.33	3.43	0.97	1.85
Security Level	-0.22	-0.66	-0.11	-0.40	0.38 *	3.25	-20.15	-11.98	18.42
Deprivation Variables									
Cell Type	-0.04	-0.11	-0.07	-0.25	0.66 ***	5.88	-3.33	-7.38	33.30
Crowding Level	0.27	0.01	0.35	0.03	-0.15	-0.02	0.45	0.87	-0.12
Deprivation Score	0.10	0.04	0.53 **	0.26	0.03	0.05	1.14	7.65	0.26
Management Variables									
Percent CO'S	-0.49	-0.04	-0.15	-0.01	-0.02	0.00	-1.18	-0.35	-0.02
Male-to-Female CO's	0.56 **	0.07	0.23	0.05	-0.22	-0.18	1.98	1.49	-1.02
Index - Racial Var.	0.56	0.03	0.06	0.00	-0.79 **	-0.10	1.07	0.10	-0.58
Importation Variables									
Percent Black Inmates	0.32	0.03	0.08	0.01	0.65 **	0.20	1.01	0.26	1.14
Percent Black Staff	-0.11	-0.02	-0.11	-0.02	0.40	0.16	-0.57	-0.56	0.90
White-to-Black Staff	0.27	0.01	-0.04	0.00	-0.10	-0.01	0.40	-0.05	-0.03

* = ASTC Significant at $\alpha = 0.05$ ** = ASTC Significant at $\alpha = 0.01$
*** = ASTC Significant at $\alpha = 0.00$

The analysis for the West region failed to present conclusive evidence to support the proposed theory of Black rage. The percentage of Black inmates had a positive impact on the staff assault rate; however, this effect was only significant in 1995. Furthermore, while the percentage of Black staff had a decreasing effect on the staff assault rate in 1984 and 1990, this factor had a noteworthy and positive impact on the staff assault rate in 1995 for both the censored and non-censored observations. For example, each additional increase in the percentage of Black staff increased the staff assault rate by 0.20 among the non-censored cases, and increased the probability of a staff assault by 0.90 among the censored observations in 1995. Hence, having 50 percent Black prison staff increased the raw staff assault rate by 10, and increased the probability of experiencing a staff assault by 45 percent. The ratio of White-to-Black staff continued its trend of non-relevance given the effect values of 0.01, 0.00, and -0.01 across the three years, respectively. Moreover, the log-likelihood ratios for the Black rage variables (importation model) were the lowest of each theoretical perspective across all three years (see Appendix C, Table 4).

Northeast Region

Table 6.10 presents the data findings for the censored and non-censored observations for facilities located in the Northeast region of the U.S. The inmate assault rate significantly increased the staff assault rate among the non-censored cases in 1990 and in 1995. Although the effect was not significant, in 1984, increasing the inmate assault rate tended to decrease the staff assault rate. The impact of security level was only significant in 1995, where being maximum-security increased the staff assault rate by 4.53. Beyond the control variables, there were very few significant effects observed among the factors used to operationalize the three theoretical perspectives on prison violence. Much like the analysis for the West, there were no consistently significant factors across years in the Northeast region. Among the independent variables, the most explanatory factor was cell type in 1984, the percentage of Black staff in 1990, and index of racial variation in 1995. In terms of which theoretical paradigm best improved the ability to explain variance in staff assault rates, there were two dominant perspectives. The deprivation model provided the best fit in 1984 and 1995 for the Northeast region, while the log-likelihood ratio for the importation model in 1990 was slightly higher than that for both the management and deprivation perspectives.

For the censored observations, four factors consistently produced substantial influences on the probability of experiencing a staff assault. The impact of the inmate assault rate went from noticeably decreasing the likelihood of a staff assault in 1984 to noticeably increasing the chances of a staff assault in 1995. Along the same lines, the influence of security level changed drastically from 1984 to 1995; for example, in 1984, maximum-security prisons had an 8.19 percent higher probability of a staff assault versus a 39.64 percent higher probability in 1995. The pattern displayed by the cell type variable was just the opposite. In 1984, housing inmates exclusively in single-cell arrangements increased the odds of staff assault by 36.33 percent, while this same factor decreased the odds by 9.83 percent in 1995. Lastly, increasing the number of conditions for which a facility was under federal court order consistently increased the probability of a staff assault among the censored observations. The drastic reduction in the maximum deprivation score across years in the Northeast region partially explains the large effect for the deprivation score observed in 1990. In both 1984 and 1990, the maximum deprivation score obtained in the Northeast was 10, while in 1990, the maximum obtained was 4. In which case, a facility under federal court order for 4 conditions in 1990 had a 63.88 percent higher probability of experiencing a staff assault.

Table 6.10 - Independent Variable Effects on Staff Assault Rates –
Northeast Region

Control Variables	Non-censored Cases						Censored Cases		
	1984 Sample		1990 Sample		1995 Sample		1984	1990	1995
	ASTC	Effect	ASTC	Effect	ASTC	Effect	Effect	Effect	Effect
Inmate Assault Rate	-0.29	-0.17	0.68***	0.42	0.30**	0.35	-1.59	3.48	3.05
Security Level	0.11	0.89	0.24	2.11	0.48***	4.53	8.19	17.28	39.64
Deprivation Variables									
Cell Type	0.58***	3.96	0.14	1.15	-0.11	-1.12	36.33	9.42	-9.83
Crowding Level	-0.29	-0.04	-0.03	0.00	0.16	0.02	-0.39	-0.03	0.20
Deprivation Score	0.25	0.37	0.31**	1.95	0.15	0.36	3.43	15.97	3.11
Management Variables									
Percent CO'S	0.14	0.04	0.29	0.13	-0.02	-0.01	0.39	1.02	-0.07
Male-to-Female CO's	0.24	0.03	-0.03	-0.01	0.12	0.02	0.24	-0.05	0.14
Index - Racial Var.	0.48	0.07	0.32	0.05	0.29	0.06	0.61	0.41	0.52
Importation Variables									
Percent Black Inmates	0.09	0.01	0.38**	0.08	0.11	0.03	0.13	0.65	0.23
Percent Black Staff	-0.28	-0.05	-0.56*	-0.10	-0.12	-0.04	-0.42	-0.81	-0.32
White-to-Black Staff	0.02	0.00	0.02	0.00	-0.02	0.00	0.01	0.01	-0.01

* = ASTC Significant at $\alpha = 0.05$ ** = ASTC Significant at $\alpha = 0.01$
*** = ASTC Significant at $\alpha = 0.00$

The regional comparisons observed in the Northeast for 1990 offered the strongest support for the Black rage theory. In 1990, the percentage of Black inmates significantly increased the staff assault rate while the percentage of Black staff significantly decreased the rate of violence against prison staff. In addition, next to the inmate assault rate, the percentage of Black staff had the largest effect on the staff assault rate based on the standardized coefficient values. The coefficient signs for both the percentage of Black inmates and the percentage of Black staff were in directions supporting the Black rage theory, however, only the 1990 coefficients were significant. As found in the previous regions, the ratio of White-to-Black staff had essentially no impact on staff violence for both the censored and non-censored observations. The percentage of Black inmates and Black staff had noticeable influences on the probability of experiencing a staff assault for the censored observations in 1990. For instance, if a facility in 1990 had 50 percent Black inmates, this increased their odds of a staff assault by 32.5 percent. Likewise, if a facility had 50 percent Black staff, this decreased the odds of a staff assault by 40.5 percent. For each year, among the censored observations, the effects of Black staff more than cancelled the positive influence of Black inmates on the probability of a staff assault; however, this negating effect progressively reduced over time.

Midwest Region

Table 6.11 provides cumulative model summaries for the censored and non-censored observations from the Midwest region. Concerning the control variables, the inmate assault rate remained highly significant across all three years of analysis, while security level was significant in 1990 and 1995. The effect of the inmate assault rate substantially increased the staff assault rate in 1990 and 1995. For instance, if a 1995 facility had an inmate violence rate of 25 inmate-on-inmate assaults per 100 inmates, their predicted staff assault rate would be 21 assaults per 100 staff members (25 * 0.84). Moreover, being maximum-security increased the staff assault rate by 5.70 in 1990 and by 3.31 in 1995.

There were two consistent findings among the variables operationalizing the three theoretical paradigms. The IRV significantly increased the staff assault rate in both 1990 and 1995. Although not significant, the IRV coefficient for 1984 was also relatively high and positive. All three years suggest that as prison staff in the Midwest increased racial diversity, the staff assault rate subsequently increased. One should note that the Midwest consistently had the lowest degree of racial diversity among prison staff (see Table 6.1). In which case, in areas with a high degree of staff diversity (i.e. major cities), there were also likely to be a high percentage of Black inmates who significantly increased the staff assault rate across all three years of analysis.

The influence of Black inmates on the staff assault rate was greatest in 1990, where for instance, if a facility had 50 percent Black inmates, based on this fact alone, their predicted rate of staff violence was 9 assaults per 100 staff members (50 * 0.18). Along with the positive effect of Black inmates, there was also a negative effect of Black staff on the staff assault rate within the Midwest; however, only the effect for 1990 was significant. In 1990, the effect of the Black staff essentially cancelled out the effect of Black inmates on the staff assault rate. The relatively equal estimated effect sizes suggest that if facilities maintained equal Black representation within the staff and inmate populations, they could negate the positive influence of Black inmates on staff assaults. For example, if a 1990 facility had 50 percent Black staff, this would have lowered their predicted staff assault rate by 8.5, which essentially cancels the predicted staff assault rate for facilities with 50 percent Black inmates. The sign of the importation coefficients were uniformly in the direction suggested by the proposed theory of Black rage. However, once again, the percentage of Black inmates was the only factor to continuously reach significance across all three years, and the ratio of White-to-Black staff continued to have a less than noticeable effect on the staff assault rate.

Table 6.11 - Independent Variable Effects on Staff Assault Rates – Midwest Region

Control Variables	Non-censored Cases						Censored Cases		
	1984 Sample		1990 Sample		1995 Sample		1984	1990	1995
	ASTC	Effect	ASTC	Effect	ASTC	Effect	Effect	Effect	Effect
Inmate Assault Rate	0.44 **	0.29	0.72 ***	0.79	0.61 ***	0.84	0.19	2.84	6.03
Security Level	0.10	0.79	0.49 ***	5.70	0.41 ***	3.31	0.51	20.58	23.80
Deprivation Variables									
Cell Type	0.19	1.51	0.10	1.03	0.09	0.76	0.97	3.74	5.44
Crowding Level	-0.07	-0.01	-0.25 *	-0.05	0.01	0.00	-0.01	-0.18	0.00
Deprivation Score	0.28	0.46	-0.14	-0.36	0.07	0.14	0.30	-1.30	1.01
Management Variables									
Percent CO'S	-0.48 **	-0.14	-0.16	-0.07	-0.08	-0.03	-0.09	-0.25	-0.24
Male-to-Female CO's	-0.24	-0.04	0.12	0.10	0.21	0.17	-0.03	0.36	1.25
Index - Racial Var.	0.57	0.12	0.60 **	0.17	0.55 *	0.10	0.08	0.60	0.75
Importation Variables									
Percent Black Inmates	0.57 *	0.11	0.65 ***	0.18	0.26 *	0.06	0.07	0.64	0.40
Percent Black Staff	-0.16	-0.05	-0.55 *	-0.17	-0.39	-0.10	-0.04	-0.61	-0.68
White-to-Black Staff	0.38	0.03	0.20	0.02	0.15	0.01	0.02	0.08	0.08

* = ASTC Significant at α = 0.05   ** = ASTC Significant at α = 0.01
*** = ASTC Significant at α = 0.00

The percentage of Black staff and Black inmates also significantly influenced the probability of a staff assault among the censored observations. For example, if a 1990 facility had 50 percent Black inmates, this fact alone increased their probability of a staff assault by 32 percent. Furthermore, if this same 1990 facility had 50 percent Black staff, their probability of a staff assault reduced by 30.5 percent. Across all three years, the effect of Black staff among the censored observations approximately cancelled the influence of Black inmates on the likelihood of a staff assault. In fact, in 1995, the decreasing effect of Black staff surpassed the increasing effect of Black inmates.

Other factors also produced noticeable influences on the probability of a staff assault for the censored observations. The inmate assault rate, security level, cell type, and the index of racial variation, regularly increased the odds of staff assault across at least two of the three years in question. Although the effect sizes for the 1990 and 1995 indexes of racial variation appeared rather small, they were actually quite significant. Consider for instance that the average Midwest facility in 1995 had an IRV value of 24.28, which implies that this variable alone increased the likelihood of staff assault by 18.21 percent.

Breakdown of the Black Rage Theory Across Region and Time

Black Inmates

Dissecting the study samples according to region revealed interesting camouflaged patterns unobserved when analyzing the data collectively. In the collective data analysis, the percentage of Black inmates had a positive influence on the staff assault rate across all three years. However, regional analysis further revealed that the positive influence of Black inmates on the staff assault rate, for non-censored observations, primarily resulted from facilities located in the Midwest. For instance, in 1990, the overall effect of Black inmates for the entire sample increased the staff assault rate by 0.07, whereas in the Midwest, Black inmates increased the staff assault rate by 0.18. Thus, based on the entire sample, if a facility had 50 percent Black inmates, this fact would increase the staff violence rate by 3.5. On the contrary, a facility with 50 percent Black inmates in the Midwest had an increase of 9 in their staff assault rate. Furthermore, the percentage of Black inmates also significantly increased staff violence in the Northeast in 1990 and in the West in 1995. The influence of Black inmates in the West for 1995 had the largest effect of Black inmates on staff violence rates among all levels of analysis. Whereas a one-unit increase in the percentage of Black inmates increased the staff assault rate by 0.03 overall, this same change increased the staff assault rate by 0.20 in the West.

In direct contradiction to theory predictions, the percentage of Black inmates consistently lowered the staff assault rate in the Southeast. This finding was particularly interesting given the large representation of Black inmates in the Southeast. For example, in 1995, the Southeast had an average prison population that was 60.08 percent Black, while the West had an average of 21.73 percent Black inmates. Based on the descriptive statistics, one could argue that the higher percentage of Black prison staff in the Southeast explains the decreasing effect of Black inmates on the staff assault rate. However, for two of the analysis years, the percentage of Black staff increased the staff assault rate, and the effect for 1990 was significant at $\alpha = 0.01$. Therefore, it appears that in the Southeast region, the Black/White dynamic between the staff and inmate population does not directly influence prison violence. Chapter VIII provides possible explanations for the observed patterns in the Southeast region.

There were also regional differences in the effect of Black inmates on the probability of a staff assault among the censored observations. Although the West consistently had the lowest percentage of Black inmates (see Table 6.1), in both 1984 and 1995, the percentage of Black inmates significantly increased the odds of staff assault. For instance, each additional unit increase in the percentage of Black inmates increased the likelihood of a staff assault by 1.14 percent. Black inmates also produced noticeable increases in the odds of experiencing a staff assault in the Northeast and Midwest across years, especially in 1990. Drawing on both the censored and non-censored observations, the influence of Black inmates necessary to support the proposed theory of Black rage was greatest in the Midwest followed by Northeast.

Black Prison Staff

A major contention of the theory of Black rage is that Black prison staff would have a "calming" effect on the violent tendencies of Black inmates, given that much of the Black inmates' anger and rage stems from the system of White oppression. In the data analysis conducted using the collective samples, all three of the years showed a decreasing effect of Black prison staff on the staff assault rate; however, only the effect observed in 1995 was significant. Regional analysis of the influence of Black staff on the staff violence level revealed that the significance of this factor in 1995 was largely due to facilities located in the Midwest. Collectively in 1995, a one-unit increase in the percentage of Black staff decreased the staff assault rate by 0.03, while in the Midwest, this same change decreased the staff assault rate by 0.10. Thus, in 1995, a facility with 50 percent Black staff in the Midwest would have reduced their staff violence rate by 5 assaults, while overall (nationwide), the rate would have only gone down by 1.5 assaults. The Northeast region also had noticeable reductions in the staff assault rate based on the percentage of Black staff.

In terms of the censored observations, the percentage of Black staff also had the largest decrease on the likelihood of a staff assault in the Northeast and Midwest regions. Whereas collectively, across all three years, a one-unit increase in the percentage of Black staff decreased the staff assault rate by an average of 0.15 percent; however, in the Northeast and Midwest, the average reductions were much larger. The average reduction associated with a one-unit increase in the percentage of Black staff was 0.52 percent in the Northeast and 0.44 percent in the Midwest. Thus, when examined collectively, if a typical prison had 50 percent Black staff, this would have decreased their average probability of experiencing a staff assault by 7.5 percent. In contrast, a prison with 50 percent Black staff would have experienced an average decrease of 26 percent and 22 percent in the probability of a staff assault in the Northeast and Midwest regions, respectively. Among the censored observations in the Southeast, the percentage of Black staff had a minimal influence in the probability of experiencing a staff assault. In the West, the percentage of Black staff had a noticeable decreasing influence in 1984 and in 1990, but a highly significant increasing influence in 1995. Thus, in terms of the censored and non-censored observations, the Northeast and the Midwest were the only regions that consistently showed a decreasing effect of Black staff on the staff assault rate. These were also the only two regions to find a significant reduction.

Ratio of White-to-Black Staff

The ratio of White-to-Black staff did not produce a significant effect among the censored or non-censored observations in both the collective sample and regional data analysis. Despite the large differences in the relative number of Black prison staff across regions, this factor was unrelated to prison violence. However, the significant effects, both positive and negative, observed for the percentage of Black staff suggests that the sheer number of Black staff influences prison violence more so than the relative numbers.

Summary

When analyzing the data sets collectively, the best support for the theory of Black rage appears in 1995. Although the final cumulative models from each analysis year yielded coefficient signs that were supportive of the Black rage theory, only the 1995 data sample produced a significant effect for the percentage of Black inmates and Black staff simultaneously. Further regional analysis demonstrated that prison violence in the Northeast and Midwest perhaps adheres more to the predictions of the Black rage theory than in the Southeast or West regions. The fact that the data analysis showed partial support for the Black rage theory in the two regions possessing the least amount of racial diversity among the staff populations was not surprising.[9] Across each year, both the Northeast and Midwest had the lowest values on the index of racial variation. For example, additional descriptive statistics (not presented) revealed that in 1995, the average percentage of White staff was 65.65 in the Southeast, 72.24 in the West, 86.41 in the Northeast, and 86.21 in the Midwest. The 1984 and 1990 data samples displayed similar patterns in terms of the distribution of White prison staff across regions. Thus, with more minority representation within the staff populations of the Southeast and the West regions, there is a lower degree of racial hostility between the staff and inmate populations. On the contrary, the predominantly White prison staffs of the Northeast and Midwest serve as constant symbols of oppression and domination to the enraged Black inmate. In which case, the violence producing process outlined by the theory of Black rage is more likely to come to fruition.

[1] Ovid, quoted in *Statistics* by Richard Larsen and Morris L. Marx (1990: 651)

[2] Voltaire, quoted in Larsen and Marx (1990: 504)

[3] Anon, quoted in Larsen and Marx (1990: 578)

[4] To verify this fact, I estimated all of the TOBIT models using ordinary least squares regression and critically assessed the changes in the variance inflation factors (VIF). Based on the values of the VIF's multicollinearity was not a problem in any of the regression models.

[5] The coefficient of determination, also known as R^2, is simply the square of an obtained Pearson correlation coefficient (r). The coefficient of determination measures the proportion of the variation in Y that is explained by X (Healey 2002).

[6] I estimated the TOBIT models using version 3.0 of the statistical software package, E-Views.

[7] See page 166 in Chapter V for a brief description of the conversion process.

[8] Tables 6.8 through 6.11 only include Model 5 from each respective year. Although I sequentially estimated all of the models as in Tables 6.2 through 6.7, to present the information in a similar fashion for each region and year would have required 24 additional tables instead of 4.

[9] What was surprising was the fact that the Southeast turned out to be the region with the most diversity among its prison staff as oppose to the least.

CHAPTER VII

Institutional Changes and Prison Violence

Including the initial level of the dependent variable is seldom justified on statistical grounds, although it may be justified on theoretical grounds.[1]

In general, whenever the present state of the dependent variable is determined directly from past states, inclusion of the lagged dependent variable in these situations is necessary to specify the model properly.[2]

Despite some powerful rhetoric questioning the value and validity of change measurement, interest in how best to represent and measure change continues unabated.[3]

Chapter Objective

When examining variation in the independent and dependent variables *across* institutions, the analysis in Chapter VI offered patterns indicating the relevance of the Black rage perspective. However, because cross-sectional designs are inherently static, Chapter VI does not provide an answer to the question: "How well does change in the independent variables explain subsequent changes in the dependent variable *within* each institution?" To answer such a question requires a longitudinal research design with multiple observation points on the same sample of subjects. By merging the 1990 and 1995 versions of the census, I was able to create a two-wave panel data set in order to attempt to answer the proposed question. The analysis in Chapter VII expands the statistical models presented in the previous chapter by incorporating the "change dynamic" into the empirical assessment of the Black rage theory. With measurement of the independent and dependent variables at two points in time, the current chapter estimates four models of change to detail precisely the factors significantly associated with increases or decreases in staff assault rates.

The four estimated change models reflect a combination of elements from the method of first differences and the static score approach. The first equation measured the influence of the pure first differences among the independent variables (ΔX) on the subsequent change in the staff assault rate from 1990 to 1995 (ΔY). The second equation used the value of the independent variables in 1990 (X_1) to predict the change in the staff assault rate across the two periods (ΔY). The third equation modeled change using the lagged effects of the independent variables (X_1) to predict staff assault rates in 1995 (Y_2). Lastly, the fourth equation modeled change using the instantaneous effects of the independent variables (X_2) to predict changes in the 1995 staff assault rate (Y_2). Equations 2-4 also included the lagged effects of the dependent variable (Y_1) among the control factors. Furthermore, given the nature of the dependent variable in equations 1 and 2, the models were estimated using ordinary least squares regression. In contrast, the large percentage of facilities with zero staff assaults in 1995 resulted in a highly skewed distribution of the dependent variable in equations 3 and 4. To correct for the non-normal distribution of Y_2, I estimated the models using the TOBIT procedure. Continuing to explore the potential regional significance of the Black rage perspective, I estimated each of the four change models, first on the entire sample, followed by an examination within the four regions.

Descriptive Statistics

Tables 7.1(a-c) provide three levels of descriptive statistics for the 533 facilities included in the panel data set; average values in 1990 and 1995, and the average change score values. Roughly 49 percent of the facilities in the panel sample were located in the Southeast, and roughly 25 percent of the sample prisons were maximum-security.[4] Not presented in Tables 7.1(a-c) are the frequency distributions for inmate housing arrangements. In 1990, approximately 19 percent of the sampled facilities housed inmates exclusively in single-cell arrangements, while in 1995 the number decreased to roughly 14 percent. The average staff assault rates for 1990 and 1995 were virtually identical, as reflected in the average change score of 0.01 for the staff assault rate across the two periods. In both years, there were approximately four assaults per 100 high-risk staff members.

In terms of the variables measuring the Black rage perspective, on average, the percentage of Black inmates and Black staff increased from 1990 to 1995. There was an average increase of 2.27 percent for Black inmates and 1.35 percent for Black prison staff. Examination of the individual region columns further revealed that the Southeast had the greatest increase in the percentage of Black inmates, while the Northeast was the only region to show a reduction in the percentage of Black inmates. The Southeast also had the largest increase in the percentage of Black prison staff and was the only region to show growth in the Black staff population across the two periods. Despite the absolute growth of Black staff, their numbers relative to the population of White prison staff remained roughly the same from 1990 to 1995 (Δ White-to-Black staff = 0.04).[5]

Table 7.1(a) - Descriptive Statistics for the 1990-1995 Merged Data Set: 1990 Values

Variables	Overall Sample	Region			
		South	West	Northeast	Midwest
	N=533	N=263	N=70	N=85	N=115
1990 Staff Assault Rate	4.01	3.11	2.78	5.38	5.83
1990 Inmate Assault Rate	2.83	2.81	2.24	3.48	2.78
1990 Percent Black Inmates	48.39	56.71	23.15	46.08	46.44
1990 Percent Black Staff	17.54	26.85	6.68	8.86	9.26
1990 White-to-Black Staff	21.66	10.51	25.10	49.43	26.39
1990 Average Crowding	10.82	4.78	6.84	23.63	17.60
1990 Deprivation Score	1.43	2.25	1.14	0.16	0.67
1990 Male-to-Female CO's	12.17	10.76	8.25	24.12	7.54
1990 % Correctional Officers	66.42	69.85	65.65	64.99	60.10
1990 IRV	35.50	43.30	42.13	22.03	23.57

Table 7.1(b) - Descriptive Statistics for the 1990-1995 Merged Data Set: 1995 Values

Variables	Overall Sample	Region			
		South	West	Northeast	Midwest
	N=533	N=263	N=70	N=85	N=115
1995 Staff Assault Rate	4.02	3.33	2.67	5.15	5.60
1995 Inmate Assault Rate	2.61	2.34	3.68	3.04	2.27
1995 Percent Black Inmates	50.66	59.96	21.96	46.62	49.85
1995 Percent Black Staff	18.89	29.95	6.50	7.98	9.22
1995 White-to-Black Staff	23.41	10.73	34.44	50.70	28.81
1995 Average Crowding	15.30	8.19	12.49	21.25	28.90
1995 Deprivation Score	1.03	1.38	0.71	0.62	0.71
1995 Male-to-Female CO's	11.26	8.15	7.00	29.64	7.03
1995 % Correctional Officers	71.97	73.58	74.01	71.28	67.54
1995 IRV	35.05	43.77	40.30	20.28	22.84

Table 7.1(c) - Descriptive Statistics for the 1990-1995
Merged Data Set: Change Score Values (Δ)

Variables	Overall Sample	Region			
		South	West	Northeast	Midwest
	N=533	N=263	N=70	N=85	N=115
Δ Staff Assault Rate	0.01	0.22	-0.11	-0.23	-0.23
Δ Inmate Assault Rate	-0.22	-0.47	1.44	-0.45	-0.52
Δ Percent Black Inmates	2.27	3.26	-1.19	0.54	3.41
Δ Percent Black Staff	1.35	3.10	-0.18	-0.88	-0.05
Δ White-to-Black Staff	0.04	-1.30	-0.98	-0.03	4.34
Δ Average Crowding	4.48	3.41	5.64	-2.38	11.30
Δ Deprivation Score	-0.40	-0.87	-0.43	0.46	0.04
Δ Male-to-Female CO's	-1.38	-4.11	-1.63	5.46	-0.98
Δ % Correctional Officers	5.55	3.73	8.35	6.29	7.44
Δ IRV	-0.44	0.48	-1.83	-1.74	-0.73

Table 7.2 presents the bivariate correlation matrix for the independent variables and the staff assault measures.[6] There was a moderate positive correlation between the 1990 and 1995 staff assault rates (Y_1 and Y_2). Because the correlation between Y_1 and Y_2 was relatively low, the reliability coefficient for the change score (ΔY) was somewhat high (0.6051). As mentioned in Chapter V, the correlation between Y_1 and Y_2 and the reliability of the change score (ΔY) vary inversely.

Thus, the higher the correlation between the individual components, the lower the reliability of the change score. Therefore, to maximize the reliability for a change score requires zero correlation between the individual components, which raises questions about whether Y_1 and Y_2 are in fact measuring the same concept. The correlation between Y_1 and Y_2 in the current study was at the optimum level. The coefficient was high enough to ensure that the individual components were measuring the same concept, but low enough to obtain more than adequate reliability for the change score on the staff assault rate.

Table 7.2(a) - Correlations for the Independent Variables and the Staff Assault Measures: 1990 Values

1990 Variable Values	1990 Staff Assault Rate (Y_1)	1995 Staff Assault Rate (Y_2)	Δ Staff Assault Rate $(ΔY)$
1990 Staff Assault Rate	1.000	0.438	**-0.622**
1995 Staff Assault Rate	**0.438**	1.000	**0.432**
Δ Staff Assault Rate	**-0.622**	**0.432**	1.000
Region	-0.113	-0.099	0.027
1990 Inmate Assault Rate	**0.328**	0.115	**-0.229**
1990 Security Level	**0.315**	**0.313**	-0.043
1990 Cell Type	**0.209**	**0.236**	-0.003
1990 Average Crowding Level	-0.023	0.076	0.090
1990 Deprivation Score	0.003	-0.014	-0.015
1990 Percent Correctional Officers	-0.087	-0.019	0.071
1990 Ratio of Male-to-Female CO's	0.003	0.039	0.031
1990 Index of Racial Variation	0.058	0.030	-0.032
1990 Percent Black Inmates	**0.141**	**0.146**	-0.015
1990 Percent Inmates	0.105	0.019	-0.089

Bold Coefficients Significant at $\alpha = 0.001$

Table 7.2(b) - Correlations for the Independent Variables and the Staff Assault Measures: 1995 Values

1995 Variable Values	1990 Staff Assault Rate (Y_1)	1995 Staff Assault Rate (Y_2)	Δ Staff Assault Rate $(ΔY)$
1995 Inmate Assault Rate	**0.190**	**0.424**	**0.179**
1995 Security Level	**0.301**	**0.363**	0.014
1995 Cell Type	**0.193**	**0.197**	-0.022
1995 Average Crowding Level	-0.008	0.026	0.031
1995 Deprivation Score	0.031	0.052	0.014
1995 Percent Correctional Officers	0.028	0.012	-0.038
1995 Ratio of Male-to-Female CO's	0.032	0.052	0.012
1995 Index of Racial Variation	0.039	0.027	-0.015
1995 Percent Black Inmates	0.114	0.109	-0.019
1995 Percent Black Staff	0.051	0.012	-0.041

Bold Coefficients Significant at $\alpha = 0.001$

Table 7.2(c) - Correlations for the Independent Variables and the Staff
Assault Measures: Change Score Values

Δ Score (Δ = 1995 Value – 1990 Value)	1990 Staff Assault Rate (Y_1)	1995 Staff Assault Rate (Y_2)	Δ Staff Assault Rate (ΔY)
Δ Inmate Assault Rate	**-0.163**	**0.201**	**0.339**
Δ Decreasing Security	0.009	-0.098	-0.095
Δ Increasing Security	-0.093	-0.049	0.051
Δ To Multiple Cell Arrangements	0.030	0.060	0.022
Δ To Single-cell Arrangements	-0.035	-0.042	-0.002
Δ Average Crowding Level	0.015	-0.049	-0.057
Δ Deprivation Score	0.022	0.057	0.027
Δ Percent Correctional Officers	**0.142**	0.010	-0.133
Δ Ratio of Male-to-Female CO's	0.057	0.048	-0.018
Δ Index of Racial Variation	-0.055	-0.010	0.046
Δ Percent Black Inmates	-0.044	-0.063	-0.011
Δ Percent Black Staff	**-0.140**	-0.017	0.126

Bold Coefficients Significant at $\alpha = 0.001$

Method of First Differences

The first change model examined using the panel data set considered the
direct influence of the change scores for the independent variables on the
subsequent change in the staff assault rate. Table 7.3 presents the
standardized and unstandardized[7] OLS regression coefficients for the
first difference equations estimated using the entire sample. Model 1
illustrates that change in the inmate assault rate from 1990 to 1995 was
the only control variable with a significant influence on the change in the
staff assault rate. Each additional unit increase in the change score for
the inmate assault rate increased the change in the staff assault rate 0.52.
Thus, if a facility experienced a 10-point increase in the inmate assault
rate from 1990 to 1995, their predicted change score for the staff assault
rate would equal 5.2. A change score of 5.2 indicated that the staff
assault rate was 5.2 points higher in 1995.[8] Although not significant,
decreasing the security level (i.e. going from maximum to medium-
security) tended to reduce the change in the staff assault rate, while
increasing the security level had the opposite effect.

Model 2 introduced the change scores for the deprivation variables.
Neither of the deprivation variables produced a significant effect on the
change in the staff assault rate. Collectively, the deprivation factors did
not contribute to the proportion of variance explained in the dependent

variable. The adjusted R^2 value for model 2 was the same as for model 1 (0.11). Unlike the deprivation variables, the management model produced a significant finding concerning changes in the staff assault rate. As indicated by model 3, each additional unit increase in the percentage of correctional officers from 1990 to 1995 decreased the subsequent change in the staff assault rate by 0.10. However, the relatively small effect size required a substantial increase in the percentage of correctional officers to produce a noticeable reduction in the staff assault rate. For instance, a 25-percentage point increase in the population of correctional officers reduced the predicted change score for the staff assault rate by 2.5.

Table 7.3 – Effects of Change in Independent Variable (ΔX) on Change in Staff Assault Rates (ΔY)

Control Variables	Model 1		Model 2		Model 3		Model 4		Model 5	
	b	β	b	β	b	β	b	β	b	β
Δ Inmate Assault Rate	0.52	0.33 ***	0.53	0.33 ***	0.56	0.35 ***	0.52	0.33 ***	0.57	0.36 ***
Δ Decreasing Security	-1.33	-0.04	-1.30	-0.04	-0.49	-0.02	-1.43	-0.05	-0.56	-0.02
Δ Increasing Security	0.92	0.03	0.96	0.04	1.03	0.04	0.91	0.03	1.06	0.04
Deprivation Variables										
Δ To Multiple Cell			0.22	0.01					-0.29	-0.01
Δ To Single-cell			0.31	0.01					0.68	0.02
Δ Crowding Level			-0.02	-0.07					-0.02	-0.06
Δ Deprivation Score			0.09	0.04					0.15	0.06
Management Variables										
Δ Percent CO'S					-0.10	-0.11 **			-0.10	-0.11 *
Δ M-to-F CO's					0.00	0.01			0.01	0.02
Δ IRV					0.03	0.03			0.00	0.00
Importation Variables										
Δ % Black Inmates							-0.01	-0.02	0.03	0.04
Δ % Black Staff							0.16	0.13 ***	0.13	0.10 *
Adjusted R^2 Value	0.11		0.11		0.13		0.13		0.14	

* = Coefficient Significant at α = 0.05   ** = Coefficient Significant at α = 0.01
*** = Coefficient Significant at α = 0.001

Among the variables operationalizing the Black rage perspective, increasing the percentage of Black staff from 1990 to 1995 significantly increased the change in the staff assault rate. This observation directly contradicted the predictions of the Black rage theory. Instead of the predicted "calming effect" of Black staff, model 4 suggests that each additional unit increase in the percentage of Black staff from 1990 to 1995 increased the change score for the staff assault rate by 0.16. However, with the relatively small effect size and the marginal increase in the average percentage of Black staff (see Table 7.1), this factor had a negligible impact on the change in the staff assault rate. Consider that in the Southeast, the region with the largest growth in the Black staff population, this factor only increased the change score for the staff assault rate by 0.50 (3.10 * 0.16).

The cumulative model duplicated the same three significant findings, although the significance levels for the change in the percentage of correctional officers and Black staff decreased considerably. All of the factors from the three perspectives combined explained only 14 percent of the variance in the dependent variable. Since the control model alone explained 11 percent, the management and importation factors added an extra 3 percent to the proportion of variance explained in the dependent variable.[9]

Table 7.4 presents the coefficient values for the first difference models across regions. Increases in the inmate assault rate from 1990 to 1995 produced significant increases in the staff assault rate for each region except the Midwest. The effect of the inmate assault rate was greatest in the Southeast, where each additional unit increase in the change score for the inmate assault rate increased the change in the staff assault rate by 0.65. Lastly, for the control variables, increasing security level significantly increased the change in the staff assault rate in the West.

In terms of the deprivation variables, changes in the deprivation score significantly influenced the change score for the staff assault rate in the West and the Northeast. Thus, from 1990 to 1995, each additional federal court order for a specific condition of confinement increased the change in the staff assault rate by 1.64 in the West and 0.98 in the Northeast. The standardized coefficient value for the deprivation score in the West suggests this factor was the most significant contributor to the change score for the staff assault rate, more so than the inmate assault rate. Despite the significance of the percentage of correctional officers in the entire sample, none of the management variables produced a noticeable impact on the change score for the staff assault rate when examined across regions.

The variables operationalizing the black rage perspective produced only one significant finding: the effect of Black staff in the Midwest. Changes in the percentage of Black inmates did not influence the subsequent change in the staff assault rates across either of the regions. This finding was unexpected given the positive influence of Black inmates on staff violence levels from the cross-sectional models of Chapter VI. Furthermore, the finding from Table 7.3 that increasing the percentage of Black staff significantly increased the change in the staff assault rate only held in the Midwest. While each additional unit increase in the percentage of Black staff overall from 1990 to 1995 increased the change in the staff assault rate by 0.13, in the Midwest this factor increased the change in the staff assault rate by 1.15. Hence, if a Midwest facility increased its percentage of Black staff by 10-points, the resulting change score for the staff assault rate increased by 11.5. However, the percentage of Black staff in the Midwest remained relatively stable from 1990 to 1995, more so than any other region.[10]

Table 7.4 – Effects of Change in Independent Variable (ΔX) on the Change in Staff Assault Rates (ΔY) by Region

Control Variables	Southeast		West		Northeast		Midwest	
	b	β	b	β	b	β	b	β
Δ Inmate Assault Rate	0.65	0.45 ***	0.47	0.40 ***	0.48	0.40 ***	0.49	0.15
Δ Decreasing Security	-0.72	-0.03	17.11	0.32 *	-2.98	-0.08	1.75	0.04
Δ Increasing Security	-0.15	-0.01	1.10	0.03	2.97	0.13	-0.64	-0.01
Deprivation Variables								
Δ To Multiple Cell	-4.22	-0.12	0.83	0.04	-1.13	-0.05	1.83	0.07
Δ To Single-cell	-0.29	-0.01	-1.84	-0.06	3.39	0.09	-0.15	0.00
Δ Crowding Level	0.03	0.07	-0.03	-0.09	-0.01	-0.06	-0.05	-0.14
Δ Deprivation Score	0.04	0.03	1.64	0.51 ***	0.98	0.26 **	-3.31	-0.19
Management Variables								
Δ Percent CO'S	-0.04	-0.05	-0.09	-0.14	-0.04	-0.04	-0.06	-0.05
Δ M-to-F CO's	0.00	0.00	0.25	0.20	0.03	0.07	-0.03	-0.01
Δ IRV	0.04	0.03	-0.07	-0.10	-0.15	-0.17	-0.11	-0.07
Importation Variables								
Δ % Black Inmates	0.00	-0.01	0.05	0.04	0.16	0.19	-0.03	-0.02
Δ % Black Staff	0.06	0.07	-0.08	-0.04	0.32	0.13	1.15	0.39 **
Adjusted R^2 Value	0.19		0.37		0.26		0.04	

* = Coefficient Significant at α = 0.05   ** = Coefficient Significant at α = 0.01
*** = Coefficient Significant at α = 0.001

The adjusted R^2 values indicate tremendous regional variation in the ability of the cumulative model to explain the variance observed in the change scores for staff assault rates. The West displayed the strongest model fit; the factors collectively explained 37 percent of the variance in the dependent variable. The Midwest had the weakest model fit, given that all of the factors combined explained only 4 percent of the variance in change scores for staff assault rates. Appendix D, Table 1, presents the individual paradigm summaries for each respective model. Based on the adjusted R^2 values presented in Appendix D, Table 1, the management variables provided the best model fit for the facilities located in the Southeast, while the deprivation variables provided the best model fit in the West and Northeast regions. Although the cumulative model for the Midwest only produced an adjusted R^2 value of 0.04, the importation model for the Midwest had an adjusted R^2 value of 0.10. In which case, the Black rage variables alone explained more of the variance in the dependent variable than the cumulative model.

Static Score with Lagged Dependent & Independent Variables

Ordinary Least Squares Regression

Although the method of first differences revealed several factors significantly associated with changes in the dependent variable, the failure to account for the influence of Y_1 biased the model findings. As noted by Lord (1963), neglecting to control for Y_1 may produce many variables that relate to the ΔY only because they significantly correlate with Y_1. In the context of the current chapter, any change score for the independent variables highly correlated with the 1990 staff assault rate would produce a misleading effect on the change score for the staff assault rate. Furthermore, Table 7.2(c) illustrated that the change scores for the inmate assault rate, percentage of correctional officers, and the percentage of Black staff, significantly correlated with the 1990 staff assault rate. In which case, one cannot accurately assess the influence of these factors on the change in the staff assault rate without the influence of Y_1 effectively partialed out or held constant statistically (Lord 1963). The second change equation estimated in the current chapter assessed the influence of the independent variables while accounting for the likely influence of Y_1 on the ΔY.

Specifically, the second equation examined the influence of the lagged independent variables (X_1) on the subsequent change in the staff assault rate (ΔY), while controlling for the lagged dependent variable (Y_1). Table 7.5 presents OLS regression coefficients for the second change equation. Model 1 revealed significant effects for the staff assault rate, security level, and region. The higher the staff assault rate in 1990, the lower the subsequent change score for the staff assault rate. Particularly, each additional unit increase in the 1990 staff assault rate reduced the change in the staff assault rate by 0.68. Thus, if a facility had a staff violence rate of 25 assaults per 100 staff members in 1990, their predicted change score for the staff assault rate would equal -17 (25 * -0.68). In order for the predicted change score to equal -17, the 1995 staff violence rate would have to reduce to 8 assaults per 100 staff members. This pattern suggests the presence of regression towards the mean, in terms of the distribution of 1990 and 1995 staff assault rates. Across all five models, the lagged effect of Y_1 was highly significant and negative. Furthermore, security level also was highly significant across all five models; however, the effect was positive. Being maximum-security increased the change in the staff violence rate by approximately 3 assaults per 100 staff members within each of the five models. After controlling for the three paradigms, being located in the Southeast no longer significantly reduced the change score for the staff assault rate.

Table 7.5 – 1990 Independent Variable Effects on the Change in Staff Assault Rates (ΔY)

Control Variables	Model 1		Model 2		Model 3		Model 4		Model 5	
	b	β	B	β	b	β	b	β	b	β
1990 Staff Assault Rate	-0.68	-0.68 ***	-0.67	-0.68 ***	-0.67	-0.70 ***	-0.69	-0.70 ***	-0.68	-0.71 ***
1990 Inmate Assault Rate	-0.04	-0.02	-0.05	-0.03	-0.05	-0.03	-0.05	-0.03	-0.06	-0.03
1990 Security Level	3.26	0.18 ***	2.79	0.15 ***	3.27	0.19 ***	3.32	0.18 ***	2.94	0.17 ***
Region	-1.04	-0.07 *	-0.33	-0.02	-0.99	-0.06	-1.61	-0.10	-1.04	-0.07
Deprivation Variables										
1990 Cell Type			1.52	0.08 *					1.16	0.06
1990 Crowding Level			0.02	0.07 *					0.02	0.06
1990 Deprivation Score			-0.05	-0.02					0.01	0.00
Management Variables										
1990 Percent CO'S					0.01	0.02			0.00	0.00
1990 M-to-F CO's					0.02	0.03			0.00	0.01
1990 IRV					0.00	-0.01			0.00	0.01
Importation Variables										
1990 % Black Inmates							0.06	0.15 ***	0.06	0.13 **
1990 % Black Staff							-0.03	-0.06	-0.02	-0.05
Adjusted R² Value	0.41		0.42		0.44		0.43		0.45	

* = Coefficient Significant at α = 0.05   ** = Coefficient Significant at α = 0.01
*** = Coefficient Significant at α = 0.001

Model 2 introduced the deprivation variables. Both cell type and the crowding level significantly increased the change in the staff assault rate; however, the effect sizes were minimal. For instance, each additional percentage over-crowded in 1990 increased the change score for the staff assault rate by 0.02. In which case, if a facility was 50 percent over-crowded in 1990, their predicted change score for the staff assault rate would equal 1. The deprivation variables also added very little to the adjusted R^2 value. The addition of these variables improved the proportion of variance explained in the dependent variable by 1 percent.

Neither of the management variables had a noticeable impact on the change in the staff assault rate. The unstandardized coefficient values for the 3 management variables ranged from 0.00 to 0.02. The increased significance of the control variables, as indicated by the slightly higher standardized coefficient values, explained the slight improvement in the adjusted R^2 value with the addition of the management factors. Model 4 introduced the importation variables and uncovered coefficient signs indicating the significance of the Black rage perspective; however, only the influence of Black inmates was significant. Specifically, each additional unit increase in the percentage of Black inmates in 1990 increased the change in the staff assault rate by 0.06. Thus, if the inmate population for a certain correctional facility were 50 percent Black, the predicted change score for the staff assault rate, based on this factor alone, would equal 3. In which case, from 1990 to 1995, the staff violence rate would increase by 3 assaults per 100 staff members. Although not significant, a 50 percent Black prison staff in 1990 would have produced a change score equal to -1.5, indicating that from 1990 to 1995, the staff violence rate would have decreased by 1.5 assaults per 100 staff members.

In the cumulative model, the two deprivation variables were no longer significant. Once controlling for all factors, only the 1990 staff assault rate, security level, and the percentage of Black inmates significantly influenced the subsequent change in the staff assault rate. Neither of the management variables had an effect on the changes in the staff assault rate; note that the unstandardized coefficients for all three of the management factors equaled 0.00. The cumulative model explained 45 percent of the variance in the dependent variable. A vast majority of the proportion of variance explained stemmed from the control variables, where the adjusted R^2 value equaled 0.41 (see model 1). Hence, the three theoretical paradigms contributed very little to overall model fit. However, the paradigms produced noticeable contributions after partitioning the sample according to region.

Table 7.6 presents the lagged independent and dependent variable effects on the change score for the staff assault rate across regions. In all four regions, the most important factor in terms of explaining changes in staff violence was the value of the staff assault rate in 1990. The lagged dependent variable had the greatest impact in the Midwest, followed closely by the West. The very strong and negative coefficient value for both regions suggests that the pitfall of regression towards the mean was more of a problem in the Midwest and West. For instance, if a Western facility had a 1990 staff violence rate of 25 assaults per 100 staff members, their predicted change score for the staff assault rate would equal -21.75. In which case, their 1995 staff violence rate would have equaled 3.25 assaults per 100 staff members. All of the regions showed patterns suggestive of regression towards the mean; however, this tendency was weakest in the Northeast.

Table 7.6 – 1990 Independent Variable Effects on the Change in Staff Assault Rates (ΔY) by Region

Control Variables	Southeast		West		Northeast		Midwest	
	b	β	b	β	b	β	b	β
1990 Staff Assault Rate	-0.62	-0.53 ***	-0.83	-0.89 ***	-0.48	-0.53 ***	-0.85	-0.97 ***
1990 Inmate Assault Rate	-0.13	-0.08	-0.05	-0.03	-0.19	-0.14	0.39	0.11
1990 Security Level	1.33	0.09	0.53	0.03	5.06	0.27	7.57	0.32 ***
Deprivation Variables								
1990 Cell Type	1.87	0.08	3.70	0.22	-2.17	-0.13	0.13	0.01
1990 Crowding Level	-0.01	-0.02	0.03	0.08	0.05	0.23 *	-0.02	-0.03
1990 Deprivation Score	-0.05	-0.03	0.04	0.02	-1.47	-0.12	0.07	0.01
Management Variables								
1990 Percent CO'S	0.00	0.01	-0.04	-0.08	-0.09	-0.07	0.07	0.07
1990 M-to-F CO's	-0.01	-0.01	0.02	0.02	0.04	0.10	-0.12	-0.06
1990 IRV	-0.01	-0.02	-0.01	-0.02	-0.02	-0.05	0.03	0.06
Importation Variables								
1990 % Black Inmates	0.03	0.08	0.13	0.23	0.01	0.02	0.15	0.24 ***
1990 % Black Staff	-0.02	-0.07	-0.03	-0.03	0.12	0.18	-0.13	-0.15
Adjusted R^2 Value	0.26		0.60		0.34		0.68	

* = Coefficient Significant at $\alpha = 0.05$ ** = Coefficient Significant at $\alpha = 0.01$
*** = Coefficient Significant at $\alpha = 0.001$

The significance of security level, indicated in Table 7.5, was primarily due to the facilities located in the Midwest. Partitioning the sample according to region revealed that the Midwest was the only region where being maximum-security significantly increased the change score for the staff assault rate. Specifically, in the Midwest, being maximum-security resulted in a staff assault rate that was 7.57 points higher from 1990 to 1995. There was also a noticeable effect size for security level in the Northeast (5.06); then again, the coefficient was not significant.

The crowding level in the Northeast was the only deprivation variable with a significant effect across the four regions. The effect of the crowding level on the subsequent change in the staff assault rate was 2.5 times higher in the Northeast, in comparison to the entire sample. While in the entire sample, being 50 percent over-crowded increased the change score for the staff assault rate by exactly one, in the Northeast, the change score for the staff assault rate increased by 2.5 under similar conditions. The management variables continued to have a negligible impact on the change score for the staff assault rate.

The percentage of Black inmates in the Midwest was the only significant importation factor. The large effect observed in the entire sample (see Table 7.5) was primarily a function of the dynamics taking place in the Midwest. Whereas in the entire sample, each additional unit increase in the percentage of Black inmates increased the change score for the staff assault rate by 0.06, in the Midwest the change score increased by 0.15. Thus, while a 50 percent Black inmate population increased the change score by 3 in the entire sample, the predicted change score for the Midwest increased by 7.5. Though not significant, the percentage of Black staff in the Midwest also had a noticeable decreasing impact on the change in the staff assault rate. For instance, each additional unit increase in the percentage of Black staff decreased the staff assault change score by 0.02 in the entire sample, but by 0.13 in the Midwest. The observed effect of Black staff in the Midwest approximately canceled the positive influence of Black inmates on the change in the staff assault rate. The pattern displayed in Table 7.6 for the Midwest supported the regional findings regarding the Black rage theory unearthed in the cross-sectional TOBIT models of Chapter VI.

The cumulative model explained significantly more of the variance in the dependent variable in the West and Midwest. For instance, in the Midwest, the estimated factors in the cumulative model accounted for 68 percent of the variance in the change scores associated with the staff assault rate. The variables provided a much weaker model fit in the Southeast and the Northeast. Examination of the individual model summaries included in Appendix D, Table 2, revealed that none of the paradigm factors contributed to the adjusted R^2 value in the Southeast region. The deprivation variables provided the strongest model fit in the West and Northeast, while the management factors provided the strongest model fit in the Midwest.

Static Score with Lagged Dependent & Independent Variables

TOBIT Models

An added luxury of the two-wave panel design is the ability to manipulate the dependent variable. In the previous two change equations, the models assessed the independent variable effects on the change in the dependent variable (ΔY). However, with the two-wave panel design it is possible to model change as a function of the independent variable effects on the value of the dependent variable at time 2 (Y_2). Using Y_2 as the dependent variable, the last two change equations explore the influence of the lagged and instantaneous effects of the independent variables on the observed staff assault rate in 1995.

Table 7.7 - ASTC and 1990 Independent Variable Effects on 1995 Staff Assault Rates by Region – Non-Censored Cases

Control Variables	Total Sample N = 345		Southeast N = 153		West N = 35		Northeast N = 72		Midwest N = 85	
	ASTC	Effect	ASTC	Effect	ASTC	Effect	ASTC	Effect	ASTC	Effect
1990 Staff Assault Rate	0.47 ***	0.18	0.46 ***	0.28	0.30	0.20	0.65 ***	0.31	0.28 *	0.08
1990 Inmate Assault Rate	-0.02	-0.01	-0.07	-0.06	-0.01	-0.01	-0.14	-0.10	0.43 *	0.27
1990 Security Level	0.28 ***	1.97	0.12	0.87	0.12	1.59	0.42 *	4.08	0.62 ***	4.50
Region	-0.14	-0.82	---	---	---	---	---	---	---	---
Deprivation Variables										
1990 Cell Type	0.12	0.91	0.16	1.97	0.38	4.49	-0.18	-1.61	-0.03	-0.19
1990 Crowding Level	0.17 **	0.02	0.06	0.01	0.44 *	0.11	0.31 **	0.04	-0.09	-0.01
1990 Deprivation Score	0.04	0.04	0.02	0.02	0.05	0.08	-0.16	-1.02	0.03	0.04
Management Variables										
1990 Percent CO'S	-0.04	-0.01	0.01	0.00	-0.17	-0.05	-0.03	-0.02	0.11	0.03
1990 M-to-F CO's	0.01	0.00	-0.05	-0.01	0.16	0.11	0.13	0.02	-0.14	-0.08
1990 IRV	0.05	0.01	0.04	0.01	0.05	0.01	-0.07	-0.01	0.30	0.05
Importation Variables										
1990 % Black Inmates	0.28 ***	0.04	0.04	0.01	0.37	0.14	0.14	0.04	0.60 ***	0.11
1990 % Black Staff	-0.13	-0.02	-0.13	-0.02	-0.04	-0.03	0.22	0.07	-0.49 *	-0.13
LL Ratio (P-value)	150.20 (0.0000)		36.05 (0.0002)		29.82 (0.0017)		40.29 (0.0000)		68.98 (0.0000)	

* = ASTC Significant at $\alpha = 0.05$ ** = ASTC Significant at $\alpha = 0.01$
*** = ASTC Significant at $\alpha = 0.001$

Table 7.7 presents the analogue standardized TOBIT coefficients (ASTC) and effect size estimates for the lagged independent variables on the 1995 staff assault rate.[11] The lagged dependent variable significantly increased the 1995 staff assault rate in the entire sample, and in every region except for the West. The effect of the lagged dependent variable was greatest in the Northeast, where each additional unit increase in the 1990 staff assault rate increased the 1995 staff assault rate 0.31. For example, in the Northeast, a staff violence rate of 25 assaults per 100 staff members in 1990 lead to a predicted staff violence rate of 7.75 assaults per 100 staff members in 1995. The lagged inmate assault rate was only significant in the Midwest. In fact, the Midwest was the only region where the lagged inmate assault rate increased the 1995 staff assault rate. The coefficients for the other regions and the entire sample were negative. The strong positive effect of security level in the entire sample was primarily a factor of the observed effect in the Midwest. Based on the entire sample, being maximum-security in 1990 increased the 1995 staff assault rate by 1.97, while in the Midwest, being maximum-security increased the staff assault rate by 4.50.

The crowding level was the only deprivation factor with a significant finding in the entire sample. The effect of the crowding variable was largest in the West. In the West region, each additional unit increase in the percentage over-crowded in 1990 increased the 1995 staff assault rate by 0.11. Hence, if a facility was 50 percent over-crowded in 1990, their predicted 1995 staff assault rate increased by 5.5. The crowding level was also significant in the Northeast, although the observed effect size was much smaller than in the West. Again, as in the previous change equations, none of the management variables produced a perceivable influence on the 1995 staff assault rate. The ASTC values for the Midwest and the marginal effect sizes suggest some importance of the management variables in the Midwest; however, the results were not significant.

Concerning the factors operationalizing the Black rage perspective, the percentage of Black inmates in 1990 significantly increased the staff assault rate in 1995. Partitioning the sample further revealed that this effect was only significant in the Midwest. The estimated effect of Black inmates on the staff assault rate was nearly 3 times as high in the Midwest compared to the entire sample. For instance, while a 50 percent Black inmate population increased the 1995 staff violence rate by 2 assaults per 100 staff members in the entire sample, this same demographic increased the staff assault rate by 5.5 in the Midwest. Furthermore, the calming effect of Black staff on the violent tendencies of Black inmates was only significant in the Midwest. The percentage of Black staff in the Southeast and the West slightly reduced the staff assault rate; however, the effect sizes were not significant and paled in comparison to the Midwest. The effect size for the percentage of Black staff in the Midwest surpassed the positive influence of Black inmates on the staff assault rate. Thus, with equal representations, the presence of Black staff effectively countered the contributions of Black inmates to the 1995 staff assault rate. In the Midwest, beyond security level, the Black rage factors were the most significant contributors to the staff assault rate based on the ASTC values.

The log-likelihood ratios provided in Appendix D, Table 3, further illustrate that the importation model explained significantly more of the variance in staff assault rates in the entire sample and in the Midwest. In the Southeast, West, and Northeast, the deprivation model provided the largest log-likelihood ratio. Nevertheless, in the West, all of the log-likelihood ratios were noticeably lower than the other regions. The weaker model fit in the West suggests the importance of other non-considered factors to explain the variation in staff assault rates.

Paralleling the structure of the TOBIT equation, Table 7.8 presents the effect size estimates for the lagged independent variables on the probability of a 1995 staff assault for the censored observations. The proportion of censored cases varied considerably across regions. For instance, 41.8 percent of the observations from the Southeast did not have a staff assault in 1995: in comparison to 50 percent in the West, 15.3 percent in the Northeast, and 26.1 percent in the Midwest. Thus, the reader should bare in mind the censored sample sizes when interpreting the effects presented in Table 7.8, especially in the Northeast.[12]

The lagged dependent variable significantly influenced the probability of a staff assault across all four regions; however, the effect was noticeably less in the Midwest. For example, in the West, if a facility had a 1990 staff violence rate of 25 assaults per 100 staff members, their probability of experiencing a 1995 staff assault increased by 53 percent. In contrast, the same staff violence rate only increased the odds of a 1995 staff assault by 19 percent in the Midwest. In the Midwest, the lagged inmate assault rate was far more significant in increasing the odds of a 1995 staff assault. Each additional unit increase in the 1990 inmate assault rate increased the likelihood of a 1995 staff assault by 2.74 percent. The lagged inmate assault rate was not significant in any other region. The influence of security level also had a uniquely different effect in the Midwest compared to the other regions. In the overall sample, being maximum-security increased the odds of a 1995 staff assault by 15.10 percent, while in the Midwest, being maximum-security increased the odds by 44.87 percent.

Two of the deprivation factors produced perceivable influences on the likelihood of a 1995 staff assault. In the West, housing inmates exclusively in single-cell arrangements increased the odds of a staff assault by nearly 50 percent (48.25). The effect of cell type in the other regions was minimal. The crowding level was also far more significant in the West than in the other regions. In the overall sample, each additional percentage point over-crowded in 1990 increased the likelihood of a 1995 staff assault by 0.17, while in the West, the probability increased by 1.19 percent. Thus, if a facility in the West was 50 percent over-crowded in 1990, their probability of experiencing a staff assault in 1995 increased by 59.5 percent.

Table 7.8 – 1990 Independent Variable Effects on the Probability of a 1995 Staff Assault – Censored Cases

Control Variables	Total Sample N = 188	Southeast N = 110	West N = 35	Northeast N = 13	Midwest N = 30
	Effect	Effect	Effect	Effect	Effect
1990 Staff Assault Rate	1.37	1.24	2.12	2.81	0.76
1990 Inmate Assault Rate	-0.11	-0.27	-0.14	-0.86	2.74
1990 Security Level	15.10	3.86	17.05	36.78	44.87
Region	-6.32	---	---	---	---
Deprivation Variables					
1990 Cell Type	7.00	8.71	48.25	-14.49	-1.90
1990 Crowding Level	0.17	0.05	1.19	0.32	-0.13
1990 Deprivation Score	0.32	0.10	0.86	-9.19	0.42
Management Variables					
1990 Percent CO's	-0.09	0.01	-0.52	-0.14	0.33
1990 M-to-F CO's	0.02	-0.06	1.19	0.21	-0.76
1990 IRV	0.05	0.03	0.11	-0.13	0.54
Importation Variables					
1990 % Black Inmates	0.34	0.04	1.46	0.33	1.05
1990 % Black Staff	-0.16	-0.10	-0.29	0.67	-1.34

Although none of the management variables were significant when considering the non-censored observations, in the censored sample analysis there were region specific effects for each management factor. For instance, the percentage of correctional officers noticeably reduced the likelihood of a 1995 staff assault in the West, while noticeably increasing the odds of staff assault in the Midwest. The ratio of male-to-female correctional officers also had opposing effects in the West and Midwest. Whereas in the West, a male-to-female correctional officer ratio of 25:1 increased the odds of a staff assault by 29.75 percent, in the

Midwest, this same ratio decreased the odds of staff assault by 19 percent. The index of racial variation had a uniquely different effect in the Midwest in comparison to the other regions. A perfectly heterogeneous staff population, in terms of race (IRV = 100), increased the odds of a staff assault by 5 percent in the entire sample. However, in the Midwest, perfect racial heterogeneity increased the odds of a staff assault by 54 percent.

The effects of the importation factors also differed across regions. Black inmates had the largest influence on the likelihood of a 1995 staff assault in the region where they possessed the lowest representation. Table 7.1 revealed that the percentage of Black inmates in the West was over 30 points lower than in the Southeast and over 20 points lower than in the Northeast and Midwest. Yet, despite the small numbers, each additional unit increase in the percentage of Black inmates increased the odds of staff assault by 1.46 percent in the West, in comparison to 0.34 percent for the entire sample. This finding supports the "*relative numbers*" theory proposed by Harer and Steffensmeier (1996). The researchers suggest that in prisons where White inmates form the majority, the smaller number of Black inmates may engage in defensive violence to deter hostile attacks by White inmates. Based on their perspective, the racial group that constitutes the numeric minority should have the most significant impact on institutional violence rates, and this appears to be the case in the West.

The influence of Black inmates was also relatively large in the Midwest. Furthermore, given the larger populations of Black inmates, the effect in the Midwest was actually greater than in the West. For instance, in the West, the maximum percentage of Black inmates in 1990 was 49.22 percent, in which case the predicted probability of a 1995 staff assault increased by 71.86 percent. In contrast, in the Midwest, the maximum percentage of Black inmates was 80 percent, which increased the predicted probability of a 1995 staff assault by 84 percent.

The effect of Black inmates, coupled with the effect of Black staff in the Midwest, offered supportive findings for the Black rage theory. Black staff had a distinctive effect in the Midwest. For the entire sample, each additional increase in the percentage of Black staff reduced the likelihood of a staff assault by 0.16 percent. However, in the Midwest, the rate of reduction in the likelihood of a staff assault was 1.34 percent. Thus, with a 50 percent Black staff population in 1990, a facility in the Midwest reduced its odds of a 1995 staff assault by 67 percent. Additionally, the calming effect of Black staff more than negated the violent effect of Black inmates. In which case, with equal representations, the effects of Black inmates on the odds of a staff assault essentially disappear.

Static Score with Lagged Dependent & Instantaneous Independent Variables – TOBIT

The previous section modeled change by describing Y_2 as a function of the lagged effects of the independent (X_1) and dependent (Y_1) variables. The question answered by this model was, "How well could one predict future staff assault rates based on past conditions, which included the past staff assault rate?" The fourth and final change equation described Y_2 as a function of the lagged effects of the dependent variable (Y_1) and the instantaneous effects of the independent variables (X_2). Here the question becomes, "How well could one predict present staff assault rates, based on present conditions, while effectively partitioning out the influence of the past staff assault rate?"

Table 7.9 presents the analogue standardized TOBIT coefficients (ASTC) and effect size estimates for the lagged dependent and instantaneous independent variables on the 1995 staff assault rate. All of the control variables were significant in the entire sample, as well as across each region except for the West. The effect of the lagged dependent variable was greatest in the Northeast, where each additional unit increase in the 1990 staff assault rate increased the 1995 staff assault rate by 0.30. In contrast, the lagged dependent variable effect was over four times lower in the Midwest (0.07). The positive effect of the inmate assault rate was greatest in the Southeast, followed by the Midwest. In the Southeast, an inmate violence rate of 25 assaults per 100 inmates resulted in a predicted staff violence rate of 15.75 ($\approx$ 16) assaults per 100 staff members. In sharp contrast, the inmate assault rate had absolutely no effect on the staff assault rate in the West (Effect = 0.00). Security level had the largest impact in the Midwest, where being maximum-security increased the staff assault rate by 3.61. Across all of the regions, being maximum-security noticeably increased the staff assault rate. The large difference in the average staff assault rate across security levels explained this result. The region coefficient for the total sample indicated that being located in the Southeast reduced the staff assault rate by 1.21; which was somewhat surprising given that this was not the region with the lowest staff assault rate (see Table 7.1 a and b).

The instantaneous effects of the deprivation variables were largely unimportant in predicting the 1995 staff assault rate. The crowding level in the Northeast was the only significant deprivation factor across any of the regions, and even there, the effect size was relatively small (0.04). The management variables had an equally marginal effect on the staff assault rate. In the entire sample, the percentage of correctional officers significantly reduced the staff violence rate; however, the effect was not significant in any particular region. Nonetheless, the Midwest was the only region where each additional unit increase in the percentage of correctional officer increased the staff assault rate. The index of racial variation also had an effect unique to the Midwest, given that each additional unit increase in staff diversity significantly increased the staff assault rate by 0.11. The small average degree of staff diversity in the Midwest weakened this finding. As indicated in Table 7.1, the average IRV score for facilities located in the Midwest was 22.84, which indicated a relatively high degree of racial homogeneity among Midwest prison staff.

Table 7.9 - ASTC and 1995 Independent Variable Effects on 1995 Staff Assault Rates by Region – Non-Censored Cases

Control Variables	Total Sample N = 345		Southeast N = 153		West N = 35		Northeast N = 72		Midwest N = 85	
	ASTC	Effect	ASTC	Effect	ASTC	Effect	ASTC	Effect	ASTC	Effect
1990 Staff Assault Rate	0.41 ***	0.14	0.28 **	0.14	0.31	0.22	0.74 ***	0.30	0.50 *	0.07
1995 Inmate Assault Rate	0.53 ***	0.40	0.81 ***	0.63	-0.00	0.00	0.42 **	0.46	0.45 ***	0.54
1995 Security Level	0.42 ***	2.65	0.39 ***	2.41	0.24	3.36	0.35 *	2.74	0.47 ***	3.61
Region	-0.22 **	-1.21	---	---	---	---	---	---	---	---
Deprivation Variables										
1995 Cell Type	0.04	0.34	0.15	1.41	0.21	3.07	-0.10	-0.75	-0.05	-0.40
1995 Crowding Level	0.10	0.01	0.11	0.02	0.19	0.05	0.30 *	0.04	-0.13	-0.01
1995 Deprivation Score	0.04	0.05	-0.02	-0.02	0.25	0.56	0.16	0.27	0.01	0.01
Management Variables										
1995 Percent CO'S	-0.15 *	-0.04	-0.19	-0.05	-0.13	-0.04	-0.21	-0.09	0.22	0.09
1995 M-to-F CO's	0.03	0.01	-0.07	-0.02	0.04	0.04	0.06	0.01	-0.06	-0.05
1995 IRV	0.14	0.02	0.12	0.02	0.08	0.02	010	0.02	0.55 *	0.11
Importation Variables										
1995 % Black Inmates	0.31 ***	0.04	0.03	0.01	0.55 *	0.25	0.21	0.04	0.17	0.04
1995 % Black Staff	-0.17	-0.02	-0.15	-0.02	-0.17	-0.10	0.02	0.01	-0.36	-0.10
Log-likelihood Ratio	255.59 (0.0000)		127.86 (0.0000)		22.88 (0.0183)		68.58 (0.0000)		65.92 (0.0000)	

* = ASTC Significant at α = 0.05   ** = ASTC Significant at α = 0.01
*** = ASTC Significant at α = 0.001

In terms of the black rage factors, the percentage of Black inmates significantly increased the staff assault rate in the entire sample and in the West. Across all of the regions, Black inmates increased the staff assault rate; however, their effect was only significant in the West. This finding confirmed the predicted influence of Black inmates on the probability of a 1995 staff assault, as indicated in Table 7.8. Recall that when examining the influence of the lagged independent variables, each additional unit increase in the 1990 percentage of Black inmates significantly increased the probability of a 1995 staff assault for the West region. In 1995, each additional unit increase in the percentage of Black inmates increased the staff assault rate by 0.25 (for the non-censored cases).

Although the percentage of Black staff did not have a significant effect in any of the regions, this factor produced a noticeable reduction in the staff assault rates for the West and Midwest. In both regions, each additional unit increase in the percentage of Black staff decreased the staff assault rate by 0.10. In which case, if the staff population of a certain facility was 50 percent Black, the staff violence rate would decrease by 5 assaults. For the West, however, the calming effect of Black staff did not surpass the violent effect of Black inmates.

The log-likelihood ratios provided in Table 7.9 indicate that the cumulative model explained significantly less of the variance in staff assault rates in the West in comparison to the other regions. This finding held true in the TOBIT models of Chapter VI, as well as in the TOBIT analysis of the current chapter. The cumulative model explained the greatest proportion of variance in the Southeast. In terms of the individual paradigms (see Appendix D, Table 4), the importation model made the largest contribution to log-likelihood ratio in the entire sample. The deprivation variables made the greatest contribution in the West, while the management variables slightly improved the model fits in the Southeast, Northeast, and Midwest regions.

Table 7.10 presents the effect size estimates for the lagged dependent and instantaneous independent variables on the probability of a 1995 staff assault for the censored observations. The lagged dependent variable had the greatest influence on the probability of a staff assault in the Northeast; however, this effect was questionable given the small sample of censored observations ($N = 13$). The West had the next largest effect for the lagged dependent variable; each additional unit increase in the 1990 staff assault rate increased the probability of a 1995 staff assault by 2.23 percent. Thus, if a Western facility had a staff violence rate of 25 assaults per 100 staff members in 1990, the probability of experiencing a staff assault in 1995 increased by 55.75 percent. The instantaneous effect of the inmate assault rate was greatest in the Midwest. Each inmate assault in the Midwest increased the odds of staff assault by an astounding 5.05 percent. Likewise, security level also had a significant influence on the probability of a staff assault in the Midwest and across all regions. The effect of being maximum-security had the smallest impact on the likelihood of experiencing a staff assault in the Southeast.

Among the deprivation variables, cell type significantly increased the odds of a staff assault in the West in comparison to the entire sample. In the West, housing inmates exclusively in single-cell arrangements increased the likelihood of a staff assault by 31.07 percent versus 2.85 percent in the total sample. The deprivation score was also highly significant in the West. Each condition of confinement for which the facility was under federal court order increased the odds of a staff assault by 5.64 percent. Hence, being under federal court order for all ten conditions increased the likelihood of experiencing a staff assault by 56.4 percent.

Table 7.10 – 1995 Independent Variable Effects on the Probability of a 1995 Staff Assault – Censored Cases

Control Variables	Total Sample N = 188	Southeast N = 110	West N = 35	Northeast N = 13	Midwest N = 30
	Effect	Effect	Effect	Effect	Effect
1990 Staff Assault Rate	1.19	0.77	2.23	3.21	0.68
1995 Inmate Assault Rate	3.36	3.40	-0.04	4.87	5.05
1995 Security Level	22.42	13.03	34.00	29.01	33.99
Region	-10.29	---	---	---	---
Deprivation Variables					
1995 Cell Type	2.85	7.63	31.07	-7.97	-3.74
1995 Crowding Level	0.09	0.10	0.52	0.37	-0.14
1995 Deprivation Score	0.38	-0.10	5.64	2.85	0.09
Management Variables					
1995 Percent CO's	-0.33	-0.27	-0.41	-0.94	0.85
1995 M-to-F CO's	0.05	-0.13	0.42	0.07	-0.44
1995 IRV	0.14	0.09	0.15	0.20	1.00
Importation Variables					
1995 % Black Inmates	0.36	0.03	2.50	0.47	0.36
1995 % Black Staff	-0.20	-0.10	-0.99	0.06	-0.97

The management variables produced two noteworthy findings. A one-unit increase in the percentage of correctional officers significantly increased the probability of a staff assault in the Midwest by 0.85. Considering the fact that the average prison in the Midwest had 67.54

percent correctional officers, this demographic alone would increase the probability of a staff assault by 57.41 percent. The index of racial variation also drastically increased the probability of experiencing a staff assault in the Midwest. Each additional unit increase on the diversity scale increased the staff assault rate by 1 percent, in which case a perfectly heterogeneous staff population would increase the staff assault rate by 100 percent. However, the maximum value on the IRV in the Midwest was 69.71, thus in the most extreme case this factor increased the odds of a staff assault by roughly 70 percent.

For the importation variables, the percentage of Black inmates increased the odds of a staff assault in the entire sample and across all regions. The effect was most noticeable in the West, where the odds of experiencing a staff assault increased by 2.50 percent with each additional unit increase in the percentage of Black inmates. The percentage of Black staff reduced the probability of a staff assault in every region except the Northeast. The effects in the West and Midwest were most noticeable. In both regions, each unit increase in the percentage of Black staff reduced the odds of a staff assault by approximately 1 percent. However, only the effect in the Midwest was large enough to negate the violent effect of the Black inmate population. The direction of the effects for both the percentage of Black inmates and Black staff support the claims of the Black rage theory in every region except for the Northeast. Nevertheless, the West was the only region to produce noticeable effect sizes for both factors simultaneously.

Summary of Change Analysis

The four change models estimated in the current chapter pale in comparison to the total number of possibilities available for capturing processes and change in panel data analysis. As indicated by the findings, the manner in which the researcher specifies the change model can produce drastically different results from equation to equation. In particular, the failure to account for the lagged dependent variable can significantly change model predictions. For instance, the cumulative model from the method of pure first differences found three factors significantly associated with changes in the staff assault rate from 1990 to 1995 (see Table 7.3). However, there was a high likelihood that the estimates were inaccurate, given that each factor significantly correlated with Y_1. After controlling for the significant influence of Y_1, the models provided more accurate, trustworthy, and consistent results.

Despite the wide variation in the change equations created through manipulation of the independent and dependent variables, a set of core factors maintained their significance, regardless of the structure of the change equation. Focusing strictly on the cumulative models for the entire sample, there were three factors with highly significant influences on the staff assault rate in each of the static score equations.[13] First, the 1990 staff assault rate significantly influenced both the 1995 staff assault rate and the change score for the staff assault rate. In the second change equation, where the change score for the staff assault rate (ΔY) served as the dependent variable, the lagged staff assault rate noticeably decreased the staff violence level, a pattern suggestive of regression towards the mean. Even with the pitfall of regression towards the mean, the 1990 staff assault rate remained one of the most important predictors of the 1995 staff assault rate (see Tables 7.7 and 7.9). Second, being maximum-security significantly increased the staff assault rate across all three static score equations. Third, the percentage of Black inmates significantly increased the level of staff violence, regardless of the nature of the dependent variable. The strong and consistently positive influence of Black inmates on the staff assault rate in the current chapter duplicated the cross-sectional TOBIT findings presented in Chapter VI. In both chapters, the influence of Black inmates provided consistent support for the theory of Black rage.

Breakdown of Black Rage Theory

Black Inmates

As indicated above, Black inmates had a significant positive impact on the staff rate when examining the panel data set collectively in all of the static score models. However, further dissection of the sample, according to region, revealed that influence of Black inmates on prison violence was not universal. The most noticeable influences of Black inmates on the staff assault rate occurred in the West and Midwest. Despite having relatively low representation in the West, Black inmates had a disproportionate impact on the staff assault rate in the West. This suggests that although the West had significantly fewer Black inmates, the Black inmates found in the West were considerably more violent than those in other regions. Harer and Steffensmeier (1996) contend that the increased propensity towards violence displayed by Black inmates (in certain situations) stems from their relative numbers, and serves as part of an elaborate defense strategy to deflect potential assaults from White inmates. Although Black inmates produced more than noticeable effects on the staff assault rate in the West, their influence was only significant in the assessment of the instantaneous effects of the independent variables on the 1995 staff assault rate.

In contrast, the impact of Black inmates on the staff assault rate in the Midwest was significant in two of the three static score models.

Specifically, the significant findings regarding the impact of Black inmates on the staff assault rates, observed in Tables 7.5 and 7.7, were only significant in the Midwest region. Table 7.5 modeled change as the influence of the lagged independent variables on the change score for the staff assault rate. Overall, each additional increase in the percentage of Black inmates in 1990 increased the change score for the staff assault rate by 0.13, while in the Midwest, the rate of increase was 0.24. Table 7.7 displayed a similar pattern in the Midwest when examining the impact of the lagged independent variables on the 1995 staff assault rate for the non-censored observations. However, when predicting the 1995 staff assault rate, the effect of Black inmates in the Midwest was over 2.5 times higher than in the entire sample. Thus, the findings from the Chapter VII data analysis offered strong support for the conclusions reached in Chapter VI regarding the influence of Black inmates on staff violence in the Midwest. Recall in Chapter VI, the Midwest was the only region where Black inmates had a significant impact of staff violence in the 1984, 1990, and 1995 cross-sectional data analysis. Finding a strong positive effect of Black inmates on the staff assault rate is the first requirement towards establishing the presence of the dynamics specified by the Black rage theory. Here, as in Chapter VI, the Midwest offers the strongest evidence in support of the first core prediction of the Black rage perspective.

Black Staff

The second requirement necessary to establish the significance of the Black rage theory is the calming effect of Black staff on the staff assault rate. In all of the change models estimated in the current chapter, the analysis using the entire sample failed to produce a significant finding regarding the influence of Black staff on the staff assault rate.[14] Although the effects were not significant, the sign of the coefficients for the percentage of Black staff in all of the cumulative change models estimated using the entire sample were negative. This indicated a general tendency for Black staff to decrease the staff assault rate.

The only significant effect observed for the influence of Black staff across all of the models occurred in the Midwest using the lagged independent variables to predict the 1995 staff assault rate (see Table 7.7). For this particular change model, each additional increase in the percentage of Black staff reduced the staff assault rate by 0.13. Although not significant, Black staff produced noticeable reductions in the staff assault rates for the Midwest in Tables 7.6 and 7.9 as well. In fact, in all of the regional static score models, the calming effect of Black staff on the staff assault rate was greatest in the Midwest.[15] Furthermore, the effect sizes for the Midwest were considerably higher than those found in the total sample. For instance, when using the lagged independent variables to predict the 1995 staff assault rate, the effect size for the percentage of Black staff in the Midwest was 6.5 times greater than the effect size found in the entire sample (see Table 7.7). Despite such large relative disparities, the effects of Black staff on prison violence in the Midwest were only significant in one of the static score models. With a larger percentage of Black staff in the Midwest, the effects would likely reach significance. Table 7.1 revealed that the average facility located in the Midwest had roughly 9 percent Black staff in both 1990 and 1995. Thus, perhaps with a Black staff population comparable to the figures found in the Southeast, the calming effect of Black staff in the Midwest would dramatically increase. However, as it stands, the Midwest continues to offer the most promising findings for the proposed theory of black rage.

[1] See Liker et al. (1985: 100), Panel Data and Models of Change: A Comparison of First Difference and Conventional Two-Wave Models, in defense of the method of first differences to assess change.

[2] See Finkel (1995: 8), Causal Analysis with Panel Data, in defense of the static score method to assess change.

[3] Burr and Nessellroade (1990: 8), Change Measurement

[4] Note the change in the distribution of security level across the two periods. From 1990 to 1995, 39 facilities decreased the level of security, while 52 facilities simultaneously increased the level of security. Consequently, the security level distributions did not match in 1990 and 1995.

[5] The ratio of White-to-Black staff did not produce a noticeable effect in any of the models presented in Chapter VI. In the vast majority of the models, the effect size for this factor equaled zero. Furthermore, the analysis for Chapter VII found the same insignificant effect for this factor. For these reasons, I removed the ratio of White-to-Black staff from the analytical models, and operationalized the Black rage perspective using only the percentage of Black inmates and the percentage of Black staff.

[6] Bivariate correlations play a vital role in change score analysis, particularly in specifying the reliabilities of change scores and detailing which factors significantly correlate with Y_1. Therefore, the correlation matrix appears in the text of the chapter as oppose to in an Appendix.

[7] The table includes both standardized and unstandardized coefficients for two reasons. 1) The unstandardized coefficients permit the direct assessment of the effect of each explanatory variable. 2) The standardized coefficients allow for effect comparison for each factor across the three theoretical paradigms.

[8] The change score equation was as follows: Δ score = 1995 Value – 1990 Value. Thus, a positive change score indicates that the 1995 value was higher than the 1990 value, while a negative change score indicates the opposite.

[9] The adjusted R^2 value did not change from model 1 to model 2, which suggests no improvement in the model fit by the adding the deprivation factors.

[10] See Table 7.1, the average Midwest facility reduced the amount of Black staff by 0.05 percent from 1990 to 1995.

[11] In efforts to minimize the number of tables, only the cumulative models from the total sample and each region appear in the remaining tables.

[12] In Tables 7.8 and 7.10, I limited the discussion on the findings from the Northeast give the relatively small sample of censored observations.

[13] There were other significant factors in the cumulative models; for instance the effect of the crowding level in Table 7.7, and the effects of region and the percentage of correctional officers in Table 7.9. However, there were only three consistently significant findings across all of the static score models.

[14] The slightly positive and significant effect of Black staff on the staff assault rate observed in the method of first differences was complicated by the strong correlation between the percentage Black staff and the unaccounted for influence of Y_1.

[15] In the change model using the instantaneous independent variable effects to predict the 1995 staff assault rate, Black staff produced the same effect size in the West and Midwest when considering the non-censored cases (see Table 7.9).

CHAPTER VIII

Prison Violence, Black Rage, and Implications

Undoubtedly, great strength allowed Black people to survive slavery and discrimination, but the notion that Black men and women can easily handle burdens that would psychologically crush other people has been oversold.[1]

Until this culture can acknowledge the pathology of White supremacy, we will never create a cultural context wherein the madness of White racist hatred of Blacks or the uncontrollable rage that surfaces as a response to that madness can be investigated, critically studied, and understood.[2]

Prison Violence in General

A major objective in the current study was to propose and test a universal theory of Black rage based on the observation that a wide variety of sources indicate the significance of this concept in explaining violent tendencies in African-Americans. More so than simply developing a theory of Black rage to explain prison violence, this study sought to explain Black violence and crime in general, in particular those offenses committed against White Americans. As a secondary objective, this study sought to make a valid contribution to criminological research, concerning prison violence, by reaffirming the significance of the importation model, while providing a more adequate assessment of the deprivation and management perspectives. Subsequently, in the process of examining the significance of the Black rage theory, the analysis uncovered two important findings with major implications for future criminological research concerning prison violence. Specifically, both the cross-sectional and longitudinal data analysis consistently revealed that *violence breeds violence*, and that significant regional variations exist concerning which paradigm best explains prison violence.

Violence Breeds Violence

In most studies of staff violence in prison, criminologists have failed to consider the *spill-over effect* of inmate violence. For instance, in one of the few studies to consider the influence of various factors on the staff assault rate, McCorkle et al. (1995) did not control for the level of inmate violence. Instead, the researchers treated both the staff and inmate assault rates as two separate dependent variables. While McCorkle et al. (1995) examined the influence of the inmate and staff assault rates on the likelihood of a prison riot, the researchers never explored the potential causal link between inmate and staff violence. This study included the inmate assault rate among the statistical controls in all of the regression models in order to provide an indication of the overall degree of violence found within the facility subculture. Intuitively, we would expect that a facility with a relatively high inmate assault rate should also have a high staff assault rate. In support of this assumption, the results from the cross-sectional data analysis illustrated that one of the best predictors of the staff assault rate for any given year was the inmate assault rate. This finding suggested that facilities with highly violent inmate subcultures produced significantly higher staff assault rates, perhaps due to the natural spill over effect of inmate aggression onto the staff population. Thus, future cross-sectional research projects that fail to consider the instantaneous influence of inmate violence on the predicted level of staff violence could produce misleading findings due to omitted variable bias.

Furthermore, based on the analysis presented in Chapter VII, omitted variable bias would also produce problematic findings in longitudinal assessments of prison violence. Finkel (1995) stated that whenever the past state of a dependent variable directly determines the present state, inclusion of the lagged dependent variable was necessary to specify the model properly. The longitudinal findings presented in Chapter VII demonstrated that the 1990 staff assault rate significantly influenced the change score for the staff assault rate (ΔY), as well as the 1995 staff assault rate (Y_2). Thus, despite the objections of proponents for the method of first differences in change score analysis (Allison 1990; Liker et al. 1985), in the current project, there appears to be sufficient statistical and theoretical reasons for including the lagged dependent variable among the control factors. Theoretically, before we can say that a particular independent variable caused a certain change in the staff assault rate, we must first be able to rule out the lingering effects of the staff assault rate at time one (Y_1). In sum, the highly significant instantaneous effect of the inmate assault rate in the cross-sectional analysis and the highly significant lagged effect of the staff assault rate in the longitudinal analysis, suggests that violence in one area of the prison subculture, or at one point in time, breeds violence in another. Therefore, future cross-sectional studies on staff violence in prison should include measures of inmate violence, and future longitudinal studies should include a lagged staff violence measure.

Regional Variations

In her study of racial differences in infraction rates, Petersilia (1983) examined data from three states representing the West, Midwest, and Southeast. The results of her study found that Black inmates were more violent than Whites in Texas, White inmates were more violent than Blacks in California, and in Michigan, there was no significant difference between the two groups. The drastically different findings from state-to-state indicate the problems with attempting to create universal theories of prison violence. Given the differing regional characteristics, the factors that produce violence in prison are contextual. Meaning that, the factors highly associated with prison violence in one region may not be in another. Furthermore, the factors associated with violence in a given region at time one may not be at time two.

The regional findings from this study lend further support to the contextual nature of prison violence. First, the average staff assault rate differed considerably across regions. For instance, the average staff assault rate for 1990 in the Northeast was over twice as high as the rate found in the West. Hence, the geographic location of the facility has major implications for the observed occurrences of the dependent variable (staff assaults). In addition to sheer differences in assault rates, the factors highly associated with staff violence also differed significantly from region-to-region. For example, one of the most consistent findings throughout Chapters VI and VII was the observation that collectively, the management, deprivation, and importation factors explained a relatively small amount of the variance in staff assault rates for the West region. Based on the log-likelihood ratios and the adjusted R^2 values, there were other more significant variables in terms of explaining staff assaults in the West.

There are two potential explanations for the relatively weak model fits in the West region. First, the racial variables focused exclusively on the Black/White dichotomy, when in the West, the appropriate dichotomy is perhaps Hispanic/White. From 1984 through 1995, the percentage of Hispanic inmates grew significantly in the West region. In fact, by 1990, the average percentage of Hispanic inmates in the West was greater than the average percentage of Black inmates. In addition, across all three years of data analysis, the average percentage of Hispanic staff in the West region was noticeably higher than the average percentage of Black staff. In which case, the higher population of Hispanic inmates is perhaps highly associated with prison violence, given the Hispanic male's proneness towards aggressive behavior. Davidson (1974) noted that Hispanic males follow a "machismo" subculture similar to the "Code of the Streets" followed by Black males (Anderson

1999). In either culture, violence is both expected and praised under certain circumstances as a natural reaction to challenges and frustrations. Therefore, Hispanic males likely have a greater influence on staff violence in the West than Black males.

A second potentially significant factor in explaining staff violence in the West concerns the level of gang activity. For example, research conducted by Hunt et al. (1993) suggests that in California, the sheer volume of gangs has increased dramatically and that gangs are becoming more ruthless and violent. In addition, Park (1976) found that gangs within the California prison system are divided along racial-ethnic lines with the Mexican-American groups having the largest membership. In all, five traditional ethnic gangs compete for dominance within the California prison system; Mexican Mafia, La Nuestra Familia, and the Texas Syndicate are all Chicano gangs; the Black Guerilla Family is the leading Black gang; and the Aryan Brotherhood is the prominent White gang (Hunt et al. 1993). Both Park (1976) and Hunt et al. (1993) concluded that gang competition over control of the market for illicit goods (sub-rosa economy) contributes significantly to the number of inmate and staff assaults in the California prison system. Furthermore, in each edition of the census, California represented the overwhelming majority of the facilities located in the West region. For example, in 1984, California represented roughly 35 percent of the facilities classified in the West region. In the 1995 data sample, California represented approximately 43 percent of the West facilities.[3] Therefore, given the overrepresentation of California facilities in the West, perhaps the lack of a measure of gang activity contributed to the weaker model fit for the facilities located in this region.

Paradigm Summaries – Deprivation and Management

As mentioned above, this study sought to assess the relative merits of the importation model while dramatically improving the empirical assessments of the deprivation and management perspectives. In a somewhat arbitrary fashion, criminologists have assigned varying degrees of significance to each of the paradigms considered. By far, the deprivation model is perhaps the most highly researched and accepted theoretical paradigm. This perspective maintains its relative importance despite the lack of consensus regarding exactly how to measure this approach.[4] This study provided more adequate measures of prison deprivation, and found two relatively consistent findings across the regression models. In the cross-sectional analysis presented in Chapter VI, cell type was the only deprivation factor with a routinely significant effect. The findings consistently revealed that housing inmates exclusively in single-cell arrangements dramatically increased the staff assault rate. However, in the longitudinal analysis, the influence of the crowding level was the only consistently significant deprivation factor, and the effect was primarily significant in the Northeast region. Both the lagged and instantaneous effects of the crowding level significantly increased the change in the staff assault rate (ΔY) as well as the 1995 staff assault rate (Y_2) in the Northeast region. The number of conditions of confinement for which the facility was under federal court order produced largely insignificant effects in both the cross-sectional and longitudinal analysis. In sum, although the deprivation factors provided the best model fit, the individual variables were not uniformly significant.

Researchers consider the management model as valuable in explaining collective acts of violence, but regard the perspective as useless when predicting individual violent acts. I sought to improve on the empirical assessment of the management model by incorporating gender demographics (male-to-female guard ratio) and a diversity indicator (index of racial variation) among the variables used to operationalize the management perspective. Unfortunately, none of the management variables were consistently significant in the cross-sectional analysis, and in the longitudinal analysis, virtually none of the factors reached significance. In which case, it appears that the management model offers little promise in terms of predicting staff assaults. However, with access to other management factors, such as the guard turnover ratio or the percentage of inmates involved in some type of rehabilitation program, the conclusions regarding the management model would likely change.

Black Rage and Prison Violence

Each of the individual components of the Black rage model were summarized at the conclusion of Chapters VI and VII. The discussion here elaborates on three unique findings regarding the empirical assessment of the proposed model. Specifically, the discussion addresses the lack of a significant effect for the ratio of White-to-Black staff, the lack of a significant model fit for the Southeast region, and the significance of the Black rage variables in the Midwest region.

White-to-Black Staff versus White-to-Black Guards

Because the ratio of White-to-Black staff used to operationalize the Black rage perspective failed to produce a noticeable effect in any of the cross-sectional TOBIT models, I removed this factor from the longitudinal data analysis.[5] At first glance, this observation appeared in stark contrast to the finding of McCorkle et al. (1995), where the researchers found that, next to security level, the ratio of White-to-Black guards was the most significant predictor of staff assaults. However, McCorkle et al. (1995) considered the ratio of White-to-Black guards, and not the ratio of White-to-Black staff. Therefore, the slightly greater representation of African-Americans among the guard population in comparison to the total staff population perhaps explains the discrepancy regarding the significance of this factor. For instance, analysis of data from the *Sourcebook of Criminal Justice Statistics* for 1994 revealed that Blacks represented 16.8 percent of the wardens and superintendents in adult correctional facilities, and 22.7 percent of the correctional officers (Maguire and Pastore 1994). This finding illustrates the higher concentration of Blacks within the guard population. Thus, combining all staff produces a relatively larger ratio of White-to-Black staff than would be found for the ratio of White-to-Black guards. Consequently, a significant effect for the White-to-Black guard ratio is likely to change after inflating the ratio by combining all prison staff. The 1990 edition of the *Census of State and Federal Adult Correctional Facilities* was the only version to include racial demographics for the guard population. Therefore, in efforts to keep the samples comparable, I computed the White-to-Black staff ratio across each year instead of the White-to-Black guard ratio.

Explaining the Southeast Region

A major assumption of the black rage theory predicted that given the well-documented history of racial discrimination in the American South (see Schuman et al. 1985; Tuch 1987), this region would display the strongest support for the proposed paradigm. However, the analysis consistently revealed that neither the percentage of Black inmates nor the percentage of Black staff significantly influenced the staff assault rate in the Southeast. I propose two reasons for the lack of a significant effect for the Black rage model in the Southeast region. First, based on the racial demographics of the staff and inmate populations found in this region, one could argue that perhaps the relatively large population of Black staff found in this region effectively countered the violent tendencies of Black inmates. Based on the data presented in Table 6.1(a-c), across all three years of data analysis, the average percentage of Black inmates in the Southeast was roughly 57 percent, while the average percentage of Black staff was approximately 27 percent. In comparison, the average percentage of Black inmates in the West across all three years was roughly 22 percent, and the average percentage of Black staff in the West was approximately 7 percent. Hence, the Southeast had the lowest ratio of Black inmates-to-Black staff. Specifically, in 1995, the average Black inmate-to-Black staff ratio equaled 19.09 in the Southeast, 19.23 in the West, 50.26 in the Northeast, and 39.42 in the Midwest. Although the West had a Black inmate-to-Black staff ratio comparable to that of the Southeast, the drastically different population sizes further indicates the unique demographic found in the Southeast. In the Northeast and the Midwest, there were significantly more Black inmates relative to the number of Black prison staff members. In which case, with the relatively high percentage of Black staff in the Southeast, Black inmates in this region perhaps experience less racial hostility towards the staff population. Consequently, both factors would essentially cancel out each other and neither would significantly influence the staff assault rate.

A second potential explanation for the lack of significance in the Black rage model in the Southeast focuses on the changing racial attitudes found in this region. In contrast to the images of racist, White southerners found during slavery and the Jim Crow era, more recent research indicates that White Americans in the Southeast have become more tolerant of racial differences (Case and Greeley 1990; Firebaugh and Davis 1988; Ellison 1991; Borg 1997). For instance, Case and Greeley (1990) analyzed data from 1965-1980 and found that individuals in the South exhibited an increasingly lower likelihood of favoring segregation in schools, opposing Blacks in their neighborhood, opposing interracial marriages, and being unhappy with Black dinner guests. Furthermore, Firebaugh and Davis (1988) analyzed trend data covering the period 1972 to 1984, and concluded that while anti-Black prejudice generally declined across the United States, such sentiments declined more rapidly in the Southeast. Therefore, with a more racially harmonious atmosphere in the Southeast than initially presumed, in conjunction with more Black representation among prison staff, the conditions believed to worsen the Black inmate's rage were not present. Consequently, the Southeast failed to generate significant findings in support of the Black rage theory. Instead, facilities in the Midwest consistently revealed the significance of Black rage in both the cross-sectional and longitudinal data analysis.

Explaining the Midwest Region

The findings for the Midwest offered the strongest support for the proposed theory of Black rage. In the cross-sectional analysis, the Midwest was the only region where the percentage of Black inmates significantly increased the staff assault rate across each year. In addition, the percentage of Black staff produced noticeable reductions in the staff assault rate in the Midwest; however, the effect only reached statistical significance in 1990. As well, in the static score change models presented in Chapter VII, the Midwest again indicated the potential significance of Black rage in predicting staff assaults. I propose two likely explanations for the observed relationship in the Midwest. First, as indicated above, the ratio of Black inmates-to-Black staff was considerably high in the Midwest. For instance, in 1995, there were approximately 39 Black inmates per each Black staff member. Next to the Southeast, the Midwest had the highest concentration of Black inmates; however, the concentration of Black staff in the Midwest was significantly lower than in the Southeast. In which case, although the regions had comparable numbers regarding Black inmates, the average percentage of Black staff across the three years was roughly 10 percent in the Midwest, in comparison to the 27 percent found in the Southeast. Therefore, the racial demographics of the staff and inmate populations in the Midwest reflected the ideal setting for observing Black rage. The relatively high percentage of Black inmates and White staff found in the Midwest likely amplified racial hostilities between the two groups by continuing the perception of White oppression over African-Americans.

The second potential explanation for the significance of Black rage in the Midwest focuses on the impoverished conditions faced by many African-Americans residing in this region. Massey and Eggers (1990) found that from 1970 to 1980, the concentration of poverty among Blacks in the Northeast and Midwest increased significantly, while Blacks in the Southeast and West showed an increase in income and affluence. Furthermore, Jargowsky (1994) analyzed census data covering the span of 1980 to 1990 and found that lower class Blacks were becoming increasingly isolated in "ghetto neighborhoods." Moreover, the increase in the concentration of Blacks in ghetto neighborhoods was greatest in the Midwest and South, while the proportions actually decreased in many Eastern states. Wilson (1994) also reported significantly higher concentrations of Black poverty in major cities located in the Midwest and Southeast. A constant theme in all three studies was the observed detrimental position of Blacks located in the Midwest. Therefore, with a higher concentration of poverty, there is perhaps a greater sense of oppression and a stronger tendency to view racism as a significant cause of one's position. As mentioned in Chapter III, marginal status in education and employment increases the level of rage in Black males by limiting their legitimate opportunities for improving their position in life. In which case, for Black inmates confined in Midwest facilities, White prison staff truly represents *symbols of oppression*. This symbolism subsequently increases the staff assault rate through the process of displaced aggression.

Data Limitations

Although findings from the Midwest suggested the significance of the Black rage theory, two limitations of the data set prohibited the formulation of strong causal statements by restricting the empirical assessment of the perspective.[6] One of the major limitations to generalizing the studies' findings pertained to the inability to understand the context surrounding inmate-on-staff assaults. By ruminative thoughts and cognitive neoassociation, the theory of Black rage predicts that certain events can trigger displaced aggression. These triggering events are typically actions that highlight, or symbolize, the history of White oppression over Blacks. For instance, in the three examples of "Black rage in Action" presented on page 140-141, the movie, *Mississippi Burning*, the confederate flag, and the word "Nigger" served as triggering events that produced violent outburst. Furthermore, in the context of the prison environment, the language and behavior of White guards can serve as triggering mechanisms for the release of violent Black rage (Fox 1982). However, without access to the context leading up to violent interactions between White prison staff and Black inmates, we can only speculate, based on racial differences, that Black rage was a significant cause of the assault. Since it is doubtful that Black rage is the only factor responsible for Black inmate assaults against White prison staff, we have to be able to rule out these other factors, which is virtually impossible without the story surrounding the event.

Given the necessity of detailing the context surrounding staff assaults, perhaps the best data set for analyzing the proposed theory of black rage would rely on the individual as the unit of analysis instead of the institution, as presented here. While criminologists contend that inmate-on-inmate assaults in prison are rare events in the inmate's institutional life (Gaes and McGuire 1985), inmate-on-staff assaults are even more of an anomaly. Most of the concerns with using the individual as the unit of analysis focused on the financial expense and difficulty in tracking inmates over a prolonged period of time. Therefore, in efforts to observe more occurrences of prison assaults, researchers suggested using the institution as the unit of analysis. However, I propose that instead of actually tracking individuals, the researcher should conduct a content analysis of all disciplinary reports filed for assaults against facility staff. This would provide the ideal type of individual level data necessary to examine the Black rage theory, as well as provide a respectable number of prison assaults from which to form generalizations. Such data sources are rich in contextual information surrounding the assault event, and provide the much needed racial demographics of the victim and the offender. Not gathering the data via self-report surveys greatly reduces the time and expense mentioned as an obstacle by criminologists such as Gaes and McGuire (1985).

A second major limitation of the current data source concerns the relatively long lag between observation points in the longitudinal analysis. While the ability to link facilities in the 1990 and 1995 data sets greatly enhanced the studies findings and conclusions, many would contend that a five-year lag is perhaps too long to formulate causal statements, and thus raises the possibility of other factors explaining the change in prison violence. In future studies on prison violence that adopt a longitudinal research design and use the institution as the unit of analysis, a shorter lag between observations, such as one-year intervals, will better protect against spurious relationships. For instance, in this study, annual figures for the percentage of Black inmates, percentage of Black prison staff, and the staff assault indicator would have allowed for a more accurate assessment of the Black rage perspective. With a relatively long window of time between observations, there is an increased possibility that changes in other variables, most notably those external to the institution, better explain the observed change in the staff assault rate. In addition, gathering data at shorter intervals will produce more observation points, which permit stronger statements regarding the association between two factors. For example, to show that changes in the Black rage variables were significantly associated with the changes in the staff assault rate when considering a five-year interval is adequate. However, routinely showing this relationship based on annual data is by far more powerful in terms of theory construction. Nevertheless, despite the data limitations, this study has major implications for the Black community, prison administrators, and most importantly, the discipline of criminology.

Implications - Black Community

Chapter III presented several historical and contemporary sources of rage in Black males. The sources considered represented historical issues, such as the emasculating experience of slavery, the fear of lynching, the injustice of the convict lease system, and the tragic cost of expressing rage during the civil rights era. The contemporary sources of rage touched on issues in the Black family, education, employment, and a variety of discrimination stages in the American criminal justice system. Collectively, the historical and contemporary sources of Black rage paint a disturbing picture for the Black community. With such a large number of Black males experiencing multiple sources of rage, *the tangle of pathology* will only worsen for the Black community. Several of the consequences of Black rage, such as suicide, or Black-on-White crime, produce a self-generating cycle of rage. The removal of adult Black males via death or incarceration contributes to the breakdown of the family structure, which in turn has implications for Black male youth in education, which in turn has implications for Black males in employment, and the saga continues. As long as the cycle of rage continues, Black males will always maintain their over-representation in American prisons and jails, an observation that has negative implications for the Black community and for prison administrators.

Implications - Prison Administrators

In accords with the frustration-aggression process described by Dollard et al. (1939), feelings of anger and rage will eventually find an avenue for expression. In addition to the inevitability of expression, there is an intrinsic desire to displace aggression onto individuals who resemble the initial source of frustration. Therefore, the arrival of Black males to the confines of prison, with well-established anger towards the larger system of White oppression, produces detrimental consequences for both White prison staff and White inmates. Awareness of the reality of Black rage can assist prison administrators in the housing patterns and the scheduling of activities involving the inmate population. It is not coincidental that research shows that as high as 75 percent of all inmates seeking protective custody are White (Jacobs 1983). The qualitative statements provided by Carroll (1974, 1977) and Robinson (1971) indicate that White inmates perhaps seek protective custody as a safe haven from the Black inmate's violent display of his pent-up anger and rage directed towards the larger system of White oppression.

Understanding Black rage also has implications for the staffing patterns in American prisons. The vast majority of Black males in prison have likely progressed through social structures where they have equated authority and domination with being White. Subsequently, the presence of Black prison guards and other staff members refute the image of the prison structure as another arena in which Whites control and oppress Blacks. Given that "the very structure of the prison, its walls and bars, its rigid hierarchy, its whiteness, seems designed to foster an image of a racist conspiracy" (Carroll 1982: 184), to staff the facility with an over-representation of Whites results in their becoming "convenient and highly visible symbol[s] of White economic dominance and authority over Blacks" (Fox 1982: 65). In which case, through the process of ruminative thought and cognitive neoassociation, White prison staff become the victims of preference for displacement of the Black inmate's anger and rage. Therefore, prison administrators could use their knowledge and understanding of Black rage to assist in not only staffing patterns, but also areas such as policies and procedures, or regulating general tone and demeanor during interactions with Black inmates. Such considerations should effectively reduce the likelihood of interracial assaults in prison involving White prison staff and Black inmates.

Implications - Discipline of Criminology

In spite of the fact that numerous literary sources routinely reference the process described here as Black rage, the discipline of criminology has largely ignored the concept. Throughout American society, episodes portraying the violent consequences of Black rage occur at a greater frequency than most would care to admit. Consider for instance, the individual portrayals of Black rage, such as the violent outburst of Colin Ferguson or group displays of Black rage, such as the 1992 LA riots following the Rodney King verdicts, or the more recent riots in Cincinnati, Ohio following the police murder of a young Black male for a traffic violation. While the examples given here were the more publicized cases, literature by Black authors from a variety of disciplines and occupations testify to the prevalence of everyday Black rage among African-Americans of all demographic and social categories.[7]   In addition to the cited literature, Black inmates in qualitative interviews, such as Carroll (1974, 1977) or literary works such as Cleaver (1968) and Jackson (1970), have testified to the role of Black rage in their decision to commit crimes and their choice of a victim.

Not only have criminologists ignored the qualitative evidence regarding the presence of Black rage, but they have also largely chosen not to see the increasing rates of interracial crime where Blacks victimize Whites. Whether examining the FBI's Uniform Crime Report, Hate Crime Statistics, or the National Crime Victimization Survey, the fact remains that Blacks victimize Whites at drastically higher frequencies than Whites victimize Blacks. Given the plethora of evidence indicating the reality of Black rage, one has to raise the question, *Why has this concept not been more thoroughly examined by mainstream criminologists?* I believe there are two main reasons for the "hands-off" approach concerning this topic within the discipline of criminology.

Krupey (1997: 197) summarize best the first explanation for avoiding the topic of Black rage when he notes, "the issue of Black-on-White crime is the dirty little secret of American society-something almost everyone knows about or suspects, but no one discusses. To discuss it, in fact is to run the risk of being stigmatized as a racist" (Krupey 1997: 197). The general fear of the racist label constricts most examinations of the connection between race and crime to, superficial or safe topics. Consequently, consideration of the likely influence of Black rage is not a safe topic, i.e. most mainstream criminologist would not pick up and explore the concept.

This leads to the second reason for the exclusion of this concept, which stems from the absence of the Black voice in criminological discourse and the underdevelopment of Black criminology. Through the absence of the Black perspective from mainstream criminology, the discipline has failed to detail more concisely *why* African-Americans have higher rates of criminal offending, which subsequently is the primary objective of a "Black criminology" as described by Russell (1992). Given that skin color appears to grant one the right to make controversial statements about Black culture,[8] criminology needs the Black voice; otherwise, the discipline will not progress to new unexplored issues regarding the connection between race and crime. The unexplored issue addressed in this study has tremendous implications for the discipline of criminology. The conceptual model of Black rage not only suggests new directions for criminological theory, but also supplements the general arguments of several classical theories of deviance. In particular, Black rage has implications for anomie and strain theories, Akers' social learning theory, Hirshi's social bonding theory, and general conflict theories of deviant behavior. With the foundation of Black rage well established by this study and the sources cited within, the question becomes *who* and *when* will mainstream criminology give serious consideration to the significance of Black rage and other topics pondered by the excluded voice.

[1] Poussiant and Alexander (2000: 102), *Lay My Burden Down*

[2] Hooks (1995: 26), *Killing Rage*

[3] The 1990 version of the census included a region indicator but not a state indicator.

[4] For example, Gaes and McGuire (1985) operationalize deprivation by the average percentage of time remaining on the inmate's sentence, the staff-to-inmate ratio, and the percentage of staff that were correctional officers. In contrast, McCorkle et al. (1995) operationalized deprivation by crowding, court order for conditions of confinement, and increases in the number of security personnel. These two studies illustrate the lack of uniformity in selecting indicators of the deprivation perspective.

[5] I removed this variable only after estimating the change score models with the ratio of White-to-Black staff included in the equation and continuously finding no noticeable effect for this factor.

[6] The limitations presented on pages 161-162 in Chapter V were pre-analysis obstacles that were obvious before conducting any form of analysis. The limitations discussed here reflect post-analysis considerations.

[7] See Hooks (1995), McCall (1995), Grier and Cobbs (1965), Cose (1993), Gibbs (1988, 1994), Peterson (2000), and many more, most of which are referenced in Chapter III.

[8] See Chapter I, page 2-3, discussing the differential reactions to controversial statements made by Moynihan (1965), and Black scholars, E. Franklin Frazier and Kenneth B. Clark.

Appendices

Appendix A: Physically Matched Facilities – Decisions

Query	Name as Reported 1995	Name as Reported 1990	Decision	
1	YOUTH CORRECT INST. A.C. WAGNER	A.C. WAGNER YOUTH CORR. INST		
2	APALACHEE CORRECT INSTIT	APALACHEE CORRECTIONAL INSTITUTIO		
3	APPALACHIAN CORRECTIONAL UNIT # 2	APPALACHIAN CORRECTIONAL UNIT		
4	ARIZONA STATE PRISON - WINSLOW	ARIZONA STATE PRISON- WINSLOW		
5	ARKANSAS VALLEY CORR FACILITY	ARKANSAS VALLEY CORRECTIONAL		
6	AVON PARK CORR INST & WORK CAMP	AVON PARK CORRECTIONAL INSTITUTIO		
7	BAKER CORR INST & WORK CAMP	BAKER CORRECTIONAL INSTITUTION		
8	BOLIVAR CO COMM WORK CTR	BOLIVAR CO COMM WORK CENTER		
9	BOTETOURT CORR. UNIT #25	BOTETOURT CORR. UNIT 25		
10	BROOKS CORRECT FACILITY	BROOKS REGIONAL FACILITY		
11	CALHOUN CORR INSTITUTION	CALHOUN CORRECTIONAL INSTITUTION		
12	CARL ROBINSON CORR INST	CARL ROBINSON CORRECTIONAL INST		
13	CAROLINE CORR. UNIT #2	CAROLINE CORR. UNIT 2		
14	CARSON CITY CORR FACILITY	CARSON CITY REGIONAL FACILITY		
15	CARSON CITY TEMP FACILITY	CARSON CITY TEMPORARY FACILITY		
16	CARYVILLE WORK CAMP	CARYVILLE VOCATIONAL CTR		
17	CENTENNIAL CORRECT FACIL - MAX SE	CENTENNIAL CORRECT FACIL		
18	CENTRAL NM CORRECT COMPLEX	CENTRAL NM CORRECT FACIL		
19	CHARLESTON CORRECT FACIL	CHARLESTON CORRECTIONAL FACILITY		
20	CHARLOTTE CORRECT. INSTITUTION	CHARLOTTE CORRECTIONAL INSTITUTIO		

249

Query	Name as Reported 1995		Name as Reported 1990		Decision
21	COASTAL CORRECT INSTIT		COASTAL WORK RELEASE CTR		Excluded
22	COLD SPRINGS UNIT		COLD SPRING GREENVILLE CORR. UN		
23	COLLINS CORRECTIONAL FAC		COLLINS CORRECTIONAL FACILITY		
24	COMM SERVICE CENTER NO 1	A	COMM SERVICE CENTER NO 1	B	Excluded All
			COMM SERVICE CENTER NO 1	C	
25	COXSACKIE CORRECT FACIL		COXSACKIE CORRECTIONAL FACILITY		
26	CROSS CTY CORR INST & WORK CAMP		CROSS CITY CORRECTIONAL INSTITUTI		
27	DADE CORR INST & WORK CAMP		DADE CORRECTIONAL INSTITUTION		
28	DEERFIELD CORR CENTER		DEERFIELD CORRECT CTR		
29	DESOTO CORR INST & WORK CAMP		DESOTO CORRECTIONAL INSTITUTION		
30	DIAGNOSTIC UNIT	A	DIAGNOSTIC UNIT	C	
	DIAGNOSTIC UNIT	B	DIAGNOSTIC UNIT	D	
31	DINWIDDIE CORR. UNIT #27		DINWIDDIE CORR. UNIT 27		
32	DRAPER CORRECTIONAL FACILITY		DRAPER CORRECTIONAL CTR		
33	EL DORADO CORRECTIONAL FACILITY		EL DORADO HONOR CAMP		Excluded
34	FAIRFAX CORR. UNIT #30		FAIRFAX CORR. UNIT 30		
35	FLORIDA STATE PRISON & WORK CAMP		FLORIDA STATE PRISON		
36	FREMONT CORRECT FACILITY -MEDIUM		FREMONT CORRECT FACILITY		
37	G K FOUNTAIN CORRECT FAC		G K FOUNTAIN CORRECT CTR		
38	G. ROBERT COTTON CORR FAC		G. ROBERT COTTON CORRECTIONAL		
39	GABILAN CONSERVATION CAMP		GABILAN CONSTRUCTION CAMP		
40	GEORGE CO COMM WORK CTR		GEORGE CO COMM WORK CENTER		

Query	Name as Reported 1995		Name as Reported 1990		Decision
41	GLADES CORR INST & WORK CAMP		GLADES CORRECTIONAL INSTITUTION		
42	GREEN BAY CORRECT INSTIT		GREEN BAY CORRECTIONAL INSTITUTIO		
43	HALIFAX CORR. UNIT # 23		HALIFAX CORR. UNIT 23		
44	HAMILTON CORR INST & WORK CAMP		HAMILTON CORRECTIONAL INSTITUTION		
45	HARRISONBURG CORR. UNIT #8		HARRISONBURG CORR. UNIT 8		
46	HAYNESVILLE CORR CENTER		HAYNESVILLE CORR. UNIT 17		Excluded
47	HENDRY CORR INST & WORK CAMP		HENDRY CORRECTIONAL INSTITUTION		
48	HIAWATHA CORECT FACILITY		HIAWATHA TEMPORARY FACILITY		
49	HIGH SECURITY CENTER – DOC		HIGH SECURITY CENTER		
50	HOLMES CORR INST & WORK CAMP		HOLMES CORRECTIONAL INSTITUTION		
51	HUTCHINS SJF	A	HUTCHINSON CORRECT WORK FACIL	C	Excluded A & C
	HUTCHINSON CORR FAC-CENTRAL UNIT	B	HUTCHINSON CORRECTIONAL FACILITY	D	
52	IDAHO MAXIMUM SECURITY INSTIT.		IDAHO MAXIMUM SEC INSTIT		
53	IL. RIVER CORRECTIONAL CENTER		IL RIVER CORRECTIONAL CENTER		
54	JACKIE BRANNON CORRECTIONS CENTER		JACKIE BRANNON		
55	JESTER UNIT III		JESTER UNIT 111		
56	KENOSHA CORRECTIONAL CENTER		KENOSHA CORRECT CTR		
57	KINROSS CORRECTIONAL FACILITY		KINROSS CORRECT FACILITY		
58	LAKE CORRECTIONAL INSTIT		LAKE CORRECTIONAL INSTITUTION		
59	LAKELAND CORRECT FACILITY		LAKELAND CORRECTIONAL FACIL.		
60	LANSIN CORR FAC-CENTRAL UNIT		LANSING CORRECTIONAL FACILITY		
61	LAWTEY CORRECT INSTIT		LAWTEY CORRECTIONAL INSTITUTION		

Query	Name as Reported 1995		Name as Reported 1990		Decision
62	LIBERTY CORR INST & WORK CAMP		LIBERTY CORRECTIONAL INSTITUTION		
63	LINCOLN CORRECTIONAL CTR	A	LINCOLN CORRECTIONAL CTR	C	
	LINCOLN CORRECTIONAL CTR	B	LINCOLN CORRECTIONAL CTR	D	
64	MADISON CORR INST & WORK CAMP	A	MADISON CORRECTIONAL INSTITUTION	B	Excluded C
			MADISON CORRECTIONAL INSTITUTION	C	
65	MARION CORR INST & WORK CAMP	A	MARION CORRECT TREAT CTR	D	
	MARION CORRECT INSTIT	B	MARION CORRECT. INSTIT	E	Excluded C & D
	MARION CORRECTIONAL INST	C	MARION CORRECTIONAL INSTITUTION	F	
66	MASS. CORR. INSTITUTION-PLYMOUTH		MASS CORR INSTITUTION PLYMOUTH		
67	MASS CORR INST-NORFOLK	A	MASS CORRECT INSTITUTION	C	
	MASS CORRECT INSTITUTION	B	MASS CORRECT INSTITUTION	D	Excluded C
			MASS CORRECT INSTITUTION	E	
68	MAX SECURITY FACILITY – DOC		MAX SECURITY FACILITY		
69	MAYO CORRECTIONAL INST		MAYO CORRECTIONAL INSTITUTION		
70	MCCAIN CORRECTIONAL HOSPITAL		MCCAIN CORRECTIONAL INSTITUTE		
71	MD CORR INSTIT-HAGERSTOWN	A	MD CORRECTIONAL INSTIT	C	
	MD CORRECTIONAL INSTIT-JESSUP	B	MD CORRECTIONAL INSTIT	D	
72	MED SECURITY FACILITY – DOC		MED SECURITY FACILITY		Excluded
73	MEDARVILLE CORR UNIT		MEDARYVILLE YOUTH CAMP		
74	MID MICHIGAN TEMP CORR FACILITY		MID-MICHIGAN TEMPORARY		
75	MILL CREEK CORRECT. FACIL.		MILL CREEK CORRECTIONAL FACILITY		
76	MIN SECURITY FACILITY – DOC		MIN SECURITY FACILITY		

252

Query	Name as Reported 1995		Name as Reported 1990		Decision
77	MN CORR FACIL-LINO LAKES		MN CORR FACIL LINO LAKES		
78	MN CORR FACIL-RED WING		MN CORR FACIL RED WING		
79	MN CORR FACIL-STILLWATER		MN CORR FACIL STILLWATER		
80	MN CORRECTIONAL FACILITY	A	MINN CORRECTIONAL FACILITY	D	
	MN CORR FACILITY-FARIBAULT	B	MN CORRECTIONAL FACILITY	E	Excluded B & D
	MN CORR FACILITY-ST. CLOUD	C	MN CORRECTIONAL FACILITY	F	
81	MOBERLY CORRECTIONAL CTR		MOBERLY CORR CTR		
82	MOORE UNIT		MOORE CORR. CENTER		Excluded
83	MULE CREEK STATE PRISON		MULE CREEK ST PRISON		
84	MULTI PURPOSE CJ FACIL MAX SEC		MULTI PURPOSE CJ FACIL		
85	MUSKOGEE COMM CORRS CENTER		MUSKOGEE COMM TREAT CTR		
86	NEW RIVER CORRECTIONAL INST		NEW RIVER CORRECTIONAL INSTITUTIO		
87	NO. FLORIDA RECEPTION CENTER		NORTH FLORIDA RECEPTION CENTER		
88	NORTHERN STATE CORR FACILITY		NORTHERN STATE PRISON		Excluded
89	NORTON STATE CORR FAC - CENT UNIT		NORTON CORRECTIONAL FACILITY		
90	OGDENSBURG CORRECT FACIL		OGDENSBURG CORRECTIONAL FACILITY		
91	OKALOOSA CORR INST & WORK CAMP		OKALOOSA CORRECTIONAL INSTITUTION		
92	ORLEANS CORRECT FACILITY		ORLEANS CORRECTIONAL FACILITY		
93	OTISVILLE CORRECT FACIL		OTISVILLE CORRECT. FACIL.		
94	PALMER CORRECTIONAL CTR		PALMER CORRECTIONAL CENTER		
95	PATRICK HENRY CORR. UNIT #28		PATRICK HENRY CORR. UNIT 28		
96	PENITENTIARY OF NM-MAIN	A	PENITENTIARY OF NEW MEXICO-NORTH	B	Excluded All

253

Query	Name as Reported 1995		Name as Reported 1990		Decision
			PENITENTIARY OF NEW MEXICO-SOUTH	C	
97	PINE BLUFF UNIT		PINE LODGE CORRECT. CTR.		
98	POLK CORR INST & WORK CAMP	A	POLK CORRECTIONAL INSTITUTION	B	Excluded C
			POLK WORK CAMP	C	
99	PRE RELEASE CENTER		PRE RELEASE UNIT		Excluded
100	QUINCY VOC CTR & WORK CAMP		QUINCY VOCATIONAL CENTER		
101	QUITMAN CO COMM WORK CTR		QUITMAN COUNTY COMMUNITY WORK CTR		
102	R J DONOVAN CORR FAC - ROCK MOUNTA		R J DONOVAN CORRECTIONAL FACILITY		
103	RAMSEY UNIT NO 3		RAMSEY UNIT 3		
104	RECEP AND DIAGNOSTIC CTR		RECEP AND GUIDANCE CTR		Excluded
105	SANTIAM CORR INST		SANTIAM CORRECTIONAL INSTITUTION		
106	SMITH UNIT		SMITH MT LAKE CORR. UNIT 24		
107	SOUTH IDAHO CORR INST		SOUTH IDAHO CORRECTIONAL INSTITUT		
108	SOUTHEAST STATE CORR FACILITY		SOUTHERN ST CORRECT FAC		
109	ST PRISON OF S. MI-SOUTH COMPLEX	A	ST PRISON OF SO MICHIGAN	C	Excluded A
	ST PRISON OF SO MICHIGAN -CENTRAL	B			
110	ST REG CORRECTIONAL FACL-MERCER		ST REG CORRECTIONAL FACL		
111	STATE CORR INST-GRATERFORD	A	STATE CORRECTIONAL INST	P	Excluded H, I, J, K, M & P
	STATE CORR INST-GREENSBURG	B	STATE CORRECTIONAL INST	Q	
	STATE CORR INST-HUNTINGDON	C	STATE CORRECTIONAL INST	R	
	STATE CORR INST-PITTSBURGH	D	STATE CORRECTIONAL INST	S	
	STATE CORR INST-RETREAT	E	STATE CORRECTIONAL INST	T	

254

Query	Name as Reported 1995		Name as Reported 1990		Decision
	STATE CORR INST-SMITHFIELD	F	STATE CORRECTIONAL INSTIT.	U	
	STATE CORR INST-WAYMART	G	STATE CORRECTIONAL INSTITUTION	V	
	STATE CORR INST AT COAL TOWNSHIP	H	STATE CORRECTIONAL INSTITUTION	W	
	STATE CORR INST AT GREENE	I	STATE CORRECTIONAL INSTITUTION	X	
	STATE CORR INST AT MAHANOY	J	STATE CORRECTIONAL INSTITUTION	Y	
	STATE CORR INST AT SOMERSET	K	STATE CORRECTIONAL INSTITUTION	Z	
	STATE CORRECTIONAL INST-DALLAS	L			
	STATE CORRECTIONAL INST ALBION	M			
	STATE CORRECTIONAL INST AT CRESSO	N			
	STATE CORRECTIONAL INST AT FRACKV	O			
112	SUMTER CORR INST & WORK CAMP	A	SUMTER CORRECTIONAL INSTITUTION	B	Excluded C
			SUMTER FORESTRY CAMP	C	
113	TAZWELL CORR. UNIT #31		TAZWELL CORR. UNIT 31		
114	THUMB CORRECTIONAL FACILITY		THUMB REG CORRECTIONAL FACILITY		
115	TOMOKA CORR INST & WORK CAMP		TOMOKA CORRECTIONAL INSTITUTION		
116	UNION CORRECT INSTIT		UNION CORRECTIONAL INSTITUTION		
117	WAKE CORRECTION CENTER		WAKE CORRECTIONS CENTER		
118	WALTON CORRECT. INSTITUTION		WALTON CORRECTIONAL INSTITUTION		
119	WARREN CORRECT. INSTITUTION		WARREN CORRECTIONAL INSTITUTION		
120	WASHINGTON CO COMM WORK CTR		WASHINGTON CO COMM WORK CENTER		
121	WENDE CORRECTIONAL FAC		WENDE CORRECTIONAL FACILITY		
122	WEST NM CORR FACILITY REC-DIAG ME		WEST NM CORR FACILITY		

255

Query	Name as Reported 1995		Name as Reported 1990		Decision	
123	WEST TN HIGH SECURITY FACILITY		WEST TN. HIGH SEC. FACILITY			
124	WESTERN IL. CORR. CENTER		WESTERN IL CORR CENTER			
125	WESTERN KY CORR. COMPLEX		WESTERN KY FARM CENTER			
126	WHITE POST CORR. UNIT #7		WHITE POST CORR. UNIT 7			
127	WILKINSON CO COMM WORK CTR		WILKINSON COUNTY COMM. WORK CTR.			
128	WISE CORR. UNIT # 18		WISE CORR. UNIT 18			
129	WOODSTOCK REGIONAL CORR FACILITY		WOODSTOCK CORRECT CTR			
130	YANCEY CORR. CTR		YANCEY CORR CTR			

Appendix B: Physically Matched Facilities – Notes

Query	Same Address	Problem
1	Y	In 1995 surveyor switched the order of the words in the facility name. Both listed as "A.C. Wagner Youth Correctional Institution" in ACA Directory.
2	Y	Inconsistent abbreviations in reporting facility name.
3	Y	Both listed as "Appalachian Correctional Unit #29" in ACA Directory.
4	Y	Extra spaces reported around the dash mark in facility name.
5	Y	Both listed as "Arkansas Valley Correctional Facility" in ACA Directory.
6	Y	Both listed as "Avon Park Correctional Institution" in ACA Directory.
7	Y	Both listed as "Baker Correctional Institution" in ACA Directory.
8	Y	Inconsistent abbreviations in reporting facility name.
9	Y	In 1990 surveyor left off the "#" sign.
10	Y	1995 listed as "Brooks Regional Facility" & 1990 listed as "E.C. Brooks Regional Facility", but both have same address.
11	Y	Inconsistent abbreviations in reporting facility name.
12	Y	Inconsistent abbreviations in reporting facility name.
13	Y	In 1990 surveyor left off the "#" sign.
14	Y	Both listed under the same name in ACA Directory. The addresses are different but the telephone numbers, contact information, etc. are all the same.
15	Y	In consistent abbreviations in reporting facility name.
16	Y	Both listed as "Caryville Work Camp" in ACA Directory.
17	Y	Both listed under the same name. The 1995 data referred to the security level in name. In 1990, the facility is also listed as maximum-security.
18	Y	Both listed under the same name in ACA Directory.
19	Y	Inconsistent abbreviations in reporting facility name.
20	Y	Inconsistent abbreviations in reporting facility name.
21	N	"Coastal Work Release CTR" not listed under the GA facilities. Both also have different construction years and security levels.
22	Y	Listed as "Greenville Correctional Unit" in 1990. Both have same construction year and telephone number.
23	Y	Inconsistent abbreviations in reporting facility name.
24	N	"Comm Service Center NO 1" not listed under PA facilities in 1990. Cannot tell which file to merge with the 1995 data.
25	Y	Inconsistent abbreviations in reporting facility name.
26	Y	Both listed as "Cross City Correctional Institution" in ACA Directory.
27	Y	Both Listed as "Dade Correctional Institution and Work Camp" in ADA Directory.

257

Query	Same Address	Problem
28	Y	Inconsistent abbreviations in reporting facility name.
29	Y	Both listed as "Desoto Correctional Institution" in ACA Directory, and construction years match.
30	Y	One of these facilities is in TX and the other in AR. However, both can be paired using the different construction dates.
31	Y	In 1990 surveyor left off the "#" sign.
32	Y	Both reported as "Draper Correctional Center" in ACA Directory.
33	N	Both facility names appear in the respective volumes of the ACA Directory, with different addresses, telephone numbers, contact information, etc.
34	Y	In 1990 surveyor left off the "#" sign.
35	Y	Both reported as "Florida State Prison" in ACA Directory.
36	Y	Both listed under the same name. The 1995 data referred to the security level in name. In 1990, the facility is also listed as medium-security.
37	Y	Both reported as "G.K. Fountain Correctional Center" in ACA Directory.
38	Y	1995 reported as "G. Robert Cotton Regional Correctional Facility", and 1990 reported as "G. Robert Cotton Correctional Facility". Both have same address.
39	NA	Neither facility name appears in the ACA directory, however based on the information in the data sets these appear to be the same facility.
40	Y	Inconsistent abbreviations in reporting facility name.
41	Y	Both listed as "Glades Correctional Institution" in ACA Directory.
42	Y	Inconsistent abbreviations in reporting facility name.
43	Y	In 1990 surveyor left off the "#" sign.
44	Y	Both listed as "Hamilton Correctional Institution" in ACA Directory.
45	Y	In 1990 surveyor left off the "#" sign.
46	N	Both are listed in the ACA Directory. They appear to be different facilities based on the name differences and other information.
47	Y	Both listed as "Hendry Correctional Institution" in ACA Directory.
48	Y	The names are listed differently in both directories, but based on the telephone numbers and facility demographics; they appear to be the same facility.
49	Y	Both listed as "High Security Center" in ACA Directory.
50	Y	Both listed as "Holmes Correctional Institution" in ACA Directory.
51	Y	The facilities on the second row of the query were listed under different names but appear to be the same based on the addresses and construction years.
52	Y	Inconsistent abbreviations in reporting facility name.
53	Y	The surveyor in 1995 added a period after the state abbreviation.
54	Y	Both listed as "Jackie Brannon Correctional Center" in the ACA Directory.

Query	Same Address	Problem
55	Y	Inconsistency in the symbols used to denote the number "111".
56	Y	Inconsistent abbreviations in reporting facility name.
57	Y	Inconsistent abbreviations in reporting facility name.
58	Y	Inconsistent abbreviations in reporting facility name.
59	Y	Inconsistent abbreviations in reporting facility name.
60	Y	In 1990, the facility is listed as "Kansas State Penitentiary". Using the internet and the cite http://www.prisons.com/calendar/ I was able to confirm that the facility changed its name to "Lansing Correctional Facility".
61	Y	Inconsistent abbreviations in reporting facility name.
62	Y	Both listed as "Liberty Correctional Institution" in the ACA Directory.
63	Y	One of these facilities is in IL and the other in NE. However, both can be paired using the different construction dates.
64	Y	1995 listed as "Madison Correctional Institution" in ACA Directory. This facility pairs with the first facility in 1990 using region and construction year.
65	Y	Based on the information in the data sets and the ACA Directory, A and F, and B and E are the same facilities, while C and D appear to be separate facilities.
66	Y	Inconsistent inclusion of periods and the dash mark in 1990.
67	Y	Based on the information in the data sets and the ACA Directory, A and D, and B and E are the same facilities, while C appears to be a separate facility.
68	Y	Based on the information in the ACA Directory and the data sets, these appear to be the same facility.
69	Y	Inconsistent abbreviations in reporting facility name.
70	Y	Both listed as "McCain Correctional Hospital" in ACA Directory, and have the same construction dates in the data sets.
71	Y	Based on the information in the data sets and the ACA Directory, A and C, and B and D are the same facilities.
72	N	Based on the information in the data sets and the ACA Directory, these appear to be two separate facilities.
73	Y	Based facility and personnel demographics these appear to be the same facility despite being listed in the ACA Directory under 2 different names.
74	N	Based on the information in the data sets both appear to be the same facility. The 1990 ACA Directory does not include "Mid-Michigan Temporary".
75	Y	Inconsistent abbreviations in reporting facility name.
76	Y	Based on the information in the data sets and the ACA Directory, these appear to be two separate facilities.
77	Y	The 1990 facility name does not include the dash mark.
78	Y	The 1990 facility name does not include the dash mark.
79	Y	The 1990 facility name does not include the dash mark.

Query	Same Address	Problem
80	Y	Based on the information in the data sets and the ACA Directory, A and F, and C and E are the same facilities, while B and D appear to be separate facilities.
81	Y	Inconsistent abbreviations in reporting facility name.
82	N	Neither facility appears in the ACA Directory nor does the information in the data sets indicate that these are the same facility.
83	Y	Inconsistent abbreviations in reporting facility name.
84	Y	Inconsistent abbreviations in reporting facility name.
85	Y	Both names appear in the ACA Directory with the same address. The information in the data sets also matches on capacity and region.
86	Y	Inconsistent abbreviations in reporting facility name.
87	Y	Inconsistent abbreviations in reporting facility name.
88	N	Neither facility appears in the ACA Directory nor does the information in the data sets indicate that these are the same facility.
89	Y	The similarities in construction year personnel indicate ACA that these are the same facility, despite the names being reversed in the ACA Directory.
90	Y	Inconsistent abbreviations in reporting facility name.
91	Y	Both listed as "Okaloosa Correctional Institution" in ACA Directory.
92	Y	Inconsistent abbreviations in reporting facility name.
93	Y	In 1990 the surveyor placed periods after the abbreviations.
94	Y	Inconsistent abbreviations in reporting facility name.
95	Y	In 1990 surveyor left off the "#" sign.
96	Y	Although these appear to be three separate facilities, they have the same addresses in the directory, but neither appears in both years of data.
97	N	Based on the ACA Directory and the information in the data sets, these appear to be separate facilities.
98	Y	Based on the information in the data sets and the ACA Directory, A and B, are the same facility, while C appears to be separate wing or institution.
99	Y	Based on the differences between the facility states and region, these appear to be separate facilities.
100	?	Neither facility appears in the ACA Directory. However, using region and construction year from the data sets, they appear to be the same facility.
101	Y	Inconsistent abbreviations in reporting facility name.
102	Y	Inconsistent reporting of facility name.
103	Y	Inconsistent reporting of facility name.
104	N	"Recep and Guidance CTR" does not appear in the ACA Directory as a facility in Indiana, and the information in the data sets does not match.
105	Y	Inconsistent abbreviations in reporting facility name.
106	Y	Based on the information in the ACA Directory and the data sets, these appear to be separate facilities.

Query	Same Address	Problem
107	Y	Inconsistent abbreviations in reporting facility name.
108	Y	Based on the information in the ACA Directory and the data sets, these appear to be separate facilities.
109	Y	Based on the information in the data sets and the ACA Directory, B and C, are the same facility, while A appears to be separate institution.
110	Y	1995 listed as "State Correctional Facility at Mercer" while 1990 listed as Regional Correctional Facility as Mercer". Appear to be the same in data.
111	NA	All of the facilities in query 13 were located in Pennsylvania. Based on the information from the ACA Directory, and using the construction year and capacity figures from the data sets, the following combinations appear to be the same facility: L & Q, A & R, C & S, D & T, F & U, B & V, N & W, O & X, E & Y, and G & Z. Most of the remaining facilities were built after 1995.
112	Y	Facilities A and B both listed as "Sumter Correctional Institution" in ACA Directory. Facility C appears to be a separate institution.
113	Y	In 1990 surveyor left off the "#" sign.
114	Y	Both listed as "Thumb Regional Correctional Facility" in ACA Directory.
115	Y	Both listed as "Tomoka Correctional Institution and Work Camp" in ACA Directory.
116	Y	Inconsistent abbreviations in reporting facility name.
117	Y	Both listed as "Wake Correctional Center" in ACA Directory.
118	Y	Inconsistent abbreviations in reporting facility name.
119	Y	Inconsistent abbreviations in reporting facility name.
120	Y	Inconsistent abbreviations in reporting facility name.
121	Y	Inconsistent abbreviations in reporting facility name.
122	Y	Both listed as "Western New Mexico Correctional Facility" in ACA Directory.
123	Y	Inconsistent abbreviations in reporting facility name.
124	Y	Surveyor in 1995 included periods after abbreviations.
125	Y	Both names appear in ACA Directory with the same address and other facility demographics.
126	Y	In 1990 surveyor left off the "#" sign.
127	Y	Inconsistent abbreviations in reporting facility name.
128	Y	In 1990 surveyor left off the "#" sign.
129	Y	Both names appear in ACA Directory under the same address, which indicates a facility name change between 1990 and 1995.
130	Y	Surveyor in 1995 included periods after abbreviations.

Appendix C: Additional Data Analysis – Cross-sectional
Table 1 - Correlation Matrix for 1984 Variables

	Staff Assault Rate	Inmate Assault Rate	Region	Security Level	Cell Type	Average Crowding Level	Deprivation Score	Percent CO's	Male-to-Female CO's	Index of Racial Variation	Percent Black Inmates	Percent Black Staff	White-to-Black Staff
Staff Assault Rate	1	**0.22**	-0.07	0.02	**0.19**	0.03	0.08	0.07	0.11	0.11	**0.15**	0.11	-0.02
Inmate Assault Rate		1	0.07	0.01	0.05	0.06	0.01	-0.02	0.12	0.02	0.05	0.04	-0.03
Region			1	0.07	-0.05	-0.03	-0.01	-0.03	-0.02	0.04	-0.02	0.04	-0.02
Security Level				1	**-0.16**	-0.08	0.10	**0.27**	-0.13	**0.31**	**0.45**	**0.41**	**-0.23**
Cell Type					1	-0.07	0.03	-0.09	0.05	0.01	-0.10	0.00	0.08
Average Crowding Level						1	**-0.15**	-0.09	**0.21**	-0.08	0.06	-0.03	0.07
Deprivation Score							1	0.05	-0.07	0.12	-0.01	0.01	-0.05
Percent CO's								1	-0.03	**0.15**	**0.23**	0.10	-0.10
Male-to-Female CO's									1	**-0.24**	0.09	**-0.18**	**0.18**
Index of Racial Variation										1	**0.38**	**0.76**	**-0.48**
Percent Black Inmates											1	**0.56**	**-0.22**
Percent Black Staff												1	**-0.36**
White-to-Black Staff													1

Bold Coefficients Significant at $\alpha = 0.001$

Table 2 - Correlation Matrix for 1990 Variables

	Staff Assault Rate	Inmate Assault Rate	Region	Security Level	Cell Type	Average Crowding Level	Deprivation Score	Percent CO's	Male-to-Female CO's	Index of Racial Variation	Percent Black Inmates	Percent Black Staff	White-to-Black Staff
Staff Assault Rate	1	**0.36**	**0.29**	-0.08	**0.23**	-0.02	0.04	-0.01	0.01	0.06	0.10	0.09	0.02
Inmate Assault Rate		1	**0.13**	0.00	0.08	0.07	-0.03	0.07	0.02	0.02	0.07	0.07	0.07
Region			1	0.06	**0.37**	-0.03	**0.18**	0.04	-0.01	0.07	0.05	0.06	0.00
Security Level				1	**-0.20**	**-0.20**	**0.26**	**0.23**	-0.06	**0.31**	**0.47**	**0.42**	**-0.21**
Cell Type					1	0.00	0.05	-0.07	0.08	-0.03	-0.01	0.03	0.05
Average Crowding Level						1	**-0.16**	**-0.15**	0.10	**-0.16**	-0.06	**-0.17**	0.13
Deprivation Score							1	0.03	-0.07	**0.19**	0.02	0.08	-0.06
Percent CO's								1	0.09	**0.12**	**0.24**	**0.13**	-0.10
Male-to-Female CO's									1	**-0.25**	0.04	**-0.21**	**0.22**
Index of Racial Variation										1	**0.32**	**0.64**	**-0.47**
Percent Black Inmates											1	**0.55**	**-0.21**
Percent Black Staff												1	**-0.36**
White-to-Black Staff													1

Bold Coefficients Significant at $\alpha = 0.001$

Table 3 - Correlation Matrix for 1995 Variables

	Staff Assault Rate	Inmate Assault Rate	Region	Security Level	Cell Type	Average Crowding Level	Deprivation Score	Percent CO's	Male-to-Female CO's	Index of Racial Variation	Percent Black Inmates	Percent Black Staff	White-to-Black Staff
Staff Assault Rate	1	**0.45**	**0.37**	**-0.12**	**0.27**	0.02	0.05	0.01	0.05	-0.01	0.07	-0.03	0.01
Inmate Assault Rate		1	**0.21**	-0.08	0.10	0.06	-0.01	**0.13**	0.03	-0.01	-0.04	-0.03	0.03
Region			1	0.06	**0.32**	-0.08	0.04	0.06	-0.02	0.10	0.08	0.07	-0.02
Security Level				1	**-0.16**	**-0.29**	**0.12**	**0.15**	**-0.19**	**0.35**	**0.46**	**0.48**	**-0.26**
Cell Type					1	**-0.13**	-0.01	0.01	0.08	-0.04	-0.03	-0.03	0.05
Average Crowding Level						1	-0.01	**-0.12**	-0.02	**-0.12**	0.03	-0.09	0.07
Deprivation Score							1	-0.08	0.00	0.11	0.11	**0.17**	-0.07
Percent CO's								1	-0.01	0.07	**0.15**	**0.14**	-0.09
Male-to-Female CO's									1	**-0.30**	-0.06	**-0.23**	**0.28**
Index of Racial Variation										1	**0.25**	**0.60**	**-0.51**
Percent Black Inmates											1	**0.59**	**-0.28**
Percent Black Staff												1	**-0.39**
White-to-Black Staff													1

Bold Coefficients Significant at $\alpha = 0.001$

Appendix D: Additional Data Analysis – Longitudinal

Table 1 – Adjusted R^2 and Mean VIF Values for Chapter VII (Table 7.3) OLS Models: Effects of Change in Independent Variables (ΔX) on Change in Staff Assault Rates (ΔY)

Sample	Model	Variables Included	Adjusted R^2	Maximum VIF	Mean VIF
Southeast	1	Control	0.16	1.05	1.03
	2	Control + Deprivation	0.16	1.08	1.05
	3	Control + Management	0.19	1.09	1.05
	4	Control + Importation	0.16	1.05	1.03
	5	Cumulative	0.19		1.09
West	1	Control	0.08	1.00	1.00
	2	Control + Deprivation	0.26	1.25	1.10
	3	Control + Management	0.25	1.53	1.21
	4	Control + Importation	0.08	1.02	1.01
	5	Cumulative	0.37		1.34
Northeast	1	Control	0.27	1.09	1.07
	2	Control + Deprivation	0.33	1.45	1.20
	3	Control + Management	0.21	1.12	1.05
	4	Control + Importation	0.29	1.49	1.21
	5	Cumulative	0.26		1.42
Midwest	1	Control	0.01	1.00	1.00
	2	Control + Deprivation	0.02	1.08	1.03
	3	Control + Management	0.00	1.11	1.05
	4	Control + Importation	0.10	1.09	1.04
	5	Cumulative	0.04		1.33

Table 2 – R^2 and Mean VIF Values for Chapter VII (Table 7.5) OLS Models: 1990 Independent Variables Effects on Change in Staff Assault Rates (ΔY)

Sample	Model	Variables Included	Adjusted R^2	Maximum VIF	Mean VIF
Southeast	1	Control	0.27	1.22	1.15
	2	Control + Deprivation	0.27	1.24	1.15
	3	Control + Management	0.27	1.27	1.13
	4	Control + Importation	0.27	1.40	1.27
	5	Cumulative	0.26	2.55	1.48
West	1	Control	0.55	2.03	1.71
	2	Control + Deprivation	0.58	2.22	1.66
	3	Control + Management	0.56	2.38	1.53
	4	Control + Importation	0.56	2.05	1.69
	5	Cumulative	0.60	3.12	2.09
Northeast	1	Control	0.33	1.46	1.33
	2	Control + Deprivation	0.35	2.45	1.68
	3	Control + Management	0.31	1.51	1.33
	4	Control + Importation	0.32	1.60	1.31
	5	Cumulative	0.33	7.27	2.74
Midwest	1	Control	0.58	1.24	1.17
	2	Control + Deprivation	0.58	1.58	1.26
	3	Control + Management	0.65	1.41	1.26
	4	Control + Importation	0.62	1.42	1.22
	5	Cumulative	0.68	5.35	2.09

Table 3 – Log Likelihood Ratios for Chapter VII (Table 7.7) TOBIT Models: 1990
Independent Variables Effects on 1995 Staff Assault Rates

Sample	Model	Variables Included	LL Ratio	P-Value
Total Sample	1	Control	134.79	0.0000
	2	Control + Deprivation	150.92	0.0000
	3	Control + Management	127.50	0.0000
	4	Control + Importation	151.48	0.0000
	5	Cumulative	150.20	0.0000
Southeast Region	1	Control	37.70	0.0000
	2	Control + Deprivation	40.84	0.0000
	3	Control + Management	32.41	0.0000
	4	Control + Importation	38.06	0.0000
	5	Cumulative	36.05	0.0002
West Region	1	Control	16.54	0.0009
	2	Control + Deprivation	31.34	0.0000
	3	Control + Management	17.51	0.0076
	4	Control + Importation	19.09	0.0019
	5	Cumulative	29.82	0.0017
Northeast Region	1	Control	31.66	0.0000
	2	Control + Deprivation	37.47	0.0000
	3	Control + Management	31.61	0.0000
	4	Control + Importation	33.48	0.0000
	5	Cumulative	40.29	0.0000
Midwest Region	1	Control	40.88	0.0000
	2	Control + Deprivation	42.65	0.0000
	3	Control + Management	51.91	0.0000
	4	Control + Importation	56.46	0.0000
	5	Cumulative	68.98	0.0000

Table 4 – Log Likelihood Ratios for Chapter VII (Table 7.9) TOBIT Models: 1995
Independent Variables Effects on 1995 Staff Assault Rates

Sample	Model	Variables Included	LL Ratio	P-Value
Total Sample	1	Control	231.13	0.0000
	2	Control + Deprivation	238.70	0.0000
	3	Control + Management	235.78	0.0000
	4	Control + Importation	245.16	0.0000
	5	Cumulative	255.59	0.0000
Southeast Region	1	Control	115.14	0.0000
	2	Control + Deprivation	119.01	0.0000
	3	Control + Management	123.43	0.0000
	4	Control + Importation	115.25	0.0000
	5	Cumulative	127.86	0.0000
West Region	1	Control	17.07	0.0007
	2	Control + Deprivation	21.34	0.0016
	3	Control + Management	17.14	0.0088
	4	Control + Importation	18.77	0.0021
	5	Cumulative	22.88	0.0184
Northeast Region	1	Control	47.85	0.0000
	2	Control + Deprivation	56.65	0.0000
	3	Control + Management	56.74	0.0000
	4	Control + Importation	52.17	0.0000
	5	Cumulative	68.58	0.0000
Midwest Region	1	Control	57.23	0.0000
	2	Control + Deprivation	57.43	0.0000
	3	Control + Management	62.85	0.0000
	4	Control + Importation	62.39	0.0000
	5	Cumulative	65.92	0.0000

References

Adams, Kenneth. (1992). Adjusting to prison life. *Crime and Justice: A Review of Research* 16, 275-359.

Adler, Patricia, and Peter Adler. (1989). Self-Censorship: The politics of presenting ethnographic data. *Arena Review* 13(1), 37-48.

African American Male Task Force. (1990). *Educating African American Males: A Dream Deferred.* Milwaukee, WI: Milwaukee Public Schools.

Agopian, M.W., D. Chappel, and G.Geis. (1974). Interracial forcible rape in a North American City: An analysis of sixty-three cases. In I. Drapkin and E. Viano (Eds.), *Victimology*, pages 93-102. Lexington, MA: Lexington Books, Heath.

Agresti, Alan, and Barbara F. Agresti. (1978). Statistical analysis of qualitative variation. *Sociological Methodology* 9, 204-237.

Albonetti, Celesta A. (1991). An integration of theories to explain judicial discretion. *Social Problems* 38, 247-266.

Allison, Paul D. (1990). Change scores as dependent variables in regression analysis. *Sociological Methodology* 20, 93-114.

Amemiya, E.C. (1963). Measurement of economic differentiation. *Journal of Regional Science* 5, 85-87.

Amemiya, Takeshi. (1973). Regression analysis when the dependent variable is truncated normal. *Econometrica* 41, 997-1016.

_____. (1984). Tobit models: A survey. *Journal of Econometrics* 24, 3-61.

American Correctional Association 1990 Directory of Juvenile and Adult Correctional Departments, Institutions, Agencies, and Paroling Authorities. Maryland: American Correctional Association.

_____. *1991 Directory of Juvenile and Adult Correctional Departments, Institutions, Agencies, and Paroling Authorities.* Maryland: American Correctional Association.

_____. *1995 Directory of Juvenile and Adult Correctional Departments, Institutions, Agencies, and Paroling Authorities.* Maryland: American Correctional Association.

_____. *1996 Directory of Juvenile and Adult Correctional Departments, Institutions, Agencies, and Paroling Authorities.* Maryland: American Correctional Association.

American Criminal Law Review. (1980). "Grisby vs Mabry" a new look at death qualified juries. Volume 18, 145-163.

Anderson, Elijah. (1999). *The Code of the Streets: Decency, Violence, and the Moral Life of the Inner City.* New York: W.W. Norton & Company.

Anderson, J. E. (1939). The limitations of infant and preschool tests in the measurement of intelligence. *Journal of Psychology*, 8, 351-379.

Armour, Jody D. (1994). Race Ipsa Loquitur: Of reasonable racists, intelligent Bayesians, and involuntary Negrophobes. *Stanford Law Review* 46, 781-816.

Aronson, E. (1980). *The Social Animal (3rd Edition).* San Francisco: Freeman & Co.

Austin, Roy L., and Mark D. Allen. (2000). Racial disparity in arrest rates as an explanation of racial disparity in commitment to Pennsylvania's prisons. *Journal of Research in Crime and Delinquency* 37(2), 200-220.

Austin, Roy L., Robert Kenner, Jr., and Andrea Johnson (1994). Sentencing guidelines and African-American overrepresentation in prison. Unpublished manuscript, Pennsylvania State University.

Averill, J.R. (1982). *Anger and Aggression: An Essay on Emotion.* New York: Springer-Verlag.

Ayers, E.L. (1984). *Vengeance and Justice: Crime and Punishment in the Nineteenth Century American South.* New York: Oxford.

_____. (1992). *The Promise of the New South: Life After Reconstruction.* New York: Oxford.

Ayers, Ian, and Joel Waldfogel. (1994). A market test for race discrimination in bail setting. *Stanford Law Review* 46, 987-1045.

Baldus, David C., Charles Pulaski, and George Woodworth. (1983). Comparative review of death sentences: An empirical study of the Georgia experience. *Journal of Criminal Law and Criminology* 74, 661-673.

Barak-Glantz, Israel L. (1985). The anatomy of another prison riot. In M. Braswell, S. Dillingham, and R. Montgomery (Eds.), *Prison Violence in America,* pages 47-71. Cincinnati, OH: Anderson.

Barnes, Carole W., and Rodney Kingsnorth. (1996). Race, drug, and criminal sentencing: Hidden effects of the criminal law. *Journal of Criminal Justice* 24, 39-55.

Bartollas, C., and C.M. Sieverdes. (1981). The victimized white in a juvenile correctional system. *Crime and Delinquency* 27, 534-543.

Bayley, David H., and Harold Mendelsohn. (1969). *Minorities and the Police: Confrontation in America.* New York: The Free Press.

Beck, A.T. (1976). *Cognitive Therapy and the Emotional Disorders.* New York: International University Press.

_____. (1983). Cognitive therapy of depression: New perspectives. In P.J. Clayton and J.E. Barrett (Eds.), *Treatment of Depression: Old Controversies and New Approaches,* pages 315-350. New York: Raven Press.

Bedau, Hugo A., and Michael L. Radelet. (1987). Miscarriages of justice in potentially capital cases. *Stanford Law Review* 40, 121-179.

Bennett, Claude. (1991). The black population in the U.S.: March 1990 and 1989. *Current Population Reports*: Series p-20 no. 448.

Benokraitis, Nijole, and Joyce A. Griffin-Keene. (1982). Prejudice and jury selection. *Journal of Black Studies* 12(4), 427-449.

Bereiter, Carl. (1963). Some persisting dilemmas in the measurement of change. In Chester W. Harris (Ed.), *Problems in Measuring Change*, pages 3 – 20. Madison, WI: University of Wisconsin Press.

Berkowitz, L. (1993). *Aggression: Its Causes, Consequences, and Control.* New York: McGraw-Hill.

Berkowitz, L., and J.A. Green. (1962). The stimulus qualities of the scapegoat. *Journal of Abnormal and Social Psychology* 64, 293-301.

Bernard, Thomas J. (1990). Angry aggression among the truly disadvantaged. *Criminology* 28, 73-96.

Bidna, Howard. (1975). Effects of increased security on prison violence. *Journal of Criminal Justice* 3, 33-46.

Bishop, Katherine. (1991, March 24). Police attacks: Hard crimes to uncover, let alone stop. *New York Times*, 1.

Black men say they are victims of profiling. (2001, June 22). *The Cincinnati Post*, Online Edition, www.cincypost.com/2001/jun/22/prof062201.html.

Blackburn, M.L., D.E. Bloom, and R.B. Freeman. (1990). The declining economic position of less-skilled American men. In G. Burtless (Ed.), *A Future of Lousy Jobs?*, pages 31-76. Washington, DC: Brookings Institute.

Blau, Judith R., and Peter M. Blau. (1982). Metropolitan structure and violent crime. *American Sociological Review* 22, 677-682.

Bloom, B. S. (1964). *Stability and Change in Human Characteristics*. New York: Wiley.

Bohrnstedt, G.W. (1969). Observations on the measurement of change. In E. F. Borgatta (Ed.), *Sociological Methodology* (pages 113-136). San Francisco: Jossey-Bass.

Bolte, Gordon L. (1978). Institutional disobedience in a maximum-security prison. *Journal of Offender Rehabilitation* 3(1), 19-31.

Bonczar, T.P. and Beck, Allen J. (1997). *Lifetime Likelihood of Going to State or Federal Prison*. Bureau of Justice Statistics, Washington DC: US Department of Justice.

Boozer, M.A., A.B. Krueger, and S. Wolkon. (1992). Race and school quality since Brown v. Board of Education. In M.N. Baily and C. Winston (Eds.), *Brookings Papers on Economic Activity*, pages 269-326. Washington, DC: Brookings Institution.

Borchard, Edwin. (1932). *Convicting the Innocent*. New Haven, CT: Yale University Press.

Borg, Marian J. (1997). The southern subculture of punitiveness? Regional variation in support for capital punishment. *Journal of Research in Crime and Delinquency* 34(1), 25-45.

Bositis, David A. (1997). *The impact of race on pretrial release decisions in the Second Circuit from July 1993 to June 1996*. Unpublished manuscript.

Bottoms, Anthony E. (1999). Interpersonal violence and social order in prisons. *Crime and Justice. A Review of Research* 26, 205-281.

Bound J., and R.B. Freeman. (1992). What went wrong?: the erosion of relative earnings and employment among young black men in the 1980's. *Quarterly Journal of Economics* 107, 201-232.

Bowers, William J. (1984). *Legal Homicide: Death As Punishment in America 1864-1982*. Boston: Northeastern University Press.

Bowers, William J., and Gleen L. Pierce. (1980). Arbitrariness and discrimination under post-Furman capital statistics. *Crime and Delinquency* 74, 563-635.

Bowker, Lee H. (1980). *Prison Victimization*. New York: Elsevier.

Boydston, John E. (1975). *San Diego Field Interrogation: Final Report.* Washington, DC: Police Foundation.

Braddock, Jomills.H. (1978). Internal colonialism and Black American education. *Western Journal of Black Studies* 2, 236-243.

Braddock, Jomills.H., and James M. McPartland. (1987). How minorities continue to be excluded from equal employment opportunities: Research on labor market and institutional barriers. *Journal of Social Issues* 43(1), 5-39.

Brazil Jeff, and Steve Berry. (1992, August 23). Color of driver is key to stops in I-95 videos. *Orlando Sentinel*, A1.

Breinin, C. (1981). Too many suspensions? Why not 'Magnetize instead? *BTF Provocator*, 11.

Breitman, George (Ed.). (1970). *By Any Means Necessary; Speeches, Interviews, and a Letter by Malcolm X*. New York: Pathfinder Press.

Brosi, Kathleen B. (1979). *A Cross-city Comparison of Felony Case Processing.* Washington, DC: Bureau of Justice Statistics, U.S. Department of Justice.

Brown, Claude. (1965). *Manchild in the Promised Land.* New York: New American Library.

Brown, Jodi M., Patrick A. Langan, and Davis J. Levin. (1999). *Felony Sentences in State Courts, 1996.* NCJ 173939, U.S. Department of Justice, Bureau of Justice Statistics.

Brown, R.M. (1975). *Strain of Violence: Historical Studies of American Violence and Vigilantism*. New York: Oxford.

Browning, Sandra L., F. Cullen, L. Cao, R. Kopache, and T. Stevenson. (1994). Race and getting hassled by the police. *Police Studies* 17(1), 1-11.

Burr, Jeffery A., and John R. Nesselroade. (1990). Change measurement. In Alexander von Eye (Ed.) *Statistical Methods in Longitudinal Research* 1, 3-33. San Diego, CA: Academic Press.

Buss, A.H. (1961). *The Psychology of Aggression*. New York: Wiley.

Bynum, T. (1982). Release on recognizance: Substantive or superficial reform? *Criminology* 20, 67-82.

Callahan, Gene, and William Anderson. (2001). The roots of racial profiling. *Reason* 33(4), 36-43.

Campbell, D.T. (1956). Enhancement of Contrast as Composite Habit. *Journal of Applied Social Psychology* 53, 350-355.

Campbell, Donald T., and David A. Kenny. (1999). *A Primer on Regression Artifacts*. New York: Guilford Press.

Cannon, Brian. (1994*). Explaining race differences in violence: An empirical test of the subculture of violence thesis*. Unpublished master's thesis, Pennsylvania State University, University Park.

Card, David, and Alan B. Kreuger. (1992a). Does school quality matter? Returns to education and the characteristics of public schools in the United States. *Journal of Political Economy* 100(1), 1-40.

_____. (1992b). School quality and black-white relative earnings: A direct assessment. *Quarterly Journal of Economics* 57(1), 151-200.

Carlson, M., A. Marcus-Newhall, and N. Miller. (1990). Effects of situational aggression cues: A quantitative review. *Journal of Personality and Social Psychology* 58, 622-633.

Carroll, Lee. (1974). *Hacks, Blacks, and Cons: Race Relations in a Maximum Security Prison*. Lexington, MA: D.C. Health and Company.

_____. (1977). Humanitarian reform and biracial sexual assault in a maximum security prison. *Urban Life* 5(4), 417-437.

_____. (1982). Race, ethnicity, and the social order of the prison. In Robert Johnson and Hans Toch (Eds.), *The Pains of Imprisonment*, pages 181-202. Beverly Hills, CA: Sage.

Carter, B. (1973). Race, sex and gangs: Reform school families. *Society* 11, 36-43.

Case, Charles E., Andrew M. Greeley. (1990). Attitudes toward racial equality. *Humbolt Journal of Social Relations* 16(1), 67-94.

Chadbourn, J. H. (1933). *Lynching and the Law*. Chapel Hill, NC: University of North Carolina Press.

Cherry, Robert. (1999). Black male employment and tight labor markets. *The Review of Black Political Economy* 27(1), 31-45.

Children's Defense Fund. (1986). *Declining Earnings of Young Men: Their Relation to Poverty, Teen Pregnancy and Family Formation*. Washington DC: CDF.

Chilton, Roland, and Jim Gavin. (1985). Race, crime and criminal justice. *Crime and Delinquency* 31, 3-14.

Christopher Commission. (1991). *Report of the Independent Commission on the Los Angeles Police Department*. Los Angeles: The Commission.

Clarke, D. B., A. M. Clarke, and R. I. Brown. (1959). Regression to the mean-A confused concept. *British Journal of Psychology* 51, 106-117.

Clark, Kenneth B. (1965). *Dark Ghetto: Dilemmas of Social Power*. New York: Harper and Row.

Cleaver, Eldridge. (1968). *Soul on Ice*. New York: Dell Publishing Company.

Clemmer, Donald. (1958). *The Prison Community*. New York: Holt, Rinehart, and Winston.

Coe, R.M. (1961). Who is the inmate? Characteristics of well adjusted and poorly adjusted inmates. *Journal of Criminal Law and Criminology Police Science* 52, 178-184.

Cole, David. (1999). *No Equal Justice*. New York: The New Press.

College to be given archives of a study on police brutality. (1991, August 27). *New York Times*, 19.

Collins, Linda M., and John L. Horn. (1991). *Best Methods for the Analysis of Change*. Washington, DC: American Psychological Association.

Colvin, M. (1997). *Penitentiaries, Reformatories, and Chain Gangs*. New York: St. Martin's Press.

Cone, James H. (1991). *Martin & Malcolm & America: A Dream or a Nightmare*. New York: Orbis Books.

Cook, L.H., and E.E. Boe. (1995). Who is teaching students with disabilities? *Teaching Exceptional Children* 28, 70-72.

Cooke, David J. (1989). Containing violent prisoners: An analysis of the Barlinnie Special Unit. *British Journal of Criminology* 29, 129-143.

Cose, Ellis. (1993). *The Rage of a Privileged Class*. New York: Harper Collins.

Covington, Jeanette. (1995). Racial classification in criminology: The reproduction of racialized crime. *Sociological Forum* 10(4), 547-568.

Crepeau, Richard C. (2001). Taboo: Why Black athletes dominate sports and why we're afraid to talk about it. *Sociology of Sport Journal* 18(2), 251-253.

Cronbach, L.J., and L. Furby. (1970). How should we measure change-or should we? *Psychological Bulletin* 74, 68-80.

Crutchfield, Robert D., George S. Bridges, and Susan R. Pitchford. (1994). Analytical and aggregation biases in analyses of imprisonment: Reconciling discrepancies in studies of racial disparity. *Journal of Research in Crime and Delinquency* 31(2), 166-182.

Culp, Jerome, and Bruce H. Dunson. (1986). Brothers of a different color: A preliminary look at employer treatment of White and Black youth. In Richard B. Freeman and Harry J. Holzer (Eds.), *The Black Youth Employment Crisis*, pages 233-260. Chicago: University of Chicago Press.

Curtis, Henry P. (1992, August 23). Statistics show pattern of discrimination. *Orlando Sentinel*, A11.

Curtis, Lynn A. (1974). *Criminal Violence: National Patterns and Behavior*. Lexington, MA: Lexington Books.

Cutler, J.E. (1905). *Lynching Law: An Investigation into the History of Lynching in the United States*. New York: Longmans, Green.

Dannefer, S. and R. Schutt. (1982). Race and juvenile justice processing in court and police agencies. *American Journal of Sociology* 87: 1113-1132.

Davidson, Theodore R. (1974). *Chicano Prisoners: The Key to San Quentin*. Prospect Heights, IL: Waveland Press, Inc.

Davies, James C. (1972). Toward a theory of revolution. *American Sociological Review* 27, 5-19.

Davis, A.J. (1968). Sexual assaults in the Philadelphia prison system and sheriff's vans. *Transaction* 6, 8-16.

Davis, Angela J. (1997). Race, cops, and traffic stops. *University of Miami Law Review* 51 (413), 425-443.

_____. (1998). Prosecution and race: the power and privilege of discretion. *Fordham Law Review* 67, 13-67.

_____. (2001). The American prosecutor: Independence, power, and the threat of tyranny. *Iowa Law Review* 86, 393-465.

Davis, James E., and Will J. Jordan. (1994). The effects of school context, structure, and experiences on African American males in middle and high school. *Journal of Negro Education* 63(4), 570-587.

Davis, Kenneth C. (1969). *Discretionary Justice*. Baton Rouge, LA: Louisiana State University Press.

D.C. Black cops don't trust fellow White cops. (1976, March). *Jet Magazine*, 5.

Death Penalty Information Center. WWW.deathpenaltyinfo.org

Dent, H., A. Mendocal, W. Pierce, and G. West. (1991). The San Francisco public schools experience with I.Q. testing: A model for non-biased assessment. In A.G. Hilliard, III (Ed.), *Testing African American Students: Special Re-issue of the Negro Educational Review*, pages 146-162. Morristown, NJ: Aaron Press.

Developments in the Law-Race and the Criminal Process. (1988). *Harvard Law Review* 101(7), 1473-1641.

DiIulio, John J. (1987). *Governing Prisons*. New York: Free Press.

DiPerna, Paula. (1984). *Juries on Trial; Faces of American Justice*. New York: Dembner Books.

Dixon, Jo and Alan J. Lizotte. (1987). Gun ownership and the southern subculture of violence. *American Journal of Sociology* 93, 383-405.

Dollard, John. (1957). *Caste and Class in a Southern Town (3rd Edition)*. New York: Doubleday Anchor Books.

Dollard, J., L.W. Doob, N.E. Miller, O.H. Mowrer., and R.R. Sears. (1939). *Frustration and Aggression*. New Haven, CT: Yale University Press.

Donziger, Steven R. (1996). *The Real War on Crime*. New York: Harper Perennial.

Douglas, Tom. (1995). *Scapegoat, Transferring Blame*. New York: Routledge.

Doyle, John H., Bettina B. Plevan, and Diane L. Zimmerman. (1997). Report of the second circuit task force on gender, racial, and ethnic fairness in the courts. *Annual Survey of American Law* 1997, 117-414.

D'Souza, Dinesh. (1995). *The End of Racism*. New York: The Free Press.

Dubois, P. H. (1957). *Multivariate Correlational Analysis*. New York: Harper.

Duncan, O. D. (1969). Some linear models for the two wave, two variable panel analysis. *Psychological Bulletin* 72, 177-182.

Ellis, A. (1962). *Reason and Emotion in Psychotherapy*. Secaucus, NJ: Lyle Stuart.

Ellis, Desmond, Harold G. Grasmick, and Bernard Gilman. (1974). Violence in prison: A sociological analysis. *American Journal of Sociology* 80, 15-43.

Ellison, Christopher G. (1991). Southern culture and firearms ownership. *Social Science Quarterly* 72, 267-283.

Epps, E.G. (1970). Interpersonal relations and motivation: Implications for teachers of disadvantaged children. *Journal of Negro Education* 39, 14-25.

_____. (1995). Race, class, and educational opportunity: Trends in the sociology of education. *Sociological Forum* 10(4), 593-608.

Erlanger, Howard S. (1974). The empirical status of the subculture of violence thesis. *Social Problems* 22, 280-292.

Eskridge, C.W. (1983). *Pretrial Release Programming: Issues and Trends*. New York: Clark Boardman Company.

Ewing, Jack, and Brant Houston. (1991, June 17). Some judges punish people without benefit of trial. *The Hartford Courant*, A1.

Eysenck, Hans J. (1991). Science, Racism, and Sexism. *Journal of Social Political and Economic Studies* 16(2), 217-250.

____. (1971). *Race, Intelligence and Education*. London: Temple Smith.

Fagan, T., and F. Lira. (1978). Profile of mood states: Racial differences in a delinquent population. *Psychological Reports* 43, 348-350.

Farnworth, Margaret, Raymond H.C. Teske Jr. and Gina Thurman. (1991). Ethnic, racial, and minority disparity in felony court processing. In Michael J. Lynch and E. Britt Patterson (Eds.), *Race and Criminal Justice*, pages 54-70. Albany, NY: Harrow & Heston.

Farrell, Ronald A., and Victoria L. Swigert. (1978). Prior offense as a self-fulfilling prophecy. *Law and Society Review* 12, 437-453.

Farmer, Paul. (1992). *Aids and Accusations*. Berkeley, CA: University of California Press.

Feagin, Joe R., and V. Hernan. (1995). *White Racism: The Basics*. New York: Routledge.

Feeley, Malcolm M. (1979). *The Process is the Punishment: Handling Cases in a Lower Criminal Court*. New York: Russell Sage Foundation.

Feld, Barry C. (1977). Neutralizing Inmate Violence: Juvenile Offenders in Institutions. Cambridge, MA: Ballinger.

Finkel, Steven E. (1995). *Causal Analysis With Panel Data*. Sage University Paper series on Quantitative Applications in the Social Sciences, 07-105. Thousands Oaks, CA: Sage.

Firebaugh, Glenn, and Kenneth E. Davis. (1988). Trends in anti-black prejudice, 1972-1984: Region and cohort effects. *American Journal of Sociology* 94(2), 251-272.

Flanagan, Timothy. (1983). Correlates of institutional misconduct among state prisoners: A research note. *Criminology* 21, 29-39.

Fletcher, Michael A. (1996, March 29). Driven to extremes black men take steps to avoid police stops. *The Washington Post*, A1.

Fong, Robert S. and Ronald E. Vogel. (1995). A comparative analysis of prison gang members, security threat group inmates, and general population prisoners in the Texas department of corrections. *The Journal of Gang Research* 2(2), 1-12.

Foote, Caleb. (1954). Compelling appearance in court: Administration of bail in Philadelphia. *University of Pennsylvania Law Review* 102, 1031-1079.

Fordham, S., and J. Ogbu. (1986). African American students' school success: Coping with the burden of "acting white". *Urban Review* 18, 176-206.

Foster, Herbert L. (1995). Educators' and non-educators' perceptions of black males: A survey. *Journal of African American Men* 1(2), 37-70.

Fox, James G. (1982). Organizational and Racial Conflict in Maximum-Security Prisons. Lexington, MA: D.C. Health and Company.

Frazier, E. F. (1939). *The Negro Family in the United States*. Chicago: University of Chicago Press.

____. (1957). *Black Bourgeoisie*. Glencoe, IL: The Free Press.

Free, Marvin D., Jr. (1999). Racial issues in contemporary criminology textbooks: The case of African-Americans. *Contemporary Justice Review* 1(4), 429-466.

Freed, David. (1991, July 1). Police brutality claims are rarely prosecuted. *Los Angeles Times* 1.

Freud, S. (1920). *A General Introduction to Psychoanalysis*. New York: Boni and Livewright.

Fridell, Lorie, Robert Lunney, Drew Diamond and Bruce Kubu. (2001). *Racially Biased Policing: A Principled Response*. Washington, DC: Police Executive Research Forum.

Fukurai, H. (1985). *Institutional Racial Inequality: A Theoretical and Empirical Examination of the Jury Selection Process*. Unpublished doctoral dissertation, University of California, Riverside.

Fukurai, Hiroshi, Edgar W. Butler, and Richard Krooth. (1991). Where did Black jurors go? A theoretical synthesis of racial disenfranchisement in the jury system and jury selection. *Journal of Black Studies* 22(2), 196-215.

Fuller, D., T. Orsagh, and D. Raber. (1977, June*). Violence and victimization within the North Carolina prison system*. Paper presented at the meeting of the Academy of Criminal Justice Sciences, San Mateo, CA.

Furby, L. (1973). Interpreting regression towards the mean in developmental research. *Developmental Psychology* 8, 172-179.

Gaes, Gerald G. and William J. McGuire. (1985). Prison violence: The contribution of crowding versus other determinants of prison assault rates. *Journal of Research in Crime & Delinquency* 22, 41-65.

Gardner, Ralph III., and Antoinette H. Miranda. (2001). Improving outcomes for urban African American students. *Journal of Negro Education* 70(4), 255-263.

Garibaldi, A.M. (1991). Black school pushouts and dropouts: Strategies for reduction. *Urban League Review* 11, 227-235.

Geen, Russell. (2001). *Human Aggression (2nd Edition)*. Buckingham, PA: Open University Press.

Geller, William A., and Hans Toch (Ed.). (1996). Understanding and controlling police abuse of force. In William A. Geller and Hans Toch (Eds.), *Police Violence*, pages 292-309. New Haven, CT: Yale University Press.

Gershman, Bennett L. (1993). Themes of injustice: Wrongful convictions, racial prejudice, and lawyer incompetence. Reprinted in Marilyn McShane and Frank P. Williams III (Eds.) (1997), *The American Court System*, pages 268-281. New York: Garland Publishing.

Gibbons, Thomas, J. (1995, August 13). Police corruption inquiry widens up to 9 officers in elite unit implicated. *Philadelphia Inquirer*, A1.

Giallombardo, R. (1966). *Society of Women: A Study of a Women's Prison*. New York: John Wiley.

Gibbs J.J. (1981). Violence in prison: Its extent, nature, and consequences. In R.R. Robert and V.J. Webb (Eds.), *Critical Issues in Corrections*, pages 110-149. St. Paul, MN: West Publishing.

Gibbs, Jewelle T. (1988). *Young, Black and Male in America.* Dover, MA: Auburn House Publishing

_____. (1994). Anger in young black males: Victims or victimizers? In Richard G. Majors and Jacob U. Gordon (Eds.) *The American Black Male*, pages 127-143. Chicago: Nelson-Hall.

_____. (1996). *Race and Justice.* San Francisco, CA: Jossey-Bass.

Gibbs, Jewelle T, and A.M. Hines. (1989). Factors related to sex differences in suicidal behavior among black youth: Implications for intervention and research. *Journal of Adolescent Research* 4(2), 152-172.

Glasgow, Douglas G. (1980). *The Black Underclass.* San Francisco: Jossey-Bass, Inc.

Goetting, Ann and Roy Michael Howsen. (1986). Correlates of prisoner misconduct. *Journal of Quantitative Criminology* 2(1), 49-67.

Goffman, Erving. (1961). *Asylums: Essays on the Social Situation of Mental Patients and Other Inmates.* Garden City, NY: Anchor.

Gold, Daniel B., and Daniel M. Wegner. (1995). Origins of ruminative thought: Trauma, incompleteness, nondisclosure, and suppression. *Journal of Applied Social Psychology* 25(14), 1245-1261.

Goldkamp, J.S. (1985). Danger and detention: A second generation of bail reform. *Journal of Criminal Law and Criminology* 76, 1-74.

Goldkamp, J.S., and M. Gottfredson. (1979). Bail decision making and pretrial detention: Surfacing judicial policy. *Law and Human Behavior* 3, 227-249.

_____. (1985). *Policy Guidelines for Bail: An Experiment in Court Reform.* Philadelphia: Temple University Press.

Gottfredson, M.R., and D.M. Gottfredson. (1988). *Decision Making in Criminal Justice: Toward the Rational Exercise of Discretion (2nd Edition).* New York: Plenum.

Gottman, John M. (1995). *The Analysis of Change.* Mahwah, NJ: Lawrence Erlbaum Associates.

Greene, Helen Taylor. (1979). *A Comprehensive Bibliography of Criminology and Criminal Justice Literature by Black Authors from 1895 to 1978.* College Park, MD: Author.

Grier, William H., and Price M. Cobbs. (1968). *Black Rage.* New York: Basic Books.

Hacker, Andrew. (1992). *Two Nations: Black and White, Separate, Hostile, Unequal.* New York: MacMillian.

Hall, A., E. Gaynes, D.A. Henry, and W.E. Smith. (1984). *Pretrial Release Program Options.* Report of the National Institute of Justice. Washington, DC: U.S. Government Printing Office.

Hall, J.D. (1979). *Revolt Against Chivalry: Jessie Daniel Ames and the Women's Campaign Against Lynching.* New York: Columbia University Press.

Hamm, Mark S., Therese Coupez, Frances E. Hoze, and Corey Weinstein. (1991). The myth of humane imprisonment: A critical analysis of severe discipline in U.S. maximum security prisons, 1945-1990. In Michael C. Braswell, Reid H. Montgomery, Jr., and Lucien X. Lombardo (Eds.), *Prison Violence in America (2nd Edition)*, pages 167-200. Cincinnati, OH: Anderson Publishing.

Hannerz, Ulf. (1969). *Soulside*. New York: Columbia University Press.

Hans, V., and N. Vidmar. (1986). *Judging the Jury*. New York: Plenum.

Harburg, E. J.C. Erfurt, and L.S. Hauestein. (1973). Socio-economical stress, suppressed hostility, skin color, and black-white male blood pressure. *Psychosomatic Medicine* 35, 276-296.

Hare, Bruce R., and Louis Castenell. (1985). No place to run, no place to hide: Comparative status and future prospects of Black boys. In Margaret B. Spencer, Geraldine K. Brookins, and Walter Allen (Eds.), *Beginnings: The Social and Affective Development of Black Children*. Hillsdale, NJ: Erlbaum.

Harer, Miles D. and Darrell Steffensmeier. (1996). Race and prison violence. *Criminology* 34(3), 323-355.

Harmsworth, Esmond. (1996). Bail and detention: An assessment and critique of the Federal and Massachusetts systems. *New England Journal of Criminal and Civil Confinement* 22, 213-290.

Harris, Chester W. (1963). *Problems in Measuring Change*. Madison, WI: University of Wisconsin Press.

Harris, David A. (1994). Factors for reasonable suspicion: When Black and poor means stopped and frisked. *Indiana Law Journal* 69, 659-688.

_____. (1998). Car wars: The Fourth Amendment's death on the highway. *George Washington Law Review* 66, 556-591.

_____. (1999). *Driving While Black, Racial Profiling on Our Nation's Highways*. American Civil Liberties Union Special Report.

Harris, Paul. (1997). *Black Rage Confronts the Law*. New York: New York University Press.

Harris, T. (1984). *Exorcising Blackness: Historical and Literary Lynching and Burning Rituals*. Bloomington, IN: Indiana University Press.

Harry, Beth., and Mary G. Anderson. (1994). The disproportionate placement of African American males in special education programs: A critique of the process. *Journal of Negro Education* 63(4), 602-619.

Hawkins, Darnell. (Ed.). (1986). *Homicide Among Black Americans*. Lanham, MD: University Press of America

Hawkins, Richard and Geoffrey P. Alpert. (1989). *American Prison System: Punishment and Justice*. Englewood Cliffs, NJ: Prentice Hall.

Healey, Joseph F. (2002). *Statistics a Tool for Social Research*. Belmont, CA: Wadsworth Group.

Held, B.S., D. Levine, and V.D. Swartz. (1979). Interpersonal aspects of dangerousness. *Criminal Justice and Behavior* 6, 49-58.

Helson, H. (1964). *Adaptation-level Theory*. New York: Harper & Row.

Hendin, Herbert. (1969). *Black Suicide*. New York: Basic Books, Inc.

Hepburn, John R. (1978). Race and the decision to arrest: An analysis of warrants issued. *Journal of Research in Crime and Delinquency* 15, 54-73.

Herton, Calvin C. (1965). *Sex and Racism in America*. New York: Grove Press.

Hewitt, John D., Eric D. Poole, and Robert M. Regoli. (1984). Self-reported and observed rule-breaking in prison: A look at disciplinary response. *Justice Quarterly* 1, 437-447.

Hicks-Bartlett, Sharon. (1991, October). *A suburb in name only: The case of Meadow View*. Paper presented at the Chicago Urban Poverty and Family Life Conference, Chicago.

Hindelang, Michael J. (1978). Race and Involvement in Common Law Personal Crimes. *American Sociological Review* 43, 93-109.

Hippler, Arthur E. (1974). *Hunter's Point*. New York: Basic Books.

Hoffman, Morris B. (1997). Peremptory challenges should be abolished: A trial judge's perspective. *University of Chicago Law Review* 64, 809-871.

Hollander-Blumoff, R. (1997). Getting to guilty: Plea bargaining as negotiation. *Harvard Negotiation Law Review* 2, 115-148.

Holmes, William M. (2001). Who are the wrongly convicted on death row? In Saundra D. Westervelt and John A. Humphrey (Eds.), *Wrongly Convicted: Perspectives on Failed Justice*, pages 99-113. New Brunswick, NJ: Rutgers University Press.

Hooks, Bell. (1995). *Killing Rage*. New York: Henry Holt and Company.

Hudson, Barbara. (1993). Racism and criminology: Concepts and controversies. In Dee Cook and Barbara Hudson (Eds.), *Racism and Criminology*, pages 1-27. Thousand Oaks, CA: Sage.

Huff, C. Ronald, Arye Rattner, and Edward Sagarin. (1986). Guilty until proved innocent: Wrongful conviction and public policy. *Crime and Delinquency* 32(4), 518-544.

_____. (1996). *Convicted but Innocent: Wrongful Conviction and Public Policy*. Thousand Oaks, CA: Sage.

Hulsey Lynn. (2001, April 28). Cincinnati tops list of police killings of blacks. *Dayton Daily News*. Retrieved March 19, 2002 from the World Wide Web: http://www.commondreams.org/headlines01/0428-04.htm

Hummel-Rossi, B. and S. L. Weinberg. (1975). *Practical Guidelines in Applying Current Theories to the Measurement of Change, Parts I and II*. Greenwich, CT: Johnson Associates.

Humprey, John A., and Timothy J. Fogarty. (1987). Race and plea bargained outcomes: A research note. *Social Forces* 66(1), 176-182.

Humphreys, L. G. (1961). Mimeographed paper on derived scores. Psychology Department, University of Illinois, Champaign-Urbana, IL.

Hunt, Geoffrey, Stephanie Riegel, Tomas Morales, and Dan Waldorf. (1993). Changes in prison culture: prison gangs and the case of the Pepsi generation. *Social Problems* 40(3), 398-409.

Inciardi, James A. (1984). *Criminal Justice*. Orlando, FL: Academic Press.

Irvine, Jacqueline J. (1990). *Black Students and School Failure: Policies, Practices, and Prescriptions.* Westport, CT: Greenwood Press.

Irvine, Jacqueline J., and Darlene E. York. (1993). Teacher perspectives: Why do African-American, Hispanic, and Vietnamese students fail? In Stanley W. Rothstein (Ed.), *Handbook of Schooling in Urban America*, pages 161-193. Westport, CT: Greenwood Press.

Irwin, John. (1971). *Some research questions of homosexuality in jails and prisons.* Paper presented at the Conference on Prison Homosexuality sponsored by the Pennsylvania Prison Society, Philadelphia.

____. (1980). *Prisons in Turmoil.* Toronto: Little, Brown and Company.

Irwin, John, and Donald R. Cressey. (1962). Thieves, convicts and the inmate culture. *Social Problems* 10, 142-155.

Jackson, Don. (1989, January 23). Police embody racism to my people. *New York Times*, A25.

Jackson, George. (1970). *Soledad Brother: The Prison Letters of George Jackson.* New York: Bantam.

Jackson, Robert. (November 10, 1995). Eagle county must pay for stopping motorists. *Denver Rocky Mountain News*, 4A.

Jacobs, Eva e., and Sohair M. Abu-Aish. (Eds.) (2000). *Handbook of U.S. Labor Statistics: Employment, Earnings, Prices, Productivity, and Other Labor Data (4th Edition).* Lanham, MD: Bernan Press.

Jacobs, James B. (1977). *Stateville: The Penitentiary in Mass Society.* Chicago: University of Chicago Press.

____. (1983). *New Perspectives on Prisons and Imprisonment.* Ithaca, NY: Cornell University Press.

Jacobs, James B., and Lawrence J. Kraft. (1978). Integrating the keepers: A comparison of black and white prison guards in Illinois. *Social Problems* 25, 304-318.

Jacobs, James B and Mary Grear. (1977). Dropouts and rejects: An analysis of the prison guard's revolving door. *Criminal Justice Review* 2(2), 57-70.

Jaman, D., P. Coburn, J. Goddard, and P. Mueller. (1971). *Behavior During the First Year in Prison – Report IV as Related to Parole Outcome.* Sacramento, CA: California Department of Corrections.

Jaman, D.P. (1972). *Behavior During the First Year in Prison – Report III Background Characteristics as Predictors of Behavior and Misbehavior.* Sacramento, CA: California Department of Corrections.

Jamison, Charles N. Jr. (1992 November). Racism: The hurt that men won't name. *Essence* 23(7), 62-66.

Jankowski, M.S. (1991). *Islands in the Street: Gangs and American Urban Society.* Berkeley, CA: University of California Press.

Jargowsky, Paul A. (1994). Ghetto poverty among Blacks in the 1980s. *Journal of Policy Analysis and Management* 13(2), 288-310.

Jencks, Christopher, and Paul Peterson. (Eds.). (1998). *The Urban Underclass.* Washington, DC: Brookings Institution Press.

Jensen, Arthur R. (1969). How much can we boost IQ and scholastic achievement. *Harvard Educational Review* 39, 1-3.

_____. (1972). *Genetics and Education*. New York: Harper and Row.

Johnson, H.M. (1961). *Sociology: A Systematic Introduction*. London: Routledge & Kegan Paul.

Johnson, James H. Jr., and Melvin L. Oliver. (1991). Economic restructuring and Black male joblessness in U.S. metropolitan areas. *Urban Geography* 12(6), 542-562.

Johnson, Robert. (1976). *Culture and Crisis in Confinement*. Lexington, MA: D.C. Health and Company.

Johnson, Sheri L. (1983). Race and the decision to detain a suspect. *Yale Law Journal* 93, 214-258.

_____. (1985). Black innocence and the white jury. *Michigan Law Review* 83, 1611-1708.

_____. (1988). Unconscious racism and the criminal law. *Cornell Law Review* 73, 1016-1037.

Jones, David A. (1976). *The Health Risks of Imprisonment*. Lexington, MA: D.C. Health and Company.

Jones-Brown, Delores D. (2000). Debunking the myth of officer friendly. *Journal of Contemporary Criminal Justice* 16(2), 209-229.

Kain, J. (1968). Housing segregation, Negro employment, and metropolitan decentralization. *Quarterly Journal of Economics* 82, 175-197.

_____. (1985). Black suburbanization in the eighties: a new beginning or a false hope? In J.M. Quigley and D.L. Rubinfeld (Eds.), *American Domestic Priorities: An Economic Appraisal*, pages 253-282. Berkeley, CA: University of California Press.

Kasarda, J.D. (1983). The implications of contemporary redistribution trends for national urban policy. In D. Hicks and N.J. Glickman (Eds.), *Transition to the Twenty-first Century: Prospect and Policies for Economic and Urban-Regional Transformation*, pages 177-247. Greenwich, CT: JAI Press.

_____. (1989). Urban industrial transition and the underclass. *Annals of the American Academy of Political and Social Science* 501, 26-47.

_____. (1990). Structural factors affecting the location and timing of underclass growth. *Urban Geography* 11(3), 234-264.

Katz, Charles M., and Cassia C. Spohn. (1995). The effect of race and gender on bail outcomes: A test of an interactive model. *American Journal of Criminal Justice* 19(2), 161-184.

Katz, I., and C. Greenbaum. (1963). Effects of anxiety, threat, and racial environment on task performance of Negro college students. *Journal of Abnormal and Social Psychology* 66, 562-567.

Katz, J. (1988). *Seductions of Crime: The Sensual and Moral Attractions of Doing Evil*. New York: Basic.

Katz, Sedelle, and Ann Mazur. (1979). *Understanding the Rape Victim: A Synthesis of Research Findings*. New York: Wiley.

Kempf, Kimberly L. (1992). *The Role of Race in Juvenile Justice Processing in Pennsylvania*. Prepared for the Juvenile Justice Training and Research Unit. Shippensburg, PA: Pennsylvania Commission on Crime and Delinquency.

Kempf, Kimberly L., and Roy L. Austin. (1986). Older and more recent evidence on racial discrimination in sentencing. *Journal of Quantitative Criminology* 2(1), 29-47.

Kerner Commission. (1968). *Report of the National Advisory Commission on Civil Disorders*. New York: Bantam Books.

Kessler, Ronald C. (1977). The use of change scores as criteria in longitudinal survey research. *Quality and Quantity* 11, 43-66.

Kessler, Ronald C., and David F. Greenberg. (1981). *Linear Panel Analysis, Models of Quantitative Change*. New York: Academic Press.

Kirschenman, Joleen, and Kathryn M. Neckerman. (1989). We'd love to hire them, but... In Christopher Jencks and Paul E. Peterson (Eds.), *The Urban Underclass*, pages 203-232. Washington, DC: The Brookings Institute.

Klein, K., and B. Creech. (1982). Race, rape and bias: Distortion of prior odds and meaning changes. *Basic and Applied Social Psychology* 3, 21-33.

Knopf, Terry Ann. (1975). *Rumors Race and Riots*. New Brunswick, NJ: Transaction Books.

Kratcoski, Peter C. (1988). The implications of research explaining prison violence and disruption. *Federal Probation* 52(1), 27-32.

Krupey, G.J. (1997). Black-on-white crime. In Peter Collier and David Horowitz (Eds.), *The Race Card: White Guilt, Black Resentment, and the Assault on Truth and Justice*, pages 196-217. Rocklin, CA: Prima Publishing.

Labouvie, E. W. (1982). Concepts of change and regression toward the mean. *Psychological Bulletin* 92, 251-257.

Labovitz, S., and J.P. Gibbs. (1964). Urbanization, technology and the division of labor: Further evidence. *Pacific Sociological Review* 7, 3-9.

Lacey, J. I., and B. C. Lacey. (1962). The law of initial value in the longitudinal study of automatic constitution: Reproducibility of autonomic responses and response patterns over a four year interval. In W. M. Wolf (Ed.) Rhythmic functions in the living system. *Annals of the New York Academy of Science* 98, 1257-1290.

LaFave, Wayne R. and Austin W. Scott. (1986). *Criminal Law, (2nd Edition)*. St. Paul, MN: West Publishing Company.

LaFree, G.D. (1980). The effect of sexual stratification by race on official reactions to rape. *American Sociological Review* 45, 842-854.

_____ (1982) Male power and female victimization: toward a theory of interracial rape. *American Journal of Sociology* 88, 311-328.

_____. (1985). Official reactions to Hispanic defendants in the Southwest. *Journal of Research in Crime and Delinquency* 22, 213-237.

LaFree, G.D., and K. Drass. (1992). *Race, crime and polarization in postwar America, 1957-1987*. Presented at the meeting of the American Society of Criminology, New Orleans, Louisiana.

Larrabee, Jennifer A. (1997). DWB (Driving While Black) and equal protection: The realities of an unconstitutional police practice. *Journal of Law and Policy* 6, 291-328.

Larsen, Richard J., and Morris L. Marx. (1990). *Statistics.* Upper Saddle River, NJ: Prentice-Hall.

Lawrence, Charles R. (1987). The Id, the ego, and equal protection: Reckoning with unconscious racism. *Stanford Law Review* 39, 317-388).

Leipold, Andrew D. (1995). Why grand juries do not (and cannot) protect the accused. *Cornell Law Review* 80: 260-324.

Leitzel Jim. (2001). Race and policing. *Society* 38(3), 38-42.

Leo, Richard A. (1996). Inside the interrogation room. *Journal of Criminal Law and Criminology* 86, 266-303.

____. (2001). False confessions: Causes, consequences, and solutions. In Saundra D. Westervelt and John A. Humphrey (Eds.), *Wrongly Convicted: Perspectives on Failed Justice*, pages 36-54. New Brunswick, NJ: Rutgers University Press.

Leo, Richard A., and Richard J. Ofshe. (1998). The consequences of false confessions: Deprivations of liberty and miscarriages of justice in the age of psychological interrogation. *Journal of Criminology and Criminal Law* 88, 429-496.

Lersch, Kim M., and Joe R. Feagin. (1996). Violent police-citizen encounters: An analysis of major newspaper accounts. *Critical Sociology* 22, 29-51.

Levin, Michael. (1991). Race differences: An overview. *Journal of Social Political and Economic Studies* 16(2), 195-216.

Levine, James P. (1992). *Juries and Politics.* Pacific Grove, CA: Brooks/Cole.

Levine, James P., Michael C. Musheno, and Dennis J. Palumbo. (1986). *Criminal Justice in America.* New York: Wiley and Sons.

Lichtenberg, Judith. (1992). Racism in the head, racism in the world. *Report from the Institute for Philosophy and Public Policy* 12, 3-5.

Liker, Jeffrey K., Sue Augustyniak, and Greg J. Duncan. (1985). Panel data and models of change: A comparison of first difference and conventional two-wave models. *Social Science Research* 14, 80-101.

Light, Stephen C. (1990). The severity of assaults on prison officers: A contextual study. *Social Science Quarterly* 71(2), 267-284.

Linn, R. L., and J. A. Slinde. (1977). The determination of the significance of change between pre and post-testing periods. *Review of Educational Research* 47, 121-150.

Lipton, J.P. (1979). Sociocultural and Personality Perspectives on Jury Behavior and Decision Making. Unpublished dissertation, University of California, Riverside.

Lizotte, Alan J. (1978). Extra-legal factors in Chicago's criminal courts: Testing the conflict model of criminal justice. *Social Problems* 25, 564-580.

Locke, Hubert G. (1996). The color of law and the issue of color: Race and the abuse of police power. In William A. Geller and Hans Toch (Eds.), *Police Violence*, pages 129-149. New Haven, CT: Yale University Press.

Lockwood, Daniel. (1980). *Prison Sexual Violence*. New York: Elsevier.

Lombroso, Gina. (1972). *Criminal Man, According to the Classification of Cesare Lombroso*. Montclair, NJ: Patterson Smith.

Long, J. Scott. (1997). *Regression Models for Categorical and Limited Dependent Variables*. Thousand Oaks, CA: Sage Publications.

Lord, Frederic M. (1956). The measurement of growth. *Educational and Psychological Measurement*, 16, 421-437.

____. (1963). Elementary models for measuring change. In Chester W. Harris (Ed.), *Problems in Measuring Change*, pages 21-38. Madison, WI: University of Wisconsin Press.

Luckenbill, David F. and Daniel P. Doyle. (1989). Structural position and violence: Developing a cultural explanation. *Criminology* 27, 419-436.

Lynch, Frederick R. (1992). Race unconsciousness and the white male. *Society* 29, 2(196), 30-35.

Lytton, H., M. E. Croxen, and F. Pysh. (1973). Regression to the mean misunderstood: A reply to Vockell and Asher. *Developmental Psychology* 8, 3-5.

Maclin, Tracey. (1998). Race and the fourth amendment. *Vanderbilt Law Review* 51(2), 333-393.

Magee, Robin K. (1994). The myth of the good cop and the inadequacy of Fourth Amendment remedies for Black men: Contrasting presumptions of innocence and guilt. *Capital University Law Review* 23, 151-219.

Maguire, Kathleen and Ann L. Pastore (Eds.). *Sourcebook of Criminal Justice Statistics 1994*. U.S. Department of Justice, Bureau of Justice Statistics. Washington, DC: USGPO, (1995).

____. *Sourcebook of Criminal Justice Statistics 1995*. U.S. Department of Justice, Bureau of Justice Statistics. Washington, DC: USGPO, (1996).

____. *Sourcebook of Criminal Justice Statistics 2000*. U.S. Department of Justice, Bureau of Justice Statistics. Washington, DC: USGPO, (2001).

Majors, R., and J.M. Billson. (1992). *Cool Pose: The Dilemmas of Black Manhood in America*. New York: Lexington Books.

Mancini, M.J. (1996). *One Dies, Get Another: Convict Leasing in the American South 1866-1928*. Columbia, SC: University of South Carolina Press.

Mann, Coramae Richey. (1993). *Unequal Justice: A Question of Color*. Bloomington, IN: Indiana University Press.

Markus, G. (1979). *Models for the Analysis of Panel Data*. Sage University Paper series on Quantitative Applications in the Social Sciences, 07-018. Beverly Hills: Sage.

Marcus-Newhall, Amy, William C. Pederson, Mike Carlson, Norman Miller. (2000). Displaced Aggression is Alive and Well: A Meta-Analytic Review. *Journal of Personality and Social Psychology* 78(4), 670-689.

Marquart, J.W. (1986). Prison guards and the use of physical coercion as a mechanism of prisoner control. *Criminology* 24, 347-366.

Martin, Leonard L., and Abraham Tesser. (1989). Toward a motivational and structural theory of ruminative thought. In J.S. Uleman and J. A. Bargh (Eds.), *Unintended Thought*, pages 306-326. New York: Guilford.

Mason, Patrick L. (1999). African American Achievement and Socioeconomic Collapse: Alternative theories and empirical evidence. In Vernon C. Polite and James E. Davis (Eds.), *African American Males in School and Society: Practices and Policies for Effective Education*, pages 149-165. New York: Teachers College Press.

Massey, Douglas S., and Kumiko Shibuya. (1995). Unraveling the tangle of pathology: The effect of spatially concentrated joblessness on the well-being of African Americans. *Social Science Research* 24, 352-366.

Massey, Douglas S., and Mitchell L. Eggers. (1990). The ecology of inequality: Minorities and the concentration of poverty, 1970-1980. *American Journal of Sociology* 95(5), 1153-1188.

Massey, Douglas S., and N.A. Denton. (1993). *American Apartheid: Segregation and the Making of the Underclass*. Cambridge, MA: Harvard University Press.

Mauer, Marc. (1995). *Young Black Americans and the Criminal Justice System: Five Years Later.* Washington. DC: The Sentencing Project.

Maxwell, N. (1994). The effect of black-white wage differences of differences in the quantity and quality of education. *Industrial and Labor Relations Review* 47(2), 249-264.

Maxwell, Scott E., and George S. Howard. (1981). Change scores-necessarily anathema? *Educational and Psychological Measurement* 41, 747-756.

May, Rollo. (1972). *Power and Innocence: A Search for the Sources of Violence.* New York: W.W. Norton & Company, Inc.

Mayer, William G. (1992). *The Changing American Mind.* Ann Arbor, MI: University of Michigan Press.

McBride, James. (1987, February 3). Convictions of Lenell Geter; Exonerated after 16 months in prison, he is looking ahead. *The Washington Post*, e01.

McCall, Nathan. (1995). *Makes Me Wanna Holler.* New York: Vintage Books.

McCorkle, Richard C., Terance D. Miethe, and Kriss A. Drass. (1995). The roots of prison violence: A test of the deprivation, management, and not-so-total institutions models. *Crime and Delinquency* 41(3), 317-331.

McGovern, J.R. (1982). *Anatomy of a Lynching: the Killing of Claude Neal.* Baton Rouge, LA: Louisiana State University Press.

McDonald, John F. and Robert A. Moffit. (1980). The uses of Tobit analysis. *The Review of Economics and Statistics* 62(2), 318-321.

McIntyre, L.D., and E. Pernell. (1985). The impact of race on teacher recommendations for special education placement. *Journal of Multicultural Counseling and Development* 6, 112-120.

McKay Commission. (1972). *Attica: The Official Report of the New York State Special Commission on Attica*. New York: Bantam Books.

McKenzie, R.B. (1991). *Competing Visions: The Political Conflict Over America's Economic Future*. Washington, DC: Cato Institute.

McLaughlin, Vance. (1992). *Police and the Use of Force*. Westport, CT: Praeger Publishers.

McNemar, Q. (1958). On growth measurement. *Educational and Psychological Measurement* 18, 47-55.

Meddis, Sam Vincent. (1993, July 26). In twin cities, a tale of two standards. *USA Today*, 6A.

Melilli, K.J. (1996). Batson in practice: What we have learned about Batson and peremptory challenges. *Notre Dame Law Review* 71, 447-503.

Menard, S. (1991). *Longitudinal Research*. Sage University Paper series on Quantitative Applications in the Social Sciences, 07-076. Newbury Park, CA: Sage.

Jerome, Miller. (1992). *Hobbling a Generation: Young-African-American Males in Washington D.C.'s Criminal Justice System.*. Alexandria, VA: National Center on Institutions and Alternatives.

Miller, N.E. (1941). The frustration-aggression hypothesis. *Psychological Review* 48, 337-342.

_____. (1948). Theory and experiment relating psychoanalytic displacement to stimulus-response generalization. *Journal of Abnormal and Social Psychology* 43, 155-178.

Miller, N., and A. Marcus-Newhall. (1997). A conceptual analysis of displaced aggression. In R. Ben-Ari and Y. Rich (Eds.), *Enhancing Education in Heterogeneous Schools*, pages 69-108. Ramat-Gan, Israel: Bar-Ilan University Press.

Miller, Marina, and Jay Hewitt. (1978). Conviction of a defendant as a function of juror-victim racial similarity. *Journal of Social Psychology* 105, 159-160.

Mollen Commission. (1994). *Commission to Investigate Allegations of Police Corruption and the Anti-Corruption Procedures of the Police Department*. New York: The Commission.

Montgomery, Reid H. Jr. (1994). American prison riots: 1774-1991. In Michael C. Braswell, Reid H. Montgomery Jr., and Lucien X. Lombardo (Eds.) *Prison Violence*, pages 227-251. Cincinnati, OH: Anderson Publishing.

Morrison, Toni. (1987). *Beloved: A Novel*. New York: Knopf.

Moss, Philip, and Christopher Tilly. (1991). *Why Black Men are Doing Worse in the Labor Market: A Review of Supply-Side and Demand-Side Explanations*. New York: Social Science Research Council.

Moynihan, Daniel P. (1965). *The Negro Family: the Case for National Action*. Washington, DC: Government Printing Office.

Mueller, J.H., and K.F. Schuessler. (1961). *Statistical Reasoning in Sociology*. Boston: Houghton Mifflin.

Myers, B.C. (1990). Hypertension as a manifestation of the stress experienced by Black families. In H.E. Cheatam and J.B. Stewart (Eds.), *Black Families: Interdisciplinary Perspectives*. New Brunswick, NJ: Transaction.

Myers, L.B., and Levy, G.W. (1978). Description and prediction of the intractable inmate. *Journal of Research in Crime and Delinquency* 15, 214-228.

Myers, Martha A., and John Hagan. (1979). Private and public trouble: Prosecutors and the allocation of court resources. *Social Problems* 26(4), 439-451.

Myrdal, Gunnar. (1944). *An American Dilemma*. New York: Harper.

NAACP Legal Defense Fund. (2000). *Death Row, USA*. New York: NAACP Legal Defense Fund, 1 April.

Nacci, P.L. (1978). Sexual assault in prisons. *American Journal of Corrections* 40, 30-31.

Nacci, P.L. and T. Kane. (1984). Inmate sexual aggressions: Some evolving propositions, empirical findings and mitigating counter forces. *Journal of Offender Counseling Services and Rehabilitation* 9, 1-20.

Naffine, Ngaire. (1987). *Female Crime: the Construction of Women in Criminology*. Boston: Allen and Unwin.

Nagel, William G. (1973). *The New Red Barn: A Critical Look at the Modern American Prison*. New York: The American Foundation, Inc.

National Academic Press. (2002). *Minority Students in Special Education and Gifted Education* Retrieved from http://books.nap.nap.edu/books/0309074398/htm#pagetop

National Advisory Commission on Criminal Justice Standards and Goals. (1973). *Task Force Report on Corrections*. Washington, DC: Government Printing Press.

National Minority Advisory Council on Criminal Justice (NMAC). (1980). *The Inequality of Justice*. Washington, DC: U.S. Department of Justice.

National Science Foundation, Division of Science Resources Studies, *Science and Engineering Doctorate Awards: 1996*, Detailed Statistical Tables, NSF 97-329, by Susan T. Hill (Arlington, VA, 1997).

National Science Foundation, *Science and Engineering Doctorates: 1960-91*, NSF 93-301, Detailed Statistical Tables, (Washington, DC, 1993).

Neff, Joseph, and Pat Stith. (1996, July 28). Highway drug unit focuses on Blacks. *News & Observer* A1.

Nesselroade, J. R., S. M. Stigler, and P. B. Baltes (1980). Regression toward the mean and the study of change. *Psychological Bulletin* 88, 622-637.

Nolen-Hoeksema, S. (1987). Sex differences in unipolar depression: Evidence and theory. *Psychological Bulletin* 101, 259-282.

O'Brien, Robert M. (1987). The interracial nature of violent crimes: A reexamination. *American Journal of Sociology* 92(4), 817-835.

Ofshe, Richard J., and Richard A. Leo. (1997). The decision to confess falsely: Rational choice and irrational action. *Denver University Law Review* 74: 979-1122.

Ogbu, J.U. (1992). Understanding cultural diversity and learning. *Educational Researcher* 21, 5-14.

Osborne, Jason W. (1997). Race and academic disidentification. *Journal of Education Psychology* 25, 59-67.

_____. (1999). Unraveling underachievement among African-American boys from as identification with academics perspective. *Journal of Negro Education* 68(4), 555-565.

Osborne, J.W., and J. Rausch. (2001, April). Identification with academics and academic outcomes in secondary students. Paper presented at the *National Meeting of the American Education Research Association*, Seattle, WA.

Oshinsky, D.M. (1996). *Worse than Slavery: Parchman Farm and the Ordeal of Jim Crow Justice*. New York: Free Press.

Ost, Laura. (1987, December 27). Innocent have died in chair, study finds. *Tallahassee Democrat* 1E, 7E.

Overall, J.E. and J. A. Woodward. (1975). Unreliability of difference scores: A paradox for measurement of change. *Psychological Bulletin* 82, 85-86.

Owen, Barbara A. (1985). Race and gender relations among prison workers. *Crime and Delinquency* 31(1), 147-159.

Park, James W. L. (1976). The organization of prison violence. In Albert K. Cohen, George F. Cole, and Robert G. Bailey (Eds.), *Prison Violence*, pages 89-96. Lexington, MA: D.C. Health and Company.

Parker, Karen F., Mari A. Dewees, and Michael L. Radelet. (2001). Racial bias in the conviction of the innocent. In Saundra D. Westervelt and John A. Humphrey (Eds.), *Wrongly Convicted: Perspectives on Failed Justice*, pages 114-131. New Brunswick, NJ: Rutgers University Press.

Patterson, E.B., and M.J. Lynch. (1991). Biases in formalized bail procedures. In M.J. Lynch and E.B. Paterson (Eds.), *Race and Criminal Justice*, pages 36-53. New York: Harrow and Heston.

Payne, Les. (1992). Up against the wall: Black men and the cops. *Essence* 23(7), 72-76.

Petee, Thomas A. (1994). Recommended for release on recognizance: Factors affecting pretrial release recommendations. *The Journal of Social Psychology* 134(3), 375-383.

Petersllla, Joan. (1983). *Racial Disparities in the Criminal Justice System*. Santa Monica, CA: RAND.

Peters, M.F. (1981). Parenting in Black families with young children: A historical perspective. In H. McAdoo (Ed.), *Black Families*. Beverly Hills, CA: Sage.

Peterson, Jesse L. (2000). *From Rage to Responsibility*. St. Paul, MN: Paragon House.

Pierce, Chester. (1970). Offensive Mechanisms. In F. Barbour (Ed.), *The Black Seventies*, pages 265-282. Boston: Porter Sargent.

Pinar, William F. (2001). *The Gender of Racial Politics and Violence in America.* New York: Peter Lang Publishing.

Piven, Frances Fox, and Richard A. Cloward. (1977). *Poor People's Movements: Why They Succeed, How They Fail.* New York: Pantheon.

Plewism, I. (1985). *Analyzing Change: Measurement and Exploration Using Longitudinal Data.* Chichester, UK: John Wiley.

Poussaint, Alvin F. (1966). The stress of the White female worker in the civil rights movement in the South. *American Journal of Psychiatry* 123, 401-407.

_____. (1983). Black on Black homicide: A psychological perspective. *Victimology* 8, 161-169.

Poussaint, Alvin F., and Amy Alexander. (2000). *Lay My Burden Down: Unraveling Suicide and the Mental Health Crisis Among African-Americans.* Boston: Beacon Press.

Powdermaker, H. (1943). The channeling of Negro aggression by the cultural process. *American Journal of Sociology*, 750-758.

Prager, Dennis. (1998). *Happiness is a Serious Problem.* New York: Harper Collins.

Prasse, D.P., and D.J. Reschly (1986). Larry P.: A case of segregation, testing, or program efficacy? *Exceptional Children* 52(4), 333-346.

President's Commission on Law Enforcement and the Administration of Justice. (1967). *The Challenge of Crime in a Free Society.* Washington, DC: Government Printing Office.

Propper, A.M. (1981). *Prison Homosexuality: Myth and Reality.* Lexington, MA: D.C. Health and Company.

Pyszczynski, T. and J. Greenberg. (1987). Self-regulatory preservation and the depressive self-focusing style: A self-awareness theory of reactive depression. *Psychological Bulletin* 102, 122-138.

Rachman, S., and R. Hodgson. (1980). *Obsessions and Compulsions.* Englewood, CA: Prentice-Hall.

Radelet, Michael L. (1981). Racial characteristics and the imposition of the death penalty. *American Sociological Review* 46, 918-927.

Radelet, Michael L., and Gleen L. Pierce. (1985). Race and prosecutorial discretion in homicide cases. *Law and Society Review* 19, 587-621.

Radelet, Michael L., William S. Lofquist, and Hugo Adam Bedau. (1996). Prisoners released from death row since 1970 because of doubts about their guilt. *Thomas M. Cooley Law Review* 13, 907-966.

Rainwater, Lee. (1970). *Behind Ghetto Walls: Black Families in a Federal Slum.* Chicago: Aldine.

Rainwater, L., and W. Yancey (Eds.). (1967). *The Moynihan Report and the Politics of Controversy.* Cambridge, MA: MIT Press.

Rampersad, Arnold (Ed.). (2001). *The Collected Works of Langston Hughes.* Columbia, MO: University of Missouri Press.

Rattner, Arye. (1988). Convicted but innocent: Wrongful conviction and the criminal justice system. *Law and Human Behavior* 12, 283-293.

Reed, R.J. (1988). Education and achievement of young black males. In Jewelle T. Gibbs (Ed.), *Young Black, and Male in America: An Endangered Species,* pages 37-96. Dover, MA: Auburn House Publishing.

Reiss, A.J. Jr. (1974). Discretionary justice in the United States. *International Journal of Criminology and Penology* 2(2), 181-200.

Rideau, W. and R. Wikberg. (1992). *Life Sentences: Rage and Survival Behind Bars*. New York: Time Books, Random House.

Riley, Kevin Jack. (1997). *Crack, Powder Cocaine, and Heroin: Drug Purchase and Use Patterns in Six U.S. Cities*. Washington, DC: National Institute of Justice.

Robinson, Billy H. (1971). Love: A hard-legged triangle. *Black Scholar* September 1971, 29.

Robinson, James L. (1995). *Racism or Attitude?* New York: Plenum Press.

Robinson, Randall. (2000). *The Debt, What America Owes to Blacks*. New York: Penguin Putnam.

Rogosa, Donald. (1995). Myths and methods: "Myths about longitudinal research" plus supplemental questions. In John M. Gottman (Ed.) *The Analysis of Change*, pages 3-66. New Jersey: Lawrence Erlbaum Associates, Inc.

Rogosa, Donald, D. Brandt, and M. Zimowski. (1982). A growth curve approach to the measurement of change. *Psychological Bulletin* 90, 726-748.

Rolison, Garry L. (1993). Nonemployment of black men in major metropolitan areas. *Sociological Inquiry* 63(3), 318-329.

Roncek, Dennis W. (1992). Learning more from Tobit coefficients: Extending a comparative analysis of political protest. *American Sociological Review* 57(4), 503-507.

Rose, Mary R. (1999). The peremptory challenge accused of race or gender discrimination? Some data from one county. *Law and Human Behavior* 23(6), 695-702.

Ross, L. E., and H. L. McMurray. (1996). Dual realities and structural challenges of African American criminologists. *Academy of Criminal Justice Sciences* XV(1), 1-9.

Russell, Katheryn K. (1992). Development of a Black criminology and the role of the Black criminologist. *Justice Quarterly* 9(4), 667-677.

_____. (1994). The racial inequality hypothesis. *Law and Human Behavior* 18(3), 305-317.

_____. (1998). *The Color of Crime: Racial Hoaxes, White Fear, Black Protectionism, Police Harassment, and Other Macroaggressions*. New York: New York University Press.

_____. (1999). "Driving while black": Corollary phenomena and collateral consequences. *Boston College Law Review* 40(3), 717-731.

Russell, Katheryn K., Heather L. Pfeifer, and Judith L. Jones. (2000). *Race and Crime: An Annotated Bibliography*. Westport, CT: Greenwood Press.

Salken, Barbara C. (1989). The general warrant of the twentieth century? A Fourth Amendment solution to unchecked discretion to arrest for traffic offenses. *Temple Law Review* 62, 221.

Sampson, Robert J., and William Julius Wilson. (1995). Toward a theory of race, crime, and urban inequality. In John Hagan and Ruth D. Peterson (Eds.), *Crime and Inequality*, pages 37-54. Stanford, CA: Stanford University Press.

Sanborn, Joseph. (1986). A historical sketch of plea-bargaining. *Justice Quarterly* 3.

Sasson, Theodore. (1995). *Crime Talk*. Hawthorne, NY: Aldine de Gruyter.

Scacco, A. M. (1975). *Rape in Prison*. Springfield, IL: Charles C. Thomas.

_____. (1982). *Male Rape: A Case Book of Sexual Aggressions*. New York: AMS Press.

Schmitt, Christopher, H. (1991, December 8). Plea bargaining favors Whites as Blacks, Hispanics pay price. *San Jose Mercury News*, 1.

Schuman, Howard, Charlotte Steeh, and Lawrence Bobo. (1985). *Racial Attitudes in America: Trends and Interpretations*. Cambridge, MA: Harvard University Press.

Schwartz, Herman. (1972). Prisoners' rights: Some hopes and realities. In Chief Justice Earl Warren Conference on Advocacy in the United States, *A Program for Prison Reform: The Final Report*. Cambridge, MA: The Roscoe Round-American Trial Lawyers Foundation.

Scott, A.J. (1988). Flexible production systems and regional development: the rise of new industrial spaces in North America and Western Europe. *International Journal of Urban and Regional Research* 12(2), 171-186.

Seigel, Larry J. (2006). *Criminology*. Belmont, CA: Thomson Wadsworth.

Seron, carroll, Martin Frankel, Douglas Mussio, and Joseph Pereira. (1997). Report of the perceptions and experiences of lawyers, judges, and court employees concerning gender, racial, and ethnic fairness in the federal courts of the second circuit of the United States. *Annual Survey of American Law* 1997: 415-528.

Serr, Brian J., and Mark Maney. (1988). Racism, peremptory challenges, and the democratic jury: The jurisprudence of a delicate balance. *The Journal of Criminal Law and Criminology* 79(1), 1-65.

Sharma, K. K., and J. K. Gupta. (1986). Optimum reliability of gain scores. *Journal of Experimental Educational* 54, 105-108.

Shoemaker, Donald and Sherwood Williams. (1987). The subculture of violence and ethnicity. *Journal of Criminal Justice* 15, 461-472.

Silberman, Matthew. (1988). Dispute meditation in the American prison: A new approach to the reduction of violence. *Policy Studies Journal* 16, 522-532.

_____. (1995). *A World of Violence*. Belmont, CA: Wadsworth Publishing Company.

Simpson, E.H. (1949). Measurement of diversity. *Nature* 163, 688.

Simpson, Patricia A. (2000). Skills shifts and Black male joblessness in major urban labor markets over the 1980's. *Social Science Research* 29, 327-355.

Singleton, Royce A., and Bruce C. Straits. (1999). *Approaches to Social Research*. New York: Oxford.

Skolnick, Jerome. (1994). *Justice Without Trial: Law Enforcement in a Democratic Society, (3rd Edition)*. New York: Macmillan.

Smith, Douglas A., Nanette Graham, and Bonney Adams. (1991). Minorities and the police: Attitudinal and behavioral questions. In Michael J. Lynch and E. Britt Patterson (Eds.), *Race and Criminal Justice*, pages 22-35. Albany, NY: Harrow and Heston Publishers.

Smith, Douglas A., Christy A. Visher, and Laura A. Davidson. (1984). Equity and discretionary justice: The influence of race on police arrest decisions. *Journal of Criminal Law and Criminology* 75(1), 234-249.

Smith, Tom W. (1990, December). Ethnic images. General Social Survey Topical Report No. 19, on file with the *Stanford Law Review*.

Soja, Ed, Rebecca Morales, and Goetz Wolff. (1983). Urban restructuring: An analysis of social and spatial change in Los Angeles. *Economic Geography* 58(2), 221-235.

Sperlich, P.W., and M.L. Jaspovice. (1975). Statistical decision theory and the selection of grand jurors: Testing for discrimination in a single panel. *Hastings Constitutional Law Quarterly* 2, 75.

Spohn, Cassia E., Susan Welch, and John Gruhl. (1985). Women defendants in court: The interaction between sex and race in convicting and sentencing. *Social Science Quarterly* 66, 176-185.

Spohn, Cassia E., John Gruhl, and Susan Welch. (1981, 1982). The effect of race on sentencing: A re-examination of an unsettled question. *Law and Society Review* 16, 71-88.

_____. (1987). The impact of ethnicity and gender of defendants on the decision to reject or dismiss felony charges. *Criminology* 25, 175-191.

Staples, Brent A. (1994). *Parallel Time: Growing Up in Black and White*. New York: Pantheon Books.

Staples, R. (1982). *Black Masculinity: The Black Man's Role in American Society*. San Francisco: Black Scholar Press.

Starchild, A. (1990). Rape of youth in prisons and juvenile facilities. *Journal of Psychohistory* 18(2), 145-150.

Starr, V.H., and M. McCormick. (1985). *Jury Selection*. Boston: Little, Brown and Company.

Steele, C. (1992). Race and the schooling of African Americans. *Atlantic Monthly*, April, 68-72.

_____. (1997). A threat in the air: How stereotypes shape intellectual identity and performance. *American Psychologist* 52, 613-629.

Steele, Shelby. (1990). *The Content of Our Character*. New York: Harper Collins.

Stevens, G. (1981). Bias in the attribution of hyperkinetic behavior as a function of ethnic identification and socio-economic status. *Psychology in the Schools* 18, 99-106.

Stevenson, Richard W. (1991, March 15). Protesting beating, many say Gates 'Has Got to Go'. *New York Times*, A16.

Stoll, Michael A. (1998). When jobs move, do Black and Latino men lose? The effect of growth in job decentralisation on young men's jobless incidence and duration. *Urban Studies* 35(12), 2221-2239.

Stycos, Steven. (1994, May 27). The force of law. *The Providence Phoenix*, 4.

Sullivan, H. S. (1953). *The Interpersonal Theory of Psychiatry*. New York: W.W. Norton & C0.

Sullivan, M. (1989). *Getting Paid: Youth Crime and Work in the Inner City*. Ithaca, NY: Cornell University Press.

Sulton, Anne. (1989). *Inner-City Crime Control*. Washington, DC: Police Foundation.

Suttles, Gerald D. (1968). *The Social Order of the Slum: Ethnicity and Territory in the Inner City*. Chicago: University of Chicago Press.

Sykes, Charles J. (1992). *A Nation of Victims*. New York: St. Martin's Press.

Sylvester, S.F., J.H. Reed, and D.O. Nelson. (1977). *Prison Homicide*. New York: Spectrum.

Tait, R., and R.C. Silver. (1989). Coming to terms with major negative life events. In J.S. Uleman and J.A. Bargh (Eds.), *Unintended Thoughts*, pages 351-382. New York: Guilford Press.

Tallis, F. G.C.L. Davey, and N. Capuzzo. (1994). The phenomenology of non-pathological worry: A preliminary investigation. In G.C.L. Davey and F. Tallis (Eds.), *Worrying: Perspectives on Theory, Assessment and Treatment*, pages 61-90. Chichester, England: John Wiley & Sons.

Taub, Richard. (1991, October). *Differing conceptions of honor and orientations toward work and marriage among low-income African-Americans and Mexican-Americans*. Paper presented at the Chicago Urban Poverty and Family Life Conference, Chicago.

Tarvis, C. (1989). *Anger: The Misunderstood Emotion*. New York: Touchstone.

Taylor, G. Flint. (1999). The case of the Ford Heights four. *Police Misconduct and Civil Rights Law Report* 6, 37-46.

Taylor, Jared, and Glayde Whitney. (1999). Crime and racial profiling by U.S. police: Is there an empirical basis? *The Journal of Social, Political, and Economic Studies* 24(4), 485-510.

Taylor, Robert L. (1994). Black males and social policy: Breaking the cycle of disadvantage. In Richard G. Majors and Jacob U. Gordon (Eds.) *The American Black Male*, pages 147-166. Chicago: Nelson-Hall.

Taylor, Yuval. (Ed.). (1999). *I Was Born a Slave (Volume 1)*. Chicago: Lawrence Hill.

The Associated Press. (2000, March 4). Police award after shooting prompts ouster. Retrieved March 5, 2002 from World Wide Web: http://www.policetalk.com/louisville.html

Thomas, Charles W. (1977). Theoretical perspectives on prisonization: A comparison of the importation and deprivation models. *The Journal of Criminal Law & Criminology* 68 (1), 135-145.

Thomas, Wayne. (1976). *Bail Reform in America.* Berkeley, CA: University of California Press.

Thorndike, R. L. (1942). Regression fallacies in the matched groups experiment. *Psychometrika* 7, 85-102.

Tiffany, Lawrence P., Donald M. McIntyre, Jr., and Daniel L. Rotenberg. (1967). *Detection of Crime: Stopping and Questioning, Search and Seizure, Encouragement and Entrapment.* Boston: Little, Brown and Company.

Tobin, James. (1958). Estimation of relationships for limited dependent variables. *Econometrica* 26, 24-36.

Toch, Hans. (1977). *Living in Prison: The Ecology of Survival.* New York: Free Press.

Tolnay, S. E., and E. M. Beck. (1995). *A Festival of Violence: An Analysis of Southern Lynchings, 1882-1930.* Urbana, IL: University of Illinois Press.

Tonry, Michael. (1995). *Malign Neglect.* New York: Oxford University Press.

Tornqvist, L. P. Vartia, and Y. O. Vartia. (1985). How should relative change be measured? *American Statistician* 39, 43-46.

Trotta, Brian M. (1994, November 22). Report: Avon police targeted minorities; Probe supports ex-officer's discrimination claims. *The Hartford Courant,* A1.

Tuch, Steven A. (1987). Urbanism, region, and tolerance revisited: The case of racial prejudice. *American Sociological Review* 52, 504-510.

Turner, Billy M., Rickie D. Lovell, John C. Young, and William F. Denny. (1986). Race and peremptory challenges during Voir Dire: Do prosecution and defense agree? *Journal of Criminal Defense* 14, 61-69.

Turner, Patricia A. (1993). *I Heard it Through the Grapevine.* Los Angeles: University of California Press (Berkeley).

Unever, James D. (1982). Direct and organizational discrimination in the sentencing of drug offenders. *Social Problems* 30, 212-225.

Unnever, James D., and Larry Hembroff. (1988). The prediction of racial/ethnic sentencing disparities: An expectation states approach. *Journal of Research in Crime and Delinquency* 25, 53-82.

U.S. Bureau of the Census. (1960). *Statistical Abstract of the United States: 1960. (81st Edition).* Washington, DC: U.S. Department of Commerce.

_____. (1980). *Statistical Abstract of the United States: 1980. (101st Edition).* Washington, DC: U.S. Department of Commerce.

_____. (1990). *Statistical Abstract of the United States: 1990. (110th Edition).* Washington, DC: U.S. Department of Commerce.

U.S. Department of Education, National Center for Education Statistics. *Digest of Education Statistics 2001.* NCES 2000-130, by Thomas D. Snyder. Production Manager, Charlene M. Hoffman. Washington, DC: 2002.

U.S. Department of Education. National Center for Education Statistics. *Findings from the Condition of Education 1994: No. 2: The Educational Progress of Black Students.* Washington DC: 1995.

U.S. Department of Health and Human Services. (1985). *Report of the Secretary's Task Force on Black and Minority Health.* Vol. 1. Washington, DC: U.S. Government Printing Office.

U.S. Department of Justice, Bureau of Justice Statistics. *Correctional Populations in the United States, 1997.*

U.S. Department of Justice, Bureau of Justice Statistics. *Census of State Adult Correctional Facilities, 1984.* Conducted by U.S. Department of Commerce, Bureau of the Census. ICPSR (Ed.) Ann Arbor, MI: Inter-university Consortium for Political and Social Research, (1997).

_____. *Census of State and Federal Adult Correctional Facilities, 1990.* Conducted by U.S. Department of Commerce, Bureau of the Census. ICPSR (Ed.) Ann Arbor, MI: Inter-university Consortium for Political and Social Research, (1993).

_____. *Census of State and Federal Adult Correctional Facilities, 1995.* Conducted by U.S. Department of Commerce, Bureau of the Census. ICPSR (Ed.) Ann Arbor, MI: Inter-university Consortium for Political and Social Research, (1998).

Van Dyke, J.M. (1977). *Jury Selection Procedures: Our Uncertain Commitment to Representative Panels.* Cambridge, MA: Ballinger.

Viscusi, W.K. (1986). Market incentives for criminal behavior. In R.B. Freeman and H.J. Holzer (Eds.), *The Black Youth Employment Crisis*, pages 301-351. Chicago: University of Chicago Press.

Vockell, E. L., and W. Asher. (1973). Methodological inaccuracies in Croxen and Lytton's reading disability and difficulties in finger localization and right-left discrimination. *Developmental Psychology* 8, 1-2.

von Eye, Alexander. (1990). *Statistical Methods in Longitudinal Research, Volume 1 – Principles and Structuring Change.* San Diego, CA: Academic Press.

Vontress, Clemmont. (1962). Patterns of segregation and discrimination: contributing factors to crime among Negroes. *Journal of Negro Education* 31, 108-116.

Waldinger, Roger. (1986). Changing ladders and musical chairs: Ethnicity and opportunity in post-industrial New York. *Politics and Society* 15(4), 369-401.

Walker, Samuel, and Molly A. Brown. (1995). Pale reflections of reality: The neglect of racial and ethnic minorities in introductory criminal justice textbooks. *Journal of Criminal Justice Education* 6(1), 61-83.

Walker, Samuel, Cassia Spohn, and Miriam DeLone. (1996). *The Color of Justice: Race, Ethnicity and Crime in America.* Belmont, CA: Wadsworth.

Warden, Rob. (2001, May 2). How mistaken and perjured eyewitness identification testimony put 46 innocent Americans on death row. *Center on Wrongful Convictions Eyewitness Study.* Retrieved March 18, 2002 from the World Wide Web: http://www.law.northwestern.edu/depts/clinic/wrongful/causes.htm.

Watkins, William H. (2002). Understanding the socialization process. In Lee Jones (Ed.), *Making it on Broken Promises: Leading African American Male Scholars Confront the Culture of Higher Education*, pages 98-105. Sterling, VA: Stylus.

Watman, W. (1966). The relationship between acting out behavior and some psychological test indices in a prison population. *Journal of Clinical Psychology* 22, 279-280.

Watson, Walter. (1995). Comedian Paul Mooney uses humor to attack racism. *National Public Radio*, September 23, 1995, Transcript #1979-7.

Weatherspoon, Floyd D. (1994). The devastating impact of the justice system on the status of African American males: An overview perspective. *Capital University Law Review* 23, 23-62.

Wegner, D.M. (1992). You can't always think what you want: Problems in the suppression of unwanted thoughts. In M. Zanna (Ed.), *Advances in Experimental Social Psychology* 25, pages 193-225. San Diego, CA: Academic.

Welch F. (1990). The employment of black men. *Journal of Labor Economics* 8, 26-74.

Wells, Ida B. (1969). *On Lynchings: Southern Horrors, A Red Record, Mob Rule in New Orleans.* New York: Arno Press.

West, Cornel. (1993). *Race Matters.* New York: Doubleday.

Westley, William A. (1970). *Violence and the Police.* Cambridge, MA: MIT Press.

Wheeler, Gerald R., and Carol L. Wheeler. (1980). Reflections on legal representation of the economically disadvantaged: Beyond assembly line justice. *Crime and Delinquency* 26(3), 319-332.

White, R.B. (1980). Prediction of adjustment to prison in a federal correctional population. *Journal of Clinical Psychology* 36, 1031-1034.

Whittaker, Gordon P. (1982). *Basic Issues in Police Performance.* Washington DC: Government Printing Office.

Wilbanks, William. (1985). Is violent crime intraracial? *Crime and Delinquency* 31(1), 117-128.

Wilder, J. (1957). The law of initial value in neurology and psychiatry. *Journal of Nervous and Mental Disease* 125, 73-86.

Williams, R.B., J.C. Baufort, and R.B. Shekelle. (1985). The health consequences of hostility. In M. Chesney and R. Rosenman (Eds.), *Anger and Hostility in Cardiovascular and Behavioral Disorders.* Washington, DC: Hemisphere.

Williams, Robin M. Jr. (1964). *Strangers Next Door.* Englewood Cliffs, NJ: Prentice Hall, Inc.

Wilson, Frank H. (1994). Urban redevelopment, housing change, and Black concentrated poverty: Reflections on the underclass controversy. Paper presented at the annual meeting for the *Society for the Study of Social Problems.*

Wilson, Lynne. (1996). Cops v. Citizen Review. *Covert Action Quarterly* 55 (Winter).

Wilson, William Julius. (1987). *The Truly Disadvantaged: The Inner City, the Underclass and Public Policy.* Chicago: The University of Chicago Press.

_____. (1996). *When Work Disappears.* New York: Alfred A. Knopf.

Wishman, Seymour. (1986). *Anatomy of a Jury: The System on Trial.* New York: Times Books.

Witte, Ann Dryden. (1980). Estimating the economic model of crime with individual data. *The Quarterly Journal of Economics* 94(1), 57-84.

Wohlwill, J.F. (1973). *The Study of Behavioral Development.* New York: Academic Press.

Wolfgang, Marvin E. (1958). *Patterns of Criminal Homicide.* New York: John Wiley & Sons.

Woodard, C.V. (1951). *The Origins of the New South, 1877-1913.* Baton Rouge, LA: Louisiana State University Press.

Wooden, Wayne S., and Jay Parker. (1983). *Men Behind Bars: Sexual Exploitation in Prison.* New York: Da Capo Press, Inc.

Worchel, P. (1960). Hostility: Theory and experimental investigation. In D. Willner (Ed.), *Decision, Values, and Groups* 1, pages 254-266. New York: Pergamon Press.

_____. (1966). Displacement and the summation of frustration. *Journal of Experimental Research in Personality* 1, 256-261.

Worden, Robert E. (1996). The Causes of police brutality: Theory and evidence on police use of force. In William A. Geller and Hans Toch (Eds.) *Police Violence: Understanding and Controlling Police Abuse of Force*, pages 23-51. New Haven, CT: Yale University Press.

Wright, G. C. (1990). *Racial Violence in Kentucky, 1865-1940: Lynchings, Mob Rule, and "Legal Lynchings."* Baton Rouge, LA: Louisiana State University Press.

Wright, Kevin N. (1989). Race and economic marginality in explaining prison adjustment. *Journal of Research in Crime and Delinquency* 26, 67-89.

_____. (1991). The violent and victimized in the male prison. *Journal of Offender Rehabilitation* 16(3/4), 1-25.

Yinger, J. (1995). *Closed Doors, Opportunities Lost: The Continuing Costs of Housing Discrimination.* New York: Russell Sage.

Young, Vernetta, and Anne Thomas Sulton. (1991). Excluded: The current status of African-American scholars in the field of criminology and criminal justice. *Journal of Research in Crime and Delinquency* 28(1), 101-116.

Zangrando, R.L. (1980). *The N.A.A.C.P. Crusade Against Lynching, 1909-1950*. Philadelphia: Temple University Press.

Zaslavsky, Alan M. (1999, May 20). Customs practices under fire. Retrieved March 18, 2002 from the World Wide Web: http://abcne.../sections/us/DailyNews/customs990520.html

Zatz, Marjorie S. (1987). The changing forms of racial/ethnic biases in sentencing. *Journal of Research in Crime and Delinquency* 24(1), 69-92.

Zimmerman, Clifford S. (2001). From the jailhouse to the courthouse: The role of informants in wrongful convictions. In Saundra D. Westervelt and John A. Humphrey (Eds.), *Wrongly Convicted: Perspectives on Failed Justice*, pages 55-76. New Brunswick, NJ: Rutgers University Press.

Zimmerman, Donald W., and Richard H. Williams. (1982). Gain scores in research can be highly reliable. *Journal of Educational Measurement* 19, 149-154.

Cases Cited

Batson v. Kentucky, 476 US 79 (1986)

Brady v. Maryland, 373 US 83 (1963)

Brown v. Board of Education, 347 US 483 (1954)

Larry P. v. Riles, 495 F. Supp. 926 (N.D. Ca. 1979)

Pugh v. Locke, 406 F. Supp. 318 (MD Ala. 1976)

Robert Wilkins v. Maryland State Police, Civil Action No. CCB-93-468 (D.Md. 1994)

Smith v. Brewer, 444 F. Supp. 490 (SD Iowa 1987)

State v. Pedro Soto, 734 A.2d 350 (N.J. Super. App. Div. 1996)

State v. Shillcut, 119 Wis.2d 788, 350 N.W.2d 686 (1984)

Strauder v. West Virginia, 100 US 303 (1880)

Taylor v. Louisiana, 419 US 522 (1975)

Tennessee v. Garner 471 US 1 (1985)

Terry v. Ohio, 392 US 1 (1968)

Tobias v. Smith, 468 F. Supp. 1287 (WDNY 1979)

United States v. Carter, 528 F.2d 844 (CA8 1975)

United States v. Cartlidge, 808 F.2d 1064 (5th Cir. 1987)

United States v. Cortez, 449 US 411 (1981)

United States v. Laymon, 730 F. Supp. 332 (D. Colo. 1990)

United States v. McDaniels, 379 F. Supp. 1243 (ED La. 1974)

United States. v. Taylor , 956 F.2d 572 (6th Circuit 1992)

Whren v. United States, 517 US 806 (1996)